D1226330

The Illustrated
Age of Fable

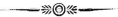

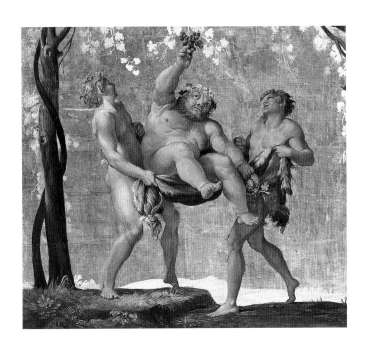

The Illustrated Age of Fable © Frances Lincoln Limited 1998

Foreword by Erika Langmuir OBE © Frances Lincoln Limited 1998
Captions by Nigel Spivey with additional art-history information from Rachel Barnes © Frances Lincoln Limited 1998

For photographic acknowledgments and copyright details, see pages 200-205 and 208

First published in Great Britain in 1998 by Frances Lincoln Limited, 4 Torriano Mews, Torriano Avenue, London NW5 2RZ

Published in 1998 and distributed in the U.S. by
Stewart, Tabori & Chang, a division of U.S. Media Holdings, Inc.
115 West 18th Street, New York, NY 10011

Distributed in Canada by General Publishing Company Ltd.
30 Lesmill Road, Don Mills, Ontario, Canada M3B 2T6

Sold in Australia by Peribo Pty Ltd.
58 Beaumont Road, Mount Kuring-gai, NSW 2080, Australia

Distributed in all other territories by Grantham Book Services Ltd.
Isaac Newton Way, Alma Park Industrial Estate
Grantham, Lincolnshire, NG31 9SD, England

Library of Congress Cataloging in Publication:
Bulfinch, Thomas, 1796-1867.
[Age of fable]
Bulfinch's Mythology. The illustrated age of fable / by Thomas Bulfinch.
p.   cm.
Originally published: 1855
Includes index.
ISBN 1-55670-825-4
1. Mythology, Classical. I. Title.
BL722.B85 1998
292. 1'3—DC21

Printed in Hong Kong
10 9 8 7 6 5 4 3 2 1

Thomas Bulfinch

The Illustrated
Age of Fable

———⬥◉⬥———

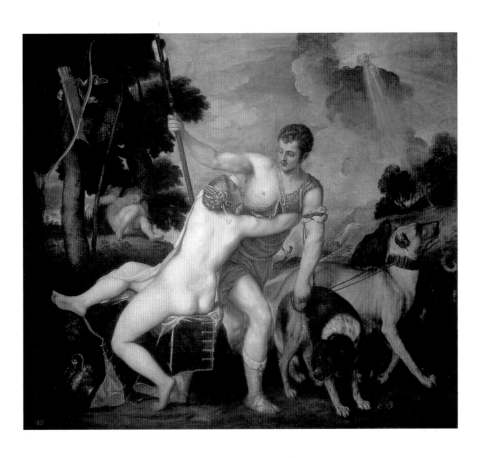

With a New Foreword by Erika Langmuir OBE

STEWART, TABORI & CHANG
New York

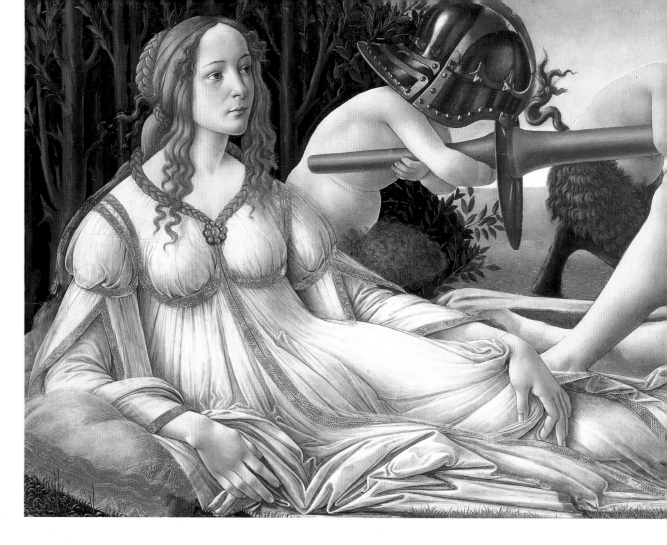

CONTENTS

Foreword   7

1. Introduction   9

2. Prometheus and Pandora   17

3. Apollo and Daphne · Pyramus and
   Thisbe · Cephalus and Procris   22

4. Juno and Her Rivals, Io and Callisto ·
   Diana and Actaeon · Latona and the Rustics   29

5. Phaëton   36

6. Midas · Baucis and Philemon   41

7. Proserpine · Glaucus and Scylla   46

8. Pygmalion · Dryope · Venus and Adonis ·
   Apollo and Hyacinthus   51

9. Ceyx and Halcyone: or The Halcyon Birds   58

10. Vertumnus and Pomona   63

11. Cupid and Psyche   65

12. Cadmus · The Myrmidons   72

13. Nisus and Scylla · Echo and Narcissus ·
    Clytie · Hero and Leander   76

14. Minerva · Niobe   81

15. Adventures of Perseus · Medusa · Atlas ·
    The Sea Monster · The Wedding Feast   86

16. Monsters: Giants · The Sphinx ·
    Pegasus and the Chimaera · The Centaurs ·
    The Pygmies · The Griffin   93

17. The Golden Fleece · Medea and Aeson   99

18. Meleager · Atalanta   103

19. Hercules · Hebe and Ganymede   107

20. Theseus · Daedalus · Castor and Pollux   111

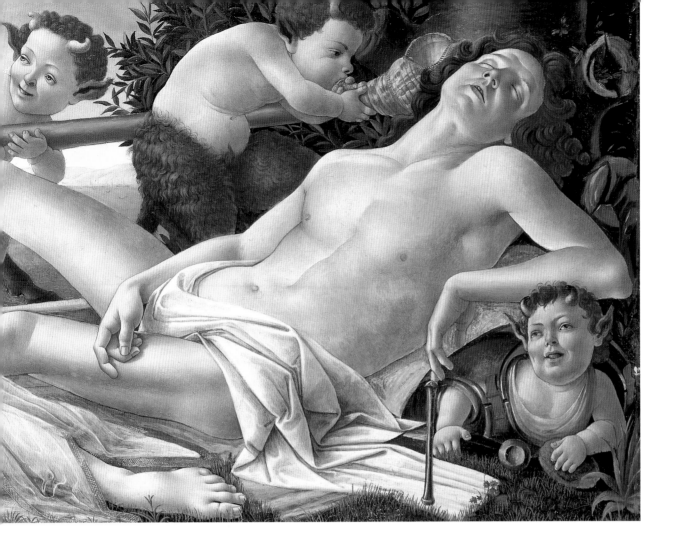

21. Bacchus · Ariadne 119

22. The Rural Deities · Erisichthon · Rhoecus · The Water Deities · The Winds 124

23. Achelous and Hercules · Admetus and Alcestis · Antigone · Penelope 131

24. Orpheus and Eurydice · Aristaeus · Amphion · Linus · Thamyris · Marsyas · Melampus · Musaeus 135

25. Endymion · Orion · Aurora and Tithonus · Acis and Galatea 143

26. The Trojan War · The Iliad 149

27. The Fall of Troy · Menelaus and Helen · Agamemnon, Orestes and Electra 163

28. Adventures of Ulysses · The Cyclopes · The Laestrygonians · Circe · The Sirens · Scylla and Charybdis · Calypso 168

29. The Phaeacians · The Fate of the Suitors 174

30. Adventures of Aeneas · The Harpies · Dido · Palinurus 179

31. The Infernal Regions · Elysium · The Sibyl 185

32. Aeneas in Italy · The Gates of Janus · Camilla · Evander · Infant Rome · Nisus and Euryalus · Mezentius ·Turnus 191

Genealogical Table of the Gods of Greece and Rome 198

Index of Artists and Paintings 200

Index 205

Photographic Acknowledgments 208

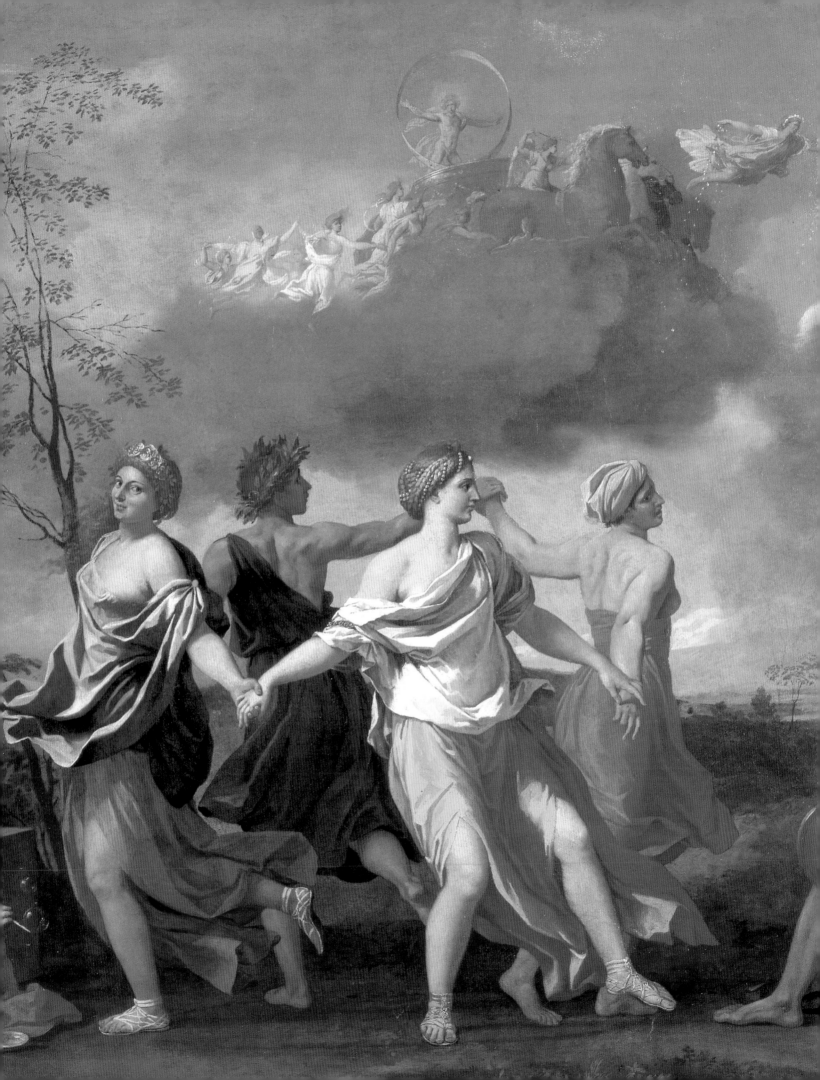

FOREWORD

THE AGE OF FABLE was the first popular retelling of Greek and Roman myths to be written for English-speaking readers who had not studied ancient languages. "Our book," wrote Thomas Bulfinch in his preface of 1855, "is not for the learned, nor for the theologian, nor for the philosopher, but for the reader of English literature, of either sex, who wishes to comprehend the allusions so frequently made by public speakers, lecturers, essayists, and poets, and those which occur in polite conversation."

The words "polite conversation" are revealing. Bulfinch, born into the New England aristocracy, was well aware that in "a practical age" when the "time even of the young is claimed by so many sciences of facts and things" many less privileged men and women felt excluded from what he called "cultivated society." His book was designed as much to remove a social barrier as to inform and delight.

Today, ancient myths are rarely the subject of "polite conversation." Social values have changed–yet in one important area of our lives, art, *The Age of Fable* retains its usefulness. Here the influence of Greek and Roman legends is clearly visible. Sensuous, frivolous, heroic, romantic, or tragic, these tales of the loves, adventures, and transformations of gods and mortals have inspired artists for the past 600 years.

In the late Middle Ages, the main purpose of painting was to assist Christian worship. But domestic decoration, such as that of bridal chests and marriage beds, continued to draw on pagan sources. Such objects, or panels cut out from them, teem with vivid incidents from Ovid's *Metamorphoses* and Virgil's *Aeneid*, the Latin sources of most of Bulfinch's material, which were based, in turn, on earlier Greek poetry and drama. To justify their use in the home, these pagan stories were presented as examples of Christian or civic virtues. Identifying the mythical subjects allows us to appreciate the skill with which the artists translated tales of violence and passion into harmless poetic ornament (pages 24, 72, 134, 150).

During the late 15th and early 16th centuries, mythology became popular again as the subject of large-scale paintings. However, while they boldly portrayed nudity "in the ancient manner," some of the most famous mythological pictures of the Renaissance still show the bias toward allegory that was a feature of medieval painting. Botticelli's *Birth of Venus* (12) embodies the philosophical notion of Ideal Beauty that draws the soul to God. Correggio's *"The School of Love"* (14) relies on astrological lore, depicting Venus and Mercury as planetary divinities. In Bronzino's *Allegory with Venus and Cupid* (53), by contrast, the goddess and her son personify lust. Most tellingly, the Sibyls on Michelangelo's Sistine Chapel ceiling (8) demonstrate the subjection of pagan thought to Christian belief: at the time the Sibyls were painted, they were thought to have prophesied the coming of Christ to the pre-Christian world.

Only with Titian's painted "poetry," as 16th-century contemporaries called it, did art recapture the power of myth to touch our deepest emotions. No pictures illustrate the gods' cruel caprice better than *Apollo and Marsyas* (141) or *The Death of Actaeon* (34). But even a master like Titian needs the viewer's help to make himself clear. To understand the pathos of *Venus and Adonis* (3), we, like Venus, must know the fate that will overtake Adonis; most viewers of the time would have been acquainted with his tragic end.

Following Titian's example, later painters have explored the capacity of myth to draw on a wide range of different emotions. The mythological landscapes of Claude (66, 154, 182, 192) and Poussin (54, 119, 144) are steeped in nostalgia; Turner's interpret myth as cosmic turbulence in which Nature echoes the drama of human life (80). From the 17th through the 19th century, myth has lent dignity to rustic anecdote (44), added fascination to the portrait (48), and made possible the uncensored depiction of erotic, sinister, or dreamlike scenes (11, 93, 95, 133).

Bulfinch hoped that his enthusiastic retelling of ancient myths would serve as "an interpreter of paintings and sculptures." I believe it can do more. Only when we have read these ageless fables, and can measure the artists' imaginations against our own, can we enjoy the infinite variety with which art speaks to the human heart.

Erika Langmuir

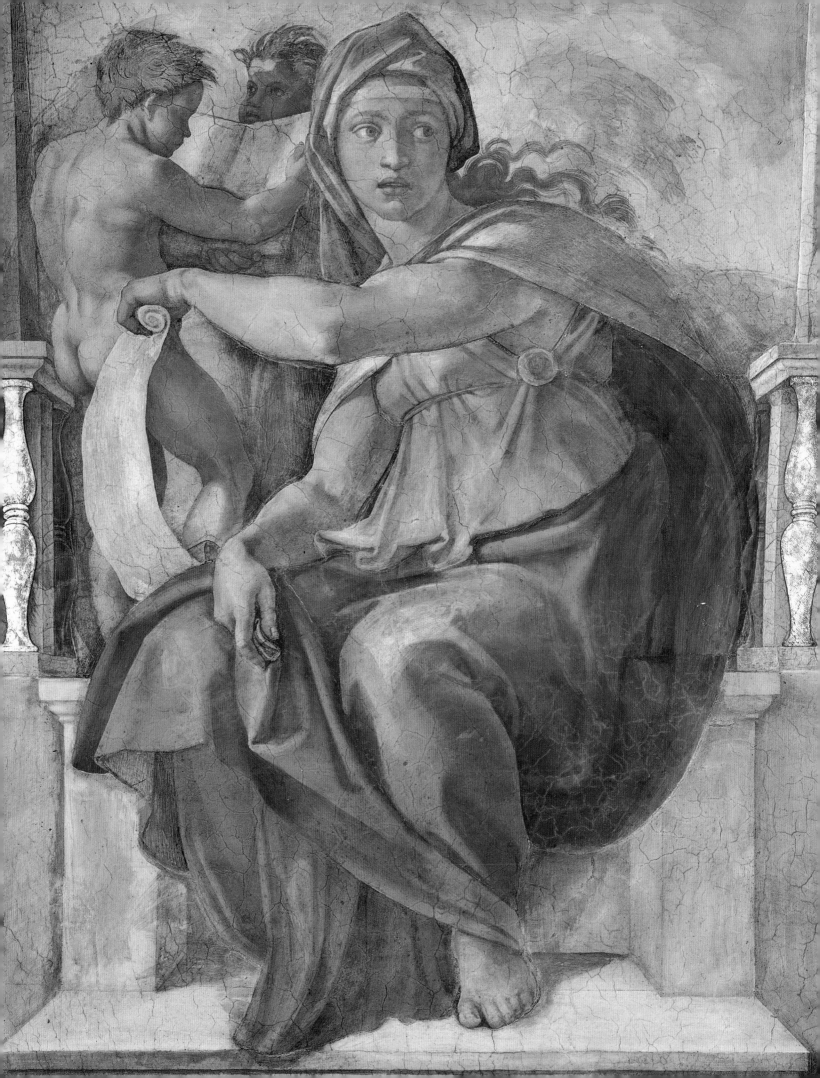

CHAPTER 1

INTRODUCTION

THE RELIGIONS OF ANCIENT GREECE AND ROME are extinct. The so-called divinities of Olympus have not a single worshipper among living men. They belong now not to the department of theology, but to those of literature and taste. There they still hold their place, and will continue to hold it, for they are too closely connected with the finest productions of poetry and art, both ancient and modern, to pass into oblivion.

We propose to tell the stories relating to them which have come down to us from the ancients and which are alluded to by modern poets, essayists, and orators. In order to understand these stories, it will be necessary to acquaint ourselves with the ideas of the structure of the universe which prevailed among the Greeks—the people from whom the Romans, and other nations through them, received their science and religion.

The Greeks believed the earth to be flat and circular, their own country occupying the middle of it, the central point being either Mount Olympus, the abode of the gods, or Delphi, so famous for its oracle.

The circular disk of the earth was crossed from west to east, and divided into two equal parts by the Sea, as they called the Mediterranean, and its continuation the Euxine, the only seas with which they were acquainted.

Around the earth flowed the River Ocean, its course being from south to north on the western side of the earth, and in a contrary direction on the eastern side. It flowed in a steady, equable current, unvexed by storm or tempest. The sea, and all the rivers on earth, received their waters from it.

The northern portion of the earth was supposed to be inhabited by a happy race named the Hyperboreans, dwelling in everlasting bliss and spring beyond the lofty mountains whose caverns were supposed to send forth the piercing blasts of the north wind, which chilled the people of Hellas (Greece). Their country was inaccessible by land or sea. They lived exempt from disease or old age, from toils and warfare.

◄ Delphic Sibyl, MICHELANGELO (1475–1564): *According to legend, the Sibyl at the sanctuary of Delphi predicted not only the coming of Christ, but events occurring until the fourth century AD.*

On the south side of the earth, close to the stream of Ocean, dwelt a people happy and virtuous as the Hyperboreans. They were named the Aethiopians. The gods favored them so highly that they were wont to leave at times their Olympian abodes and go to share their sacrifices and banquets.

On the western margin of the earth, by the stream of Ocean, lay a happy place named the Elysian Plain, whither mortals favored by the gods were transported without tasting of death, to enjoy an immortality of bliss. This happy region was also called the Fortunate Fields and the Isles of the Blessed.

We thus see that the Greeks of the early ages knew little of any real people except those to the east and south of their own country, or near the coast of the Mediterranean. Their imagination meantime peopled the western portion of this sea with giants, monsters and enchantresses, while they placed around the disk of the earth, which they probably regarded as of no great width, nations enjoying the peculiar favor of the gods and blessed with happiness and longevity.

The Dawn, the Sun, and the Moon were supposed to rise out of the Ocean, on the eastern side, and to drive through the air, giving light to gods and men. The stars also, except those forming the Wain or Bear, and others near them, rose out of and sank into the stream of Ocean. There the sun god embarked in a winged boat, which conveyed him round by the northern part of the earth, back to his place of rising in the east.

The abode of the gods was on the summit of Mount Olympus, in Thessaly. A gate of clouds, kept by the goddesses named the Seasons, opened to permit the passage of the celestials to earth and to receive them on their return. The gods had their separate dwellings; but all, when summoned, repaired to the palace of Jupiter, as did also those deities whose usual abode was the earth, the waters, or the underworld. It was also in the great hall of the palace of the Olympian king that the gods feasted each day on ambrosia and nectar, their food and drink, the latter being handed round by the lovely goddess Hebe. Here they conversed of the affairs of heaven and earth; and as they quaffed their nectar, Apollo, the god of music, delighted them with the tones of his lyre, to which the Muses sang in responsive strains. When the sun was set, the gods retired to sleep in their respective dwellings.

The robes and other parts of the dress of the goddesses were woven by Minerva and the Graces, and everything of a more solid nature was formed of the various metals. Vulcan was architect, smith, armorer, chariot builder, and artist of all work in Olympus. He built of brass the houses of the gods; he made for them the golden shoes with which they trod the air or the water, and moved from place to place with the speed of the wind, or even of thought. He also shod with brass the celestial steeds, which whirled the chariots of the gods through the air or along the surface of the sea. He was able to bestow on his workmanship self-motion, so that the tripods (chairs and tables) could move of themselves in and out of the celestial hall. He even endowed with intelligence the golden handmaidens whom he made to wait on himself.

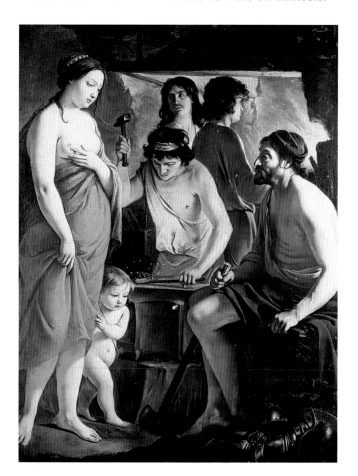

Jupiter, or Jove (Zeus), though called the father of gods and men, had himself a beginning. Saturn (Cronos) was his father, and Rhea (Ops) his mother. Saturn and Rhea were of the race of Titans, who were the children of Earth and Heaven, which sprang from Chaos, of which we shall give a further account in our next chapter.

There is another cosmogony, or account of the creation, according to which Earth, Erebus, and Love were the first of beings. Love (Eros) issued from the egg of Night, which floated on Chaos. By his arrows and torch he pierced and vivified all things, producing life and joy.

Saturn and Rhea were not the only Titans. There were others, whose names were Oceanus, Hyperion, Iapetus, and Ophion, males; and Themis, Mnemosyne, Eurynome, females. They are spoken of as the elder gods, whose dominion was afterwards transferred to others. Saturn yielded to Jupiter, Oceanus to Neptune, Hyperion to Apollo. Hyperion was the father of the Sun, Moon, and Dawn. He is therefore the original sun god, and is painted with the splendor and beauty that were afterward bestowed on Apollo.

Ophion and Eurynome ruled over Olympus till they were dethroned by Saturn and Rhea.

The representations given of Saturn are not very consistent; for on the one hand his reign is said to have been the golden age of innocence and purity, and on the other he is described as a monster who devoured his own children. Jupiter, however, escaped this fate, and when grown up espoused Metis (Prudence), who administered a draught to Saturn that caused him to disgorge his children. Jupiter, with his brothers and sisters, now rebelled against their father, Saturn, and his brothers the Titans; vanquished them, and imprisoned some of them in Tartarus, inflicting other penalties on others. Atlas was condemned to bear up the heavens on his shoulders.

◄ Venus at Vulcan's Forge, MATHIEU LE NAIN (about 1607–1677): *Like the Greek craftsmen over whom he presided, the smith-god Vulcan was portrayed as disfigured and made dirty by his work. Here Le Nain contrasts the ingenuity of Vulcan and his assistants with the unsullied grace of Vulcan's wife Venus.*

Jupiter and Thetis, JEAN-AUGUSTE-DOMINIQUE INGRES ► (1780–1867): *Ingres modeled his enthroned Jupiter on a description of the colossal statue of Zeus at Olympia created by Pheidias in the fifth century BC.*

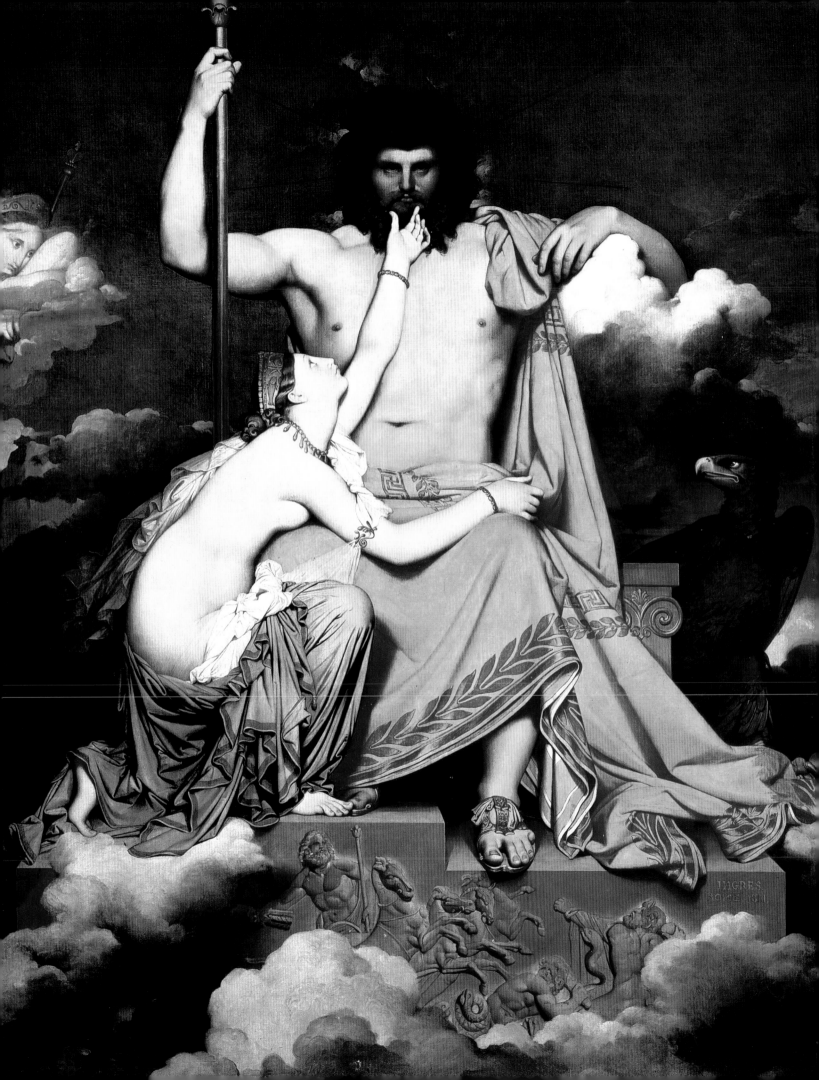

On the dethronement of Saturn, Jupiter with his brothers Neptune (Poseidon) and Pluto (Dis) divided his dominions. Jupiter's portion was the heavens, Neptune's the ocean, and Pluto's the realms of the dead. Earth and Olympus were common property. Jupiter was king of gods and men. The thunder was his weapon, and he bore a shield called Aegis, made for him by Vulcan. The eagle was his favorite bird, and bore his thunderbolts.

Juno (Hera) was the wife of Jupiter, and queen of the gods. Iris, the goddess of the rainbow, was her attendant and messenger. The peacock was her favorite bird.

Vulcan (Hephaestos), the celestial artist, was the son of Jupiter and Juno. He was born lame, and his mother was so displeased at the sight of him that she flung him out of heaven. Other accounts say that Jupiter kicked him out for taking part with his mother in a quarrel that occurred between them. Vulcan's lameness, according to this account, was the consequence of his fall. He was a whole day falling, and at last alighted on the island of Lemnos, which was thenceforth sacred to him.

Mars (Ares), the god of war, was the son of Jupiter and Juno.

Phoebus Apollo, the god of archery, prophecy, and music, was the son of Jupiter and Latona, and brother of Diana (Artemis). He was god of the sun, as Diana, his sister, was the goddess of the moon.

Venus (Aphrodite), the goddess of love and beauty, was the daughter of Jupiter and Dione. Others say that Venus sprang from the foam of the sea. The zephyr wafted her along the waves to the Isle of Cyprus, where she was received and attired by the Seasons, and then led to the assembly of the gods. All were charmed with her beauty, and each one demanded her for his wife. Jupiter gave her to Vulcan, in gratitude for the service he had rendered in forging thunderbolts. So the most beautiful of the goddesses became the wife of the most ill-favored of gods. Venus possessed an embroidered girdle called Cestus, which had the power of inspiring love. Her favorite birds were swans and doves, and the plants sacred to her were the rose and the myrtle.

Cupid (Eros), the god of love, was the son of Venus. He was her constant companion; and, armed with bow and arrows, he shot the darts of desire into the bosoms of both gods and men.

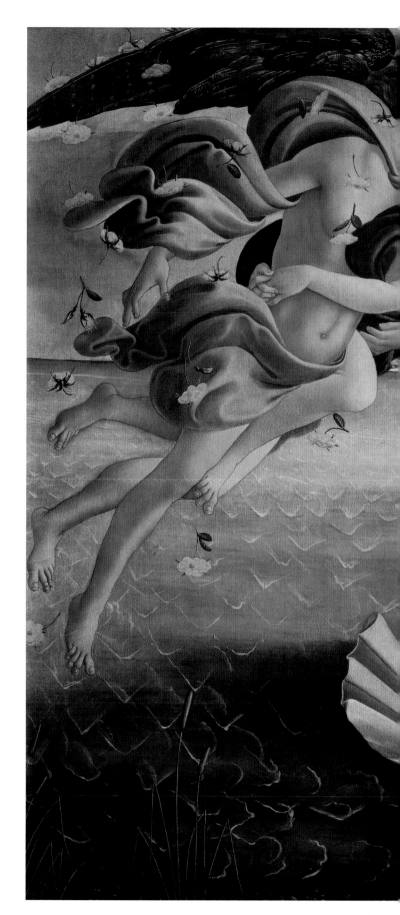

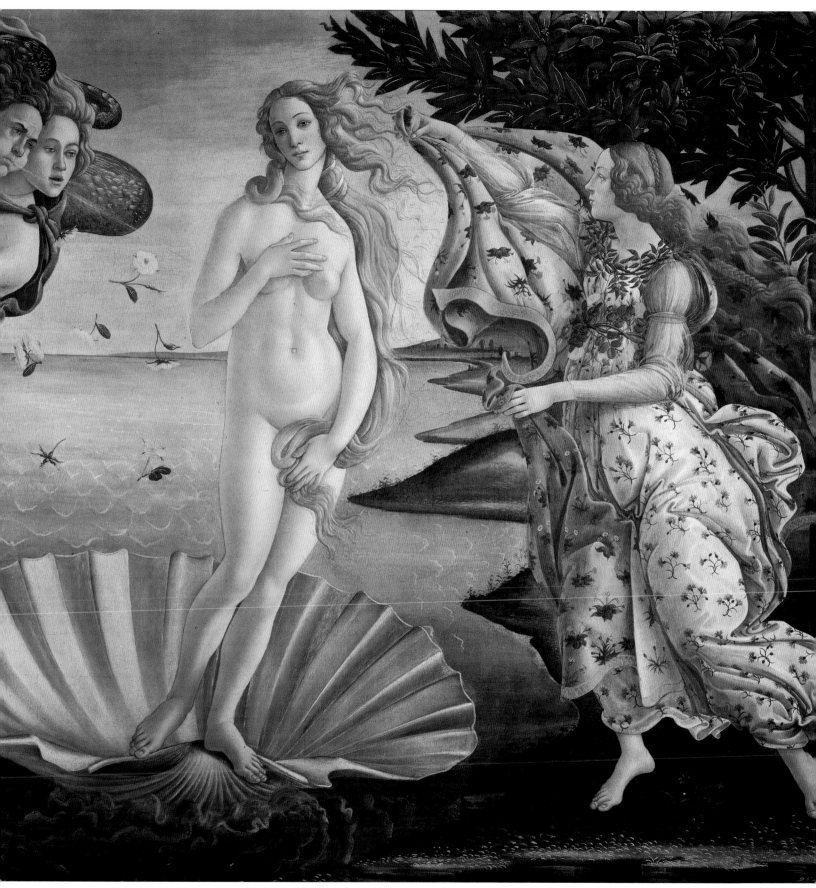

▲ The Birth of Venus, SANDRO BOTTICELLI (about 1445–1510)
*Venus was born of surf and foam; the Greek word for this, aphros, may contribute
to her name Aphrodite. As Botticelli would have known, one version of her birth specifies
that she sprang from the sheared-off genitalia of Heaven (Uranus)—
which, according to legend, were dropped into the sea off the coast of Cyprus.*

There was a deity named Anteros, who was sometimes represented as the avenger of slighted love, and sometimes as the symbol of reciprocal affection. The following legend is told of him:

Venus, complaining to Themis that her son Eros continued always a child, was told by her that it was because he was solitary, and that if he had a brother he would grow apace. Anteros was soon afterward born, and Eros immediately was seen to increase rapidly in size and strength.

Minerva (Pallas Athene), the goddess of wisdom, was the offspring of Jupiter, without a mother. She sprang forth from Jupiter's head completely armed.

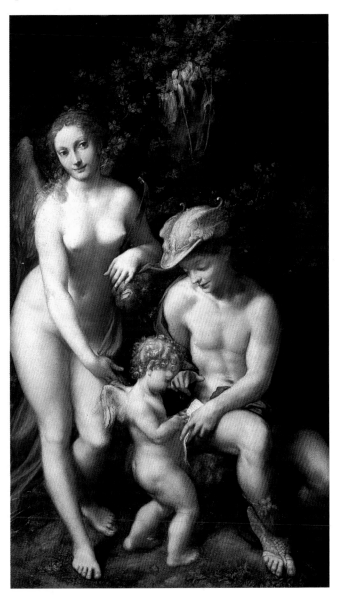

▲ Venus with Mercury and Cupid ("The School of Love"),
CORREGGIO (circa 1494; died 1534)
Cupid was both Venus's son and her errand-runner. Here Correggio shows Mercury teaching the boy the art of delivering messages.

Her favorite bird was the owl, and the plant sacred to her the olive.

Mercury (Hermes) was the son of Jupiter and Maia. He presided over commerce, wrestling and other gymnastic exercises, even over thieving, and everything, in short, which required skill and dexterity. He was the messenger of Jupiter, and wore a winged cap and winged shoes. He bore in his hand a rod entwined with two serpents, called the caduceus.

Mercury is said to have invented the lyre. He found, one day, a tortoise, of which he took the shell, made holes in the opposite edges of it, and drew cords of linen through them, and the instrument was complete. The cords were nine, in honor of the nine Muses. Mercury gave the lyre to Apollo, and received from him in exchange the caduceus.

Ceres (Demeter) was the daughter of Saturn and Rhea. She had a daughter named Proserpine (Persephone), who became the wife of Pluto and queen of the realms of the dead. Ceres presided over agriculture.

Bacchus (Dionysus), the god of wine, was the son of Jupiter and Semele. He represents not only the intoxicating power of wine, but its social and beneficent influences likewise, so that he is viewed as the promoter of civilization and a lawgiver and lover of peace.

The Muses were the daughters of Jupiter and Mnemosyne (Memory). They presided over song, and prompted the memory. They were nine in number, to each of whom was assigned the presidency over some particular department of literature, art, or science. Calliope was the muse of epic poetry, Clio of history, Euterpe of lyric poetry, Melpomene of tragedy, Terpsichore of choral dance and song, Erato of love poetry, Polyhymnia of sacred poetry, Urania of astronomy, Thalia of comedy.

The Graces were goddesses presiding over the banquet, the dance, and all social enjoyments and elegant arts. They were three in number. Their names were Euphrosyne, Aglaia, and Thalia.

The Fates were also three—Clotho, Lachesis, and Atropos. Their office was to spin the thread of human destiny, and they were armed with shears, with which they cut it off when they pleased. They were the daughters of Themis (Law), who sits by Jove on his throne to give him counsel.

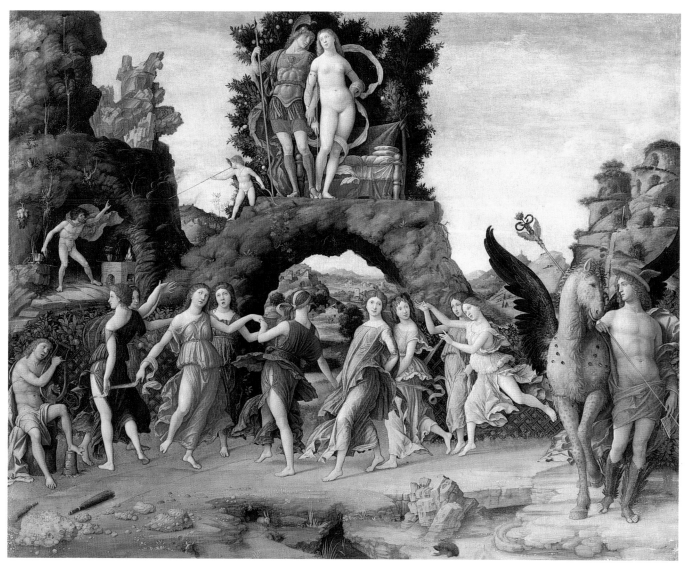

▲ Mars and Venus, Known as Parnassus, ANDREA MANTEGNA (circa 1430/1–1506)
From a lofty mountain setting (Parnassus), Mars and Venus survey the chorus and dancing of the nine Muses. Apollo, god of music, provides the chords. Mantegna harmonizes the Muses' movements in a symmetrical Renaissance composition.

The Erinnyes, or Furies, were three goddesses who punished by their secret stings the crimes of those who escaped or defied public justice. The heads of the Furies were wreathed with serpents, and their whole appearance was terrific and appalling. Their names were Alecto, Tisiphone, and Megaera. They were also called Eumenides.

Nemesis was also an avenging goddess. She represents the righteous anger of the gods, particularly toward the proud and insolent.

Pan was the god of flocks and shepherds. His favorite residence was in Arcadia.

The Satyrs were deities of the woods and fields. They were conceived to be covered with bristly hair, their heads decorated with short, sprouting horns, and their feet like goats' feet.

Momus was the god of laughter, and Plutus the god of wealth.

ROMAN DIVINITIES

The preceding are Grecian divinities, though received also by the Romans. Those which follow are peculiar to Roman mythology:

Saturn was an ancient Italian deity. It was attempted to identify him with the Grecian god Cronos, and fabled that after his dethronement by Jupiter he fled to Italy, where he reigned during what was called the Golden Age. In memory of his beneficent dominion, the feast of Saturnalia was held every year in the winter season. Then all public business was suspended, declarations of war and criminal executions were postponed, friends made presents to one another, and the slaves were indulged with great liberties. A feast was given them at which they sat at table, while their masters served them, to show the natural equality of men, and that all things belonged equally to all, in the reign of Saturn.

Faunus, the grandson of Saturn, was worshipped as the god of fields and shepherds, and also as a prophetic god. His name in the plural, Fauns, expressed a class of gamesome deities, like the Satyrs of the Greeks.

Quirinus was a war god, said to be no other than Romulus, the founder of Rome, exalted after his death to a place among the gods.

Bellona, a war goddess.

Terminus, the god of landmarks. His statue was a rude stone or post, set in the ground to mark the boundaries of fields.

Pales, the goddess presiding over cattle and pastures.

Pomona presided over fruit trees.

Flora, the goddess of flowers.

Lucina, the goddess of childbirth.

Vesta (the Hestia of the Greeks) was a deity presiding over the public and private hearth. A sacred fire, tended by six virgin priestesses called Vestals, flamed in her temple. As the safety of the city was held to be connected with its conservation, the neglect of the virgins, if they let it go out, was severely punished, and the fire was rekindled from the rays of the sun.

Liber is the Latin name of Bacchus; and Mulciber of Vulcan.

Janus was the porter of heaven. He opens the year, the first month being named after him. He is the guardian deity of gates, on which account he is commonly represented with two heads, because every door looks two ways. His temples at Rome were numerous. In wartime the gates of the principal one were always open. In peace they were closed; but they were shut only once between the reign of Numa and that of Augustus.

The Penates were the gods who were supposed to attend to the welfare and prosperity of the family. Their name is derived from Penus, the pantry, which was sacred to them. Every master of a family was the priest to the Penates of his own house.

The Lares, or Lars, were also household gods, but differed from the Penates in being regarded as the deified spirits of mortals. The family Lars were held to be the souls of ancestors, who watched over and protected their descendants. The words Lemur and Larva more nearly correspond to our word Ghost.

The Romans believed that every man had his Genius, and every woman her Juno: that is, a spirit who had given them being, and was regarded as their protector through life. On their birthdays men made offerings to their Genius, women to their Juno.

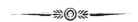

Prometheus, ARNOLD BÖCKLIN (1827–1901) ➤
The Swiss artist Böcklin puts Prometheus and the chaos of primal discord into a landscape more Alpine than Mediterranean, executed in dramatic chiaroscuro.

CHAPTER 2

PROMETHEUS AND PANDORA

THE CREATION OF THE WORLD IS A PROBLEM naturally fitted to excite the liveliest interest of man, its inhabitant. The ancient pagans, not having the information on the subject which we derive from the pages of Scripture, had their own way of telling the story, which is as follows:

Before earth and sea and heaven were created, all things wore one aspect, to which we give the name of Chaos—a confused and shapeless mass, nothing but dead weight, in which, however, slumbered the seeds of things. Earth, sea, and air were all mixed up together; so the earth was not solid, the sea was not fluid, and the air was not transparent. God and Nature at last interposed and put an end to this discord, separating earth from sea, and heaven from both. The fiery part, being the lightest, sprang up and formed the skies; the air was next in weight and place. The earth, being heavier, sank below; and the water took the lowest place, and buoyed up the earth.

Here, some god—it is not known which—gave his good offices in arranging and disposing the earth. He appointed rivers and bays their places, raised mountains, scooped out valleys, distributed woods, fountains, fertile fields, and stony plains. The air being cleared, the stars began to appear, fishes took possession of the sea, birds of the air, and four-footed beasts of the land.

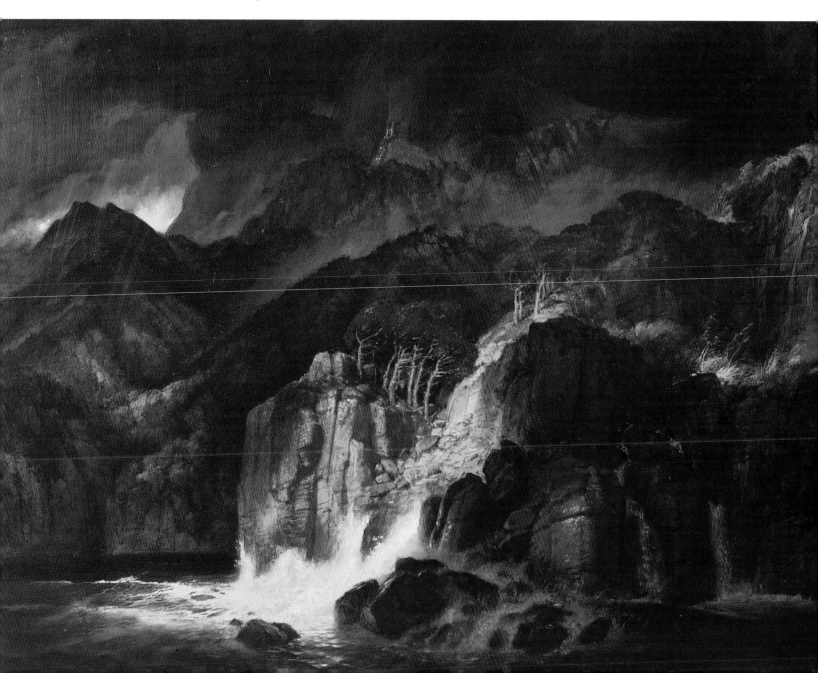

But a nobler animal was wanted, and Man was made. It is not known whether the Creator made him of divine materials, or whether in the earth, so lately separated from heaven, there lurked still some heavenly seeds. Prometheus took some of this earth, and kneading it up with water, made man in the image of the gods. He gave him an upright stature, so that while all other animals turn their faces downward and look to the earth, he raises his to heaven and gazes on the stars.

Prometheus was one of the Titans, a gigantic race who inhabited the earth before the creation of man. To him and his brother Epimetheus was committed the office of making man, and providing him and all other animals with the faculties necessary for their preservation. Epimetheus undertook to do this, and Prometheus was to overlook his work, when it was done. Epimetheus accordingly proceeded to bestow upon the different animals the various gifts of courage, strength, swiftness, sagacity; wings to one, claws to another, a shelly covering to a third, etc. But when man came to be provided for, who was to be superior to all other animals, Epimetheus had been so prodigal of his resources that he had nothing left to bestow upon him. In his perplexity he resorted to his brother Prometheus, who, with the aid of Minerva, went up to heaven and lighted his torch at the chariot of the sun, and brought down fire to man. With this gift man was more than a match for all other animals. It enabled him to make weapons wherewith to subdue them; tools with which to cultivate the earth; to warm his dwelling, so as to be comparatively independent of climate; and finally to introduce the arts and to coin money, the means of trade and commerce.

Woman was not yet made. The story (absurd enough!) is that Jupiter made her and sent her to Prometheus and his brother, to punish them for their presumption in stealing fire from heaven; and man, for accepting the gift. The first woman was named Pandora (all-gifted). She was made in heaven, every god contributing something to perfect her. Venus gave her beauty, Mercury persuasion, Apollo music, etc. Thus equipped, she was conveyed to earth and presented to Epimetheus, who gladly accepted her, though cautioned by his brother to beware of Jupiter and his gifts. Epimetheus had in his house a jar, in which were kept certain noxious articles for which,

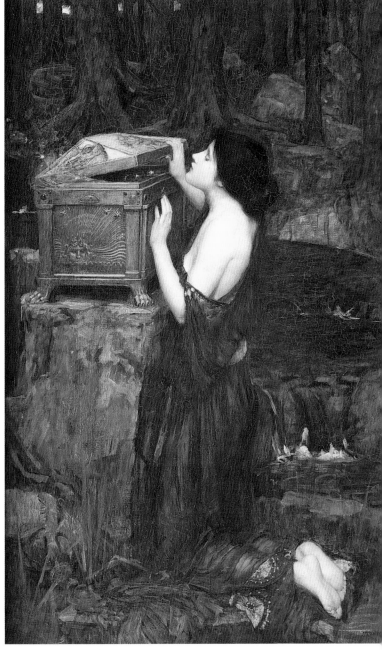

▲ Pandora, JOHN WILLIAM WATERHOUSE (1849-1917): *Pandora tentatively opens the box from which all worldly evils will flow. The myth epitomizes the keen misogyny present in ancient Greek society—in the seventh century BC, the poet Hesiod cursed women as a blight upon the earth.*

in fitting man for his new abode, he had had no occasion. Pandora was seized with an eager curiosity to know what this jar contained; and one day she slipped off the cover and looked in. Forthwith there escaped a multitude of plagues for hapless man— such as gout, rheumatism and colic for his body, and envy, spite and revenge for his mind—and scattered themselves far and wide. Pandora hastened to replace the lid; but, alas! the whole contents of the jar had escaped, one thing only excepted, which lay at the bottom, and that was hope. So we see at this day, whatever evils are abroad, hope never entirely leaves us; and while we have that, no amount of other ills can make us completely wretched.

Another story is that Pandora was sent in good faith, by Jupiter, to bless man; that she was furnished with a box containing her marriage presents, into which every god had put some blessing. She opened the box incautiously, and the blessings all escaped, hope only excepted. This story seems more probable than the former; for how could hope, so precious a jewel as it is, have been kept in a jar full of all manner of evils, as in the former statement?

The world being thus furnished with inhabitants, the first age was an age of innocence and happiness, called the Golden Age. Truth and right prevailed, though not enforced by law, nor was there any magistrate to threaten or punish. The forest had not yet been robbed of its trees to furnish timbers for vessels, nor had men built fortifications round their towns. There were no such things as swords, spears, or helmets. The earth brought forth all things necessary for man, without his labor in plowing or sowing. Perpetual spring reigned, flowers sprang up without seed, the rivers flowed with milk and wine, and yellow honey distilled from the oaks.

Then succeeded the Silver Age, inferior to the golden, but better than that of brass. Jupiter shortened the spring and divided the year into seasons. Then, first, men had to endure the extremes of heat and cold, and houses became necessary. Caves were the first dwellings, and leafy coverts of the woods, and huts woven of twigs. Crops would no longer grow without planting. The farmer was obliged to sow the seed, and the toiling ox to draw the plow.

Next came the Brazen Age, more savage of temper and readier to the strife of arms yet not altogether wicked. The hardest and worst was the Iron Age. Crime burst in like a flood; modesty, truth and honor fled. In their places came fraud and cunning, violence, and the wicked love of gain. Then seamen spread sails to the wind, and the trees were torn from the mountains to serve for keels to ships, and vex the face of ocean. The earth, which till now had been cultivated in common, began to be divided off

into possessions. Men were not satisfied with what the surface produced, but must dig into its bowels and draw forth from thence the ores of metals. Mischievous iron, and more mischievous gold, were produced. War sprang up, using both as weapons; the guest was not safe in his friend's house; and sons-in-law and fathers-in-law, brothers and sisters, husbands and wives could not trust one another. Sons wished their fathers dead, that they might come to the inheritance; family love lay prostrate. The earth was wet with slaughter, and the gods abandoned it, one by one, till Astraea alone was left, and finally she also took her departure.

Jupiter, seeing this state of things, burned with anger. He summoned the gods to council. They obeyed the call and took the road to the palace of heaven. The road, which anyone may see in a clear night, stretches across the face of the sky and is called the Milky Way. Along the road stand the palaces of the illustrious gods; the common people of the skies live apart, on either side. Jupiter addressed the assembly. He set forth the frightful condition of things on the earth and closed by announcing his intention to destroy the whole of its inhabitants, and provide a new race, unlike the first, who would be more worthy of life and much better worshippers of the gods. So saying he took a thunderbolt, and was about to launch it at the world and destroy it by burning; but recollecting the danger that such a conflagration might set heaven itself on fire, he changed his plan and resolved to drown it. The north wind, which scatters the clouds, was chained up; the south was sent out, and soon covered all the face of heaven with a cloak of pitchy darkness. The clouds, driven together, resound with a crash; torrents of rain fall; the crops are laid low; the year's labor of the husbandman perishes in an hour. Jupiter, not satisfied with his own waters, calls on his brother Neptune to aid him with his. He lets loose the rivers and pours them over the land. At the same time, he heaves the land with an earthquake and brings in the reflux of the ocean over the shores. Flocks, herds, men, and houses are swept away, and temples, with their sacred enclosures, profaned. If any edifice remained standing, it was overwhelmed, and its turrets lay hid beneath the waves. Now all was sea, sea without shore. Here and there an individual remained on a projecting hilltop, and a few, in boats,

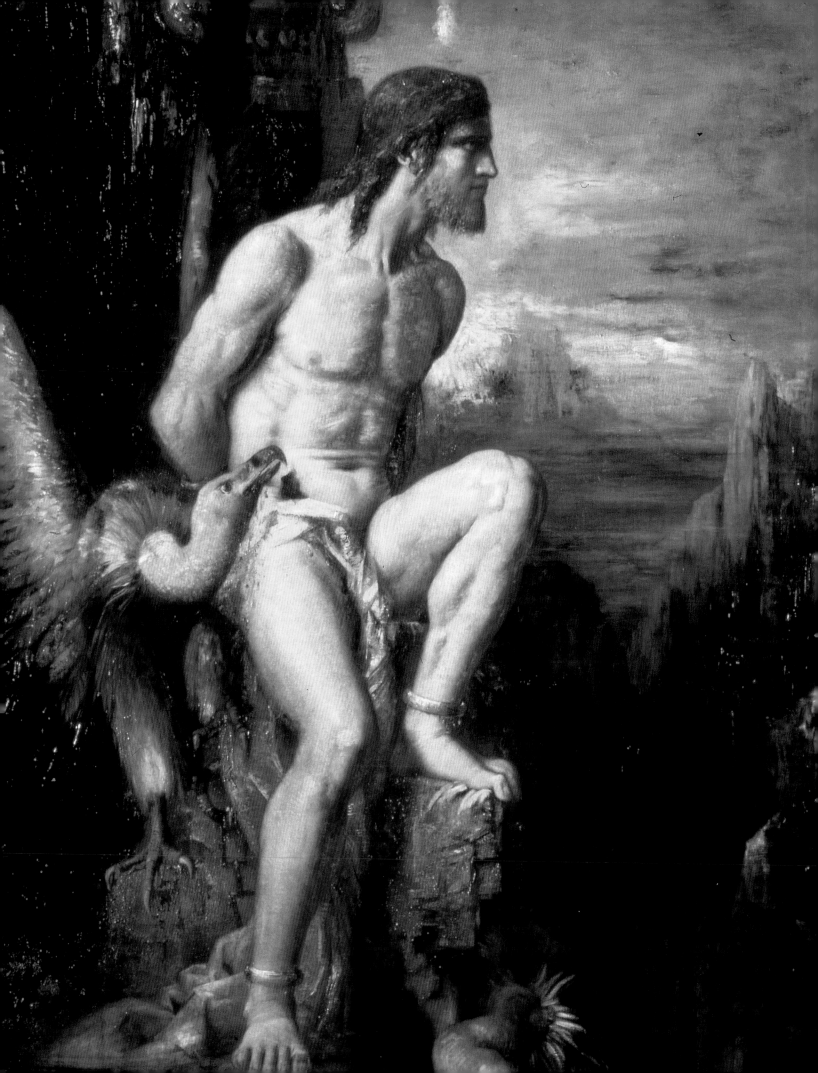

pulled the oar where they had lately driven the plow. The fishes swim among the treetops; the anchor is let down into a garden. Where the graceful lambs played but now, unwieldy sea calves gambol. The wolf swims among the sheep, the yellow lions and tigers struggle in the water. The strength of the wild boar serves him not, nor his swiftness the stag. The birds fall with weary wing into the water, having found no land for a resting place. These living beings whom the water spared fell a prey to hunger.

Parnassus alone, of all the mountains, overtopped the waves; and there Deucalion and his wife Pyrrha, of the race of Prometheus, found refuge—he a just man, and she a faithful worshipper of the gods. Jupiter, when he saw none left alive but this pair and remembered their harmless lives and pious demeanor, ordered the north winds to drive away the clouds, and disclose the skies to earth, and earth to the skies. Neptune also directed Triton to blow on his shell and sound a retreat to the waters. The waters obeyed, and the sea returned to its shores, and the rivers to their channels. Then Deucalion thus addressed Pyrrha: "Oh, wife, only surviving woman, joined to me first by the ties of kindred and marriage, and now by a common danger, would that we possessed the power of our ancestor Prometheus and could renew the race as he at first made it! But as we cannot, let us seek yonder temple and enquire of the gods what remains for us to do." They entered the temple, deformed as it was with slime, and approached the altar, where no fire burned. There they fell prostrate on the earth and prayed the goddess to inform them how they might retrieve their miserable affairs. The oracle answered, "Depart from the temple with head veiled and garments unbound, and cast behind you the bones of your mother." They heard the words with astonishment. Pyrrha first broke silence: "We cannot obey; we dare not profane the remains of our parents." They sought the thickest shades of

the wood, and revolved the oracle in their minds. At length Deucalion spoke: "Either my sagacity deceives me, or the command is one we may obey without impiety. The earth is the great parent of all; the stones are her bones; these we may cast behind us; and I think this is what the oracle means. At least, it will do no harm to try." They veiled their faces, unbound their garments, and picked up stones and cast them behind them. The stones (wonderful to relate) began to grow soft and assume shape. By degrees, they put on a rude resemblance to the human form, like a block half-finished in the hands of the sculptor. The moisture and slime that were about them became flesh; the stony part became bones; the veins remained veins, retaining their name, only changing their use. Those thrown by the hand of the man became men, and those by the woman became women. It was a hard race and well adapted to labor, as we find ourselves to be at this day, giving plain indications of our origin.

Prometheus has been a favorite subject with the poets. He is represented as the friend of mankind, who interposed on their behalf when Jove was incensed against them and who taught them civilization and the arts. But as, in so doing, he transgressed the will of Jupiter, he drew down on himself the anger of the ruler of gods and men. Jupiter had him chained to a rock on Mount Caucasus, where a vulture preyed on his liver, which was renewed as fast as devoured. This state of torment might have been brought to an end at any time by Prometheus, if he had been willing to submit to his oppressor; for he possessed a secret which involved the stability of Jove's throne, and if he would have revealed it, he might have been at once taken into favor. But that he disdained to do. He has therefore become the symbol of magnanimous endurance of unmerited suffering, and strength of will resisting oppression.

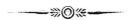

◄ The Torture of Prometheus, GUSTAVE MOREAU (1826–1898)
A Christ-like Prometheus, set in the distorted perspective of a fantastical landscape, is tortured by an eagle repeatedly gnawing at his gizzards. Prometheus's crime was to deceive the gods when performing animal sacrifice: he kept the prime steaks for himself while offering the gods mere offal and bones.

CHAPTER 3

APOLLO AND DAPHNE
PYRAMUS AND THISBE
CEPHALUS AND PROCRIS

THE SLIME WITH WHICH THE EARTH WAS COVERED by the waters of the flood produced an excessive fertility, which called forth every variety of production, both bad and good. Among the rest, Python, an enormous serpent, crept forth, the terror of the people, and lurked in the caves of Mount Parnassus. Apollo slew him with his arrows—weapons which he had not before used against any but feeble animals, hares, wild goats and such game. In commemoration of this illustrious conquest he instituted the Pythian games, in which the victor in feats of strength, swiftness of foot, or in the chariot race, was crowned with a wreath of beech leaves; for the laurel was not yet adopted by Apollo as his own tree.

APOLLO AND DAPHNE

Daphne was Apollo's first love. It was not brought about by accident, but by the malice of Cupid. Apollo saw the boy playing with his bow and arrows, and being himself elated with his recent victory over Python, he said to him, "What have you to do with warlike weapons, saucy boy? Leave them for hands worthy of them. Behold the conquest I have won by means of them over the vast serpent who stretched his poisonous body over acres of the plain! Be content with your torch, child, and kindle up your flames, as you call them, where you will, but presume not to meddle with my weapons."

Venus's boy heard these words and rejoined, "Your arrows may strike all things else, Apollo, but mine shall strike you." So saying, he took his stand on a rock of Parnassus and drew from his quiver two arrows of different workmanship, one to excite love, the other to repel it. The former was of gold and sharp pointed, the latter blunt and tipped with lead. With the leaden shaft he struck the nymph Daphne, the daughter of the river god Peneus, and with the golden one Apollo, through the heart. Forthwith the god was seized with love for the maiden, and she abhorred the thought of loving. Her delight was in woodland sports and in the spoils of the chase. Many lovers sought her, but she spurned them all, ranging the woods, and taking no thought of Cupid nor of Hymen. Her father often said to her, "Daughter, you owe me a son-in-law; you owe me grandchildren." She, hating the thought of marriage as a crime, with her beautiful face tinged all over with blushes, threw her arms around her father's neck and said, "Dearest father, grant me this favor, that I may always remain unmarried, like Diana." He consented, but at the same time said, "Your own face will forbid it."

Apollo loved her and longed to obtain her; and he who gives oracles to all the world was not wise enough to look into his own fortunes. He saw her hair flung loose over her shoulders and said, "If so charming in disorder, what would it be if arranged?" He saw her eyes bright as stars; he saw her lips, and was not satisfied with only seeing them. He admired her hands and arms, naked to the shoulder, and whatever was hidden from view he imagined more beautiful still. He followed her; she fled, swifter than the wind, and delayed not a moment at his entreaties. "Stay," said he, "daughter of Peneus; I am not a foe. Do not fly me as a lamb flies the wolf, or a dove the hawk. It is for love I pursue you. You make me miserable, for fear you should fall and hurt yourself on these stones, and I should be the cause. Pray run slower, and I will follow slower. I am no clown, no rude peasant. Jupiter is my father, and I am lord of Delphos and Tenedos, and know all things, present and future. I am the god of song and the lyre. My arrows fly true to the mark; but alas! an arrow more fatal than mine has pierced my heart! I am the god of medicine, and know the virtues of all healing plants. Alas! I suffer a malady that no balm can cure!"

The nymph continued her flight and left his plea half uttered. And even as she fled she charmed him. The wind blew her garments, and her unbound hair streamed loose behind her. The god grew impatient to find his wooings thrown away, and, sped by Cupid,

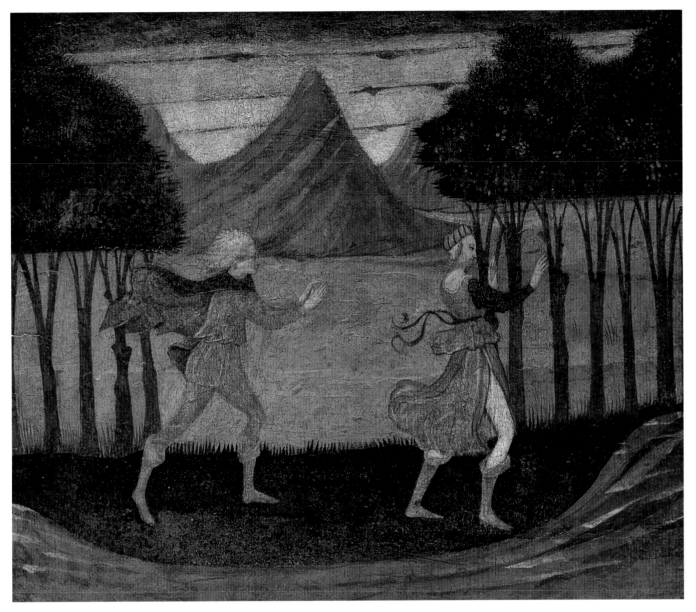

▲ Daphne Pursued by Apollo, MASTER OF THE JUDGMENT OF PARIS (Italian, active mid-15th century)
*As Daphne excapes Apollo's embrace, she is transformed into a tree. Such metamorphoses, versified
by the Roman poet Ovid, were popular subjects in medieval art.*

gained upon her in the race. It was like a hound pursuing a hare, with open jaws ready to seize, while the feebler animal darts forward, slipping from the very grasp. So flew the god and the virgin—he on the wings of love and she on those of fear. The pursuer is the more rapid, however, and gains upon her, and his panting breath blows upon her hair. Her strength begins to fail, and, ready to sink, she calls upon her father, the river god: "Help me, Peneus! Open the earth to enclose me, or change my form, which has brought me into this danger!" Scarcely had she spoken, when a stiffness seized all her limbs; her bosom began to be enclosed in a tender bark; her

hair became leaves; her arms became branches; her foot stuck fast in the ground, as a root; her face became a treetop, retaining nothing of its former self but its beauty. Apollo stood amazed. He touched the stem, and felt the flesh tremble under the new bark. He embraced the branches and lavished kisses on the wood. The branches shrank from his lips. "Since you cannot be my wife," said he, "you shall assuredly be my tree. I will wear you for my crown. I will decorate with you my harp and my quiver; and when the great Roman conquerors lead up the triumphal pomp to the Capitol, you shall be woven into wreaths for their brows. And, as eternal

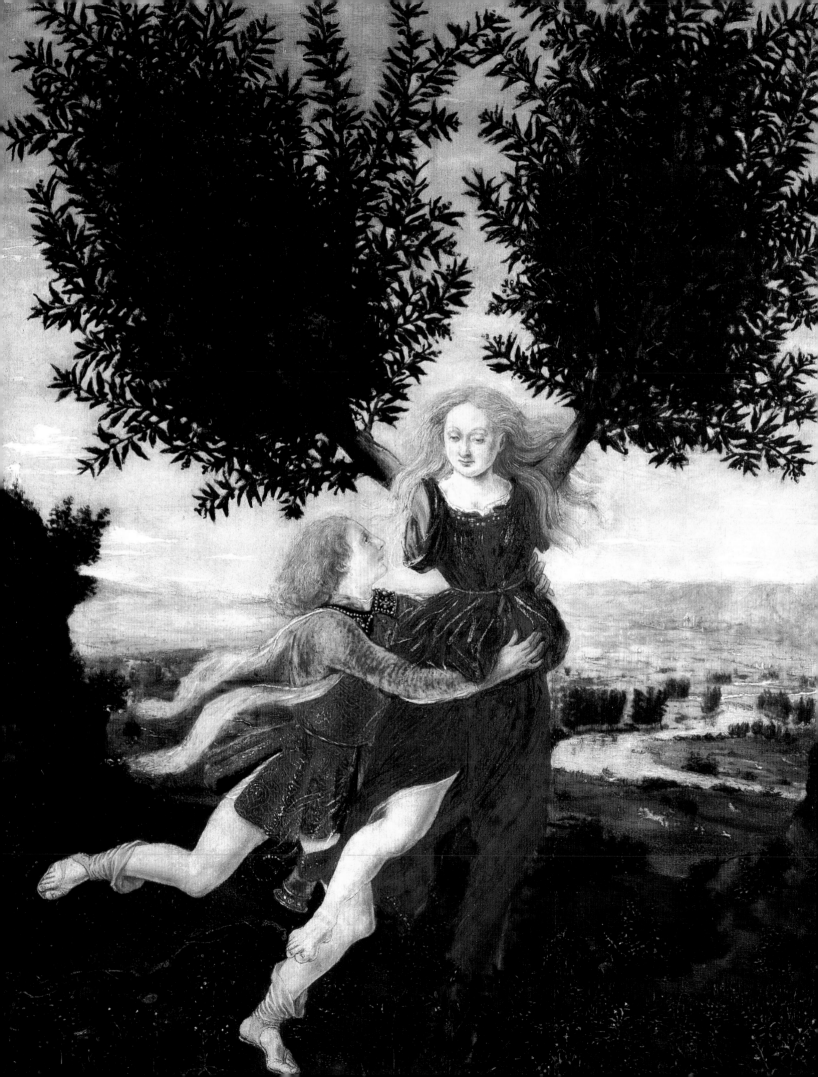

youth is mine, you also shall be always green, and your leaf know no decay." The nymph, now changed into a laurel tree, bowed its head in grateful acknowledgment.

PYRAMUS AND THISBE

Pyramus was the handsomest youth, and Thisbe the fairest maiden, in all Babylonia, where Semiramis reigned. Their parents occupied adjoining houses; and neighborhood brought the young people together, and acquaintance ripened into love. They would gladly have married, but their parents forbade. One thing, however, they could not forbid—that love should glow with equal ardor in the bosoms of both. They conversed by signs and glances, and the fire burned more intensely for being covered up. In the wall that parted the two houses there was a crack, caused by some fault in the structure. No one had remarked it before, but the lovers discovered it. What will not love discover! It afforded a passage to the voice; and tender messages used to pass backward and forward through the gap. As they stood, Pyramus on this side, Thisbe on that, their breaths would mingle. "Cruel wall," they said, "why do you keep two lovers apart? But we will not be ungrateful. We owe you, we confess, the privilege of transmitting loving words to willing ears." Such words they uttered on different sides of the wall; and when night came and they must say farewell, they pressed their lips upon the wall, she on her side, he on his, as they could come no nearer.

Next morning, when Aurora had put out the stars and the sun had melted the frost from the grass, they met at the accustomed spot. Then, after lamenting their hard fate, they agreed that next night, when all was still, they would slip away from watchful eyes, leave their dwellings, and walk out into the fields; and to ensure a meeting, repair to a well-known edifice standing without the city's bounds, called the Tomb of Ninus, and that the one who came first should await the other at the foot of a certain tree. It was a white mulberry tree, and stood near a cool spring. All was agreed on, and they waited impatiently for the sun to go down beneath the waters

◄ Apollo and Daphne, ANTONIO DEL POLLAIUOLO (circa 1432–1498): *Daphne in mid-transformation, set in a landscape inspired by Pollaiuolo's native Tuscany. The laurel wreath became a coveted prize for all who practiced Apollo's gift of music and poetry.*

and night to rise up from them. Then cautiously Thisbe stole forth, unobserved by the family, her head covered with a veil, made her way to the monument and sat down under the tree. As she sat alone in the dim light of the evening she descried a lioness, her jaws reeking with recent slaughter, approaching the fountain to slake her thirst. Thisbe fled at the sight and sought refuge in the hollow of a rock. As she fled she dropped her veil. The lioness, after drinking at the spring, turned to retreat to the woods, and seeing the veil on the ground, tossed and rent it with her bloody mouth.

Pyramus, having been delayed, now approached the place of meeting. He saw in the sand the footsteps of the lion, and the color fled from his cheeks at the sight. Presently he found the veil all rent and bloody. "Oh, hapless girl," said he, "I have been the cause of thy death! Thou, more worthy of life than I, hast fallen the first victim. I will follow. I am the guilty cause, in tempting thee forth to a place of such peril, and not being myself on the spot to guard thee. Come forth, ye lions, from the rocks, and tear this guilty body with your teeth." He took up the veil, carried it with him to the appointed tree, and covered it with kisses and with tears. "My blood also shall stain your texture," said he, and drawing his sword plunged it into his heart. The blood spurted from the wound and tinged the white mulberries of the tree all red; and sinking into the earth, reached the roots, so that the red color mounted through the trunk to the fruit.

By this time, Thisbe, still trembling with fear, yet wishing not to disappoint her lover, stepped cautiously forth, looking anxiously for the youth, eager to tell him the danger she had escaped. When she came to the spot and saw the changed color of the mulberries, she doubted whether it was the same place. While she hesitated, she saw the form of one struggling in the agonies of death. She started back, a shudder ran through her frame as a ripple on the face of the still water when a sudden breeze sweeps over it. But as soon as she recognized her lover, she screamed and beat her breast; embracing the lifeless body, pouring tears into its wounds, and imprinting kisses on the cold lips. "Oh, Pyramus," she cried, "what has done this? Answer me, Pyramus; it is your own Thisbe that speaks. Hear me, dearest, and lift that drooping head!" At the name of Thisbe, Pyramus

25

opened his eyes, then closed them again. She saw her veil stained with blood and the scabbard empty of its sword. "Thy own hand has slain thee, and for my sake," she said. "I too can be brave for once, and my love is as strong as thine. I will follow thee in death, for I have been the cause; and death, which alone could part us, shall not prevent my joining thee. And ye, unhappy parents of us both, deny us not our united request. As love and death have joined us, let one tomb contain us. And thou, tree, retain the marks of slaughter. Let thy berries still serve for memorials of our blood." So saying, she plunged the sword into her breast. Her parents ratified her wish, the gods also ratified it. The two bodies were buried in one sepulchre, and the tree ever after brought forth purple berries, as it does to this day.

CEPHALUS AND PROCRIS

Cephalus was a beautiful youth and fond of manly sports. He would rise before the dawn to pursue the chase. Aurora saw him when she first looked forth, fell in love with him, and stole him away. But Cephalus was just married to a charming wife whom he devotedly loved. Her name was Procris. She was a favorite of Diana, the goddess of hunting, who had given her a dog that could outrun every rival and a javelin that would never fail of its mark; and Procris gave these presents to her husband. Cephalus was so happy in his wife that he resisted all the entreaties of Aurora, and she finally dismissed him in displeasure, saying, "Go, ungrateful mortal, keep your wife, whom, if I am not much mistaken, you will one day be very sorry you ever saw again."

Cephalus returned, and was as happy as ever in his wife and his woodland sports. Now it happened some angry deity had sent a ravenous fox to annoy the country; and the hunters turned out in great strength to capture it. Their efforts were all in vain; no dog could run it down; and at last they came to Cephalus to borrow his famous dog, whose name was Lelaps. No sooner was the dog let loose than he darted off, quicker than their eye could follow him.

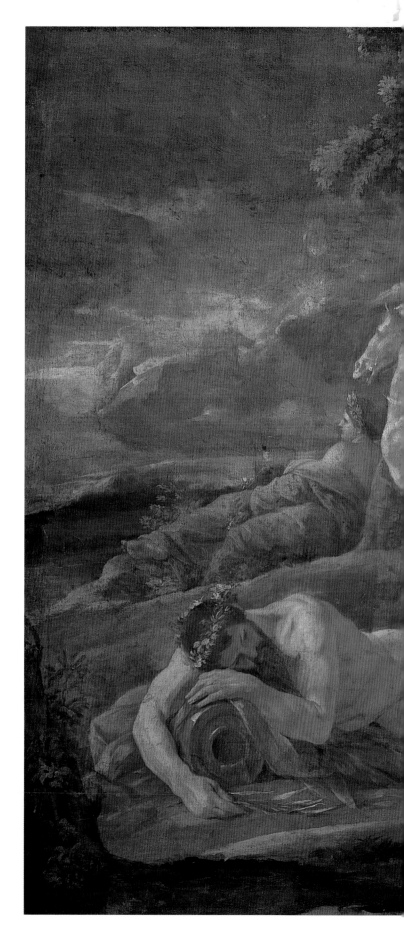

Cephalus and Aurora, NICOLAS POUSSIN (1594–1665) ➤
Aurora, "rosy-fingered" goddess of dawn, attempts to embrace Cephalus; he breaks away, as Cupid flourishes before him the image of his wife, Procris. Poussin bathes his figures in a golden light characteristic of his treatment of classical myths.

26

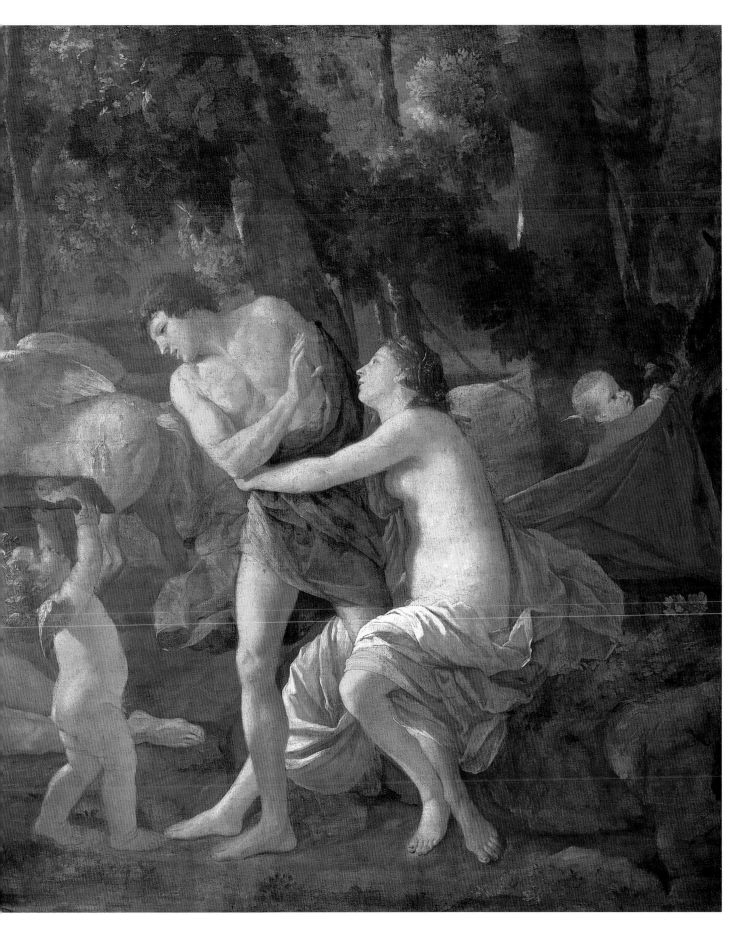

If they had not seen his footprints in the sand they would have thought he flew. Cephalus and others stood on a hill and saw the race. The fox tried every art; he ran in a circle and turned on his track, the dog close upon him, with open jaws, snapping at his heels, but biting only the air. Cephalus was about to use his javelin when, suddenly, he saw both dog and game stop instantly. The heavenly powers, who had given both, were not willing that either should conquer. In the very attitude of life and action they were turned into stone. So lifelike and natural did they look, you would have thought, as you looked at them, that one was going to bark, the other to leap forward.

Cephalus, though he had lost his dog, still continued to take delight in the chase. He would go out at early morning, ranging the woods and hills unaccompanied by anyone, needing no help, for his javelin was a sure weapon in all cases. Fatigued with hunting, when the sun got high he would seek a shady nook where a cool stream flowed, and, stretched on the grass, with his garments thrown aside, would enjoy the breeze. Sometimes he would say aloud, "Come, sweet breeze, come and fan my breast, come and allay the heat that burns me."

Someone passing by one day heard him talking in this way to the air, and, foolishly believing that he was talking to some maiden, went and told the secret to Procris, Cephalus's wife. Love is credulous. Procris, at the sudden shock, fainted away. Presently recovering, she said, "It cannot be true; I will not believe it unless I myself am a witness to it." So she waited, with anxious heart, till the next morning, when Cephalus went to hunt as usual. Then she stole out after him and concealed herself in the place where the informer directed her.

Cephalus came, as he was wont when tired with sport, and stretched himself on the green bank, saying, "Come, sweet breeze, come and fan me; you know how I love you! You make the groves and my solitary rambles delightful." He was running on in this way when he heard, or thought he heard, a sound as of a sob in the bushes. Supposing it some wild animal, he threw his javelin at the spot.

A cry from his beloved Procris told him that the weapon had too surely met its mark. He rushed to the place and found her bleeding and, with sinking strength, endeavoring to draw forth from the wound the javelin, her own gift. Cephalus raised her from the earth, strove to stanch the blood, and called her to revive and not to leave him miserable, to reproach himself with her death. She opened her feeble eyes and forced herself to utter these few words: "I implore you, if you have ever loved me, if I have ever deserved kindness at your hands, my husband, grant me this last request; do not marry that odious Breeze!" This disclosed the whole mystery: but alas! what advantage to disclose it now? She died; but her face wore a calm expression, and she looked pityingly and forgivingly on her husband when he made her understand the truth.

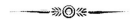

Chapter 4

Juno and Her Rivals, Io and Callisto
Diana and Actaeon
Latona and the Rustics

Juno one day perceived it suddenly grow dark and immediately suspected that her husband had raised a cloud to hide some of his doings that would not bear the light. She brushed away the cloud and saw her husband on the banks of a glassy river, with a beautiful heifer standing near him. Juno suspected the heifer's form concealed some fair nymph of mortal mould—as was, indeed, the case; for it was Io, the daughter of the river god Inachus, whom Jupiter had been flirting with and, when he became aware of the approach of his wife, had changed into that form.

Juno joined her husband, and noticing the heifer, praised its beauty, and asked whose it was, and of what herd. Jupiter, to stop questions, replied that it was a fresh creation from the earth. Juno asked to have it as a gift. What could Jupiter do? He was loath to give his mistress to his wife; yet how refuse so trifling a present as a simple heifer? He could not, without exciting suspicion; so he consented. The goddess was not yet relieved of her suspicions; so she delivered the heifer to Argus, to be strictly watched.

Now Argus had a hundred eyes in his head and never went to sleep with more than two at a time, so that he kept watch on Io constantly. He suffered her to feed through the day and at night tied her up with a vile rope round her neck. She would have stretched out her arms to implore freedom of Argus, but she had no arms to stretch out, and her voice was a bellow that frightened even herself. She saw her father and her sisters, went near them, and suffered them to pat her back, and heard them admire her beauty. Her father reached her a tuft of grass, and she licked the outstretched hand. She longed to make herself known to him, and would have uttered her wish; but, alas! words were wanting. At length she bethought herself of writing, and inscribed her name—it was a short one—with her hoof on the sand. Inachus recognized it, and discovering that his daughter, whom he had long sought in vain, was hidden under this disguise, mourned over her, and, embracing her white neck, exclaimed, "Alas! my daughter, it would have been a less grief to have lost you altogether!" While he thus lamented, Argus, observing, came and drove her away, and took his seat on a high bank, from whence he could see all around in every direction.

Jupiter was troubled at beholding the sufferings of his mistress and, calling Mercury, told him to go and dispatch Argus. Mercury made haste, put his winged slippers on his feet, and cap on his head, took his sleep-producing wand, and leaped down from the heavenly towers to the earth. There he laid aside his wings and kept only his wand, with which he presented himself as a shepherd driving his flock. As he strolled on, he blew upon his pipes. These were what are called the Syrinx or Pandean pipes. Argus listened with delight, for he had never seen the instrument before. "Young man," said he, "come and take a seat by me on this stone. There is no better place for your flock to graze in than hereabouts, and here is a pleasant shade such as shepherds love." Mercury sat down, talked, and told stories till it grew late, and played upon his pipes his most soothing strains, hoping to lull the watchful eyes to sleep, but all in vain; for Argus still contrived to keep some of his eyes open though he shut the rest.

Among other stories, Mercury told him how the instrument on which he played was invented. "There was a certain nymph, whose name was Syrinx, who was much beloved by the satyrs and spirits of the wood; but she would have none of them, but was a faithful worshipper of Diana and followed the chase. You would have thought it was Diana herself, had you seen her in her hunting dress, only that her bow was of horn and Diana's of silver. One day, as she was returning from the chase, Pan met her, told her just this, and added more of the same sort. She ran away, without stopping to hear his compliments, and he pursued till she came to the bank of the river, where he overtook her, and she had only time to call for help on her friends the water nymphs. They heard and consented. Pan threw his arms around what he supposed to be the form of the nymph and found he embraced only a tuft of reeds! As he breathed a sigh, the air sounded through the reeds and produced a plaintive melody. The god, charmed with the novelty and with the sweetness of the music, said, 'Thus, then, at least, you shall be mine.' And he took some of the reeds, and placing them together, of unequal lengths, side by side, made an instrument which he called Syrinx, in honor of the nymph." Before Mercury had finished his story he saw Argus's eyes all asleep. As his head nodded forward on his breast, Mercury with one stroke cut his neck through, and tumbled his head down the rocks. Oh, hapless Argus! the light of your hundred eyes is quenched at once! Juno took them and put them as ornaments on the tail of her peacock, where they remain to this day.

But the vengeance of Juno was not yet satiated. She sent a gadfly to torment Io, who fled over the whole world from its pursuit. She swam through the Ionian Sea, which derived its name from her, then roamed over the plains of Illyria, ascended Mount Haemus, and crossed the Thracian strait, thence named the Bosphorus (cow ford), rambled on through Scythia and the country of the Cimmerians, and arrived at last on the banks of the Nile. At length, Jupiter interceded for her, and upon his promising not to pay her any more attentions Juno consented to restore her to her form. It was curious to see her gradually recover her former self. The coarse hairs fell from her body, her horns shrank up, her eyes grew narrower, her mouth shorter; hands and fingers came instead of hoofs to her forefeet; in fine there was nothing left of the heifer, except her beauty. At first she was afraid to speak for fear she should low, but gradually she recovered her confidence, and was restored to her father and sisters.

CALLISTO

Callisto was another maiden who excited the jealousy of Juno, and the goddess changed her into a bear. "I will take away," said she, "that beauty with which you have captivated my husband." Down fell Callisto on her hands and knees; she tried to stretch out her arms in supplication—they were already beginning to be covered with black hair. Her hands grew rounded, became armed with crooked claws, and served for feet; her mouth, which Jove used to praise for its beauty, became a horrid pair of jaws;

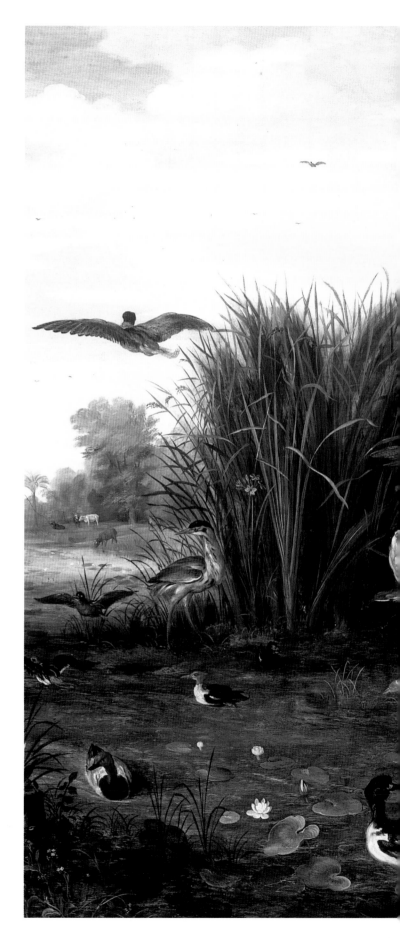

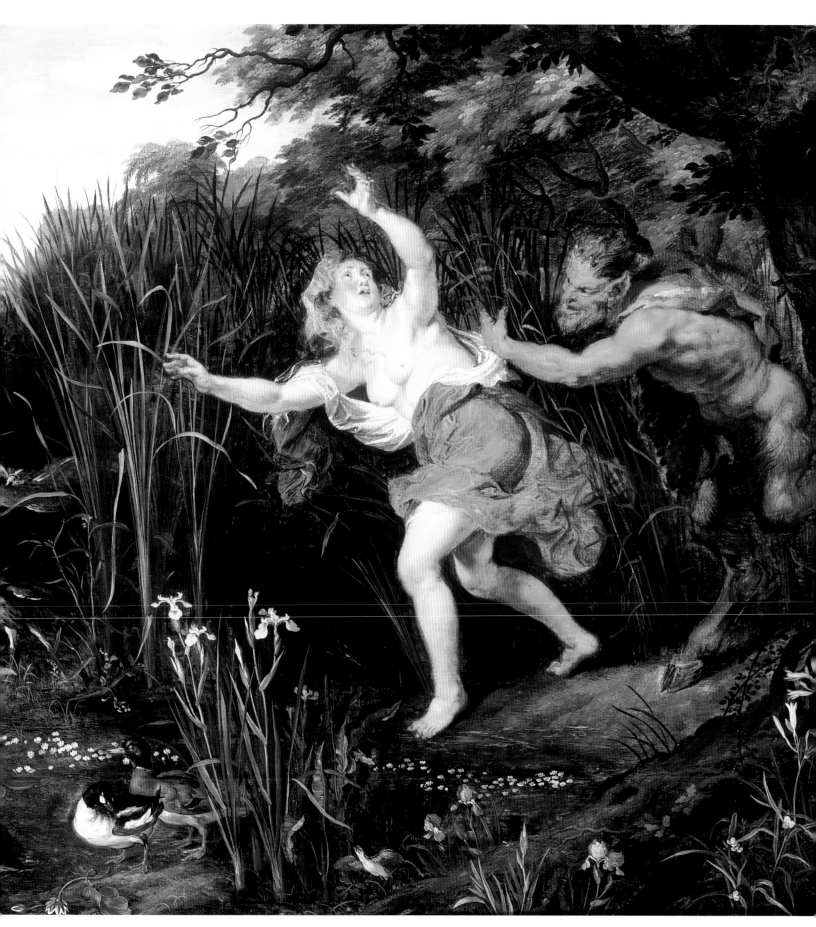

▲ Landscape with Pan and Syrinx, PETER PAUL RUBENS (1577–1640) AND JAN BRUEGHEL THE ELDER (1568–1625)
In Greek, Pan simply means "all." As cloven-hoofed deity of the countryside, however, he was especially dear to shepherds, whose delight was to play the reed pipe or syrinx. The grotesque face of Pan may owe more to Brueghel than to Rubens.

her voice, which if unchanged would have moved the heart to pity, became a growl, more fit to inspire terror. Yet her former disposition remained, and with continual groaning, she bemoaned her fate and stood upright as well as she could, lifting up her paws to beg for mercy; and felt that Jove was unkind, though she could not tell him so. Ah, how often, afraid to stay in the woods all night alone, she wandered about the neighborhood of her former haunts; how often, frightened by the dogs, did she, so lately a huntress, fly in terror from the hunters! Often she fled from the wild beasts, forgetting that she was now a wild beast herself; and, bear as she was, was afraid of the bears.

One day a youth espied her as he was hunting. She saw him and recognized him as her own son, now grown a young man. She stopped and felt inclined to embrace him. As she was about to approach, he, alarmed, raised his hunting spear, and was on the point of transfixing her, when Jupiter, beholding, arrested the crime, and snatching away both of them, placed them in the heavens as the Great and Little Bear.

Juno was in a rage to see her rival so set in honor, and hastened to ancient Tethys and Oceanus, the powers of ocean, and in answer to their enquiries, thus told the cause of her coming: "Do you ask why I, the queen of the gods, have left the heavenly plains and sought your depths? Learn that I am supplanted in heaven—my place is given to another. You will hardly believe me; but look when night darkens the world, and you shall see the two of whom I have so much reason to complain exalted to the heavens, in that part where the circle is the smallest, in the neighborhood of the pole. Why should anyone hereafter tremble at the thought of offending Juno, when such rewards are the consequence of my displeasure! See what I have been able to effect! I forbade her to wear the human form—she is placed among the stars! So do my punishments result—such is the extent of my power! Better that she should have resumed her former shape, as I permitted Io to do. Perhaps he means to marry her, and put me away! But you, my foster parents, if you feel for me, and see with displeasure this unworthy treatment of me, show it, I beseech you, by forbidding this guilty couple from coming into your waters." The powers of the ocean assented, and consequently the two constellations of the Great and Little Bear move round and round in heaven, but never sink, as the other stars do, beneath the ocean.

DIANA AND ACTAEON

Thus, in two instances, we have seen Juno's severity to her rivals; now let us learn how a virgin goddess punished an invader of her privacy.

It was midday, and the sun stood equally distant from either goal, when young Actaeon, son of King Cadmus, thus addressed the youths who with him were hunting the stag in the mountains:

"Friends, our nets and our weapons are wet with the blood of our victims; we have had sport enough for one day, and tomorrow we can renew our labors. Now, while Phoebus parches the earth, let us put by our implements and indulge ourselves with rest."

There was a valley thick enclosed with cypresses and pines, sacred to the huntress queen, Diana. In the extremity of the valley was a cave, not adorned with art, but nature had counterfeited art in its construction, for she had turned the arch of its roof with stones as delicately fitted as if by the hand of man. A fountain burst out from one side, whose open basin was bounded by a grassy rim. Here the goddess of the woods used to come when weary with hunting and lave her virgin limbs in the sparkling water.

One day, having repaired thither with her nymphs, she handed her javelin, her quiver, and her bow to one, her robe to another, while a third unbound the sandals from her feet. Then Crocale, the most skillful of them, arranged her hair, and Nephele, Hyale, and the rest drew water in capacious urns. While the goddess was thus employed in the labors of the toilet, behold Actaeon, having quitted his companions and rambling without any especial object, came to the place, led thither by his destiny. As he presented himself at the entrance of the cave, the nymphs, seeing a man, screamed and rushed toward the goddess to hide her with their bodies. But she was taller than the rest and overtopped them all by a head. Such a color as tinges the clouds at sunset or at dawn came over the countenance of Diana thus taken by surprise. Surrounded as she was by her nymphs, she

Diana the Huntress, SCHOOL OF FONTAINEBLEAU ➤
(about 1530–1560): *Diana was goddess not only of the hunt, but also of the moon and of the female cycle; she is often shown with a crescent moon on her forehead. Her weapon, the bow and arrow, and her attendant hounds, signaled her as a goddess to be widely feared by men and women alike.*

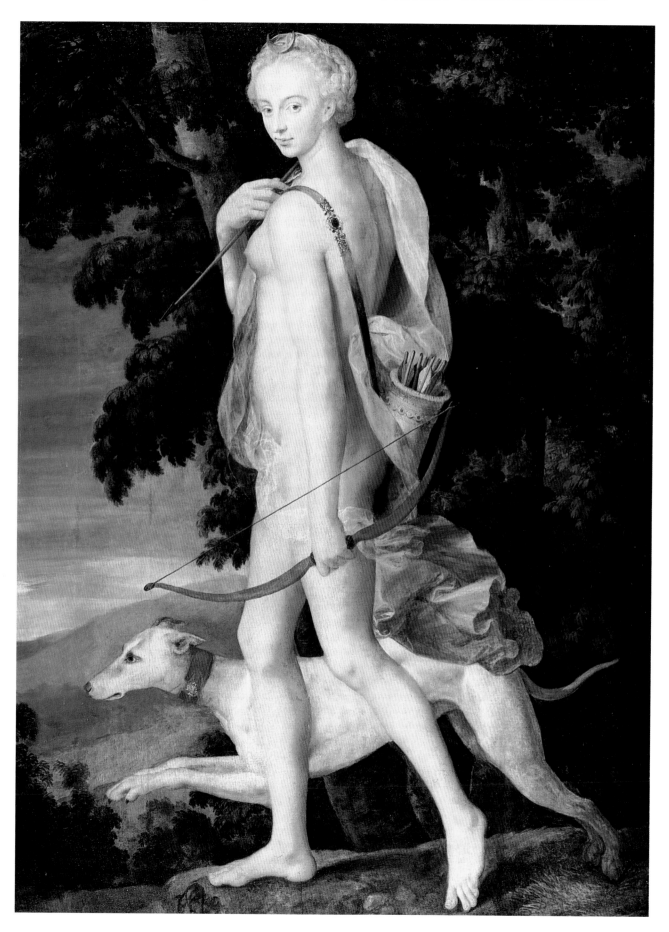

yet turned half away and sought with a sudden impulse for her arrows. As they were not at hand, she dashed the water into the face of the intruder, adding these words: "Now go and tell, if you can, that you have seen Diana unappareled." Immediately, a pair of branching stag's horns grew out of his head, his neck gained in length, his ears grew sharp-pointed, his hands became feet, his arms long legs, his body was covered with a hairy spotted hide. Fear took the place of his former boldness, and the hero fled. He could not but admire his own speed; but when he saw his horns in the water, "Ah, wretched me!" he would have said, but no sound followed the effort. He groaned, and tears flowed down the face which had taken the place of his own. Yet his consciousness remained. What shall he do— go home to seek the palace or lie hid in the woods? The latter he was afraid, the former he was ashamed to do. While he hesitated, the dogs saw him. First Melampus, a Spartan dog, gave the signal with his bark, then Pamphagus, Dorceus, Lelaps, Theron, Nape, Tigris, and all the rest rushed after him

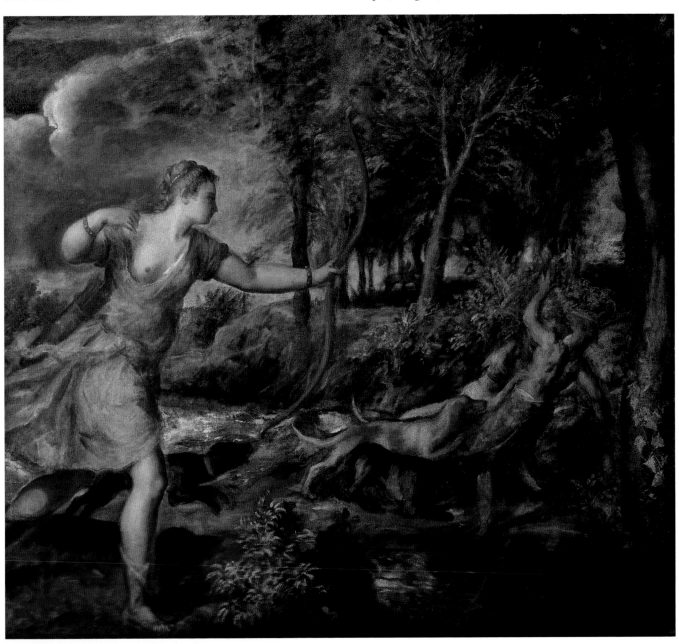

⋏ The Death of Actaeon, TITIAN (active circa 1506; died 1576)
Actaeon transgressed by watching Diana as she bathed. His punishment, to be torn apart by her pack of hounds, echoes the bloodletting practices at ancient temples, such as Artemis Orthia, near Sparta, where Diana was worshipped.

swifter than the wind. Over rocks and cliffs, through mountain gorges that seemed impracticable, he fled and they followed. Where he had often chased the stag and cheered on his pack, his pack now chased him, cheered on by his huntsmen. He longed to cry out, "I am Actaeon; recognize your master!" but the words came not at his will. The air resounded with the bark of the dogs. Presently one fastened on his back, another seized his shoulder. While they held their master, the rest of the pack came up and buried their teeth in his flesh. He groaned—not in a human voice, yet certainly not in a stag's—and falling on his knees, raised his eyes, and would have raised his arms in supplication, if he had had them. His friends and fellow huntsmen cheered on the dogs, and looked everywhere for Actaeon, calling on him to join the sport. At the sound of his name, he turned his head, and heard them regret that he should be away. He earnestly wished he was. He would have been well pleased to see the exploits of his dogs, but to feel them was too much. They were all around him, rending and tearing; and it was not till they had torn his life out that the anger of Diana was satisfied.

LATONA AND THE RUSTICS

Some thought the goddess in this instance more severe than was just, while others praised her conduct as strictly consistent with her virgin dignity. As usual, the recent event brought older ones to mind, and one of the bystanders told this story: "Some countrymen of Lycia once insulted the goddess Latona, but not with impunity. When I was young, my father, who had grown too old for active labors, sent me to Lycia to drive thence some choice oxen, and there I saw the very pond and marsh where the wonder happened. Nearby stood an ancient altar, black with the smoke of sacrifice and almost buried among the reeds. I enquired whose altar it might be, whether of Faunus or the Naiads or some god of the neighboring mountain, and one of the country people replied, 'No mountain or river god possesses this altar but she whom royal Juno in her jealousy drove from land to land, denying her any spot of earth whereon to rear her twins. Bearing in her arms the infant deities,

Latona reached this land, weary with her burden and parched with thirst. By chance she espied in the bottom of the valley this pond of clear water, where the country people were at work gathering willows and osiers. The goddess approached, and kneeling on the bank, would have slaked her thirst in the cool stream, but the rustics forbade her. "Why do you refuse me water?" said she. "Water is free to all. Nature allows no one to claim as property the sunshine, the air, or the water. I come to take my share of the common blessing. Yet I ask it of you as a favor. I have no intention of washing my limbs in it, weary though they be, but only to quench my thirst. My mouth is so dry that I can hardly speak. A draught of water would be nectar to me; it would revive me, and I would own myself indebted to you for life itself. Let these infants move your pity, who stretch out their little arms as if to plead for me—'" and the children, as it happened, were stretching out their arms.

"Who would not have been moved with these gentle words of the goddess? But these clowns persisted in their rudeness; they even added jeers and threats of violence if she did not leave the place. Nor was this all. They waded into the pond and stirred up the mud with their feet, so as to make the water unfit to drink. Latona was so angry that she ceased to mind her thirst. She no longer supplicated the clowns, but lifting her hands to heaven exclaimed, 'May they never quit that pool, but pass their lives there!' And it came to pass accordingly. They now live in the water, sometimes totally submerged, then raising their heads above the surface or swimming upon it. Sometimes they come out upon the bank, but soon leap back again into the water. They still use their base voices in railing, and though they have the water all to themselves, are not ashamed to croak in the midst of it. Their voices are harsh, their throats bloated, their mouths have become stretched by constant railing, their necks have shrunk up and disappeared, and their heads are joined to their bodies. Their backs are green, their disproportioned bellies white, and in short they are now frogs and dwell in the slimy pool."

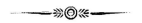

CHAPTER 5

PHAËTON

PHAËTON WAS THE SON OF APOLLO AND THE NYMPH Clymene. One day a schoolfellow laughed at the idea of his being the son of the god, and Phaëton went in rage and shame and reported it to his mother. "If," said he, "I am indeed of heavenly birth, give me, mother, some proof of it and establish my claim to the honor." Clymene stretched forth her hands toward the skies and said, "I call to witness the Sun, which looks down upon us, that I have told you the truth. If I speak falsely, let this be the last time I behold his light. But it needs not much labor to go and enquire for yourself; the land whence the Sun rises lies next to ours. Go and demand of him whether he will own you as a son." Phaëton heard with delight. He traveled to India, which lies directly in the regions of sunrise; and, full of hope and pride, approached the goal whence his parent begins his course.

The palace of the Sun stood reared aloft on columns, glittering with gold and precious stones, while polished ivory formed the ceilings, and silver the doors. The workmanship surpassed the material; for upon the walls Vulcan had represented earth, sea, and skies, with their inhabitants. In the sea were the nymphs, some sporting in the waves, some riding on the backs of fishes, while others sat upon the rocks and dried their sea-green hair. Their faces were not all alike, nor yet unlike—but such as sisters' ought to be. The earth had its towns and forests and rivers and rustic divinities. Over all was carved the likeness of the glorious heaven; and on the silver doors the twelve signs of the zodiac, six on each side.

Clymene's son advanced up the steep ascent and entered the halls of his disputed father. He approached the paternal presence, but stopped at a distance, for the light was more than he could bear. Phoebus, arrayed in a purple vesture, sat on a throne which glittered as with diamonds. On his right hand and his left stood the Day, the Month, and the Year, and, at regular intervals, the Hours. Spring stood with her head crowned with flowers, and Summer, with garment cast aside and a garland formed of spears of ripened grain, and Autumn, with his feet stained with grape juice, and icy Winter, with his hair stiffened with hoar frost. Surrounded by these attendants, the Sun, with the eye that sees everything, beheld the youth dazzled with the novelty and splendor of the scene, and enquired the purpose of his errand. The youth replied, "O light of the boundless world, Phoebus, my father—if you permit me to use that name—give me some proof, I beseech you, by which I may be known as yours." He ceased; and his father, laying aside the beams that shone all around his head, bade him approach, and embracing him, said, "My son, you deserve not to be disowned, and I confirm what your mother has told you. To put an end to your doubts, ask what you will, the gift shall be yours. I call to witness that dreadful lake, which I never saw, but which we gods swear by in our most solemn engagements."

Phaëton immediately asked to be permitted for one day to drive the chariot of the sun. The father repented of his promise; thrice and four times he shook his radiant head in warning. "I have spoken rashly," said he; "this only request I would fain deny. I beg you to withdraw it. It is not a safe boon, nor one, my Phaëton, suited to your youth and strength. Your lot is mortal, and you ask what is beyond a mortal's power. In your ignorance you aspire to do that which not even the gods themselves may do. None but myself may drive the flaming car of day. Not even Jupiter, whose terrible right arm hurls the thunderbolts. The first part of the way is steep and such as the horses when fresh in the morning can hardly climb; the middle is high up in the heavens, whence I myself can scarcely, without alarm, look down and behold the earth and sea stretched beneath me. The last part of the road descends rapidly and requires most careful driving. Tethys, who is waiting to receive me, often trembles for me lest I should fall headlong. Add to all this, the heaven is all the time turning around and carrying the stars with it. I have to be perpetually on my guard lest that movement, which sweeps everything else along, should hurry me also away. Suppose I should lend you the chariot, what would you do? Could you keep your course while the sphere was revolving under you? Perhaps you think that there are forests and cities, the abodes of gods, and palaces and temples on the way. On the contrary, the road is through the midst of frightful monsters. You pass

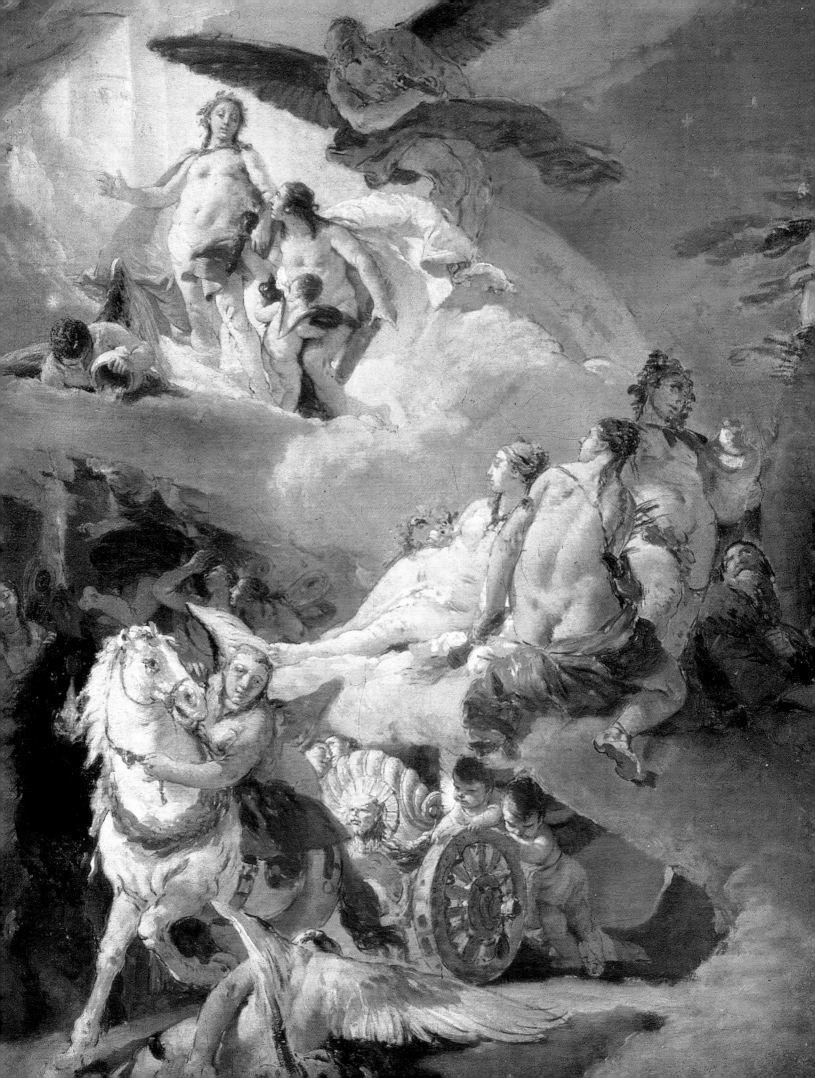

by the horns of the Bull, in front of the Archer, and near the Lion's jaws, and where the Scorpion stretches its arms in one direction and the Crab in another. Nor will you find it easy to guide those horses, with their breasts full of fire that they breathe forth from their mouths and nostrils. I can scarcely govern them myself, when they are unruly and resist the reins. Beware, my son, lest I be the donor of a fatal gift; recall your request while yet you may. Do you ask me for a proof that you are sprung from my blood? I give you a proof in my fears for you. Look at my face—I would that you could look into my breast, you would there see all a father's anxiety. Finally," he continued, "look around the world and choose whatever you will of what earth or sea contains most precious—ask it and fear no refusal. This only I pray you not to urge. It is not honor but destruction you seek. Why do you hang round my neck and still entreat me? You shall have it if you persist—the oath is sworn and must be kept—but I beg you to choose more wisely."

He ended; but the youth rejected all admonition and held to his demand. So, having resisted as long as he could, Phoebus at last led the way to where stood the lofty chariot.

It was of gold, the gift of Vulcan; the axle was of gold, the pole and wheels of gold, the spokes of silver. Along the seat were rows of chrysolites and diamonds, which reflected all around the brightness of the sun. While the daring youth gazed in admiration, the early Dawn threw open the purple doors of the east and showed the pathway strewn with roses. The stars withdrew, marshaled by the Day star, which last of all retired also. The father, when he saw the earth beginning to glow and the Moon preparing to retire, ordered the Hours to harness up the horses. They obeyed, and led forth from the lofty stalls the steeds full fed with ambrosia, and attached the reins.

Then the father bathed the face of his son with a powerful unguent, and made him capable of enduring the brightness of the flame. He set the rays on his head and, with a foreboding sigh, said, "If, my son,

◄ Phaëton and Apollo, GIAMBATTISTA TIEPOLO (1696–1770)
In another aspect, Apollo was Helios, the sun god; his symbol was a horse-drawn chariot. Here the wreathed Apollo reluctantly allows his son to take the reins. The over-eager appearance of the horse suggests that the ride will be disastrous.

you will in this at least heed my advice, spare the whip and hold tight the reins. They go fast enough of their own accord; the labor is to hold them in. You are not to take the straight road directly between the five circles, but turn off to the left. Keep within the limit of the middle zone, and avoid the northern and the southern alike. You will see the marks of the wheels, and they will serve to guide you. And, that the skies and the earth may each receive their due share of heat, go not too high, or you will burn the heavenly dwellings, nor too low, or you will set the earth on fire; the middle course is safest and best. And now I leave you to your chance, which I hope will plan better for you than you have done for yourself. Night is passing out of the western gates and we can delay no longer. Take the reins; but if at last your heart fails you, and you will benefit by my advice, stay where you are in safety, and suffer me to light and warm the earth."

The agile youth sprang into the chariot, stood erect and grasped the reins with delight, pouring out thanks to his reluctant parent.

Meanwhile, the horses fill the air with their snortings and fiery breath and stamp the ground impatient. Now the bars are let down, and the boundless plain of the universe lies open before them. They dart forward and cleave the opposing clouds, and outrun the morning breezes which started from the same eastern goal. The steeds soon perceived that the load they drew was lighter than usual; and as a ship without ballast is tossed hither and thither on the sea, so the chariot, without its accustomed weight, was dashed about as if empty. They rush headlong and leave the traveled road. He is alarmed, and knows not how to guide them; nor, if he knew, has he the power. Then, for the first time, the Great and Little Bear were scorched with heat, and would fain, if it were possible, have plunged into the water; and the Serpent which lies coiled up round the north pole, torpid and harmless, grew warm, and with warmth felt its rage revive. Boötes, they say, fled away, though encumbered with his plow, and all unused to rapid motion.

When hapless Phaëton looked down upon the earth, now spreading in vast extent beneath him, he grew pale and his knees shook with terror. In spite of the glare all around him, the sight of his eyes grew dim. He wished he had never touched his father's horses, never learned his parentage, never prevailed in his request. He is borne along like a vessel that flies before a tempest, when the pilot can do no more and betakes himself to his prayers. What shall he do? Much of the heavenly road is left behind, but more remains before. He turns his eyes from one direction to the other; now to the goal whence he began his course, now to the realms of sunset which he is not destined to reach. He loses his self-command, and knows not what to do—whether to draw tight the reins or throw them loose; he forgets the names of the horses. He sees with terror the monstrous forms scattered over the surface of heaven. Here the Scorpion extended his two great arms, with his tail and crooked claws stretching over two signs of the zodiac. When the boy beheld him, reeking with poison and menacing with his fangs, his courage failed, and the reins fell from his hands. The horses, when they felt them loose on their backs, dashed headlong, and unrestrained went off into unknown regions of the sky, in among the stars, hurling the chariot over pathless places, now up in high heaven, now down almost to the earth. The moon saw with astonishment her brother's chariot running beneath her own. The clouds begin to smoke, and the mountaintops take fire; the fields are parched with heat, the plants wither, the trees with their leafy branches burn, the harvest is ablaze! But these are small things. Great cities perished, with their walls and towers; whole nations with their people were consumed to ashes! The forest-clad mountains burned, Athos and Taurus and Tmolus and Oeta; Ida, once celebrated for fountains, but now all dry; the Muses' mountain Helicon, and Haemus; Aetna, with fires within and without, and Parnassus, with his two peaks, and Rhodope, forced at last to part with his snowy crown. Her cold climate was no protection to Scythia, Caucasus burned, and Ossa and Pindus, and, greater than both, Olympus; the Alps high in air, and the Apennines crowned with clouds.

Then Phaëton beheld the world on fire, and felt the heat intolerable. The air he breathed was like the air of a furnace and full of burning ashes, and the smoke was of a pitchy darkness. He dashed forward he knew not whither. Then, it is believed, the people of Aethiopia became black by the blood being forced so suddenly to the surface, and the Libyan desert was dried up to the condition in which it remains to this day.

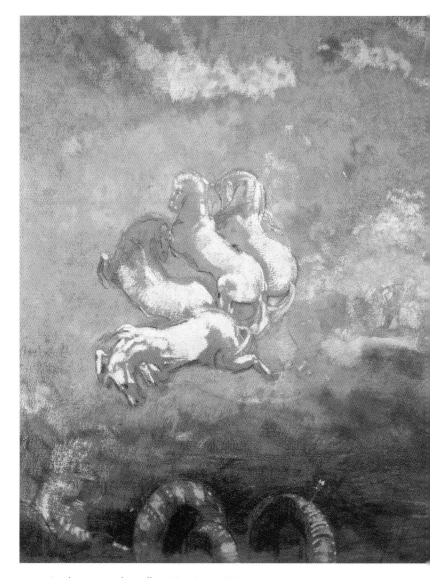

▲ Phaëton and Apollo, ODILON REDON (1840–1916)
Apollo's son Phaëton loses control, and Jupiter strikes his blazing chariot with a thunderbolt, lest the earth be consumed by flames. The visionary quality of this painting was later to exert a major influence on the Surrealist movement.

The nymphs of the fountains, with disheveled hair, mourned their waters, nor were the rivers safe beneath their banks; Tanais smoked, and Caicus, Xanthus and Maeander. Babylonian Euphrates and Ganges, Tagus with golden sands, and Caÿster where the swans resort. Nile fled away and hid his head in the desert, and there it still remains concealed. Where he used to discharge his waters through seven mouths into the sea, there seven dry channels alone remained. The earth cracked open, and through the chinks light broke into Tartarus and frightened the king of shadows and his queen. The sea shrank up. Where before was water it became a dry plain;

39

and the mountains that lie beneath the waves lifted up their heads and became islands. The fishes sought the lowest depths, and the dolphins no longer ventured as usual to sport on the surface. Even Nereus, and his wife Doris, with the Nereids, their daughters, sought the deepest caves for refuge. Thrice Neptune essayed to raise his head above the surface, and thrice was driven back by the heat. Earth, surrounded as she was by waters, yet with head and shoulders bare, screening her face with her hand, looked up to heaven, and with a husky voice called on Jupiter.

"O ruler of the gods, if I have deserved this treatment, and it is your will that I perish with fire, why withhold your thunderbolts? Let me at least fall by your hand. Is this the reward of my fertility, of my obedient service? Is it for this that I have supplied herbage for cattle, and fruits for men, and frankincense for your altars? But if I am unworthy of regard, what has my brother Ocean done to deserve such a fate? If neither of us can excite your pity, think, I pray you, of your own heaven, and behold how both the poles are smoking which sustain your palace, which must fall if they be destroyed. Atlas faints, and scarce holds up his burden. If sea, earth, and heaven perish, we fall into ancient Chaos. Save what yet remains to us from the devouring flame. Oh, take thought for our deliverance in this awful moment!"

Thus spoke Earth, and overcome with heat and thirst, could say no more. Then Jupiter omnipotent, calling to witness all the gods, including him who had lent the chariot, and showing them that all was lost unless some speedy remedy were applied, mounted the lofty tower from whence he diffuses clouds over the earth, and hurls the forked lightnings. But at that time not a cloud was to be found to interpose for a screen to earth, nor was a shower remaining unexhausted. He thundered, and brandishing a lightning bolt in his right hand launched it against the charioteer, and struck him at the same moment from his seat and from existence! Phaëton, with his hair on fire, fell headlong, like a shooting star which marks the heavens with its brightness as it falls, and Eridanus, the great river, received him and cooled his burning frame. The Italian Naiads reared a tomb for him, and inscribed these words upon the stone:

> Driver of Phoebus's chariot, Phaëton,
> Struck by Jove's thunder, rests beneath this stone.
> He could not rule his father's car of fire,
> Yet was it much so nobly to aspire.

His sisters, the Heliades, as they lamented his fate were turned into poplar trees on the banks of the river, and their tears, which continued to flow, became amber as they dropped into the stream.

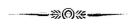

CHAPTER 6

MIDAS · BAUCIS AND PHILEMON

Bacchus, on a certain occasion, found his old schoolmaster and foster father, Silenus, missing. The old man had been drinking, and in that state wandered away, and was found by some peasants, who carried him to their king, Midas. Midas recognized him and treated him hospitably, entertaining him for ten days and nights with an unceasing round of jollity. On the eleventh day he brought Silenus back and restored him in safety to his pupil. Whereupon Bacchus offered Midas his choice of a reward, whatever he might wish. He asked that whatever he might touch should be changed into gold. Bacchus consented, though sorry that he had not made a better choice. Midas went his way, rejoicing in his new-acquired power, which he hastened to put to the test. He could scarce believe his eyes when he found a twig of an oak, which he plucked from the branch, become gold in his hand.

He took up a stone; it changed to gold. He touched a sod; it did the same. He took an apple from the tree; you would have thought he had robbed the garden of the Hesperides. His joy knew no bounds, and as soon as he got home, he ordered the servants to set a splendid repast on the table. Then he found to his dismay that whenever he touched bread, it hardened in his hand; or put a morsel to his lips, it defied his teeth. He took a glass of wine, but it flowed down his throat like melted gold.

In consternation at the unprecedented affliction, he strove to divest himself of his power; he hated the gift he had lately coveted. But all in vain; starvation seemed to await him. He raised his arms, all shining with gold, in prayer to Bacchus, begging to be delivered from his glittering destruction. Bacchus, merciful deity, heard and consented. "Go," said he, "to the River Pactolus, trace the stream to its

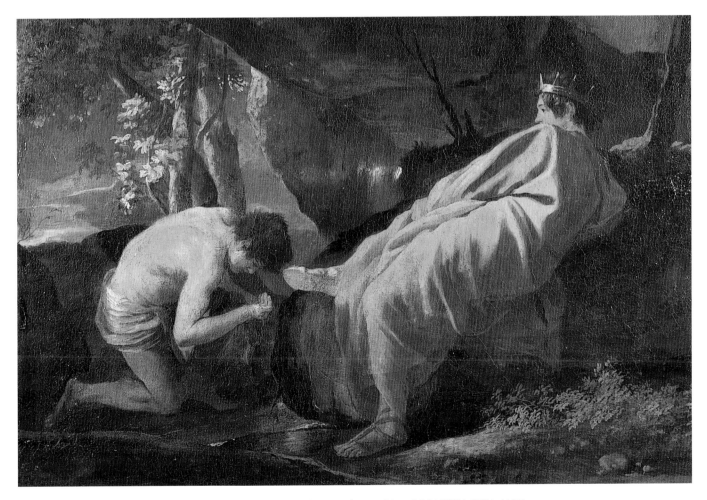

▲ Midas at the Source of the Pactolus, NICOLAS POUSSIN (1594–1665)
The River Pactolus was in Phrygia (now part of Turkey) where Midas was once legendary and historical king. Here Midas, cured of his own addiction, watches a youth search the river's yellow sands for gold. Poussin's implicit moral is that greed for what glitters is never ending.

fountainhead, there plunge your head and body in and wash away your fault and its punishment." He did so, and scarce had he touched the waters before the gold-creating power passed into them, and the river sands became changed into gold, as they remain to this day.

Thenceforth Midas, hating wealth and splendor, dwelt in the country, and became a worshipper of Pan, the god of the fields. On a certain occasion Pan had the temerity to compare his music with that of Apollo and to challenge the god of the lyre to a trial of skill. The challenge was accepted, and Tmolus, the mountain god, was chosen umpire. The senior took his seat and cleared away the trees from his ears to listen. At a given signal Pan blew on his pipes, and with his rustic melody gave great satisfaction to himself and his faithful follower Midas, who happened to be present. Then Tmolus turned his head toward the sun god, and all his trees turned with him. Apollo rose, his brow wreathed with Parnassian laurel, while his robe of Tyrian purple swept the ground. In his left hand he held the lyre, and with his right hand struck the strings. Ravished with the harmony, Tmolus at once awarded the victory to the god of the lyre, and all but Midas acquiesced in the judgment. He dissented and questioned the justice of the award. Apollo would not suffer such a depraved pair of ears any longer to wear the human form, but caused them to increase in length, grow hairy, within and without, and movable on their roots; in short, to be on the perfect pattern of those of an ass.

Mortified enough was King Midas at this mishap; but he consoled himself with the thought that it was possible to hide his misfortune, which he attempted to do by means of an ample turban or headdress. But his hairdresser of course knew the secret. He was charged not to mention it and threatened with dire punishment if he presumed to disobey. But he found it too much for his discretion to keep such a secret; so he went out into the meadow, dug a hole in the ground, and stooping down, whispered the story and covered it up. Before long a thick bed of reeds sprang up in the meadow, and as soon as it had gained its growth, began whispering the story, and has continued to do so, from that day to this, every time a breeze passes over the place.

Midas was king of Phrygia. He was the son of Gordius, a poor countryman, who was taken by the people and made king, in obedience to the command of the oracle, which had said that their future king should come in a wagon. While the people were deliberating, Gordius with his wife and son came driving his wagon into the public square.

Gordius, being made king, dedicated his wagon to the deity of the oracle, and tied it up in its place with a fast knot. This was the celebrated Gordian knot, which, in aftertimes it was said, whoever should untie should become lord of all Asia. Many tried to untie it, but none succeeded, till Alexander the Great, in his career of conquest, came to Phrygia. He tried his skill with as ill success as others, till growing impatient he drew his sword and cut the knot. When he afterward succeeded in subjecting all Asia to his sway, people began to think that he had complied with the terms of the oracle according to its true meaning.

BAUCIS AND PHILEMON

On a certain hill in Phrygia stand a linden tree and an oak, enclosed by a low wall. Not far from the spot is a marsh, formerly good habitable land, but now indented with pools, the resort of fen birds and cormorants. Once upon a time, Jupiter, in human shape, visited this country, and with him his son Mercury (he of the caduceus), without his wings. They presented themselves as weary travelers at many a door, seeking rest and shelter, but found all closed, for it was late, and the inhospitable inhabitants would not rouse themselves to open for their reception. At last a humble mansion received them, a small thatched cottage where Baucis, a pious old dame, and her husband, Philemon, united when young, had grown old together. Not ashamed of their poverty, they made it endurable by moderate desires and kind dispositions. One need not look there for master or for servant; they two were the whole household, master and servant alike. When the two heavenly guests crossed the humble threshold and bowed their heads to pass under the low door, the old man placed a seat on which Baucis, bustling and attentive, spread a cloth, and begged

The Judgment of Midas, DOMENICHINO AND ASSISTANTS ➤
(1581–1641): Apollo rebukes Midas for asinine judgment.
The painting is one of a series of ten frescoes depicting
stories of Apollo from Ovid's Metamorphoses.

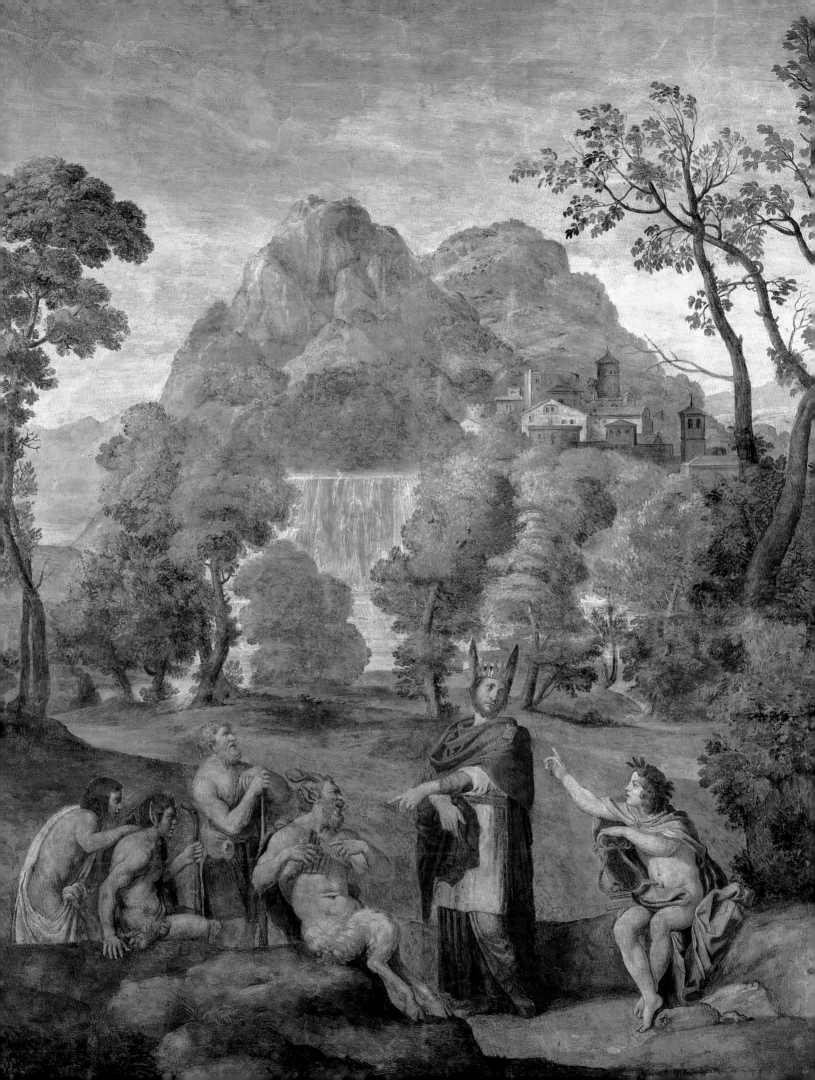

them to sit down. Then she raked out the coals from the ashes, and kindled up a fire, fed it with leaves and dry bark, and with her scanty breath blew it into a flame. She brought out of a corner split sticks and dry branches, broke them up, and placed them under the small kettle. Her husband collected some pot-herbs in the garden, and she shred them from the stalks and prepared them for the pot. He reached down with a forked stick a flitch of bacon hanging in the chimney, cut a small piece, and put it in the pot to boil with the herbs, setting away the rest for another time. A beechen bowl was filled with warm water, that their guests might wash. While all was doing they beguiled the time with conversation.

On the bench designed for the guests was laid a cushion stuffed with seaweed, and a cloth, only produced on great occasions, but ancient and coarse enough, was spread over that. The old lady, with her apron on, with trembling hand set the table. One leg was shorter than the rest, but a piece of slate put under restored the level. When fixed, she rubbed the table down with some sweet-smelling herbs. Upon it she set some of chaste Minerva's olives, some cornel berries preserved in vinegar, and added radishes and cheese, with eggs lightly cooked in the ashes. All were served in earthen dishes, and an earthenware pitcher, with wooden cups, stood beside them. When all was ready, the stew, smoking hot,

Y Jupiter and Mercury beside Philemon and Baucis, ADAM ELSHEIMER (1578–1610)
The story of Philemon and Baucis as told by Ovid has often been cited for its rustic piety and the virtues of simple living: this ensured its popularity with moralizing artists throughout the ages.

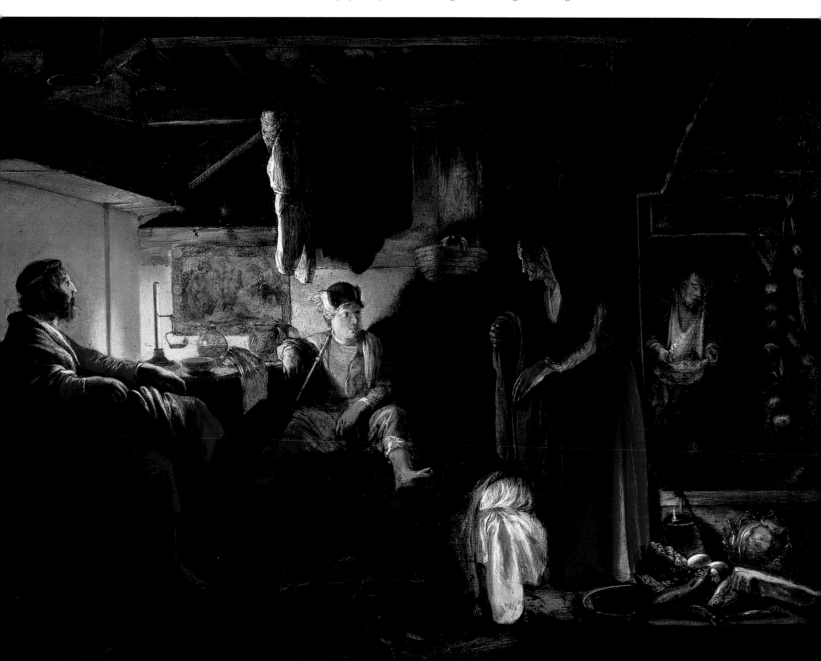

was set on the table. Some wine, not of the oldest, was added; and for dessert, apples and wild honey; and over and above all, friendly faces and simple but hearty welcome.

Now while the repast proceeded, the old folks were astonished to see that the wine, as fast as it was poured out, renewed itself in the pitcher, of its own accord. Struck with terror, Baucis and Philemon recognized their heavenly guests, fell on their knees, and with clasped hands implored forgiveness for their poor entertainment. There was an old goose, which they kept as the guardian of their humble cottage; and they bethought them to make this a sacrifice in honor of their guests. But the goose, too nimble, with the aid of feet and wings, for the old folks, eluded their pursuit and at last took shelter between the gods themselves. They forbade it to be slain; and spoke in these words: "We are gods. This inhospitable village shall pay the penalty of its impiety; you alone shall go free from the chastisement. Quit your house and come with us to the top of yonder hill."

They hastened to obey, and, staff in hand, labored up the steep ascent. They had reached to within an arrow's flight of the top, when turning their eyes below, they beheld all the country sunk in a lake, only their own house left standing. While they gazed with wonder at the sight, and lamented the fate of their neighbors, that old house of theirs

was changed into a temple. Columns took the place of the corner posts, the thatch grew yellow and appeared a gilded roof, the floors became marble, the doors were enriched with carving and ornaments of gold. Then spoke Jupiter in benignant accents: "Excellent old man, and woman worthy of such a husband, speak, tell us your wishes; what favor have you to ask of us?"

Philemon took counsel with Baucis a few moments, then declared to the gods their united wish. "We ask to be priests and guardians of this your temple; and since here we have passed our lives in love and concord, we wish that one and the same hour may take us both from life, that I may not live to see her grave, nor be laid in my own by her." Their prayer was granted. They were the keepers of the temple as long as they lived. When grown very old, as they stood one day before the steps of the sacred edifice, and were telling the story of the place, Baucis saw Philemon begin to put forth leaves, and old Philemon saw Baucis changing in like manner. And now a leafy crown had grown over their heads, while exchanging parting words, as long as they could speak. "Farewell, dear spouse," they said, together, and at the same moment the bark closed over their mouths. The Tyanean shepherd still shows the two trees, standing side by side, made out of the two good old people.

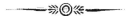

Chapter 7

Proserpine
Glaucus and Scylla

When Jupiter and his brothers had defeated the Titans and banished them to Tartarus, a new enemy rose up against the gods. They were the giants Typhon, Briareus, Enceladus, and others. Some of them had a hundred arms, others breathed out fire. They were finally subdued and buried alive under Mount Aetna, where they still sometimes struggle to get loose and shake the whole island with earthquakes. Their breath comes up through the mountain and is what men call the eruption of the volcano.

The fall of these monsters shook the earth, so that Pluto was alarmed, and feared that his kingdom would be laid open to the light of day. Under this apprehension, he mounted his chariot, drawn by black horses, and took a circuit of inspection to satisfy himself of the extent of the damage. While he was thus engaged, Venus, who was sitting on Mount Eryx playing with her boy Cupid, espied him and said, "My son, take your darts with which you conquer all, even Jove himself, and send one into the breast of yonder dark monarch, who rules the realm of Tartarus. Why should he alone escape? Seize the opportunity to extend your empire and mine. Do you not see that even in heaven some despise our power? Minerva the wise, and Diana the huntress, defy us; and there is that daughter of Ceres, who threatens to follow their example. Now do you, if you have any regard for your own interest or mine, join these two in one." The boy unbound his quiver and selected his sharpest and truest arrow; then, straining the bow against his knee, he attached the string and, having made ready, shot the arrow with its barbed point right into the heart of Pluto.

In the vale of Enna there is a lake embowered in woods, which screen it from the fervid rays of the sun, while the moist ground is covered with flowers, and Spring reigns perpetual. Here Proserpine was playing with her companions, gathering lilies and violets, and filling her basket and her apron with them, when Pluto saw her, loved her, and carried her off. She screamed for help to her mother and her companions; and when in her fright she dropped the corners of her apron and let the flowers fall, childlike she felt the loss of them as an addition to her grief. The ravisher urged on his steeds, calling them each by name and throwing loose over their heads and necks his iron-colored reins. When he reached the River Cyane, and it opposed his passage, he struck the riverbank with his trident, and the earth opened and gave him a passage to Tartarus.

Ceres sought her daughter all the world over. Bright-haired Aurora, when she came forth in the morning, and Hesperus, when he led out the stars in the evening, found her still busy in the search. But it was all unavailing. At length weary and sad, she sat down upon a stone, and continued sitting nine days and nights, in the open air, under the sunlight and moonlight and falling showers. It was where now stands the city of Eleusis, then the home of an old man named Celeus. He was out in the field, gathering acorns and blackberries, and sticks for his fire. His little girl was driving home their two goats, and as she passed the goddess, who appeared in the guise of an old woman, she said to her, "Mother,"— and the name was sweet to the ears of Ceres—"why do you sit here alone upon the rocks?" The old man also stopped, though his load was heavy, and begged her to come into his cottage, such as it was. She declined, and he urged her. "Go in peace," she replied, "and be happy in your daughter; I have lost mine." As she spoke, tears—or something like tears, for the gods never weep—fell down her cheeks upon her bosom. The compassionate old man and his child wept with her. Then said he, "Come with us, and despise not our humble roof; so may your daughter be restored to you in safety." "Lead on," said she, "I cannot resist that appeal!" So she rose from the stone and went with them. As they walked he told her that his only son, a little boy, lay very sick, feverish and sleepless. She stooped and gathered some poppies. As they entered the cottage, they found all in great distress, for the boy seemed past hope of recovery. Metanira, his mother, received her kindly, and the goddess stooped and kissed the lips of the sick child. Instantly the paleness left his face,

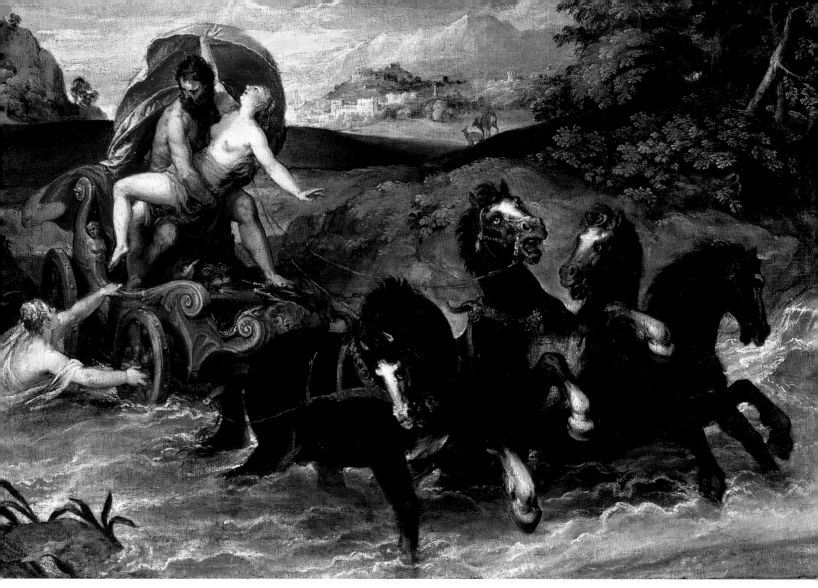

▲ The Rape of Proserpine, CHRISTOPH SCHWARTZ (1545–1592)
The story of Proserpine's abduction reflects the annual turn of the seasons: hence the decay of vegetation during her six months in the underworld (autumn–winter) and its revival when she rejoins her mother (spring–summer).

and healthy vigor returned to his body. The whole family were delighted—that is, the father, mother, and little girl, for they were all; they had no servants. They spread the table and put upon it curds and cream, apples and honey in the comb. While they ate, Ceres mingled poppy juice in the milk of the boy. When night came and all was still, she arose, and taking the sleeping boy, moulded his limbs with her hands, and uttered over him three times a solemn charm, then went and laid him in the ashes. His mother, who had been watching what her guest was doing, sprang forward with a cry and snatched the child from the fire. Then Ceres assumed her own form, and a divine splendor shone all around. While they were overcome with astonishment, she said, "Mother, you have been cruel in your fondness to your son. I would have made him immortal, but you have frustrated my attempt. Nevertheless, he shall

be great and useful. He shall teach men the use of the plow, and the rewards which labor can win from the cultivated soil." So saying, she wrapped a cloud about her and, mounting her chariot, rode away.

Ceres continued her search for her daughter, passing from land to land, and across seas and rivers, till at length she returned to Sicily, whence she at first set out, and stood by the banks of the River Cyane, where Pluto made himself a passage with his prize to his own dominions. The river nymph would have told the goddess all she had witnessed, but dared not, for fear of Pluto; so she only ventured to take up the girdle which Proserpine had dropped in her flight, and waft it to the feet of the mother. Ceres, seeing this, was no longer in doubt of her loss, but she did not yet know the cause and laid the blame on the innocent land. "Ungrateful soil," said she, "which I have endowed with fertility and clothed

47

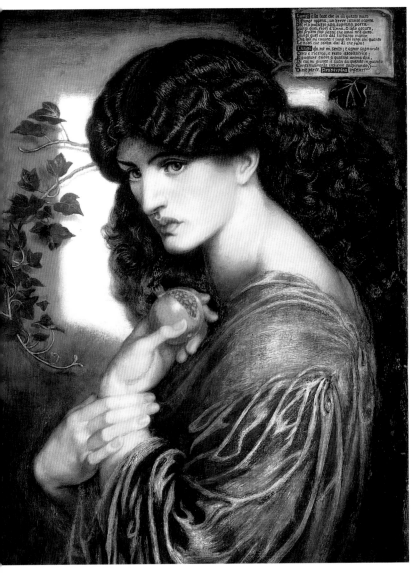

▲ Proserpine, DANTE GABRIEL ROSSETTI (1828–1882)
Rossetti's mistress Jane Morris was his model for this Pre-Raphaelite
Proserpine. The painting was a highly personal one for the artist,
who saw Jane–like Proserpine–trapped in an unhappy marriage.
In ancient Greece, the pomegranate was a traditional
votive offering to Ceres.

beauty, but I cared nothing for it, and rather boasted of my hunting exploits. One day I was returning from the wood, heated with exercise, when I came to a stream silently flowing, so clear that you might count the pebbles on the bottom. The willows shaded it, and the grassy bank sloped down to the water's edge. I approached, I touched the water with my foot. I stepped in knee-deep, and not content with that, I laid my garments on the willows and went in. While I sported in the water, I heard an indistinct murmur coming up as out of the depths of the stream; and made haste to escape to the nearest bank. The voice said, 'Why do you fly, Arethusa? I am Alpheus, the god of this stream.' I ran, he pursued; he was not more swift than I, but he was stronger, and gained upon me, as my strength failed. At last, exhausted, I cried for help to Diana. 'Help me, goddess! Help your votary!' The goddess heard and wrapped me suddenly in a thick cloud. The river god looked now this way and now that, and twice came close to me, but could not find me. 'Arethusa! Arethusa!' he cried. O, how I trembled— like a lamb that hears the wolf growling outside the fold. A cold sweat came over me, my hair flowed down in streams; where my foot stood there was a pool. In short, in less time than it takes to tell it, I became a fountain. But in this form Alpheus knew me, and attempted to mingle his stream with mine. Diana cleft the ground, and I, endeavoring to escape him, plunged into the cavern, and through the bowels of the earth came out here in Sicily. While I passed through the lower parts of the earth, I saw your Proserpine. She was sad, but no longer showing alarm in her countenance. Her look was such as became a queen—the queen of Erebus; the powerful bride of the monarch of the realms of the dead."

When Ceres heard this, she stood for a while like one stupefied; then turned her chariot toward heaven and hastened to present herself before the throne of Jove. She told the story of her bereavement, and implored Jupiter to interfere to procure the restitution of her daughter. Jupiter consented on one condition, namely, that Proserpine should not during her stay in the lower world have taken any food; otherwise, the Fates forbade her release. Accordingly, Mercury was sent, accompanied by Spring, to demand Proserpine of Pluto. The wily monarch consented; but alas!

with herbage and nourishing grain, no more shall you enjoy my favors." Then the cattle died, the plow broke in the furrow, the seed failed to come up; there was too much sun, there was too much rain; the birds stole the seeds—thistles and brambles were the only growth. Seeing this, the fountain Arethusa interceded for the land. "Goddess," said she, "blame not the land; it opened unwillingly to yield a passage to your daughter. I can tell you of her fate, for I have seen her. This is not my native country; I came hither from Elis. I was a woodland nymph, and delighted in the chase. They praised my

48

the maiden had taken a pomegranate which Pluto offered her, and had sucked the sweet pulp from a few of the seeds. This was enough to prevent her complete release; but a compromise was made, by which she was to pass half the time with her mother, and the rest with her husband Pluto.

Ceres allowed herself to be pacified with this arrangement and restored the earth to her favor. Now she remembered Celeus and his family, and her promise to his infant son Triptolemus. When the boy grew up, she taught him the use of the plow, and how to sow the seed. She took him in her chariot, drawn by winged dragons, through all the countries of the earth, imparting to mankind valuable grains, and the knowledge of agriculture. After his return, Triptolemus built a magnificent temple to Ceres in Eleusis, and established the worship of the goddess, under the name of the Eleusinian mysteries, which, in the splendor and solemnity of their observance,

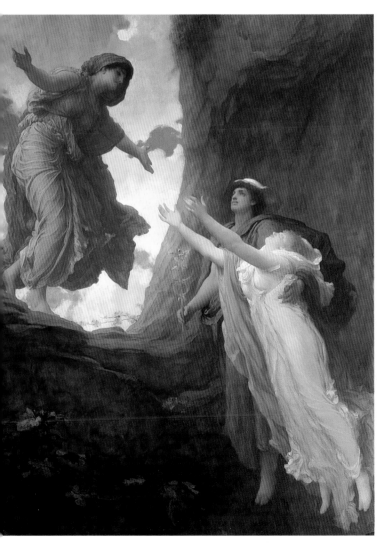

surpassed all other religious celebrations among the Greeks.

There can be little doubt of this story of Ceres and Proserpine being an allegory. Proserpine signifies the seed-corn which, when cast into the ground, lies there concealed—that is, she is carried off by the god of the underworld; it reappears—that is, Proserpine is restored to her mother. Spring leads her back to the light of day.

GLAUCUS AND SCYLLA

Glaucus was a fisherman. One day he had drawn his nets to land and had taken a great many fishes of various kinds. So he emptied his net and proceeded to sort the fishes on the grass. The place where he stood was a beautiful island in the river, a solitary spot, uninhabited, and not used for pasturage of cattle, nor ever visited by any but himself. On a sudden, the fishes, which had been laid on the grass, began to revive and move their fins as if they were in the water; and while he looked on astonished, they one and all moved off to the water, plunged in and swam away. He did not know what to make of this, whether some god had done it, or some secret power in the herbage. "What herb has such a power?" he exclaimed; and gathering some of it, he tasted it. Scarce had the juices of the plant reached his palate when he found himself agitated with a longing desire for the water. He could no longer restrain himself, but bidding farewell to earth, he plunged into the stream. The gods of the water received him graciously and admitted him to the honor of their society. They obtained the consent of Oceanus and Tethys, the sovereigns of the sea, that all that was mortal in him should be washed away. A hundred rivers poured their waters over him. Then he lost all sense of his former nature and all consciousness. When he recovered, he found himself changed in form and mind. His hair was sea-green, and trailed behind him on the water; his shoulders grew broad, and what had been thighs and legs assumed the form of a fish's tail. The sea gods complimented him on the change of his appearance, and he fancied himself rather a good-looking personage.

◄ The Return of Persephone, LORD FREDERIC LEIGHTON (1830–1896): *Leighton excelled in neo-classical subjects such as this. According to classical topography, Proserpine's return to earth took place in the flower-strewn fields of Sicily. The artist's use of light emphasizes the darkness of the underworld below.*

One day Glaucus saw the beautiful maiden Scylla, the favorite of the water nymphs, rambling on the shore, and when she had found a sheltered nook, laving her limbs in the clear water. He fell in love with her, and showing himself on the surface, spoke to her, saying such things as he thought most likely to win her to stay; for she turned to run immediately on the sight of him, and ran till she had gained a cliff overlooking the sea. Here she stopped and turned around to see whether it was a god or a sea animal, and observed with wonder his shape and color. Glaucus, partly emerging from the water and supporting himself against a rock, said, "Maiden, I am no monster, nor a sea animal, but a god; and neither Proteus nor Triton ranks higher than I. Once I was a mortal, and followed the sea for a living; but now I belong wholly to it." Then he told the story of his metamorphosis, and how he had been promoted to his present dignity, and added, "But what avails all this if it fails to move your heart?" He was going on in this strain, but Scylla turned and hastened away.

Glaucus was in despair, but it occurred to him to consult the enchantress Circe. Accordingly he repaired to her island—the same where afterward Ulysses landed, as we shall see in one of our later stories. After mutual salutations, he said, "Goddess, I entreat your pity; you alone can relieve the pain I suffer. The power of herbs I know as well as anyone, for it is to them I owe my change of form. I love Scylla. I am ashamed to tell you how I have sued and promised to her, and how scornfully she has treated me. I beseech you to use your incantations, or potent herbs, if they are more prevailing, not to cure me of my love—for that I do not wish—but to make her share it and yield me a like return." To which Circe replied, for she was not insensible to the attractions of the sea-green deity, "You had better pursue a willing object; you are worthy to be sought, instead of having to seek in vain. Be not diffident, know your own worth. I protest to you that even I, goddess though I be, and learned in the virtues of plants and spells, should not know how to refuse you. If she scorns you, scorn her; meet one who is ready to meet you halfway, and thus make a due return to both at once." To these words Glaucus replied, "Sooner shall trees grow at the bottom of the ocean, and seaweed on the top of the mountains, than I will cease to love Scylla, and her alone."

The goddess was indignant, but she could not punish him, neither did she wish to do so, for she liked him too well; so she turned all her wrath against her rival, poor Scylla. She took plants of poisonous powers and mixed them together, with incantations and charms. Then she passed through the crowd of gamboling beasts, the victims of her art, and proceeded to the coast of Sicily, where Scylla lived. There was a little bay on the shore to which Scylla used to resort in the heat of the day, to breathe the air of the sea and to bathe in its waters. Here the goddess poured her poisonous mixture, and muttered over it incantations of mighty power. Scylla came as usual and plunged into the water up to her waist. What was her horror to perceive a brood of serpents and barking monsters surrounding her! At first she could not imagine they were a part of herself, and tried to run from them and to drive them away; but as she ran she carried them with her, and when she tried to touch her limbs, she found her hands touch only the yawning jaws of monsters. Scylla remained rooted to the spot. Her temper grew as ugly as her form, and she took pleasure in devouring hapless mariners who came within her grasp. Thus she destroyed six of the companions of Ulysses, and tried to wreck the ships of Aeneas, till at last she was turned into a rock, and as such still continues to be a terror to mariners.

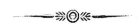

CHAPTER 8

PYGMALION · DRYOPE
VENUS AND ADONIS
APOLLO AND HYACINTHUS

Pygmalion saw so much to blame in women that he came at last to abhor the sex, and resolved to live unmarried. He was a sculptor, and had made with wonderful skill a statue of ivory, so beautiful that no living woman came anywhere near it. It was indeed the perfect semblance of a maiden that seemed to be alive, and only prevented from moving by modesty. His art was so perfect that it concealed itself, and its product looked like the workmanship of nature. Pygmalion admired his own work and at last fell in love with the counterfeit creation. Oftentimes he laid his hand upon it as if to assure himself whether it were living or not, and could not even then believe that it was only ivory. He caressed it and gave it presents such as young girls love—bright shells and polished stones, little birds and flowers of various hues, beads and amber. He put raiment on its limbs, and jewels on its fingers, and a necklace about its neck. To the ears he hung earrings, and strings of pearls upon the breast. Her dress became her, and she looked not less charming than when unattired. He laid her on a couch spread with cloths of Tyrian dye, and called her his wife, and put her head upon a pillow of the softest feathers, as if she could enjoy their softness.

The festival of Venus was at hand—a festival celebrated with great pomp at Cyprus. Victims were offered, the altars smoked, and the odor of incense filled the air. When Pygmalion had performed his part in the solemnities, he stood before the altar and timidly said, "Ye gods, who can do all things, give me, I pray you, for my wife"—he dared not say 'my ivory virgin,' but said instead—"one like my ivory virgin." Venus, who was present at the festival, heard him and knew the thought he would have uttered; and as an omen of her favor, caused the flame on the altar to shoot up thrice in a fiery point into the air. When he returned home, he went to see his statue, and leaning over the couch, gave a kiss to the mouth. It seemed to be warm. He pressed its lips again, he laid his hand upon the limbs; the ivory felt soft to his touch and yielded to his fingers like the wax of Hymettus. While he stands astonished and glad, though doubting, and fears he may be mistaken, again and again with a lover's ardor, he touches the object of his hopes. It was indeed alive!

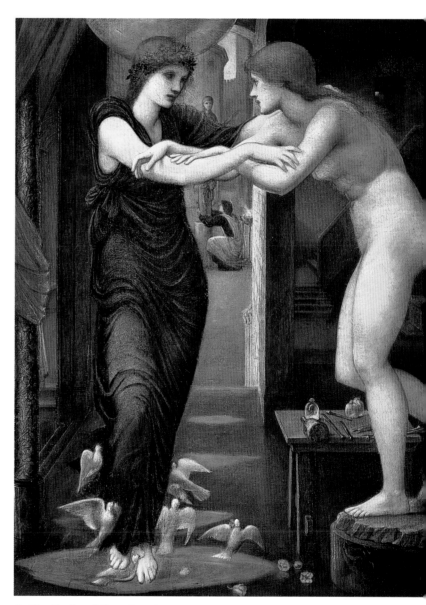

▲ The Godhead Fires, SIR EDWARD BURNE-JONES (1833–1898)
Burne-Jones depicts the very moment when Venus, accompanied by her sacred doves and roses, works her miracle. Legend has it that Pygmalion once ruled Cyprus—Venus's own island. The artist's nudes echo the Renaissance ideal of beauty.

51

The veins when pressed yielded to the finger and again resumed their roundness. Then at last the votary of Venus found words to thank the goddess, and pressed his lips upon lips as real as his own. The virgin felt the kisses and blushed, and opening her timid eyes to the light, fixed them at the same moment on her lover. Venus blessed the nuptials she had formed, and from this union Paphos was born, from whom the city sacred to Venus received its name.

DRYOPE

Dryope and Iole were sisters. The former was the wife of Andraemon, beloved by her husband, and happy in the birth of her first child. One day the sisters strolled to the bank of a stream that sloped gradually down to the water's edge, while the upland was overgrown with myrtles. They were intending to gather flowers for forming garlands for the altars of the nymphs, and Dryope carried her child at her bosom, a precious burden, and nursed him as she walked. Near the water grew a lotus plant, full of purple flowers. Dryope gathered some and offered them to the baby, and Iole was about to do the same, when she perceived blood dropping from the places where her sister had broken them off the stem. The plant was no other than the nymph Lotis, who, running from a base pursuer, had been changed into this form. This they learned from the country people when it was too late.

Dryope, horror-struck when she perceived what she had done, would gladly have hastened from the spot, but found her feet rooted to the ground. She tried to pull them away, but moved nothing but her upper limbs. The woodiness crept upward, and by degrees invested her body. In anguish she attempted to tear her hair, but found her hands filled with leaves. The infant felt his mother's bosom begin to harden and the milk cease to flow. Iole looked on at the sad fate of her sister and could render no assistance. She embraced the growing trunk, as if she would hold back the advancing wood, and would gladly have been enveloped in the same bark. At this moment, Andraemon, the husband of Dryope, with her father, approached; and when they asked for Dryope, Iole pointed them to the new-formed lotus. They embraced the trunk of the yet warm tree and showered their kisses on its leaves.

Now there was nothing left of Dryope but her face. Her tears still flowed and fell on her leaves, and while she could she spoke. "I am not guilty. I deserve not this fate. I have injured no one. If I speak falsely, may my foliage perish with drought and my trunk be cut down and burned. Take this infant and give it to a nurse. Let it often be brought and nursed under my branches, and play in my shade; and when he is old enough to talk, let him be taught to call me mother, and to say with sadness, 'My mother lies hid under this bark.' But bid him be careful of riverbanks, and beware how he plucks flowers, remembering that every bush he sees may be a goddess in disguise. Farewell, dear husband, and sister, and father. If you retain any love for me, let not the axe wound me, nor the flocks bite and tear my branches. Since I cannot stoop to you, climb up hither and kiss me, and while my lips continue to feel, lift up my child that I may kiss him. I can speak no more, for already the bark advances up my neck, and will soon shoot over me. You need not close my eyes, the bark will close them without your aid." Then the lips ceased to move, and life was extinct; but the branches retained for some time longer the vital heat.

VENUS AND ADONIS

Venus, playing one day with her boy Cupid, wounded her bosom with one of his arrows. She pushed him away, but the wound was deeper than she thought. Before it healed she beheld Adonis, and was captivated with him. She no longer took any interest in her favorite resorts—Paphos and Cnidos and Amathos, rich in metals. She absented herself even from heaven, for Adonis was dearer to her than heaven. Him she followed and bore him company. She who used to love to recline in the shade, with no care but to cultivate her charms, now rambles through the woods and over the hills, dressed like the huntress Diana; and calls her dogs, and chases hares and stags, or other game that it is safe to hunt, but keeps clear of the wolves and bears, reeking with the slaughter of the herd. She charged Adonis, too,

An Allegory with Venus and Cupid, BRONZINO (1503–1572) ➤
Venus, holding the prize apple given to her by Paris, disarms Cupid, who kisses her with blatant affection. Careless Pleasure tosses rose petals at Venus, heedless of the thorn piercing his foot. Deceit offers honeycomb, concealing the sting in her tail with her other hand. Jealousy screams in agony, while Oblivion tries to draw the veil across, but is prevented by Father Time.

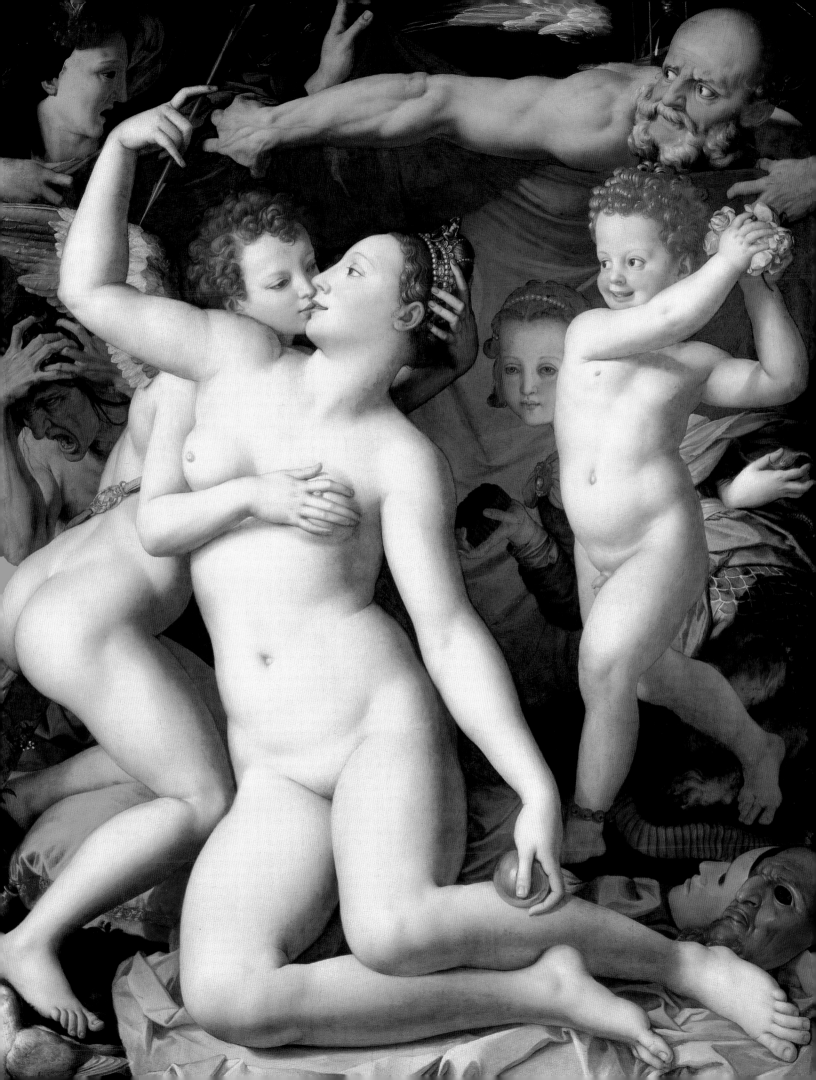

to beware of such dangerous animals. "Be brave towards the timid," said she; "courage against the courageous is not safe. Beware how you expose yourself to danger and put my happiness to risk. Attack not the beasts that Nature has armed with weapons. I do not value your glory so high as to consent to purchase it by such exposure. Your youth, and the beauty that charms Venus, will not touch the hearts of lions and bristly boars. Think of their terrible claws and prodigious strength! I hate the whole race of them. Do you ask me why?" Then she told him the story of Atalanta and Hippomenes,

who were changed into lions for their ingratitude to her.

Having given him this warning, she mounted her chariot drawn by swans and drove away through the air. But Adonis was too noble to heed such counsels. The dogs had roused a wild boar from his lair, and the youth threw his spear and wounded the animal with a sidelong stroke. The beast drew out the weapon with his jaws and rushed after Adonis, who turned and ran; but the boar overtook him, and buried his tusks in his side, and stretched him dying upon the plain.

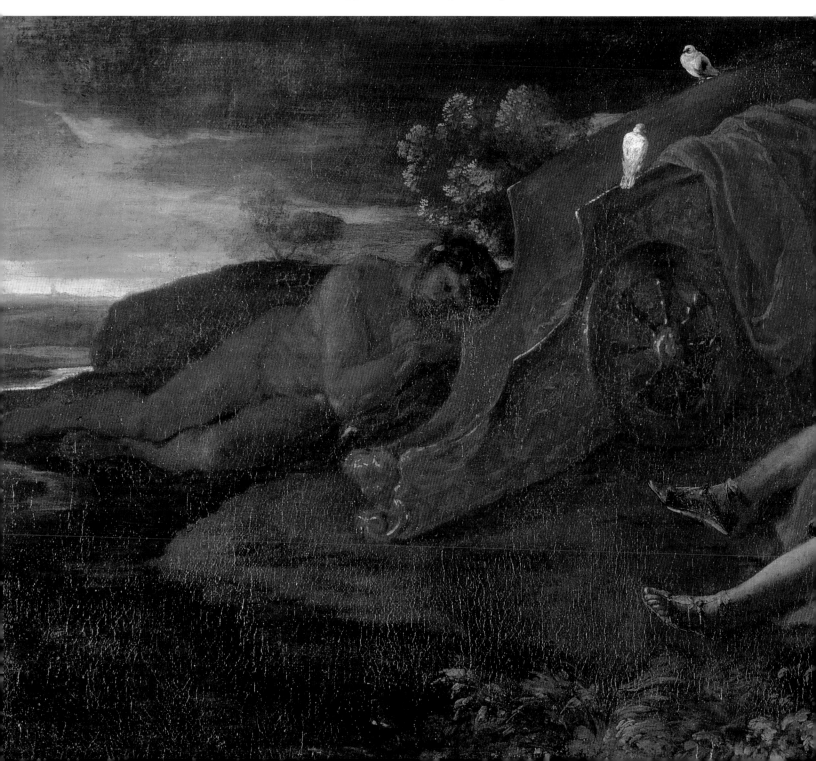

Venus, in her swan-drawn chariot, had not yet reached Cyprus, when she heard coming up through mid-air the groans of her beloved, and turned her white-winged coursers back to earth. As she drew near and saw from on high his lifeless body bathed in blood, she alighted, and bending over it beat her breast and tore her hair. Reproaching the Fates, she said, "Yet theirs shall be but a partial triumph; memorials of my grief shall endure, and the spectacle of your death, my Adonis, and of my lamentation shall be annually renewed. Your blood shall be changed into a flower; that consolation none can envy me." Thus speaking, she sprinkled nectar on the blood; and as they mingled, bubbles rose as in a pool, on which raindrops fall, and in an hour's time there sprang up a flower of bloody hue like that of the pomegranate. But it is short-lived. It is said the wind blows the blossoms open, and afterward blows

▼ Venus Weeping over Adonis, NICOLAS POUSSIN (1594–1665)
A distraught Venus sprinkles ambrosia on the blood of her young lover. The cult of Adonis was dominated by libations of perfume and rare fragrances; gardens and bowers were a distinct feature of places where he was worshipped.

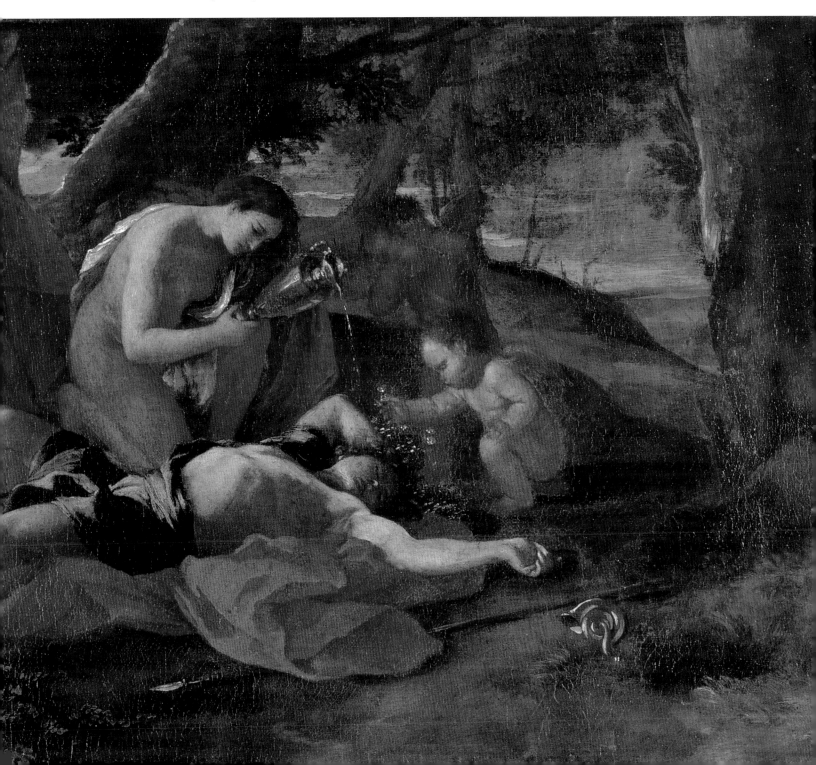

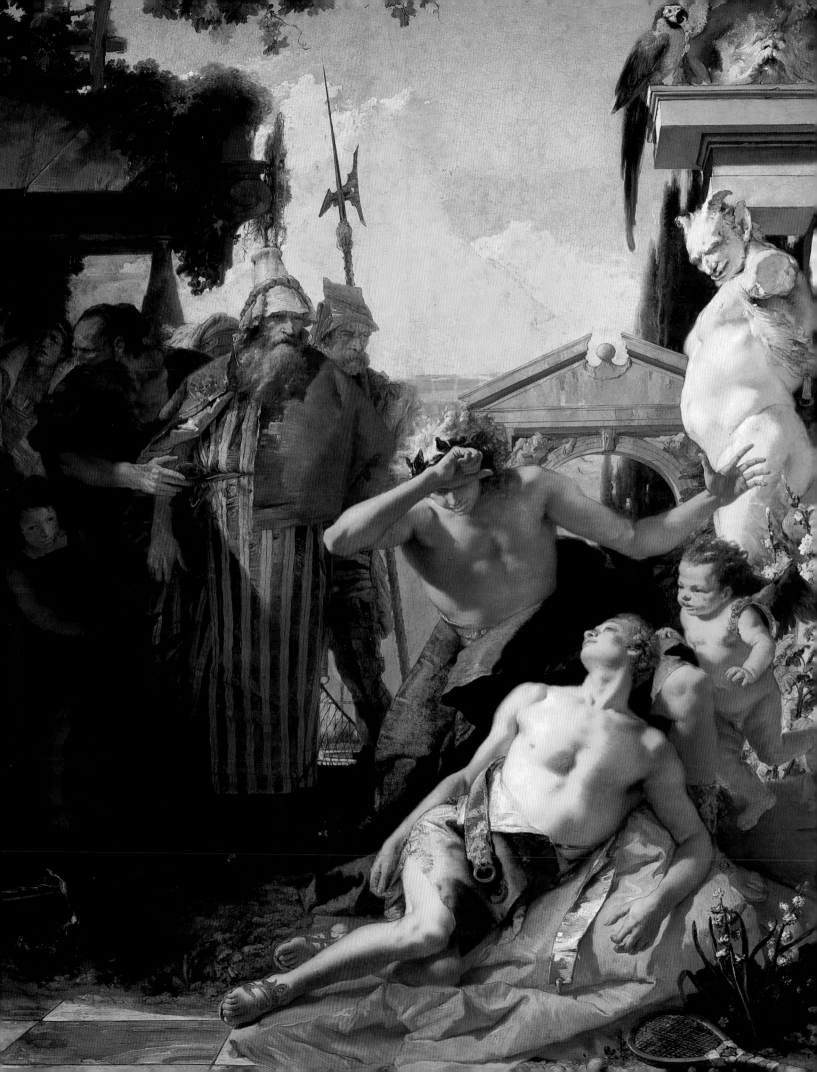

the petals away; so it is called Anemone, or Wind Flower, from the cause which assists equally in its production and its decay.

APOLLO AND HYACINTHUS

Apollo was passionately fond of a youth named Hyacinthus. He accompanied him in his sports, carried the nets when he went fishing, led the dogs when he went to hunt, followed him in his excursions in the mountains, and neglected for him his lyre and his arrows. One day they played a game of quoits together, and Apollo, heaving aloft the discus, with strength mingled with skill, sent it high and far. Hyacinthus watched it as it flew, and excited with the sport ran forward to seize it, eager to make his throw, when the quoit bounded from the earth and struck him in the forehead. He fainted and fell. The god, as pale as himself, raised him and tried all his art to stanch the wound and retain the flitting life, but all in vain; the hurt was past the power of medicine. As when one has broken the stem of a lily in the garden it hangs its head and turns its flowers to the earth, so the head of the dying boy, as if too heavy for his neck, fell over on his shoulder. "Thou diest, Hyacinth," so spoke Phoebus, "robbed of thy youth by me. Thine is the suffering, mine the crime. Would that I could die for thee! But since that may not be, thou shalt live with me in memory and in song. My lyre shall celebrate thee, my song shall tell thy fate, and thou shalt become a flower inscribed with my regrets." While Apollo spoke, behold the blood which had flowed on the ground and stained the herbage ceased to be blood; but a flower of hue more beautiful than the Tyrian sprang up, resembling the lily, if it were not that this is purple and that silvery white. And this was not enough for Phoebus; but to confer still greater honor, he marked the petals with his sorrow and inscribed "Ah! Ah!" upon them, as we see to this day. The flower bears the name of Hyacinthus, and with every returning spring revives the memory of his fate.

It was said that Zephyrus (the West wind), who was also fond of Hyacinthus and jealous of his preference for Apollo, blew the quoit out of its course to make it strike Hyacinthus.

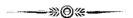

◄ The Death of Hyacinth, GIAMBATTISTA TIEPOLO (1696–1770): *The Greek discus, or quoit, was a large, solid metal object. Hyacinthus's exclamation upon being struck by a discus—"Ai Ai!" ("Alas, alas!")—was a common lament in Greek tragedy. Here Apollo claps his brow with remorse; Hyacinthus is decidedly effeminate; and the tennis racket in the foreground is a shameless anachronism.*

CHAPTER 9

CEYX AND HALCYONE: OR, THE HALCYON BIRDS

EYX WAS KING OF THESSALY, WHERE HE REIGNED in peace, without violence or wrong. He was son of Hesperus, the day star, and the glow of his beauty reminded one of his father. Halcyone, the daughter of Aeolus, was his wife, and devotedly attached to him. Now Ceyx was in deep affliction for the loss of his brother, and direful prodigies following his brother's death made him feel as if the gods were hostile to him. He thought best, therefore, to make a voyage to Claros in Ionia, to consult the oracle of Apollo. But as soon as he disclosed his intention to his wife Halcyone, a shudder ran through her frame, and her face grew deadly pale. "What fault of mine, dearest husband, has turned your affection from me? Where is that love of me that used to be uppermost in your thoughts? Have you learned to feel easy in the absence of Halcyone? Would you rather have me away?" She also endeavored to discourage him, by describing the violence of the winds, which she had known familiarly when she lived at home in her father's house, Aeolus being the god of the winds, and having as much as he could do to restrain them. "They rush together," said she, "with such fury that fire flashes from the conflict. But if you must go," she added, "dear husband, let me go with you, otherwise I shall suffer not only the real evils which you must encounter but those also which my fears suggest."

These words weighed heavily on the mind of King Ceyx, and it was no less his own wish than hers to take her with him, but he could not bear to expose her to the dangers of the sea. He answered, therefore, consoling her as well as he could, and finished with these words: "I promise, by the rays of my father the day star, that if fate permits I will return before the moon shall have twice rounded her orb." When he had thus spoken, he ordered the vessel to be drawn out of the shiphouse and the oars and sails to be put aboard. When Halcyone saw these preparations, she shuddered, as if with a presentiment of evil. With tears and sobs she said farewell, and then fell senseless to the ground.

Ceyx would still have lingered, but now the young men grasped their oars and pulled vigorously through the waves, with long and measured strokes. Halcyone raised her streaming eyes and saw her husband standing on the deck, waving his hand to her. She answered his signal till the vessel had receded so far that she could no longer distinguish his form from the rest. When the vessel itself could no more be seen, she strained her eyes to catch the last glimmer of the sail, till that too disappeared. Then, retiring to her chamber, she threw herself on her solitary couch.

Meanwhile they glide out of the harbor, and the breeze plays among the ropes. The seamen draw in their oars and hoist their sails. When half or less of their course was passed, as night drew on, the sea began to whiten with swelling waves, and the east wind to blow a gale. The master gave the word to take in sail, but the storm forbade obedience, for such is the roar of the winds and waves his orders are unheard. The men, of their own accord, busy themselves to secure the oars, to strengthen the ship, to reef the sail. While they thus do what to each one seems best, the storm increases. The shouting of the men, the rattling of the shrouds, and the dashing of the waves mingle with the roar of the thunder. The swelling sea seems lifted up to the heavens, to scatter its foam among the clouds; then sinking away to the bottom assumes the color of the shoal—a Stygian blackness.

The vessel shares all these changes. It seems like a wild beast that rushes on the spears of the hunters. Rain falls in torrents, as if the skies were coming down to unite with the sea. When the lightning ceases for a moment, the night seems to add its own darkness to that of the storm; then comes the flash, rending the darkness asunder and lighting up all with a glare. Skill fails, courage sinks, and death seems to come on every wave. The men are stupefied with terror. The thought of parents, and kindred and pledges left at home, comes over their minds. Ceyx thinks of Halcyone. No name but hers is on his lips, and while he yearns for her, he yet rejoices in her absence. Presently the mast is shattered by a stroke of lightning, the rudder broken, and the triumphant surge curling over looks down upon the wreck, then falls, and crushes it to fragments. Some of the seamen, stunned by the stroke, sink, and rise no more; others cling to fragments of the wreck. Ceyx, with the hand that used to grasp the scepter, holds fast to a plank, calling for help—alas, in vain—upon his father and his father-in-law. But oftenest on his lips was the name of Halcyone. To her his thoughts cling. He prays that the waves may bear his body to her sight and that it may receive burial at her hands. At length the waters overwhelm him, and he sinks. The day star looked dim that night. Since it could not leave the heavens, it shrouded its face with clouds.

In the meanwhile Halcyone, ignorant of all these horrors, counted the days till her husband's promised return. Now she gets ready the garments which he shall put on, and now what she shall wear when he arrives. To all the gods she offers frequent incense, but more than all to Juno. For her husband, who was no more, she prayed incessantly; that he might be safe; that he might come home; that he might not, in his absence, see any one that he would love better than her. But of all these prayers, the last was the only one destined to be granted. The goddess, at length, could not bear any longer to be pleaded with for one already dead, and to have hands raised to her altars that ought rather to be offering funeral rites. So, calling Iris, she said, "Iris, my faithful messenger, go to the drowsy dwelling of Somnus and tell him to send a vision to Halcyone, in the form of Ceyx, to make known to her the event."

Iris puts on her robe of many colors, and tinging the sky with her bow, seeks the palace of the King of Sleep. Near the Cimmerian country, a mountain cave is the abode of the dull god, Somnus. Here Phoebus dares not come, either rising, at midday, or setting. Clouds and shadows are exhaled from the ground, and the light glimmers faintly. The bird of dawning, with crested head, never there calls aloud to Aurora, nor watchful dog, nor more sagacious goose disturbs the silence. No wild beast, nor cattle, nor branch moved with the wind, nor sound of human conversation, breaks the stillness. Silence reigns there; but from the bottom of the rock the River Lethe flows, and by its murmur invites to sleep. Poppies grow abundantly before the door of the cave, and other herbs, from whose juices

Night collects slumbers, which she scatters over the darkened earth. There is no gate to the mansion, to creak on its hinges, nor any watchman; but in the midst, a couch of black ebony, adorned with black plumes and black curtains. There the god reclines, his limbs relaxed with sleep. Around him lie dreams, resembling all various forms, as many as the harvest bears stalks, or the forest leaves, or the seashore sand grains.

As soon as the goddess entered and brushed away the dreams that hovered around her, her brightness lit up all the cave. The god, scarce opening his eyes and ever and anon dropping his beard upon his breast, at last shook himself free from himself, and leaning on his arm, enquired her errand—for he knew who she was. She answered, "Somnus, gentlest of the gods, tranquilizer of minds and soother of careworn hearts, Juno sends you her commands that you despatch a dream to Halcyone, in the city of Trachine, representing her lost husband and all the events of the wreck."

Having delivered her message, Iris hasted away, for she could not longer endure the stagnant air, and as she felt drowsiness creeping over her, she made her escape and returned by her bow the way she came. Then Somnus called one of his numerous sons, Morpheus—the most expert in counterfeiting forms and in imitating the walk, the countenance, and mode of speaking, even the clothes and attitudes most characteristic of each. But he only imitates men, leaving it to another to personate birds, beasts, and serpents. Him they call Icelos; and Phantasos is a third, who turns himself into rocks, waters, woods, and other things without life. These wait upon kings and great personages in their sleeping hours, while others move among the common people. Somnus chose, from all the brothers, Morpheus, to perform the command of Iris; then laid his head on his pillow and yielded himself to grateful repose.

Morpheus flew, making no noise with his wings, and soon came to the Haemonian city, where, laying aside his wings, he assumed the form of Ceyx. Under that form, but pale like a dead man, naked, he stood before the couch of the wretched wife. His beard seemed soaked with water, and water trickled from his drowned locks. Leaning over the bed, tears streaming from his eyes, he said, "Do you recognize your Ceyx, unhappy wife, or has death too much changed my visage? Behold me, know me, your husband's shade, instead of himself. Your prayers, Halcyone, availed me nothing. I am dead. No more deceive yourself with vain hopes of my return. The stormy winds sunk my ship in the Aegean Sea, waves filled my mouth while it called aloud on you. No uncertain messenger tells you this, no vague rumor brings it to your ears. I come in person, a shipwrecked man, to tell you my fate. Arise! Give me tears, give me lamentations, let me not go down to Tartarus unwept." To these words Morpheus added the voice which seemed to be that of her husband; he seemed to pour forth genuine tears; his hands had the gestures of Ceyx.

Halcyone, weeping, groaned and stretched out her arms in her sleep, striving to embrace his body, but grasping only the air. "Stay!" she cried; "Whither do you fly? Let us go together." Her own voice awakened her. Starting up, she gazed eagerly around, to see if he was still present, for the servants, alarmed by her cries, had brought a light. When she found him not, she smote her breast and rent her garments. She cares not to unbind her hair, but tears it wildly. Her nurse asks what is the cause of her grief. "Halcyone is no more," she answers, "she perished with her Ceyx. Utter not words of comfort, he is shipwrecked and dead. I have seen him, I have recognized him. I stretched out my hands to seize

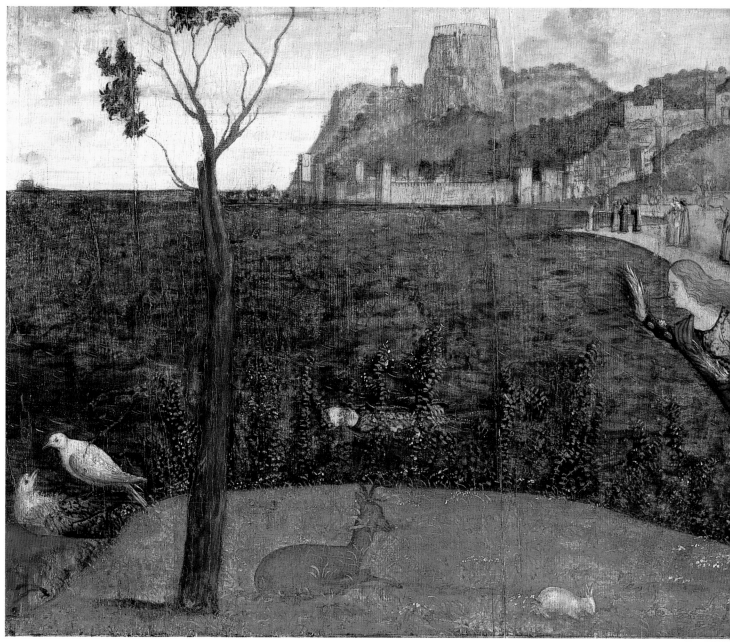

▲ The Metamorphosis of Alcyone, VITTORE CARPACCIO (active 1490; died 1523/6)
Halcyone's ornithological transformation takes place in Carpaccio's favored local setting of the Veneto: a shoreline made complete by the stylized figures of courtly love, reminiscent of earlier, medieval painting.

him and detain him. His shade vanished, but it was the true shade of my husband. Not with the accustomed features, not with the beauty that was his, but pale, naked, and with his hair wet with seawater, he appeared to wretched me. Here, in this very spot, the sad vision stood"—and she looked to find the mark of his footsteps. "This it was, this that my presaging mind foreboded, when I implored him not to leave me, to trust himself to the waves. Oh, how I wish, since thou wouldst go, thou hadst taken me with thee! It would have been far better. Then I should have had no remnant of life to spend without thee, nor a separate death to die. If I could bear to live and struggle to endure, I should be more cruel

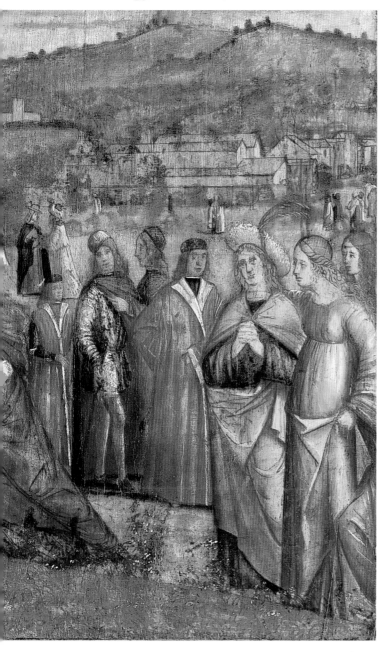

to myself than the sea has been to me. But I will not struggle, I will not be separated from thee, unhappy husband. This time, at least, I will keep thee company. In death, if one tomb may not include us, one epitaph shall; if I may not lay my ashes with thine, my name, at least, shall not be separated." Her grief forbade more words, and these were broken with tears and sobs.

It was now morning. She went to the seashore and sought the spot where she last saw him, on his departure. "While he lingered here, and cast off his tacklings, he gave me his last kiss." While she reviews every object and strives to recall every incident, looking out over the sea, she descries an indistinct object floating in the water. At first she was in doubt what it was, but by degrees the waves bore it nearer, and it was plainly the body of a man. Though unknowing of whom, yet, as it was of some shipwrecked one, she was deeply moved, and gave it her tears, saying, "Alas! Unhappy one, and unhappy, if such there be, thy wife!" Borne by the waves, it came nearer. As she more and more nearly views it, she trembles more and more. Now, now it approaches the shore. Now marks that she recognizes appear. It is her husband! Stretching out her trembling hands towards it, she exclaims, "O, dearest husband, is it thus you return to me?"

There was built out from the shore a mole, constructed to break the assaults of the sea and stem its violent ingress. She leaped upon this barrier and (it was wonderful she could do so) she flew, and striking the air with wings produced on the instant, skimmed along the surface of the water, an unhappy bird. As she flew, her throat poured forth sounds full of grief, and like the voice of one lamenting. When she touched the mute and bloodless body, she enfolded its beloved limbs with her new-formed wings and tried to give kisses with her horny beak. Whether Ceyx felt it, or whether it was only the action of the waves, those who looked on doubted, but the body seemed to raise its head. But indeed he did feel it, and by the pitying gods both of them were changed into birds. They mate and have their young ones. For seven placid days, in wintertime, Halcyone broods over her nest, which floats upon the sea. Then the way is safe to seamen. Aeolus guards the winds and keeps them from disturbing the deep. The sea is given up, for the time, to his grandchildren.

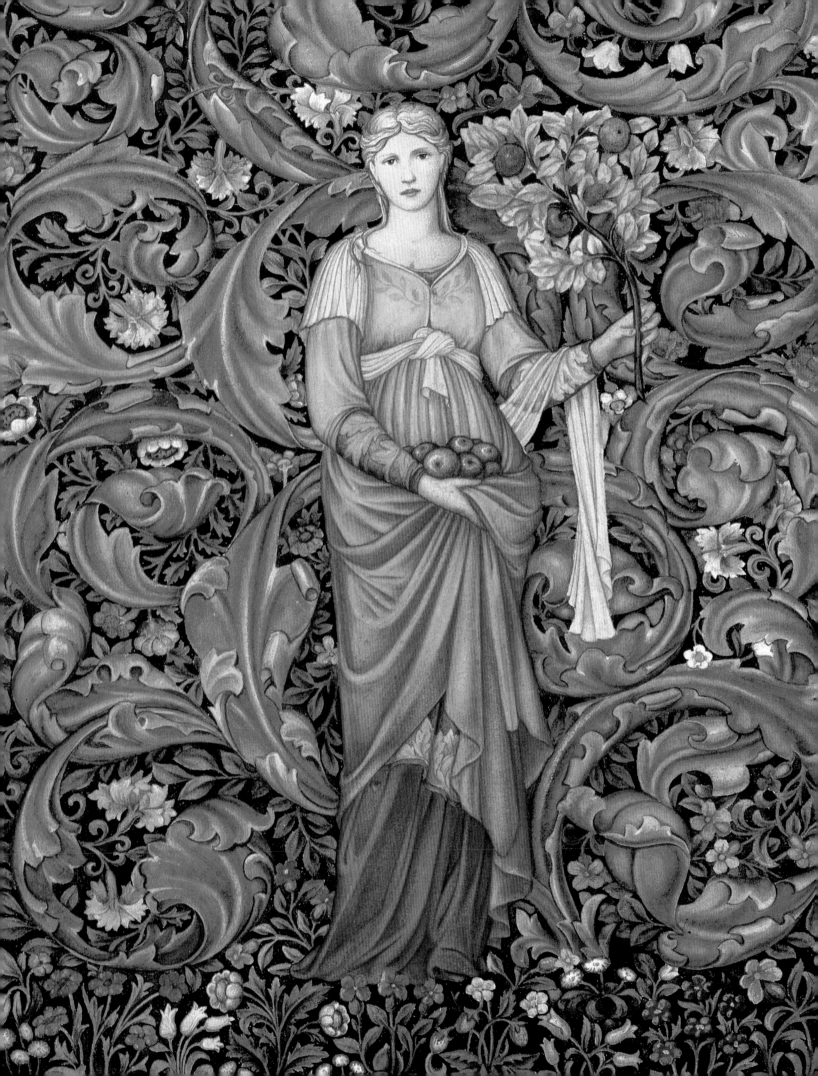

CHAPTER 10

VERTUMNUS AND POMONA

THE HAMADRYADS WERE WOOD NYMPHS. POMONA was of this class, and no one excelled her in love of the garden and the culture of fruit. She cared not for the forests and rivers, but loved the cultivated country and trees that bear delicious apples. Her right hand bore for its weapon not a javelin, but a pruning knife. Armed with this, she busied herself at one time to repress the too luxuriant growths, and curtail the branches that straggled out of place; at another, to split the twig and insert therein a graft, making the branch adopt a nursling not its own. She took care, too, that her favorites should not suffer from drought, and led streams of water by them that the thirsty roots might drink. This occupation was her pursuit, her passion; and she was free from that which Venus inspires. She was not without fear of the country people, and kept her orchard locked, and allowed not men to enter. The Fauns and Satyrs would have given all they possessed to win her, and so would old Sylvanus, who looks young for his years, and Pan, who wears a garland of pine leaves around his head. But Vertumnus loved her best of all; yet he sped no better than the rest. Oh, how often, in the disguise of a reaper, did he bring her corn in a basket, and looked the very image of a reaper! With a hay band tied round him, one would think he had just come from turning over the grass. Sometimes he would have an ox goad in his hand, and you would have said he had just unyoked his weary oxen. Now he bore a pruning hook and personated a vine-dresser; and again, with a ladder on his shoulder, he seemed as if he was going to gather apples. Sometimes he trudged along as a discharged soldier, and again he bore a fishing rod as if going to fish. In this way, he gained admission to her, again and again, and fed his passion with the sight of her.

One day he came in the guise of an old woman, her gray hair surmounted with a cap and a staff in her hand. She entered the garden and admired the fruit. "It does you credit, my dear," she said and kissed her, not exactly with an old woman's kiss.

◄ Pomona Tapestry Design, SIR EDWARD BURNE-JONES (1833–1898): *Pomona was the goddess of fruit (poma), especially apples and pears; her cult, Italian rather than Greek, was associated with fertility and ripeness.*

She sat down on a bank and looked up at the branches laden with fruit which hung over her. Opposite was an elm entwined with a vine loaded with swelling grapes. She praised the tree and its associated vine equally. "But," said she, "if the tree stood alone, and had no vine clinging to it, it would have nothing to attract or offer us but its useless leaves. And equally the vine, if it were not twined round the elm, would lie prostrate on the ground. Why will you not take a lesson from the tree and the vine and consent to unite yourself with someone? I wish you would. Helen herself had not more numerous suitors, nor Penelope, the wife of shrewd Ulysses. Even while you spurn them, they court you—rural deities and others of every kind that frequent these mountains. But if you are prudent and want to make a good alliance, and will let an old woman advise you—who loves you better than you have any idea of—dismiss all the rest and accept Vertumnus, on my recommendation. I know him as well as he knows himself. He is not a wandering deity, but belongs to these mountains. Nor is he like too many of the lovers nowadays, who love anyone they happen to see; he loves you and you only. Add to this, he is young and handsome, and has the art of assuming any shape he pleases, and can make himself just what you command him. Moreover, he loves the same things that you do, delights in gardening, and handles your apples with admiration. But now he cares nothing for fruits, nor flowers, nor anything else, but only yourself. Take pity on him and fancy him speaking now with my mouth. Remember that the gods punish cruelty, and that Venus hates a hard heart, and will visit such offences sooner or later. To prove this, let me tell you a story, which is well known in Cyprus to be a fact; and I hope it will have the effect to make you more merciful.

"Iphis was a young man of humble parentage, who saw and loved Anaxarete, a noble lady of the ancient family of Teucer. He struggled long with his passion, but when he found he could not subdue it, he came a suppliant to her mansion. First he told his passion to her nurse and begged her as she loved her foster child to favor his suit. And then he tried to win her domestics to his side. Sometimes he committed his vows to written tablets, and often hung at her door garlands which he had moistened with his tears. He stretched himself on her threshold and uttered his complaints to the cruel bolts and bars. She was deafer than the surges which rise in the November gale; harder than steel from the German forges, or a rock that still clings to its native cliff. She mocked and laughed at him, adding cruel words to her ungentle treatment, and gave not the slightest gleam of hope.

"Iphis could not any longer endure the torments of hopeless love, and, standing before her doors, he spake these last words: 'Anaxarete, you have conquered, and shall no longer have to bear my importunities. Enjoy your triumph! Sing songs of joy, and bind your forehead with laurel—you have conquered! I die; stony heart, rejoice! This at least I can do to gratify you, and force you to praise me; and thus shall I prove that the love of you left me but with life. Nor will I leave it to rumor to tell you of my death. I will come myself, and you shall see me die, and feast your eyes on the spectacle. Yet, O ye gods, who look down on mortal woes, observe my fate! I ask but this: let me be remembered in coming ages, and add those years to my fame which you have reft from my life.' Thus he said, and, turning his pale face and weeping eyes toward her mansion, he fastened a rope to the gatepost, on which he had often hung garlands, and putting his head into the noose, he murmured, 'This garland at least will please you, cruel girl!' and falling, hung suspended with his neck broken. As he fell he struck against the gate, and the sound was as the sound of a groan. The servants opened the door and found him dead, and with exclamations of pity raised him and carried

him home to his mother, for his father was not living. She received the dead body of her son and folded the cold form to her bosom, while she poured forth the sad words which bereaved mothers utter. The mournful funeral passed through the town, and the pale corpse was borne on a bier to the place of the funeral pile. By chance the home of Anaxarete was on the street where the procession passed, and the lamentations of the mourners met the ears of her whom the avenging deity had already marked for punishment.

"'Let us see this sad procession,' said she, and mounted to a turret, whence through an open window she looked upon the funeral. Scarce had her eyes rested upon the form of Iphis stretched on the bier, when they began to stiffen, and the warm blood in her body to become cold. Endeavoring to step back, she found she could not move her feet; trying to turn away her face, she tried in vain; and by degrees all her limbs became stony like her heart. That you may not doubt the fact, the statue still remains, and stands in the temple of Venus at Salamis, in the exact form of the lady. Now think of these things, my dear, and lay aside your scorn and your delays, and accept a lover. So may neither the vernal frosts blight your young fruits, nor furious winds scatter your blossoms!"

When Vertumnus had spoken thus, he dropped the disguise of an old woman, and stood before her in his proper person, as a comely youth. It appeared to her like the sun bursting through a cloud. He would have renewed his entreaties, but there was no need; his arguments and the sight of his true form prevailed, and the nymph no longer resisted, but owned a mutual flame.

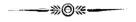

CHAPTER 11

CUPID AND PSYCHE

A CERTAIN KING AND QUEEN HAD THREE DAUGHTERS. The charms of the two elder were more than common, but the beauty of the youngest was so wonderful that the poverty of language is unable to express its due praise. The fame of her beauty was so great that strangers from neighboring countries came in crowds to enjoy the sight, and looked on her with amazement, paying her that homage which is due only to Venus herself. In fact Venus found her altars deserted, while men turned their devotion to this young virgin. As she passed along, the people sang her praises and strewed her way with chaplets and flowers.

This perversion of homage due only to the immortal powers to the exaltation of a mortal gave great offence to the real Venus. Shaking her ambrosial locks with indignation, she exclaimed, "Am I then to be eclipsed in my honors by a mortal girl? In vain then did that royal shepherd, whose judgment was approved by Jove himself, give me the palm of beauty over my illustrious rivals, Pallas and Juno. But she shall not so quietly usurp my honors. I will give her cause to repent of so unlawful a beauty."

Thereupon she calls her winged son Cupid, mischievous enough in his own nature, and rouses and provokes him yet more by her complaints. She points out Psyche to him and says, "My dear son, punish that contumacious beauty; give thy mother a revenge as sweet as her injuries are great; infuse into the bosom of that haughty girl a passion for some low, mean, unworthy being, so that she may reap a mortification as great as her present exultation and triumph."

Cupid prepared to obey the commands of his mother. There are two fountains in Venus's garden, one of sweet waters, the other of bitter. Cupid filled two amber vases, one from each fountain, and suspending them from the top of his quiver, hastened to the chamber of Psyche, whom he found asleep. He shed a few drops from the bitter fountain over her lips, though the sight of her almost moved him to pity; then touched her side with the point of his arrow. At the touch she awoke, and opened eyes upon Cupid (himself invisible), which so startled him that in his confusion he wounded himself with his own arrow. Heedless of his wound his whole thought now was to repair the mischief he had done, and he poured the balmy drops of joy over all her silken ringlets.

Psyche, henceforth frowned upon by Venus, derived no benefit from all her charms. True, all eyes were cast eagerly upon her, and every mouth spoke her praises; but neither king, royal youth, nor plebeian presented himself to demand her in marriage. Her two elder sisters of moderate charms had now long been married to two royal princes; but Psyche, in her lonely apartment, deplored her solitude, sick of that beauty which, while it procured abundance of flattery, had failed to awaken love.

Her parents, afraid that they had unwittingly incurred the anger of the gods, consulted the oracle of Apollo and received this answer: "The virgin is destined for the bride of no mortal lover. Her future husband awaits her on the top of the mountain. He is a monster whom neither gods nor men can resist."

This dreadful decree of the oracle filled all the people with dismay, and her parents abandoned themselves to grief. But Psyche said, "Why, my dear parents, do you now lament me? You should rather have grieved when the people showered upon me undeserved honors and with one voice called me a Venus. I now perceive that I am a victim to that name. I submit. Lead me to that rock to which my unhappy fate has destined me." Accordingly, all things being prepared, the royal maid took her place in the procession, which more resembled a funeral than a nuptial pomp, and with her parents, amid the lamentations of the people, ascended the mountain, on the summit of which they left her alone, and with sorrowful hearts returned home.

While Psyche stood on the ridge of the mountain, panting with fear and with eyes full of tears, the gentle Zephyr raised her from the earth and bore her with an easy motion into a flowery dale. By degrees her mind became composed, and she laid herself down on the grassy bank to sleep. When she awoke refreshed with sleep, she looked round and beheld

Landscape with Psyche outside the Palace of Cupid ➤
("The Enchanted Castle"), CLAUDE (1604/5–1682)
The story of Psyche has strong Gothic overtones: Cupid, instructed to make Psyche enamored of a beast, himself falls for her charms, and hides her in this fairy-tale castle.

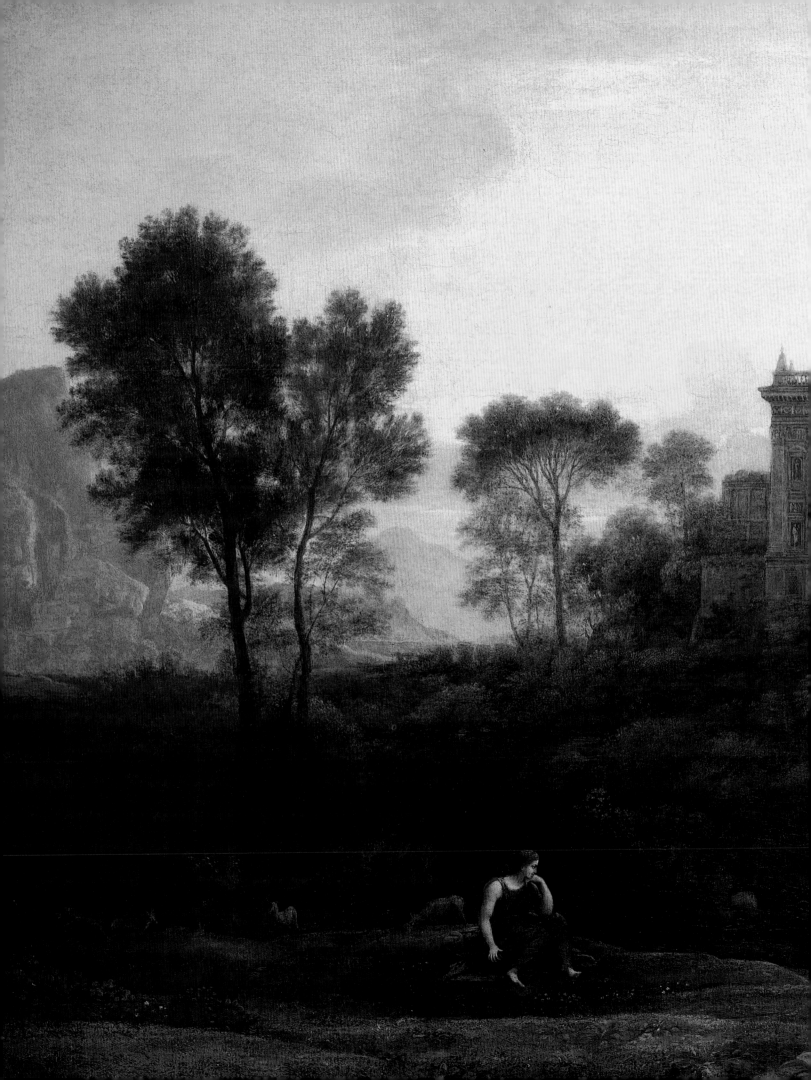

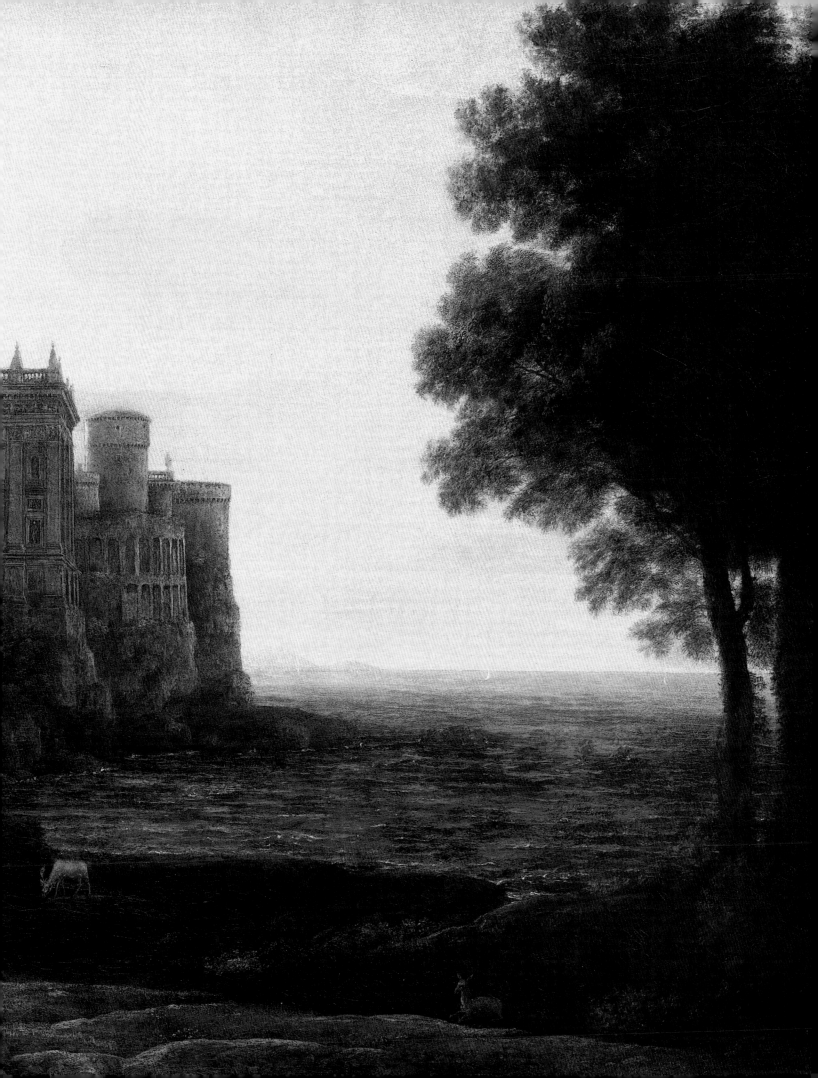

nearby a pleasant grove of tall and stately trees. She entered it, and in the midst discovered a fountain, sending forth clear and crystal waters, and fast by, a magnificent palace whose august front impressed the spectator that it was not the work of mortal hands, but the happy retreat of some god. Drawn by admiration and wonder, she approached the building and ventured to enter. Every object she met filled her with pleasure and amazement. Golden pillars supported the vaulted roof, and the walls were enriched with carvings and paintings representing beasts of the chase and rural scenes, adapted to delight the eye of the beholder. Proceeding onward, she perceived that besides the apartments of state there were others filled with all manner of treasures, and beautiful and precious productions of nature and art.

While her eyes were thus occupied, a voice addressed her, though she saw no one, uttering these words: "Sovereign lady, all that you see is yours. We whose voices you hear are your servants and shall obey all your commands with our utmost care and diligence. Retire therefore to your chamber and repose on your bed of down, and when you see fit, repair to the bath. Supper awaits you in the adjoining alcove when it pleases you to take your seat there."

Psyche gave ear to the admonitions of her vocal attendants, and after repose and the refreshment of the bath, seated herself in the alcove, where a table immediately presented itself, without any visible aid from waiters or servants, and covered with the greatest delicacies of food and the most nectareous wines. Her ears too were feasted with music from invisible performers; of whom one sang, another played on the lute, and all closed in the wonderful harmony of a full chorus.

She had not yet seen her destined husband. He came only in the hours of darkness and fled before the dawn of morning, but his accents were full of love and inspired a like passion in her. She often begged him to stay and let her behold him, but he would not consent. On the contrary he charged her to make no attempt to see him, for it was his pleasure, for the best of reasons, to keep concealed. "Why should you wish to behold me?" he said; "Have you any doubt of my love? Have you any wish ungratified? If you saw me, perhaps you would fear me, perhaps adore me, but all I ask of you is to love me. I would rather you would love me as an equal than adore me as a god."

This reasoning somewhat quieted Psyche for a time, and while the novelty lasted she felt quite happy. But at length the thought of her parents, left in ignorance of her fate, and of her sisters, precluded from sharing with her the delights of her situation, preyed on her mind and made her begin to feel her palace as but a splendid prison. When her husband came one night, she told him her distress, and at last drew from him an unwilling consent that her sisters should be brought to see her.

So calling Zephyr, she acquainted him with her husband's commands, and he, promptly obedient, soon brought them across the mountain down to their sister's valley. They embraced her and she returned their caresses. "Come," said Psyche, "enter with me my house and refresh yourselves with whatever your sister has to offer." Then taking their hands she led them into her golden palace, and committed them to the care of her numerous train of attendant voices, to refresh them in her baths and at her table and to show them all her treasures. The view of these celestial delights caused envy to enter their bosoms, at seeing their young sister possessed of such state and splendor, so much exceeding their own.

They asked her numberless questions, among others what sort of a person her husband was. Psyche replied that he was a beautiful youth, who generally spent the daytime in hunting upon the mountains. The sisters, not satisfied with this reply, soon made her confess that she had never seen him. Then they proceeded to fill her bosom with dark suspicions. "Call to mind," they said, "the Pythian oracles that declared you destined to marry a direful and tremendous monster. The inhabitants of this valley say that your husband is a terrible and monstrous serpent, who nourishes you for a while with dainties that he may by and by devour you. Take our advice. Provide yourself with a lamp and a sharp knife; put them in concealment that your husband may not discover them, and when he is sound asleep, slip out of bed, bring forth your lamp and see for yourself whether what they say is true or not. If it is, hesitate not to cut off the monster's head and thereby recover your liberty."

Psyche resisted these persuasions as well as she could, but they did not fail to have their effect on her mind, and when her sisters were gone, their words

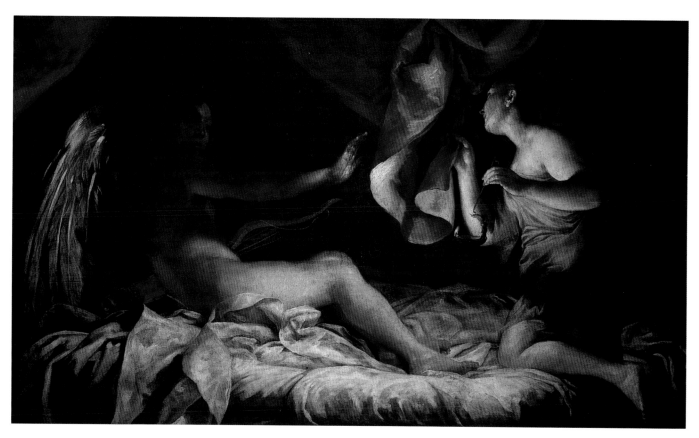

▲ Cupid and Psyche, GIUSEPPE MARIA CRESPI (1665–1747)
*The viewer voyeuristically sees Cupid through Psyche's eyes as she catches sight of her lover for the first time, shrouded in half-darkness.
Crespi's use of chiaroscuro imbues the moment with mystery.*

and her own curiosity were too strong for her to resist. So she prepared her lamp and a sharp knife and hid them out of sight of her husband. When he had fallen into his first sleep, she silently rose and uncovering her lamp beheld not a hideous monster, but the most beautiful and charming of the gods, with his golden ringlets wandering over his snowy neck and crimson cheek, with two dewy wings on his shoulders, whiter than snow, and with shining feathers like the tender blossoms of spring. As she leaned the lamp over to have a nearer view of his face a drop of burning oil fell on the shoulder of the god, startled with which he opened his eyes and fixed them full upon her; then, without saying one word, he spread his white wings and flew out of the window. Psyche, in vain endeavoring to follow him, fell from the window to the ground. Cupid, beholding her as she lay in the dust, stopped his flight for an instant and said, "O foolish Psyche, is it thus you repay my love? After having disobeyed my mother's commands and made you my wife, will you think me a monster and cut off my head? But go; return to your sisters, whose advice you

seem to think preferable to mine. I inflict no other punishment on you than to leave you forever. Love cannot dwell with suspicion." So saying, he fled away, leaving poor Psyche prostrate on the ground, filling the place with mournful lamentations.

When she had recovered some degree of composure she looked around her, but the palace and gardens had vanished, and she found herself in the open field not far from the city where her sisters dwelt. She repaired thither and told them the whole story of her misfortunes, at which, pretending to grieve, those spiteful creatures inwardly rejoiced; "For now," said they, "he will perhaps choose one of us." With this idea, without saying a word of her intentions, each of them rose early the next morning and ascended the mountain, and having reached the top, called upon Zephyr to receive her and bear her to his lord; then leaping up, and not being sustained by Zephyr, fell down the precipice and was dashed to pieces.

Psyche, meanwhile, wandered day and night, without food or repose, in search of her husband. Casting her eyes on a lofty mountain having on its brow a magnificent temple, she sighed and said to herself, "Perhaps my love, my lord, inhabits there," and directed her steps thither.

She had no sooner entered than she saw heaps of corn, some in loose ears and some in sheaves, with mingled ears of barley. Scattered about lay sickles and rakes and all the instruments of harvest, without order, as if thrown carelessly out of the weary reapers' hands in the sultry hours of the day.

This unseemly confusion the pious Psyche put an end to, by separating and sorting everything to its proper place and kind, believing that she ought to neglect none of the gods, but endeavor by her piety to engage them all on her behalf. The holy Ceres, whose temple it was, finding her so religiously employed, thus spoke to her: "Oh, Psyche, truly worthy of our pity, though I cannot shield you from the frowns of Venus, yet I can teach you how best to allay her displeasure. Go then and voluntarily surrender yourself to your lady and sovereign, and try by modesty and submission to win her forgiveness, and perhaps her favor will restore you the husband you have lost."

Psyche obeyed the commands of Ceres and took her way to the temple of Venus, endeavoring to fortify her mind and ruminating on what she should say and how best propitiate the angry goddess, feeling that the issue was doubtful and perhaps fatal.

Venus received her with angry countenance. "Most undutiful and faithless of servants," said she, "do you at last remember that you really have a mistress? Or have you rather come to see your sick husband, yet laid up of the wound given him by his loving wife? You are so ill-favored and disagreeable that the only way you can merit your lover must be by dint of industry and diligence. I will make trial of your housewifery." Then she ordered Psyche to be led to the storehouse of her temple, where was laid up a great quantity of wheat, barley, millet, vetches, beans, and lentils prepared for food for her pigeons, and said, "Take and separate all these grains, putting all of the same kind in a parcel by themselves, and see that you get it done before evening." Then Venus departed and left her to her task.

But Psyche, in a perfect consternation at the enormous work, sat stupid and silent, without moving a finger to the inextricable heap.

While she sat despairing, Cupid stirred up the little ant, a native of the fields, to take compassion on her. The leader of the ant hill, followed by whole hosts of his six-legged subjects, approached the heap, and with the utmost diligence taking grain by grain, they separated the pile, sorting each kind to its parcel; and when it was all done, they vanished out of sight in a moment.

Venus, at the approach of twilight, returned from the banquet of the gods, breathing odors and crowned with roses. Seeing the task done, she exclaimed, "This is no work of yours, wicked one, but his, whom to your own and his misfortune you have enticed." So saying, she threw her a piece of black bread for her supper and went away.

Next morning Venus ordered Psyche to be called and said to her, "Behold yonder grove which stretches along the margin of the water. There you will find sheep feeding without a shepherd, with golden-shining fleeces on their backs. Go, fetch me a sample of that precious wool gathered from every one of their fleeces."

Psyche obediently went to the riverside, prepared to do her best to execute the command. But the river god inspired the reeds with harmonious murmurs, which seemed to say, "Oh, maiden, severely tried, tempt not the dangerous flood, nor venture among the formidable rams on the other side, for as long as they are under the influence of the rising sun, they burn with a cruel rage to destroy mortals with their sharp horns or rude teeth. But when the noontide sun has driven the cattle to the shade, and the serene spirit of the flood has lulled them to rest, you may then cross in safety, and you will find the woolly gold sticking to the bushes and the trunks of the trees."

Thus the compassionate river god gave Psyche instructions how to accomplish her task, and by observing his directions she soon returned to Venus with her arms full of the golden fleece; but she received not the approbation of her implacable mistress, who said, "I know very well it is by none of your own doings that you have succeeded in this task, and I am not satisfied yet that you have any capacity to make yourself useful. But I have another task for you. Here, take this box, and go your way to the infernal shades, and give this box to Proserpine and say, 'My mistress Venus desires you to send her a little of your beauty, for in tending her sick son she has lost some of her own.' Be not too long on your errand, for I must paint myself with it to appear at the circle of the gods and goddesses this evening."

Psyche was now satisfied that her destruction was at hand, being obliged to go with her own feet directly down to Erebus. Wherefore, to make no delay of what was not to be avoided, she goes to the top of a high tower to precipitate herself headlong, thus to descend the shortest way to the shades below. But a voice from the tower said to her, "Why, poor unlucky girl, dost thou design to put an end to thy days in so dreadful a manner? And what cowardice makes thee sink under this last danger who hast been so miraculously supported in all thy former?" Then the voice told her how by a certain cave she might reach the realms of Pluto, and how to avoid all the dangers of the road, to pass by Cerberus, the three-headed dog, and prevail on Charon, the ferryman, to take her across the black river and bring her back again. But the voice added, "When Proserpine has given you the box filled with her beauty, of all things this is chiefly to be observed by you, that you never once open or look into the box nor allow your curiosity to pry into the treasure of the beauty of the goddesses."

Psyche, encouraged by this advice, obeyed it in all things, and taking heed to her ways traveled safely to the kingdom of Pluto. She was admitted to the palace of Proserpine, and without accepting the delicate seat or delicious banquet that was offered her, but contented with coarse bread for her food, she delivered her message from Venus. Presently the box was returned to her, shut and filled with the precious commodity. Then she returned the way she came, and glad was she to come out once more into the light of day.

But having got so far successfully through her dangerous task a longing desire seized her to examine the contents of the box. "What," said she, "shall I, the carrier of this divine beauty, not take the least bit to put on my cheeks to appear to more advantage in the eyes of my beloved husband!" So she carefully opened the box, but found nothing there of any beauty at all, but an infernal and truly Stygian sleep, which being thus set free from its prison, took possession of her, and she fell down in the midst of the road, a sleepy corpse without sense or motion.

But Cupid, being now recovered from his wound, and not able longer to bear the absence of his beloved Psyche, slipping through the smallest crack of the window of his chamber, which happened to

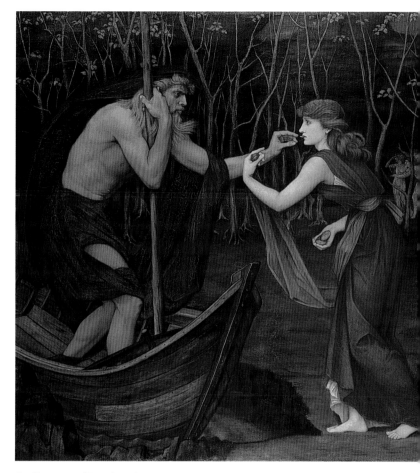

▲ Charon and Psyche, JOHN SPENCER STANHOPE (1829–1908)
Charon, ferryman of the underworld, presses on Psyche's lips the coin (obol) customarily required for passage across the River Styx.

be left open, flew to the spot where Psyche lay, and gathering up the sleep from her body closed it again in the box, and waked Psyche with a light touch of one of his arrows. "Again," said he, "hast thou almost perished by the same curiosity. But now perform exactly the task imposed on you by my mother, and I will take care of the rest."

Then Cupid, as swift as lightning penetrating the heights of heaven, presented himself before Jupiter with his supplication. Jupiter lent a favoring ear and pleaded the cause of the lovers so earnestly with Venus that he won her consent. On this he sent Mercury to bring Psyche up to the heavenly assembly, and when she arrived, handing her a cup of ambrosia, he said, "Drink this, Psyche, and be immortal; nor shall Cupid ever break away from the knot in which he is tied, but these nuptials shall be perpetual."

Thus Psyche became at last united to Cupid, and in due time they had a daughter born to them whose name was Pleasure.

CHAPTER 12

CADMUS · THE MYRMIDONS

Jupiter, under the disguise of a bull, had carried away Europa, the daughter of Agenor, King of Phoenicia. Agenor commanded his son Cadmus to go in search of his sister, and not to return without her. Cadmus went and sought long and far for his sister, but could not find her, and not daring to return unsuccessful, consulted the oracle of Apollo to know what country he should settle in. The oracle informed him that he should find a cow in the field, and should follow her wherever she might wander, and where she stopped, should build a city and call it Thebes. Cadmus had hardly left the Castalian cave, from which the oracle was delivered, when he saw a young cow slowly walking before him. He followed her close, offering at the same time his prayers to Phoebus. The cow went on till she passed the shallow channel of Cephisus and came out into the plain of Panope. There she stood still, and raising her broad forehead to the sky, filled the air with her lowings. Cadmus gave thanks and, stooping down, kissed the foreign soil, then lifting his eyes, greeted the surrounding mountains. Wishing to offer a sacrifice to Jupiter, he sent his servants to seek pure water for a libation. Nearby there stood an ancient grove which had never been profaned by the axe, in the midst of which was a cave, thick covered with the growth of bushes, its roof forming a low arch, from beneath which burst forth a fountain of purest water. In the cave lurked a horrid serpent with a crested head and scales glittering like gold. His eyes shone like fire, his body was swollen with venom, he vibrated a triple tongue, and showed a triple row of teeth. No sooner had the Tyrians dipped their pitchers in the fountain, and the ingushing waters made a sound, than the glittering serpent raised his head out of the cave and uttered a fearful hiss. The vessels fell from their hands, the blood left their cheeks, they trembled in every limb. The serpent, twisting his scaly body in a huge coil, raised his head so as to overtop the tallest trees, and while the Tyrians from terror could neither fight nor fly, slew some with his fangs, others in his folds, and others with his poisonous breath.

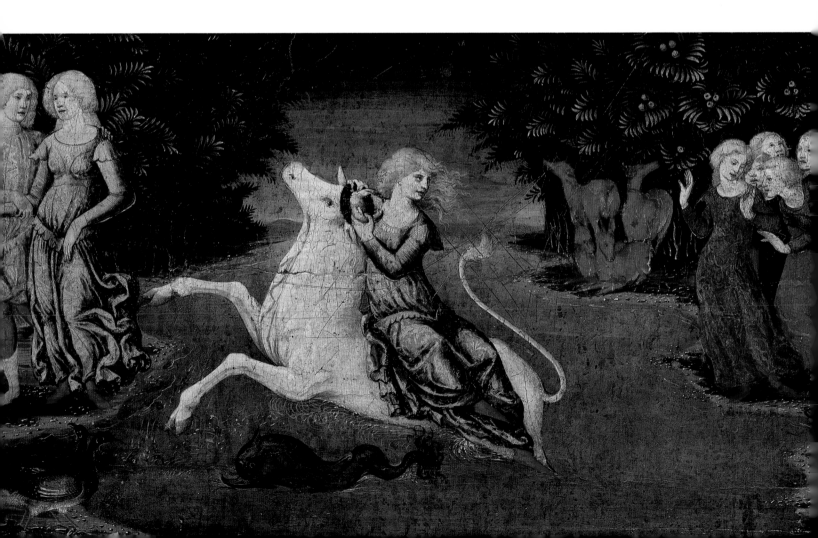

Cadmus, having waited for the return of his men till midday, went in search of them. His covering was a lion's hide, and besides his javelin he carried in his hand a lance, and in his breast a bold heart, a surer reliance than either. When he entered the wood, and saw the lifeless bodies of his men and the monster with his bloody jaws, he exclaimed, "Oh, faithful friends, I will avenge you or share your death." So saying, he lifted a huge stone and threw it with all his force at the serpent. Such a block would have shaken the wall of a fortress, but it made no impression on the monster. Cadmus next threw his javelin, which met with better success, for it penetrated the serpent's scales and pierced through to his entrails. Fierce with pain, the monster turned back his head to view the wound and attempted to draw out the weapon with his mouth, but broke it off, leaving the iron point rankling in his flesh. His neck swelled with rage, bloody foam covered his jaws, and the breath of his nostrils poisoned the air around. Now he twisted himself into a circle, then stretched himself out on the ground like the trunk of a fallen tree. As he moved onward, Cadmus retreated before him, holding his spear opposite to the monster's opened jaws. The serpent snapped at the weapon and attempted to bite its iron point. At last Cadmus, watching his chance, thrust the spear at a moment when the animal's head thrown back came against the trunk of a tree, and so succeeded in pinning him to its side. His weight bent the tree as he struggled in the agonies of death.

While Cadmus stood over his conquered foe, contemplating its vast size, a voice was heard (from whence he knew not, but he heard it distinctly) commanding him to take the dragon's teeth and sow them in the earth. He obeyed. He made a furrow in the ground, and planted the teeth, destined to produce a crop of men. Scarce had he done so when the clods began to move, and the points of spears to appear above the surface. Next, helmets with their nodding plumes came up, and next the shoulders and breasts and limbs of men with weapons, and in time a harvest of armed warriors. Cadmus, alarmed, prepared to encounter a new enemy, but one of them said to him, "Meddle not with our civil war."

▼ Europa and the Bull, LIBERALE DA VERONA (circa 1445–1527/9)
On this panel from a cassone or wedding chest, Zeus carries away the Phoenician princess Europa. Her name was later given to a continent.

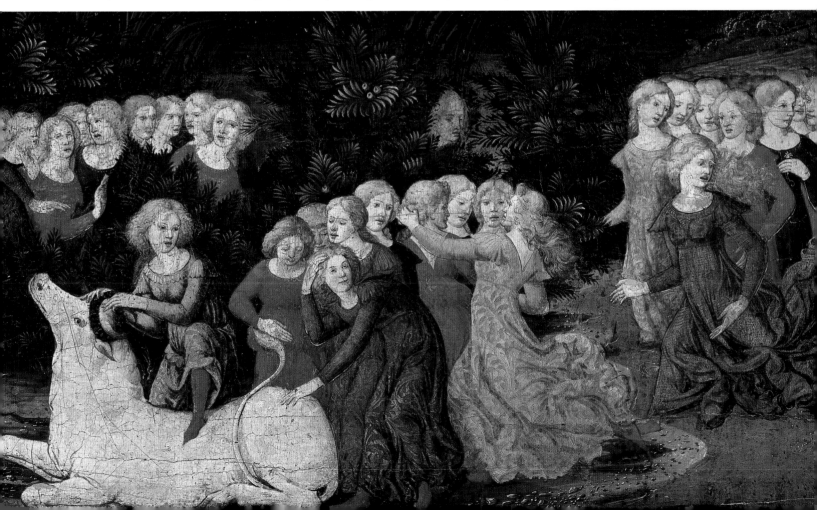

With that, he who had spoken smote one of his earth-born brothers with a sword, and he himself fell pierced with an arrow from another. The latter fell victim to a fourth, and in like manner the whole crowd dealt with each other till all fell slain with mutual wounds, except five survivors. One of these cast away his weapons and said, "Brothers, let us live in peace!" These five joined with Cadmus in building his city, to which they gave the name of Thebes.

Cadmus obtained in marriage Harmonia, the daughter of Venus. The gods left Olympus to honor the occasion with their presence, and Vulcan presented the bride with a necklace of surpassing brilliancy, his own workmanship. But a fatality hung over the family of Cadmus in consequence of his killing the serpent sacred to Mars. Semele and Ino, his daughters, and Actaeon and Pentheus, his grandchildren, all perished unhappily, and Cadmus and Harmonia quitted Thebes, now grown odious to them, and emigrated to the country of the Enchelians, who received them with honor and made Cadmus their king. But the misfortunes of their children still weighed upon their minds; and one day Cadmus exclaimed, "If a serpent's life is so dear to the gods, I would I were myself a serpent." No sooner had he uttered the words than he began to change his form. Harmonia beheld it and prayed to the gods to let her share his fate. Both became serpents. They live in the woods, but mindful of their origin, they neither avoid the presence of man, nor do they ever injure anyone.

There is a tradition that Cadmus introduced into Greece the letters of the alphabet which were invented by the Phoenicians.

THE MYRMIDONS

The Myrmidons were the soldiers of Achilles in the Trojan war. From them, all zealous and unscrupulous followers of a political chief are called by that name, down to this day. But the origin of the Myrmidons would not give one the idea of a fierce and bloody race, but rather of a laborious and peaceful one.

Cephalus, King of Athens, arrived in the island of Aegina to seek assistance of his old friend and ally Aeacus, the king, in his war with Minos, King of Crete. Cephalus was most kindly received, and the desired assistance readily promised. "I have people enough," said Aeacus, "to protect myself and spare

you such a force as you need." "I rejoice to see it," replied Cephalus, "and my wonder has been raised, I confess, to find such a host of youths as I see around me, all apparently of about the same age. Yet there are many individuals whom I previously knew that I look for now in vain. What has become of them?" Aeacus groaned and replied with a voice of sadness, "I have been intending to tell you, and will now do so, without more delay, that you may see how from the saddest beginning a happy result sometimes flows. Those whom you formerly knew are now dust and ashes! A plague sent by angry Juno devastated the land. She hated it because it bore the name of one of her husband's female favorites. While the disease appeared to spring from natural causes we resisted it as we best might by natural remedies; but it soon appeared that the pestilence was too powerful for our efforts, and we yielded. At the beginning the sky seemed to settle down upon the earth, and thick clouds shut in the heated air. For four months together a deadly south wind prevailed. The disorder affected the wells and springs; thousands of snakes crept over the land and shed their poison in the fountains. The force of the disease was first spent on the lower animals, dogs, cattle, sheep, and birds. The luckless plowman wondered to see his oxen fall in the midst of their work and lie helpless in the unfinished furrow. The wool fell from the bleating sheep, and their bodies pined away. The horse once foremost in the race contested the palm no more, but groaned at his stall and died an inglorious death. The wild boar forgot his rage, the stag his swiftness, the bears no longer attacked the herds. Everything languished; dead bodies lay in the roads, the fields, and the woods; the air was poisoned by them. I tell you what is hardly credible, but neither dogs nor birds would touch them, nor starving wolves. Their decay spread the infection. Next the disease attacked the country people, and then the dwellers in the city. At first the cheek was flushed and the breath drawn with difficulty. The tongue grew rough and swelled, and the dry mouth stood open with its veins enlarged and gasped for the air. Men could not bear the heat of their clothes or their beds, but preferred to lie on the bare ground; and the ground did not cool them, but on the contrary, they heated the spot where they lay. Nor could the physicians help, for the disease attacked them also, and the contact of the sick gave them infection, so that the most faithful were the first victims. At last all hope of relief vanished, and men learned to look upon death as the only deliverer from disease. Then they gave way to every inclination and cared not to ask what was expedient, for nothing was expedient. All restraint laid aside, they crowded around the wells and fountains and drank till they died, without quenching thirst. Many had not strength to get away from the water, but died in the midst of the stream, and others would drink of it notwithstanding. Such was their weariness of their sick beds that some would creep forth, and if not strong enough to stand, would die on the ground. They seemed to hate their friends, and got away from their homes, as if, not knowing the cause of their sickness, they charged it on the place of their abode. Some were seen tottering along the road, as long as they could stand, while others sank on the earth and turned their dying eyes around to take a last look, then closed them in death.

"What heart had I left me, during all this, or what ought I to have had, except to hate life and wish to be with my dead subjects? On all sides lay my people, strewn like overripened apples beneath the tree, or acorns under the storm-shaken oak. You see yonder a temple on the height. It is sacred to Jupiter. Oh, how many offered prayers there, husbands for wives, fathers for sons, and died in the very act of supplication! How often, while the priest made ready for sacrifice, the victim fell, struck down by disease without waiting for the blow. At length all reverence for sacred things was lost. Bodies were thrown out unburied, wood was wanting for funeral piles, men fought with one another for the possession of them. Finally there were none left to mourn; sons and husbands, old men and youths, perished alike unlamented.

"Standing before the altar I raised my eyes to heaven. 'O Jupiter,' I said, 'if thou art indeed my father, and art not ashamed of thy offspring, give me back my people, or take me also away!' At these words a clap of thunder was heard. 'I accept the omen,' I cried; 'oh, may it be a sign of a favorable disposition toward me!' By chance there grew by the place where I stood an oak with wide-spreading branches, sacred to Jupiter. I observed a troop of ants busy with their labor, carrying minute grains in their mouths and following one another in a line up the trunk of the tree. Observing their numbers with admiration I said, 'Give me, O father, citizens as numerous as these, and replenish my empty city.' The tree shook and gave a rustling sound with its branches though no wind agitated them. I trembled in every limb, yet I kissed the earth and the tree. I would not confess to myself that I hoped, yet I did hope. Night came on and sleep took possession of my frame oppressed with cares. The tree stood before me in my dreams, with its numerous branches all covered with living, moving creatures. It seemed to shake its limbs and throw down over the ground a multitude of those industrious grain-gathering animals, which appeared to gain in size, and grow larger and larger, and by-and-by to stand erect, lay aside their superfluous legs and their black color, and finally to assume the human form. Then I awoke, and my first impulse was to chide the gods who had robbed me of a sweet vision and given me no reality in its place. Being still in the temple my attention was caught by the sound of many voices without; a sound of late unusual to my ears.

While I began to think I was yet dreaming, Telamon, my son, throwing open the temple gates, exclaimed, 'Father, approach, and behold things surpassing even your hopes!' I went forth; I saw a multitude of men, such as I had seen in my dream, and they were passing in procession in the same manner. "While I gazed with wonder and delight they approached and, kneeling, hailed me as their king. I paid my vows to Jove and proceeded to allot the vacant city to the new-born race and to parcel out the fields among them. I called them Myrmidons from the ant (*myrmex*) from which they sprang. You have seen these persons; their dispositions resemble those which they had in their former shape. They are a diligent and industrious race, eager to gain, and tenacious of their gains. Among them you may recruit your forces. They will follow you to the war, young in years and bold in heart."

75

CHAPTER 13

NISUS AND SCYLLA
ECHO AND NARCISSUS
CLYTIE · HERO AND LEANDER

Minos, King of Crete, made war upon Megara. Nisus was king of Megara, and Scylla was his daughter. The siege had now lasted six months, and the city still held out, for it was decreed by fate that it should not be taken so long as a certain purple lock, which glittered among the hair of King Nisus, remained on his head. There was a tower on the city walls, which overlooked the plain where Minos and his army were encamped. To this tower Scylla used to repair, and look abroad over the tents of the hostile army. The siege had lasted so long that she had learned to distinguish the persons of the leaders. Minos, in particular, excited her admiration. Arrayed in his helmet, and bearing his shield, she admired his graceful deportment; if he threw his javelin, skill seemed combined with force in the discharge; if he drew his bow, Apollo himself could not have done it more gracefully. But when he laid aside his helmet, and in his purple robes bestrode his white horse with its gay caparisons, and reined in its foaming mouth, the daughter of Nisus was hardly mistress of herself; she was almost frantic with admiration. She envied the weapon that he grasped, the reins that he held. She felt as if she could, if it were possible, go to him through the hostile ranks; she felt an impulse to cast herself down from the tower into the midst of his camp, or to open the gates to him, or to do anything else, so only it might gratify Minos. As she sat in the tower, she talked thus with herself: "I know not whether to rejoice or grieve at this sad war. I grieve that Minos is our enemy; but I rejoice at any cause that brings him to my sight. Perhaps he would be willing to grant us peace and receive me as a hostage. I would fly down, if I could, and alight in his camp, and tell him that we yield ourselves to his mercy. But, then, to betray my father! No! Rather would I never see Minos again. And yet no doubt it is sometimes the best thing for a city to be conquered, when the conqueror is clement and generous. Minos certainly has right on his side.

I think we shall be conquered; and if that must be the end of it, why should not love unbar the gates to him, instead of leaving it to be done by war? Better spare delay and slaughter if we can. And oh, if anyone should wound or kill Minos! No one surely would have the heart to do it; yet ignorantly, not knowing him, one might. I will, I will surrender myself to him, with my country as a dowry, and so put an end to the war. But how? The gates are guarded, and my father keeps the keys; he only stands in my way. Oh, that it might please the gods to take him away! But why ask the gods to do it? Another woman, loving as I do, would remove with her own hands whatever stood in the way of her love. And can any other woman dare more than I? I would encounter fire and sword to gain my object; but here there is no need of fire and sword. I only need my father's purple lock. More precious than gold to me, that will give me all I wish."

While she thus reasoned night came on, and soon the whole palace was buried in sleep. She entered her father's bedchamber and cut off the fatal lock; then passed out of the city and entered the enemy's camp. She demanded to be led to the king, and thus addressed him: "I am Scylla, the daughter of Nisus. I surrender to you my country and my father's house. I ask no reward but yourself; for love of you I have done it. See here the purple lock! With this I give you my father and his kingdom." She held out her hand with the fatal spoil. Minos shrunk back and refused to touch it. "The gods destroy thee, infamous woman," he exclaimed; "disgrace of our time! May neither earth nor sea yield thee a resting place! Surely, my Crete, where Jove himself was cradled, shall not be polluted with such a monster!" Thus he said, and gave orders that equitable terms should be allowed to the conquered city, and that the fleet should immediately sail from the island.

Scylla was frantic. "Ungrateful man," she exclaimed, "is it thus you leave me?—me who have given you victory—who have sacrificed for you parent and country! I am guilty, I confess, and deserve to die, but not by your hand." As the ships left the shore, she leaped into the water, and seizing the rudder of the one which carried Minos, she was borne along, an unwelcome companion of their course. A sea eagle soaring aloft—it was her father who had been changed into that form—seeing her, pounced down upon her and struck her with his beak and claws. In terror she let go the ship, and would have fallen into the water, but some pitying deity changed her into a bird. The sea eagle still cherishes the old animosity; and whenever he espies her in his lofty flight, you may see him dart down upon her, with beak and claws, to take vengeance for the ancient crime.

ECHO AND NARCISSUS

Echo was a beautiful nymph, fond of the woods and hills, where she devoted herself to woodland sports. She was a favorite of Diana, and attended her in the chase. But Echo had one failing: she was fond of talking, and whether in chat or argument, would have the last word. One day Juno was seeking her husband, who, she had reason to fear, was amusing himself among the nymphs. Echo by her talk contrived to detain the goddess till the nymphs made their escape. When Juno discovered it, she passed sentence upon Echo in these words: "You shall forfeit the use of that tongue with which you have cheated me, except for that one purpose you are so fond of—reply. You shall still have the last word, but no power to speak first."

This nymph saw Narcissus, a beautiful youth, as he pursued the chase upon the mountains. She loved him and followed his footsteps. Oh, how she longed to address him in the softest accents, and win him to converse! But it was not in her power. She waited with impatience for him to speak first, and had her answer ready. One day the youth, being separated from his companions, shouted aloud, "Who's here?" Echo replied, "Here." Narcissus looked around, but seeing no one, called out, "Come." Echo answered, "Come." As no one came, Narcissus called again, "Why do you shun me?" Echo asked the same question. "Let us join one another," said the youth. The maid answered with all her heart in the same words, and hastened to the spot, ready to throw her arms about his neck. He started back, exclaiming,

"Hands off! I would rather die than you should have me!" "Have me," said she; but it was all in vain. He left her, and she went to hide her blushes in the recesses of the woods. From that time forth she lived in caves and among mountain cliffs. Her form faded with grief, till at last all her flesh shrank away. Her bones were changed into rocks, and there was nothing left of her but her voice. With that she is still ready to reply to anyone who calls her, and keeps up her old habit of having the last word.

Narcissus's cruelty in this case was not the only instance. He shunned all the rest of the nymphs, as he had done poor Echo. One day a maiden, who had in vain endeavored to attract him, uttered a prayer that he might sometime or other feel what it was to love and meet no return of affection. The avenging goddess heard and granted the prayer.

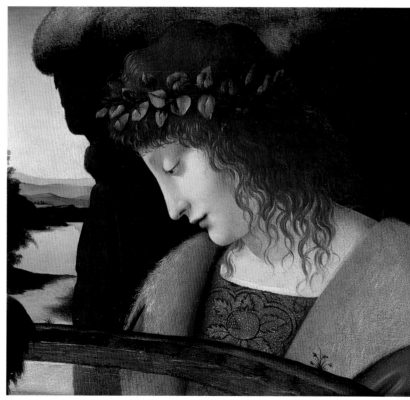

▲ Narcissus, FOLLOWER OF LEONARDO (1452–1519)
The founder of self-love or narcissism gazes longingly (and fatally) at his own reflection. The androgynous image may have been inspired by Ovid's description in his Metamorphoses.

There was a clear fountain, with water like silver, to which the shepherds never drove their flocks, nor the mountain goats resorted, nor any of the beasts of the forest; neither was it defaced with fallen leaves or branches; but the grass grew fresh around it,

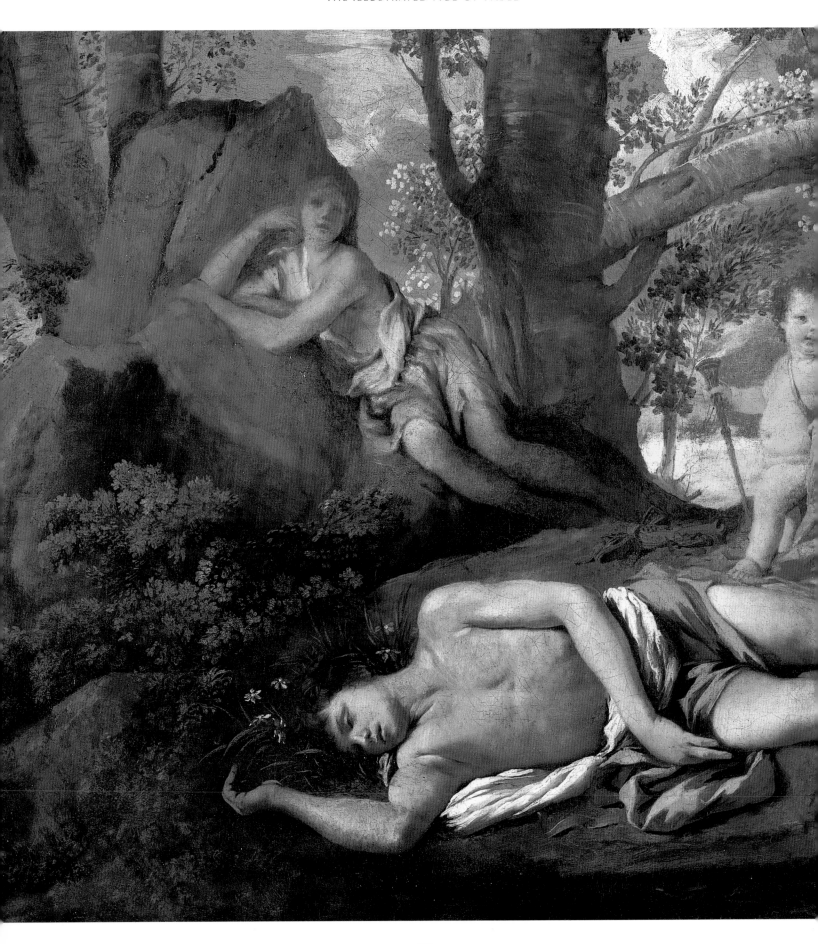

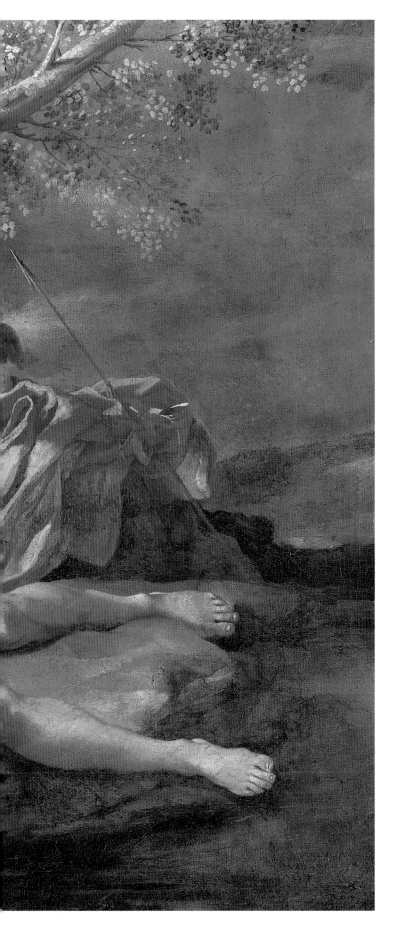

and the rocks sheltered it from the sun. Hither came one day the youth fatigued with hunting, heated and thirsty. He stooped down to drink, and saw his own image in the water; he thought it was some beautiful water spirit living in the fountain. He stood gazing with admiration at those bright eyes, these locks curled like the locks of Bacchus or Apollo, the rounded cheeks, the ivory neck, the parted lips, and the glow of health and exercise over all. He fell in love with himself. He brought his lips near to take a kiss; he plunged his arms in to embrace the beloved object. It fled at the touch, but returned again after a moment and renewed the fascination. He could not tear himself away; he lost all thought of food or rest, while he hovered over the brink of the fountain gazing upon his own image. He talked with the supposed spirit: "Why, beautiful being, do you shun me? Surely, my face is not one to repel you. The nymphs love me, and you yourself look not indifferent upon me. When I stretch forth my arms you do the same; and you smile upon me and answer my beckonings with the like." His tears fell into the water and disturbed the image. As he saw it depart, he exclaimed, "Stay, I entreat you! Let me at least gaze upon you, if I may not touch you." With this, and much more of the same kind, he cherished the flame that consumed him, so that by degrees he lost his color, his vigor, and the beauty which formerly had so charmed the nymph Echo. She kept near him, however, and when he exclaimed, "Alas! Alas!" she answered him with the same words. He pined away and died; and when his shade passed the Stygian river, it leaned over the boat to catch a look of itself in the waters. The nymphs mourned for him, especially the water nymphs; and when they smote their breasts, Echo smote hers also. They prepared a funeral pile, and would have burned the body, but it was nowhere to be found; but in its place a flower, purple within, and surrounded with white leaves, which bears the name and preserves the memory of Narcissus.

◄ Echo and Narcissus, NICOLAS POUSSIN (1594–1665)
Poussin shows the love-stricken Echo gazing hopelessly at Narcissus. The artist makes much of the god's great beauty; his recumbent form prefigures a wasting death.

CLYTIE

Clytie was a water nymph and in love with Apollo, who made her no return. So she pined away, sitting all day long upon the cold ground, with her unbound tresses streaming over her shoulders. Nine days she sat and tasted neither food nor drink, her own tears and the chilly dew her only food. She gazed on the Sun when he rose and as he passed through his daily course to his setting; she saw no other object, her face turned constantly on him. At last, they say, her limbs rooted in the ground, her face became a flower, which turns on its stem so as always to face the sun throughout its daily course; for it retains to that extent the feeling of the nymph from whom it sprang.

HERO AND LEANDER

Leander was a youth of Abydos, a town of the Asian side of the strait which separates Asia and Europe. On the opposite shore in the town of Sestos lived the maiden Hero, a priestess of Venus. Leander loved her, and used to swim the strait nightly to enjoy the company of his mistress, guided by a torch which she reared upon the tower, for the purpose. But one night a tempest arose and the sea was rough; his strength failed, and he was drowned. The waves bore his body to the European shore, where Hero became aware of his death, and in her despair cast herself down from the tower into the sea and perished.

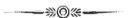

▼ The Parting of Hero and Leander, JOSEPH MALLORD WILLIAM TURNER (1775–1851)
A moonlit landscape dwarfs the sea-borne passion of the hero and heroine. To this day, Leander remains a favorite name for sea-going craft.

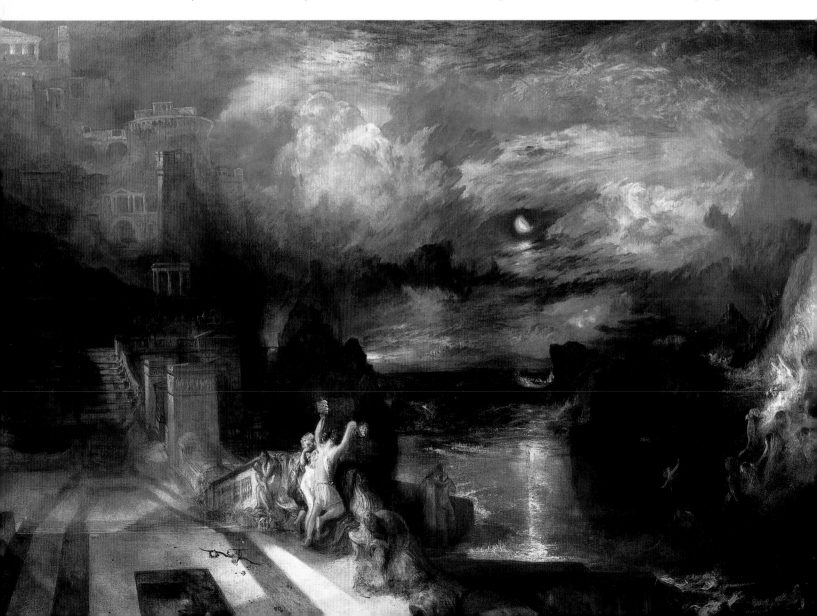

CHAPTER 14

MINERVA · NIOBE

MINERVA, THE GODDESS OF WISDOM, WAS THE daughter of Jupiter. She was said to have leaped forth from his brain, mature and in complete armor. She presided over the useful and ornamental arts, both those of men—such as agriculture and navigation—and those of women—spinning, weaving and needlework. She was also a warlike divinity; but it was defensive war only that she patronized, and she had no sympathy with Mars's savage love of violence and bloodshed. Athens was her chosen seat, her own city, awarded to her as the prize of a contest with Neptune, who also aspired to it. The tale ran that in the reign of Cecrops, the first king of Athens, the two deities contended for the possession of the city. The gods decreed that it should be awarded to that one who produced the gift most useful to mortals. Neptune gave the horse; Minerva produced the olive. The gods gave judgment that the olive was the more useful of the two, and awarded the city to the goddess; and it was named after her, Athens, her name in Greek being Athene.

There was another contest, in which a mortal dared to come in competition with Minerva. That mortal was Arachne, a maiden who had attained such skill in the arts of weaving and embroidery that the nymphs themselves would leave their groves and fountains to come and gaze upon her work. It was not only beautiful when it was done, but beautiful also in the doing. To watch her, as she took the wool in its rude state and formed it into rolls, or separated it with her fingers and carded it till it looked as light and soft as a cloud, or twirled the spindle with skillful touch, or wove the web, or, after it was woven, adorned it with her needle, one would have said that Minerva herself had taught her. But this she denied, and could not bear to be thought a pupil even of a goddess. "Let Minerva try her skill with mine," said she; "if beaten, I will pay the penalty." Minerva heard this and was displeased. She assumed the form of an old woman and went and gave Arachne some friendly advice. "I have had much experience," said she, "and I hope you will not despise my counsel. Challenge your fellow mortals as you will, but do not compete with a goddess. On the contrary, I advise you to ask her forgiveness for

what you have said, and as she is merciful, perhaps she will pardon you." Arachne stopped her spinning and looked at the old dame with anger in her countenance. "Keep your counsel," said she, "for your daughters or handmaids; for my part, I know

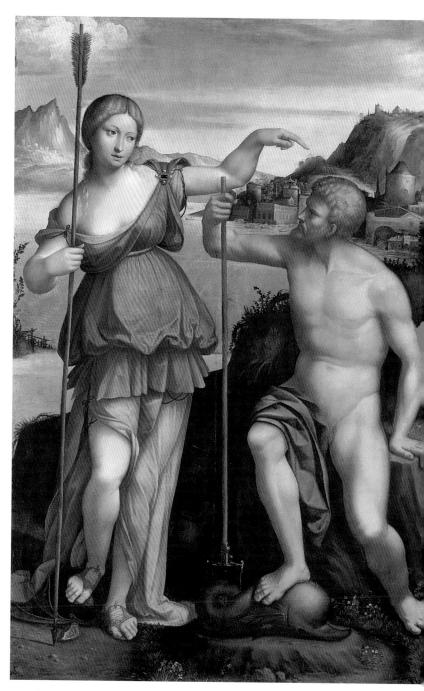

▲ Neptune and Minerva, GAROFALO (circa 1481–1559)
The sea-god Neptune, recognizable by his trident and dolphin footrest, disputes with Minerva the territory of Attica. The story occupied a central place on the west pediment of the Athenian Parthenon.

what I say, and I stand to it. I am not afraid of the goddess; let her try her skill, if she dare venture." "She comes," said Minerva; and dropping her disguise, stood confessed. The nymphs bent low in homage, and all the bystanders paid reverence. Arachne alone was unterrified. She blushed, indeed; a sudden color dyed her cheek, and then she grew pale. But she stood to her resolve, and with a foolish conceit of her own skill rushed on her fate. Minerva forbore no longer, nor interposed any further advice. They proceed to the contest. Each takes her station and attaches the web to the beam. Then the slender shuttle is passed in and out among the threads. The

reed with its fine teeth strikes up the woof into its place and compacts the web. Both work with speed; their skillful hands move rapidly, and the excitement of the contest makes the labor light. Wool of Tyrian dye is contrasted with that of other colors, shaded off into one another so adroitly that the joining deceives the eye. Like the bow, whose long arch tinges the heavens, formed by sunbeams reflected from the shower, in which, where the colors meet they seem as one, but at a little distance from the point of contact are wholly different.

Minerva wrought on her web the scene of her contest with Neptune. Twelve of the heavenly powers

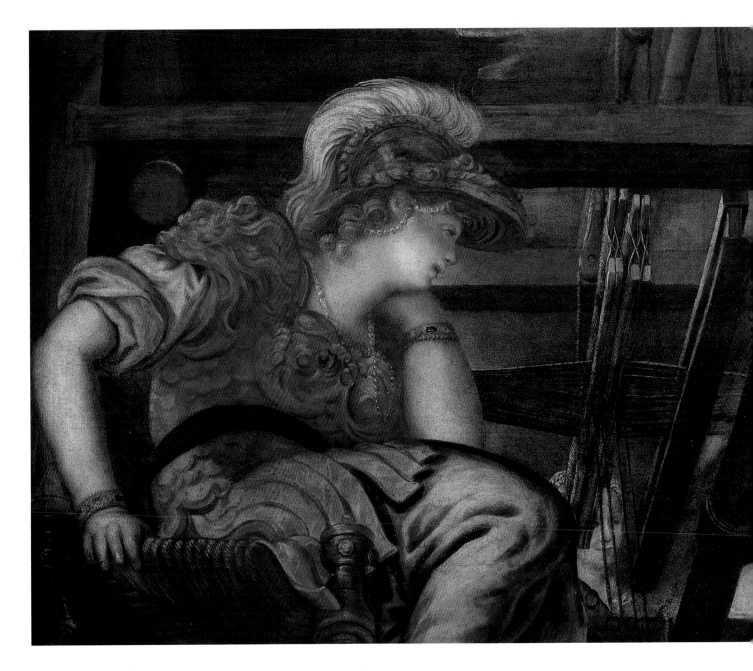

are represented, Jupiter, with august gravity, sitting in the midst. Neptune, the ruler of the sea, holds his trident, and appears to have just smitten the earth, from which a horse has leaped forth. Minerva depicted herself with helmeted head, her Aegis covering her breast. Such was the central circle; and in the four corners were represented incidents illustrating the displeasure of the gods at such presumptuous mortals as had dared to contend with them. These were meant as warnings to her rival to give up the contest before it was too late.

Arachne filled her web with subjects designedly chosen to exhibit the failings and errors of the gods. One scene represented Leda caressing the swan, under which form Jupiter had disguised himself; and another, Danaë, in the brazen tower in which her father had imprisoned her, but where the god effected his entrance in the form of a golden shower. Still another depicted Europa deceived by Jupiter under the disguise of a bull. Encouraged by the tameness of the animal, Europa ventured to mount his back, whereupon Jupiter advanced into the sea and swam

▼ Minerva and Arachne, JACOPO TINTORETTO (1518–1594)
Minerva's contest with Arachne would once have had a social resonance. The citizen women of ancient Athens spent most of their days at the loom, weaving clothes for the general populace and to adorn the statues of their deities.

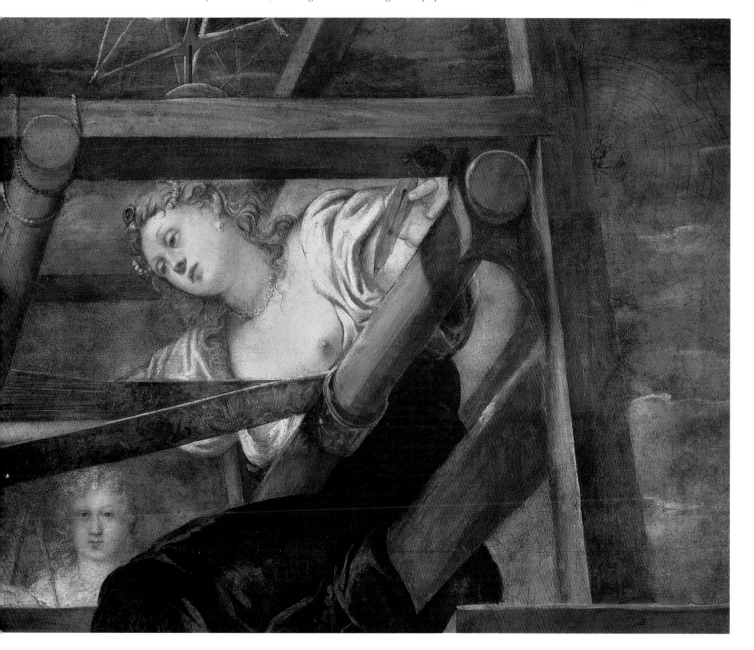

with her to Crete. You would have thought it was a real bull, so naturally was it wrought and so natural the water in which it swam. She seemed to look with longing eyes back upon the shore she was leaving, and to call to her companions for help. She appeared to shudder with terror at the sight of the heaving waves, and to draw back her feet from the water.

Arachne filled her canvas with similar subjects, wonderfully well done, but strongly marking her presumption and impiety. Minerva could not forbear to admire, yet felt indignant at the insult. She struck the web with her shuttle and rent it in pieces; she then touched the forehead of Arachne and made her feel her guilt and shame. She could not endure it, and went and hanged herself. Minerva pitied her as she saw her suspended by a rope. "Live," she said, "guilty woman—and that you may preserve the memory of this lesson continue to hang, both you and your descendants, to all future times." She sprinkled her with the juices of aconite, and immediately her hair came off, and her nose and ears likewise. Her form shrank up, and her head grew smaller yet; her fingers cleaved to her side and served for legs. All the rest of her is body, out of which she spins her thread, often hanging suspended by it, in the same attitude as when Minerva touched her and transformed her into a spider.

NIOBE

The fate of Arachne was noised abroad through all the country, and served as a warning to all presumptuous mortals not to compare themselves with the divinities. But one, and she a matron too, failed to learn the lesson of humility. It was Niobe, the queen of Thebes. She had indeed much to be proud of; but it was not her husband's fame, nor her own beauty, nor their great descent, nor the power of their kingdom that elated her. It was her children; and truly the happiest of mothers would Niobe have been, if only she had not claimed to be so. It was on occasion of the annual celebration in honor of Latona and her offspring, Apollo and Diana—when the people of Thebes were assembled, their brows crowned with laurel, bearing frankincense to the altars and paying their vows— that Niobe appeared among the crowd. Her attire was splendid with gold and gems, and her aspect beautiful as the face of an angry woman can be. She stood and surveyed the people with haughty looks.

"What folly," said she, "is this!—to prefer beings whom you never saw to those who stand before your eyes! Why should Latona be honored with worship, and none be paid to me? My father was Tantalus, who was received as a guest at the table of the gods; my mother was a goddess. My husband built and rules this city, Thebes, and Phrygia is my paternal inheritance. Wherever I turn my eyes I survey the elements of my power; nor is my form and presence unworthy of a goddess. To all this let me add, I have seven sons and seven daughters, and look for sons-in-law and daughters-in-law of pretensions worthy of my alliance. Have I not cause for pride? Will you prefer to me this Latona, the Titan's daughter, with her two children? I have seven times as many. Fortunate indeed am I, and fortunate I shall remain! Will any one deny this? My abundance is my security. I feel myself too strong for Fortune to subdue. She may take from me much; I shall still have much left. Were I to lose some of my children, I should hardly be left as poor as Latona with her two only. Away with you from these solemnities— put off the laurel from your brows—have done with this worship!" The people obeyed and left the sacred services uncompleted.

The goddess was indignant. On the Cynthian mountaintop where she dwelt, she thus addressed her son and daughter: "My children, I who have been so proud of you both and have been used to hold myself second to none of the goddesses except Juno alone, begin now to doubt whether I am indeed a goddess. I shall be deprived of my worship altogether unless you protect me." She was proceeding in this strain, but Apollo interrupted her. "Say no more," said he; "speech only delays punishment." So said Diana also. Darting through the air, veiled in clouds, they alighted on the towers of the city. Spread out before the gates was a broad plain, where the youth of the city pursued their warlike sports. The sons of Niobe were there with the rest—some mounted on spirited horses richly caparisoned, some driving gay chariots. Ismenos, the firstborn, as he guided his foaming steeds, struck with an arrow from above, cried out, "Ah me!"—dropped the reins and fell lifeless. Another, hearing the sound of the bow—like a boatman who sees the storm gathering and makes all sail for the port—gave the rein to his horses and attempted to escape. The inevitable arrow overtook him as he fled. Two others, younger boys, just from their tasks, had gone to the playground to have a game of wrestling. As they stood breast to breast, one arrow pierced them both. They uttered a cry together, together cast a parting look around them, and together breathed their last. Alphenor, an elder brother, seeing them fall, hastened to the spot to render assistance and fell stricken in the act of brotherly duty. One only was left, Ilioneus. He raised his arms to heaven to try whether prayer might not avail. "Spare me, ye gods!" he cried, addressing all, in his ignorance that all needed not his intercessions; and Apollo would have spared him, but the arrow had already left the string, and it was too late.

The terror of the people and grief of the attendants soon made Niobe acquainted with what had taken place. She could hardly think it possible; she was indignant that the gods had dared and amazed that they had been able to do it. Her husband, Amphion, overwhelmed with the blow, destroyed himself. Alas! How different was this Niobe from her who had so lately driven away the people from the sacred rites, and held her stately course through the city, the envy of her friends, now the pity even of her foes! She knelt over the lifeless bodies, and kissed, now one, now another of her dead sons. Raising her pallid arms to heaven, "Cruel Latona," said she, "feed full your rage with my anguish! Satiate your hard heart, while I follow to the grave my seven sons. Yet where is your triumph? Bereaved as I am, I am still richer than you, my conqueror." Scarce had she spoken, when the bow sounded and struck terror into all hearts except Niobe's alone. She was brave from excess of grief. The sisters stood in garments of mourning over the biers of their dead brothers. One fell, struck by an arrow, and died on the corpse she was bewailing. Another, attempting to console her mother, suddenly ceased to speak, and sank lifeless to the earth. A third tried to escape by flight, a fourth by concealment, another stood trembling, uncertain what course to take. Six were now dead, and only one remained, whom the mother held clasped in her arms, and covered as it were with her whole body. "Spare me one, and that the youngest! Oh, spare me one of so many!" she cried; and while she spoke, that one fell dead. Desolate she sat, among sons, daughters, husband, all dead, and seemed torpid with grief. The breeze moved not her hair, no color was on her cheek, her eyes glared fixed and immovable, there was no sign of life about her. Her very tongue cleaved to the roof of her mouth, and her veins ceased to convey the tide of life. Her neck bent not, her arms made no gesture, her foot no step. She was changed to stone, within and without. Yet tears continued to flow; and, borne on a whirlwind to her native mountain, she still remains, a mass of rock, from which a trickling stream flows, the tribute of her never-ending grief.

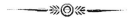

Adventures of Perseus
Medusa · Atlas · The Sea Monster
The Wedding Feast

THE GRAEAE WERE THREE SISTERS WHO WERE gray-haired from their birth, whence their name. The Gorgons were monstrous females with huge teeth like those of swine, brazen claws, and snaky hair. None of these beings make much figure in mythology except Medusa, the Gorgon, whose story we shall next advert to. We mention them chiefly to introduce an ingenious theory of some modern writers, namely, that the Gorgons and Graeae were only personifications of the terrors of the sea, the former denoting the strong billows of the wide-open main, and the latter the white-crested waves that dash against the rocks of the coast. Their names in Greek signify the above epithets.

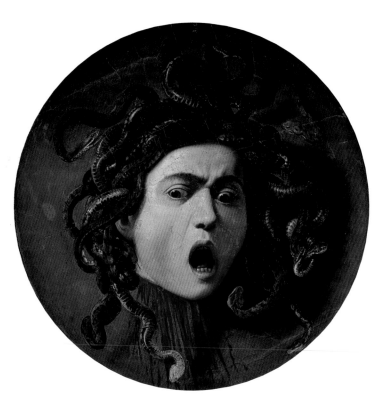

▲ Medusa, CARAVAGGIO (1571–1610)
Caravaggio shows Medusa in her full "apotropaic" mode—a visage intended to terrify onlookers. As such, the Gorgon's mask was often painted on the shields of Greek soldiers, or sculpted, like a gargoyle, on the gables of Greek temples.

MEDUSA

Perseus was the son of Jupiter and Danaë. His grandfather Acrisius, alarmed by an oracle that had told him that his daughter's child would be the instrument of his death, caused the mother and child to be shut up in a chest and set adrift on the sea. The chest floated toward Seriphus, where it was found by a fisherman who conveyed the mother and infant to Polydectes, king of the country, by whom they were treated with kindness. When Perseus was grown up, Polydectes sent him to attempt the conquest of Medusa, a terrible monster who had laid waste the country. She was once a beautiful maiden whose hair was her chief glory, but as she dared to vie in beauty with Minerva, the goddess deprived her of her charms and changed her beautiful ringlets into hissing serpents. She became a cruel monster of so frightful an aspect that no living thing could behold her without being turned into stone. All around the cavern where she dwelt might be seen the stony figures of men and animals that had chanced to catch a glimpse of her and had been petrified with the sight. Perseus, favored by Minerva and Mercury, the former of whom lent him her shield and the latter his winged shoes, approached Medusa while she slept, and taking care not to look directly at her, but guided by her image reflected in the bright shield which he bore, he cut off her head, and gave it to Minerva, who fixed it in the middle of her Aegis.

ATLAS

After the slaughter of Medusa, Perseus, bearing with him the head of the Gorgon, flew far and wide, over land and sea. As night came on, he reached the western limit of the earth, where the sun goes down. Here he would gladly have rested till morning. It was the realm of King Atlas, whose bulk surpassed that of all other men. He was rich in flocks and herds and had no neighbor or rival to dispute his state. But his chief pride was in his gardens, whose fruit was of gold,

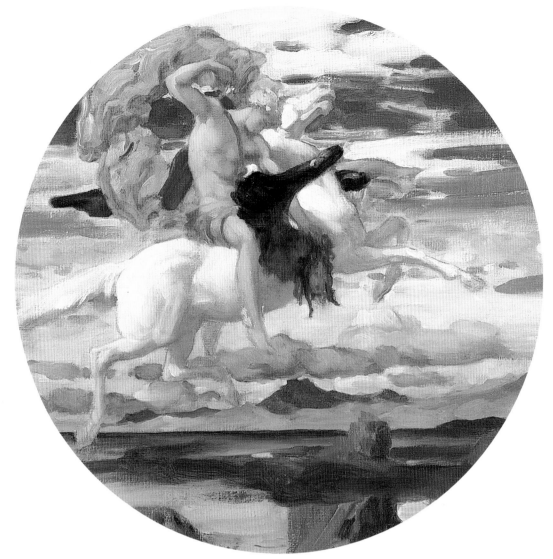

▲ *Study for* Perseus on Pegasus Hastening to the Rescue of Andromeda, LORD FREDERIC LEIGHTON (1830–1896)
From the decapitated Medusa sprang the winged horse Pegasus. Later, Pegasus was to become the mount of the hero Bellerophon.

hanging from golden branches, half hid with golden leaves. Perseus said to him, "I come as a guest. If you honor illustrious descent, I claim Jupiter for my father; if mighty deeds, I plead the conquest of the Gorgon. I seek rest and food." But Atlas remembered that an ancient prophecy had warned him that a son of Jove should one day rob him of his golden apples. So he answered, "Begone! or neither your false claims of glory or parentage shall protect you;" and he attempted to thrust him out. Perseus, finding the giant too strong for him, said, "Since you value my friendship so little, deign to accept a present;" and turning his face away, he held up the Gorgon's head. Atlas, with all his bulk, was changed into stone. His beard and hair became forests, his arms and shoulders cliffs, his head a summit and his bones rocks. Each part increased in bulk till he became a mountain, and

(such was the pleasure of the gods) heaven with all its stars rests upon his shoulders.

THE SEA MONSTER

Perseus, continuing his flight, arrived at the country of the Aethiopians, of which Cepheus was king. Cassiopeia, his queen, proud of her beauty, had dared to compare herself to the sea nymphs, which roused their indignation to such a degree that they sent a prodigious sea monster to ravage the coast. To appease the deities, Cepheus was directed by the oracle to expose his daughter Andromeda to be devoured by the monster. As Perseus looked down

Andromeda Saved by Perseus, PIERO DI COSIMO ➤
(circa 1462–1521): *Andromeda was an Ethiopian, hence the turban-wearing spectators witnessing Perseus's heroism. The sea monster was sent by Neptune who was insulted by a claim that Andromeda excelled his own Nereids in beauty.*

87

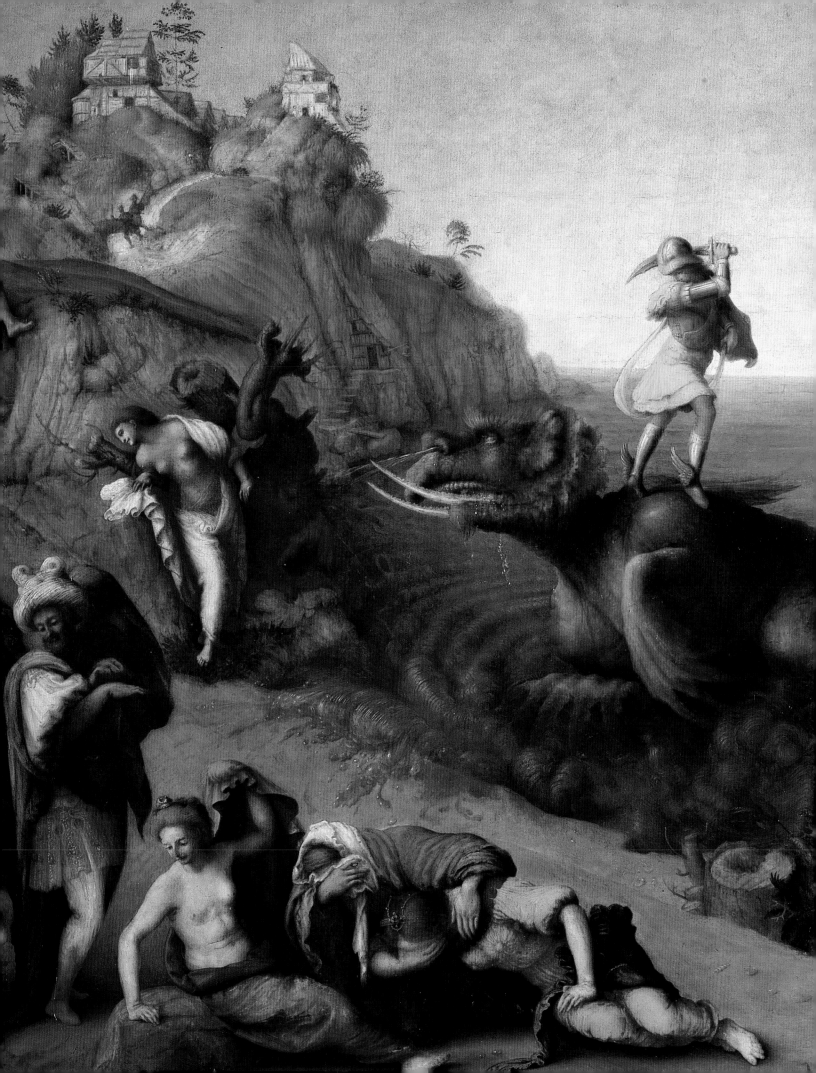

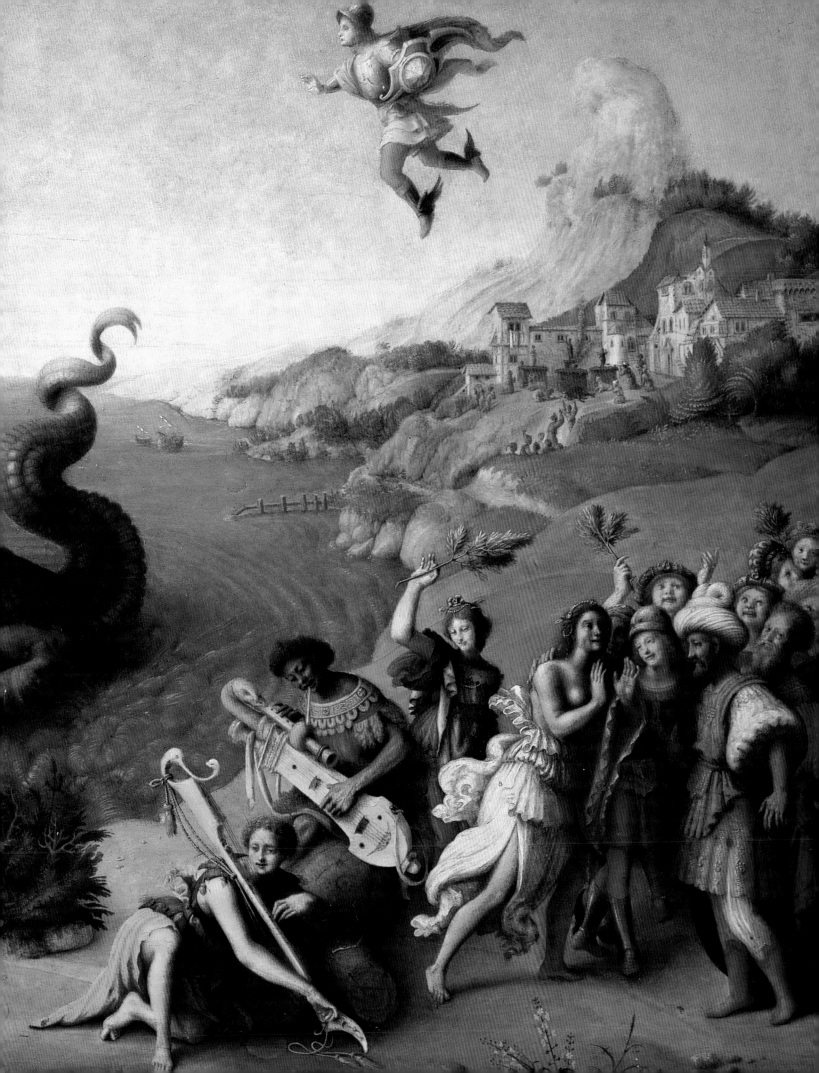

from his aerial height he beheld the virgin chained to a rock, waiting the approach of the serpent. She was so pale and motionless that if it had not been for her flowing tears and her hair that moved in the breeze, he would have taken her for a marble statue. He was so startled at the sight that he almost forgot to wave his wings. As he hovered over her he said, "Oh, virgin, undeserving of those chains, but rather of such as bind fond lovers together, tell me, I beseech you, your name, and the name of your country, and why you are thus bound." At first she was silent from modesty, and, if she could, would have hid her face with her hands; but when he repeated his questions, for fear she might be thought guilty of some fault which she dared not tell, she disclosed her name and that of her country, and her mother's pride of beauty. Before she had done speaking, a sound was heard off upon the water, and the sea monster appeared, with his head raised above the surface, cleaving the waves with his broad breast. The virgin shrieked, the father and mother, who had now arrived at the scene, wretched both, but the mother more justly so, stood by, not able to afford protection, but only to pour forth lamentations and to embrace the victim. Then spoke Perseus: "There will be time enough for tears; this hour is all we have for rescue. My rank as the son of Jove and my renown as the slayer of the Gorgon might make me acceptable as a suitor; but I will try to win her by services rendered, if the gods will only be propitious. If she be rescued by my valor, I demand that she be my reward." The parents consent (how could they hesitate?) and promise a royal dowry with her.

And now the monster was within the range of a stone thrown by a skillful slinger, when with a sudden bound the youth soared into the air. As an eagle, when from his lofty flight he sees a serpent basking in the sun, pounces upon him and seizes him by the neck to prevent him from turning his head around and using his fangs, so the youth darted down upon the back of the monster and plunged his sword into its shoulder. Irritated by the wound, the monster raised himself into the air, then plunged into the depth; then, like a wild boar surrounded by a pack of barking dogs, turned swiftly from side to side, while the youth eluded its attacks by means of his wings. Wherever he can find a passage for his sword between the scales he makes a wound, piercing now the side,

now the flank, as it slopes toward the tail. The brute spouts from his nostrils water mixed with blood. The wings of the hero are wet with it, and he dares no longer trust to them. Alighting on a rock that rose above the waves, and holding on by a projecting fragment, as the monster floated near he gave him a death stroke. The people who had gathered on the shore shouted so that the hills echoed the sound. The parents, transported with joy, embraced their future son-in-law, calling him their deliverer and the savior of their house, and the virgin, both cause and reward of the contest, descended from the rock.

THE WEDDING FEAST

The joyful parents, with Perseus and Andromeda, repaired to the palace, where a banquet was spread for them, and all was joy and festivity. But suddenly a noise was heard of warlike clamor, and Phineus, the betrothed of the virgin, with a party of his adherents, burst in, demanding the maiden as his own. It was in vain that Cepheus remonstrated— "You should have claimed her when she lay bound to the rock, the monster's victim. The sentence of the gods dooming her to such a fate dissolved all engagements, as death itself would have done." Phineus made no reply, but hurled his javelin at Perseus, but it missed its mark and fell harmless. Perseus would have thrown his in turn, but the cowardly assailant ran and took shelter behind the altar. But his act was a signal for an onset by his band upon the guests of Cepheus. They defended themselves and a general conflict ensued, the old king retreating from the scene after fruitless expostulations, calling the gods to witness that he was guiltless of this outrage on the rights of hospitality.

Perseus and his friends maintained for some time the unequal contest; but the numbers of the assailants were too great for them, and destruction seemed inevitable, when a sudden thought struck Perseus— "I will make my enemy defend me." Then with a loud voice he exclaimed, "If I have any friend here let him turn away his eyes!" and held aloft the Gorgon's head.

The Baleful Head, SIR EDWARD BURNE-JONES (1833–1898) ➤
Even when decapitated, the Medusa's gaze was deadly. Perseus therefore shows it to his bride Andromeda only as a reflection. Burne-Jones sets the incident in a Pre-Raphaelite garden burgeoning with fruit and flowers.

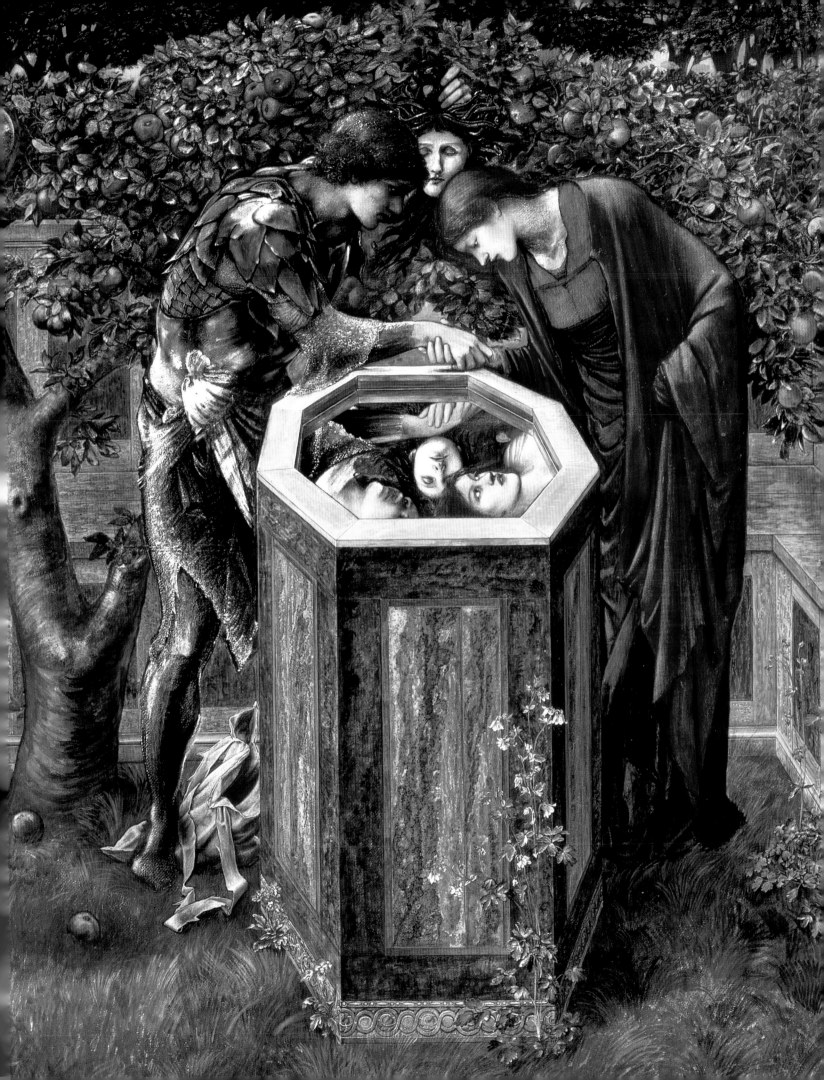

"Seek not to frighten us with your jugglery," said Thescelus, and raised his javelin in act to throw, and became stone in the very attitude. Ampyx was about to plunge his sword into the body of a prostrate foe, but his arm stiffened and he could neither thrust forward nor withdraw it. Another, in the midst of a vociferous challenge, stopped; his mouth open, but no sound issuing. One of Perseus' friends, Aconteus, caught sight of the Gorgon and stiffened like the rest. Astyages struck him with his sword, but instead of wounding, it recoiled with a ringing noise.

Phineus beheld this dreadful result of his unjust aggression and felt confounded. He called aloud to his friends but got no answer; he touched them and found them stone. Falling on his knees and stretching out his hands to Perseus, but turning his head away, he begged for mercy. "Take all," said he, "give me but my life." "Base coward," said Perseus, "thus much I will grant you; no weapon shall touch you; moreover, you shall be preserved in my house as a memorial of these events." So saying, he held the Gorgon's head to the side where Phineus was looking, and in the very form in which he knelt, with his hands outstretched and face averted, he became fixed immovably, a mass of stone!

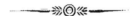

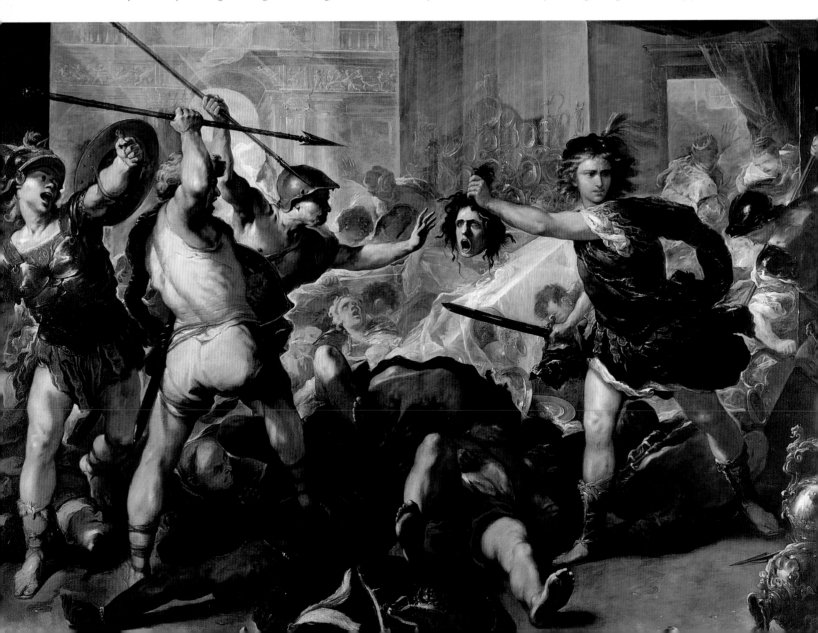

▼ Perseus Turning Phineas and His Followers to Stone, LUCA GIORDANO (1634–1705)
Perseus slew the sea monster in order to win Andromeda for his bride. Seeking to deny him that prize, Phineus and his followers are literally petrified by the Gorgon's visage. Giordano gives the scene a baroque sense of movement by showing the figures in contrapposto.

CHAPTER 16

MONSTERS: GIANTS · THE SPHINX PEGASUS AND THE CHIMAERA THE CENTAURS · THE PYGMIES · THE GRIFFIN

ONSTERS, IN THE LANGUAGE OF MYTHOLOGY, WERE beings of unnatural proportions or parts, usually regarded with terror, as possessing immense strength and ferocity, which they employed for the injury and annoyance of men. Some of them were supposed to combine the members of different animals; such were the Sphinx and Chimaera; and to these all the terrible qualities of wild beasts were attributed, together with human sagacity and faculties. Others, as the giants, differed from men chiefly in their size; and in this particular we must recognize a wide distinction among them. The human giants, if so they may be called, such as the Cyclopes, Antaeus, Orion, and others, must be supposed not to be altogether disproportioned to human beings, for they mingled in love and strife with them. But the superhuman giants, who warred with the gods, were of vastly larger dimensions. Tityus, we are told, when stretched on the plain, covered nine acres, and Enceladus required the whole of Mount Aetna to be laid upon him to keep him down.

We have already spoken of the war which the giants waged against the gods, and of its result. While this war lasted the giants proved a formidable enemy. Some of them, like Briareus, had a hundred arms; others, like Typhon, breathed out fire. At one time they put the gods to such fear that they fled into Egypt and hid themselves under various forms. Jupiter took the form of a ram, whence he was afterward worshipped in Egypt as the god Ammon, with curved horns. Apollo became a crow, Bacchus a goat, Diana a cat, Juno a cow, Venus a fish, Mercury a bird. At another time the giants attempted to climb up into heaven, and for that purpose took up the mountain Ossa and piled it on Pelion. They were at last subdued by thunderbolts, which Minerva invented and taught Vulcan and his Cyclopes to make for Jupiter.

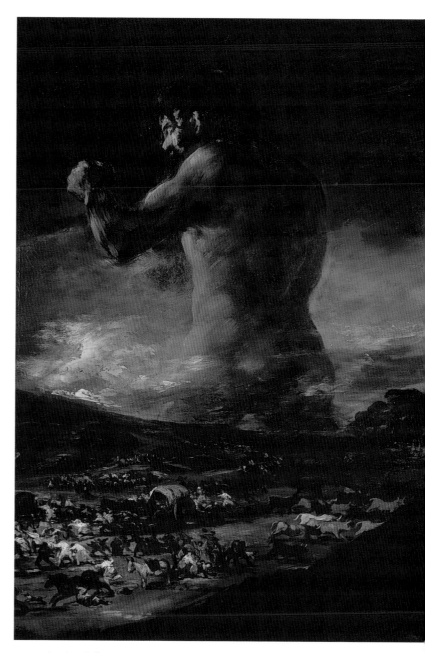

▲ The Colossus, FRANCISCO DE GOYA (1746–1828)
In Greek mythology, mountains were explained as the dead or fossilized bodies of toppled giants—mostly felled in elemental battle with the Olympian deities, but always symbolic of revolt against divine order.

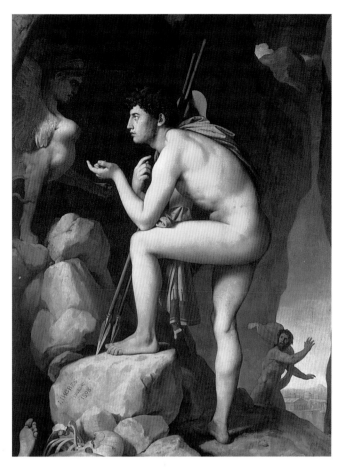

▲ Oedipus Explains the Riddle of the Sphinx,
JEAN-AUGUSTE-DOMINIQUE INGRES (1780–1867)
The Egyptian Sphinx of Greek and Roman iconography is usually associated with death or funerary passage.

THE SPHINX

Laius, King of Thebes, was warned by an oracle that there was danger to his throne and life if his newborn son should be suffered to grow up. He therefore committed the child to the care of a herdsman with orders to destroy him; but the herdsman, moved with pity, yet not daring entirely to disobey, tied up the child by the feet, and left him hanging to the branch of a tree. In this condition the infant was found by a peasant, who carried him to his master and mistress, by whom he was adopted and called Oedipus, or Swollen-foot.

Many years afterward Laius, being on his way to Delphi, accompanied only by one attendant, met in a narrow road a young man also driving in a chariot. On his refusal to leave the way at their command, the attendant killed one of his horses, and the stranger, filled with rage, slew both Laius and his attendant. The young man was Oedipus, who thus unknowingly became the slayer of his own father.

Shortly after this event, the city of Thebes was afflicted with a monster that infested the high road. It was called the Sphinx. It had the body of a lion, and the upper part of a woman. It lay crouched on the top of a rock and arrested all travelers who came that way, proposing to them a riddle, with the condition that those who could solve it should pass safe, but those who failed should be killed. Not one had yet succeeded in solving it, and all had been slain. Oedipus was not daunted by these alarming accounts, but boldly advanced to the trial. The Sphinx asked him, "What animal is that which in the morning goes on four feet, at noon on two, and in the evening upon three?" Oedipus replied, "Man, who in childhood creeps on hands and knees, in manhood walks erect, and in old age with the aid of a staff." The Sphinx was so mortified at the solving of her riddle that she cast herself down from the rock and perished.

The gratitude of the people for their deliverance was so great that they made Oedipus their king, giving him in marriage their queen Jocasta. Oedipus, ignorant of his parentage, had already become the slayer of his father; in marrying the queen he became the husband of his mother. These horrors remained undiscovered, till at length Thebes was afflicted with famine and pestilence, and the oracle being consulted, the double crime of Oedipus came to light. Jocasta put an end to her own life, and Oedipus, seized with madness, tore out his eyes and wandered away from Thebes, dreaded and abandoned by all except his daughters, who faithfully adhered to him; till after a tedious period of miserable wandering, he found the termination of his wretched life.

PEGASUS AND THE CHIMAERA

When Perseus cut off Medusa's head, the blood sinking into the earth produced the winged horse Pegasus. Minerva caught and tamed him and presented him to the Muses. The fountain Hippocrene, on the Muses' mountain Helicon, was opened by a kick from his hoof.

The Chimaera was a fearful monster, breathing fire. The forepart of its body was a compound of the lion and the goat, and the hind part a dragon's. It made great havoc in Lycia, so that the king,

Iobates, sought for some hero to destroy it. At that time there arrived at his court a gallant young warrior whose name was Bellerophon. He brought letters from Proetus, the son-in-law of Iobates, recommending Bellerophon in the warmest terms as an unconquerable hero, but added at the close a request to his father-in-law to put him to death. The reason was that Proetus was jealous of him, suspecting that his wife Antea looked with too much admiration on the young warrior. From this instance of Bellerophon being unconsciously the bearer of his own death warrant, the expression 'Bellerophontic letters' arose, to describe any species of communication which a person is made the bearer of, containing matter prejudicial to himself.

Iobates, on perusing the letters, was puzzled what to do, not willing to violate the claims of hospitality, yet wishing to oblige his son-in-law. A lucky thought occurred to him, to send Bellerophon to combat with the Chimaera. Bellerophon accepted the proposal, but before proceeding to the combat consulted the soothsayer Polyidus, who advised him to procure if possible the horse Pegasus for the conflict. For this purpose he directed him to pass the night in the temple of Minerva. He did so, and as he slept Minerva came to him and gave him a golden bridle. When he awoke the bridle remained in his hand. Minerva also showed him Pegasus drinking at the well of Pirene, and at sight of the bridle, the winged steed came willingly and suffered himself to be taken. Bellerophon mounted him, rose with him into the air, soon found the Chimaera, and gained an easy victory over the monster.

After the conquest of the Chimaera, Bellerophon was exposed to further trials and labors by his unfriendly host, but by the aid of Pegasus he triumphed in them all; till at length Iobates, seeing that the hero was a special favorite of the gods, gave him his daughter in marriage and made him his successor on the throne. At last Bellerophon, by his pride and presumption, drew upon himself the anger of the gods; it is said he even attempted to fly up into heaven on his winged steed; but Jupiter sent a gadfly which stung Pegasus and made him throw his rider, who became lame and blind in consequence. After this Bellerophon wandered lonely through the Aleian field, avoiding the paths of men, and died miserably.

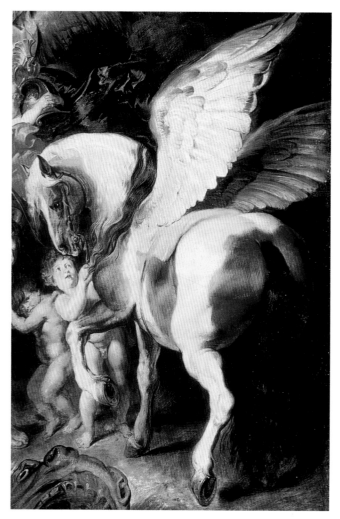

⋏ Perseus and Andromeda, PETER PAUL RUBENS (1577–1640)
The stories of Pegasus stem mostly from the Peloponnese, in particular around Corinth—the city for which the winged horse became a special emblem. Rubens depicts Pegasus as a naturalistic pony with wings rather than as a fantastical creature.

THE CENTAURS

These monsters were represented as men from the head to the loins, while the remainder of the body was that of a horse. The ancients were too fond of a horse to consider the union of his nature with man's as forming a very degraded compound, and accordingly the centaur is the only one of the fancied monsters of antiquity to which any good traits are assigned. The centaurs were admitted to the companionship of man, and at the marriage of Pirithous with Hippodamia, they were among the guests. At the feast, Eurytion, one of the centaurs, becoming intoxicated with the wine, attempted to offer violence to the bride; the other centaurs followed his example, and a dreadful conflict arose in which several of them were slain. This is the

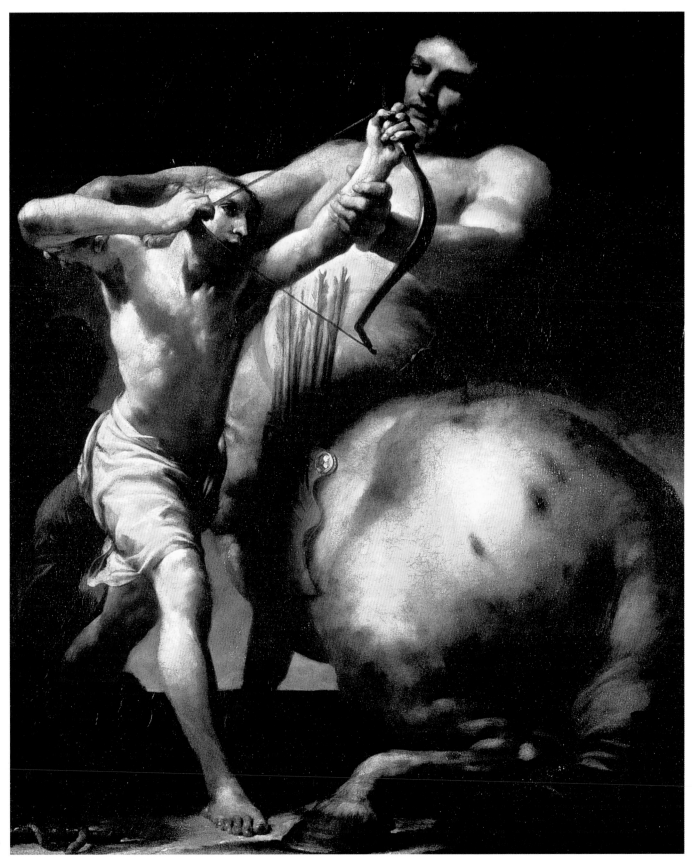

▲ The Centaur Chiron Teaches the Young Achilles Archery, GIUSEPPE MARIA CRESPI (1665–1747)
Centaurs were generally troublemakers in Greek mythology, but Chiron was an exception. Here, the irony of young Achilles learning archery lies in his eventual fate—he was struck in the heel by an arrow and died of the wound.

celebrated battle of the Lapithae and centaurs, a favorite subject with the sculptors and poets of antiquity.

But not all the centaurs were like the rude guests of Pirithous. Chiron was instructed by Apollo and Diana, and was renowned for his skill in hunting, medicine, music, and the art of prophecy. The most distinguished heroes of Grecian story were his pupils. Among the rest the infant Aesculapius was entrusted to his charge, by Apollo, his father. When the sage returned to his home bearing the infant, his daughter Ocyroe came forth to meet him, and at sight of the child burst forth into a prophetic strain (for she was a prophetess), foretelling the glory that he was to achieve. Aesculapius when grown up became a renowned physician, and even in one instance succeeded in restoring the dead to life. Pluto resented this, and Jupiter, at his request, struck the bold physician with lightning and killed him, but after his death received him into the number of the gods.

Chiron was the wisest and justest of all the centaurs, and at his death Jupiter placed him among the stars as the constellation Sagittarius.

THE PYGMIES

The Pygmies were a nation of dwarfs, so called from a Greek word which means the cubit or measure of about thirteen inches, which was said to be the height of these people. They lived near the sources of the Nile, or according to others, in India. Homer tells us that the cranes used to migrate every winter to the Pygmies' country, and their appearance was the signal of bloody warfare to the puny inhabitants, who had to take up arms to defend their cornfields against the rapacious strangers. The Pygmies and their enemies the cranes form the subject of several works of art.

Later writers tell of an army of Pygmies which, finding Hercules asleep, made preparations to attack him, as if they were about to attack a city. But the hero, awaking, laughed at the little warriors, wrapped some of them up in his lion's skin, and carried them to Eurystheus.

THE GRIFFIN, OR GRYPHON

The griffin is a monster with the body of a lion, the head and wings of an eagle, and back covered with feathers. Like birds it builds its nest, and instead of an egg lays an agate therein. It has long claws and talons of such a size that the people of that country make them into drinking cups. India was assigned as the native country of the griffins. They found gold in the mountains and built their nests of it, for which reason their nests were very tempting to the hunters and they were forced to keep vigilant guard over them. Their instinct led them to know where buried treasures lay, and they did their best to keep plunderers at a distance. The Arimaspians, among whom the griffins flourished, were a one-eyed people of Scythia.

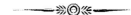

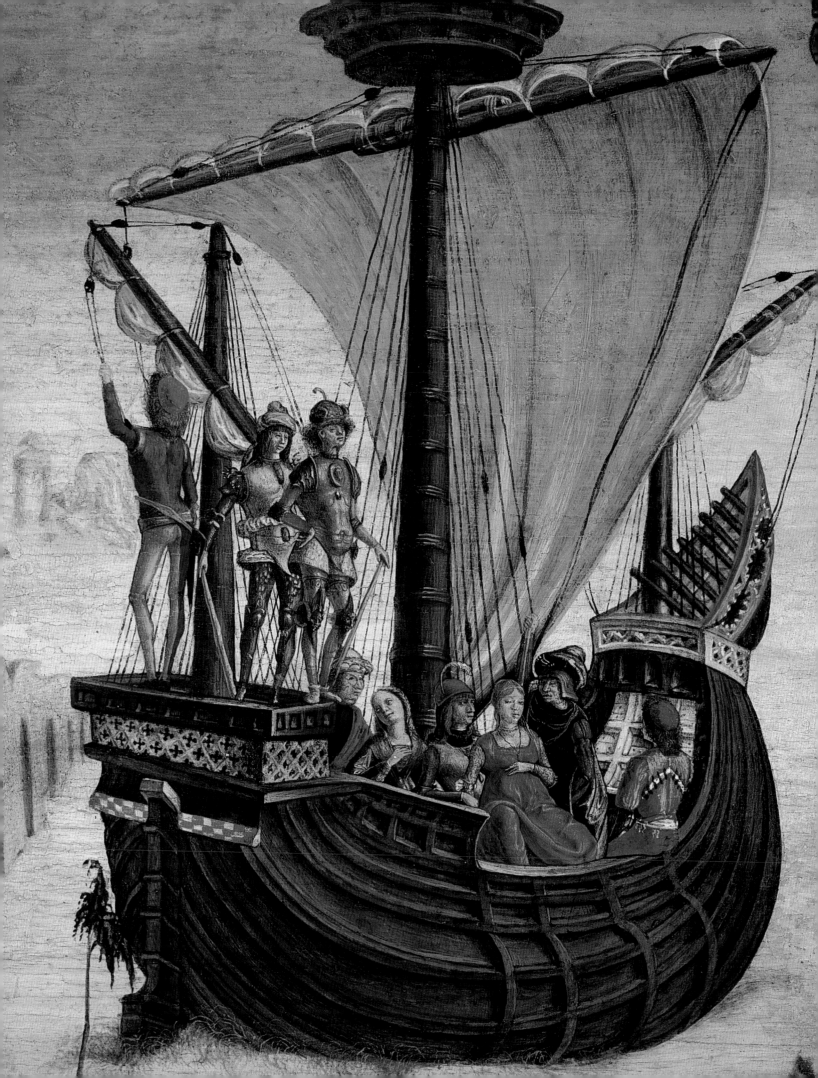

CHAPTER 17

THE GOLDEN FLEECE · MEDEA AND AESON

In very ancient times there lived in Thessaly a king and queen named Athamas and Nephele. They had two children, a boy and a girl. After a time Athamas grew indifferent to his wife, put her away, and took another. Nephele suspected danger to her children from the influence of the stepmother and took measures to send them out of her reach. Mercury assisted her and gave her a ram, with a golden fleece, on which she set the two children, trusting that the ram would convey them to a place of safety. The ram vaulted into the air with the children on his back, taking his course to the east, till when crossing the strait that divides Europe and Asia, the girl, whose name was Helle, fell from his back into the sea, which from her was called the Hellespont—now the Dardanelles. The ram continued his career till he reached the kingdom of Colchis, on the eastern shore of the Black Sea, where he safely landed the boy Phryxus, who was hospitably received by Aetes, the king of the country. Phryxus sacrificed the ram to Jupiter, and gave the golden fleece to Aetes, who placed it in a consecrated grove, under the care of a sleepless dragon.

There was another kingdom in Thessaly near to that of Athamas and ruled over by a relative of his. The king, Aeson, being tired of the cares of government, surrendered his crown to his brother Pelias, on condition that he should hold it only during the minority of Jason, the son of Aeson. When Jason was grown up and came to demand the crown from his uncle, Pelias pretended to be willing to yield it, but at the same time suggested to the young man the glorious adventure of going in quest of the golden fleece, which it was well known was in the kingdom of Colchis and was, as Pelias pretended, the rightful property of their family. Jason was pleased with the thought and forthwith made preparations for the expedition. At that time the only species of navigation known to the Greeks consisted of small boats or canoes hollowed out from trunks of trees, so that when Jason employed Argus to build him a vessel capable of containing fifty men, it was considered a gigantic undertaking. It was accomplished, however, and the vessel named *Argo*, from the name of the builder. Jason sent his invitation to all the adventurous young men of Greece and soon found himself at the head of a band of bold youths, many of whom afterward were renowned among the heroes and demigods of Greece. Hercules, Theseus, Orpheus, and Nestor were among them. They are called the Argonauts, from the name of their vessel.

The *Argo* with her crew of heroes left the shores of Thessaly and, having touched at the island of Lemnos, thence crossed to Mysia and thence to Thrace. Here they found the sage Phineus, and from him received instruction as to their future course. It seems the entrance of the Euxine Sea was impeded by two small rocky islands which floated on the surface and, in their tossings and heavings, occasionally came together, crushing and grinding to atoms any object that might be caught between them. They were called the Symplegades, or Clashing Islands. Phineus instructed the Argonauts how to pass this dangerous strait. When they reached the islands they let go a dove, which took her way between the rocks and passed in safety, only losing some feathers of her tail. Jason and his men seized the favorable moment of the rebound, plied their oars with vigor, and passed safe through, though the islands closed behind them and actually grazed their stern. They now rowed along the shore till they arrived at the eastern end of the sea, and landed at the kingdom of Colchis.

Jason made known his message to the Colchian king, Aetes, who consented to give up the golden fleece if Jason would yoke to the plow two fire-breathing bulls with brazen feet, and sow the teeth of the dragon, which Cadmus had slain, and from which it was well known that a crop of armed men would spring up, who would turn their weapons against their producer. Jason accepted the conditions, and a time was set for making the experiment. Previously, however, he found means to plead his cause to Medea, daughter of the king. He promised her marriage, and as they stood before the altar of Hecate, called the goddess to witness his oath.

◄ The Argonauts Leaving Colchis,
ERCOLE de'ROBERTI (active 1479; died 1496)
Homer called the Argo "the ship which is all men's concerns."
Colchis was the turning point of the voyage.

99

Medea yielded—and by her aid, for she was a potent sorceress, he was furnished with a charm, by which he could encounter safely the breath of the fire-breathing bulls and the weapons of the armed men.

At the time appointed, the people assembled at the grove of Mars, and the king assumed his royal seat, while the multitude covered the hillsides. The brazen-footed bulls rushed in, breathing fire from their nostrils, that burned up the herbage as they passed. The sound was like the roar of a furnace, and the smoke like that of water upon quicklime. Jason advanced boldly to meet them. His friends, the chosen heroes of Greece, trembled to behold him. Regardless of the burning breath, he soothed their rage with his voice, patted their necks with fearless hand, and adroitly slipped over them the yoke, and compelled them to drag the plow. The Colchians were amazed; the Greeks shouted for joy. Jason next proceeded to sow the dragon's teeth and plow them in. And soon the crop of armed men sprang up, and—wonderful to relate!—no sooner had they reached the surface than they began to brandish their weapons and rush upon Jason. The Greeks trembled for their hero, and even she who had provided him a way of safety and taught him how to use it, Medea herself, grew pale with fear. Jason for a time kept his assailants at bay with his sword and shield, till finding their numbers overwhelming, he resorted to the charm which Medea had taught him, seized a stone, and threw it in the midst of his foes. They immediately turned their arms against one another, and soon there was not one of the dragon's brood left alive. The Greeks embraced their hero, and Medea, if she dared, would have embraced him, too.

It remained to lull to sleep the dragon that guarded the fleece, and this was done by scattering over him a few drops of a preparation, which Medea had supplied. At the smell he relaxed his rage, stood for a moment motionless, then shut those great round eyes, that had never been known to shut before, and turned over on his side, fast asleep. Jason seized the fleece and, with his friends and Medea accompanying, hastened to their vessel, before Aetes the king could arrest their departure, and made

▾ Hylas and the Nymphs, JOHN WILLIAM WATERHOUSE (1849–1917)
The seduction of Hylas provided a perfect vehicle for the coy sensuality permitted to Victorian painters by "respectable" classical subjects.

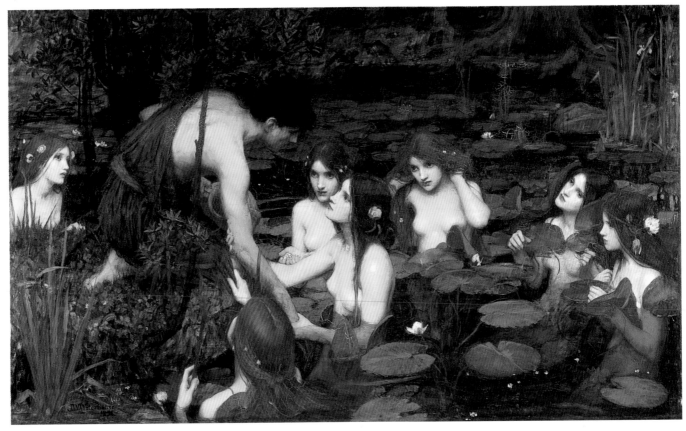

the best of their way back to Thessaly, where they arrived safe, and Jason delivered the fleece to Pelias, and dedicated the *Argo* to Neptune. What became of the fleece afterward we do not know, but perhaps it was found after all, like many other golden prizes, not worth the trouble it had cost to procure it.

Hercules left the expedition at Mysia, for Hylas, a youth beloved by him, who, having gone for water, was laid hold of and kept by the nymphs of the spring, who were fascinated by his beauty. Hercules went in quest of the lad, and while he was absent the *Argo* put to sea and left him.

MEDEA AND AESON

Amid the rejoicings for the recovery of the golden fleece, Jason felt that one thing was wanting, the presence of Aeson, his father, who was prevented by his age and infirmities from taking part in them. Jason said to Medea, "My spouse, would that your arts, whose power I have seen so mighty for my aid, could do me one further service, take some years from my life and add them to my father's." Medea replied, "Not at such a cost shall it be done, but if my art avails me, his life shall be lengthened without abridging yours." The next full moon she issued forth alone, while all creatures slept; not a breath stirred the foliage, and all was still. To the stars she addressed her incantations, and to the moon; to Hecate, the goddess of the underworld, and to Tellus, the goddess of the earth, by whose power plants potent for enchantments are produced. She invoked the gods of the woods and caverns, of mountains and valleys, of lakes and rivers, of winds and vapors. While she spoke the stars shone brighter, and presently a chariot descended through the air, drawn by flying serpents. She ascended it and, borne aloft, made her way to distant regions, where potent plants grew which she knew how to select for her purpose. Nine nights she employed in her search, and during that time came not within the doors of her palace nor under any roof, and shunned all intercourse with mortals.

She next erected two altars, the one to Hecate, the other to Hebe, the goddess of youth, and sacrificed a black sheep, pouring libations of milk and wine. She implored Pluto and his stolen bride that they would not hasten to take the old man's life. Then she directed that Aeson should be led forth, and having

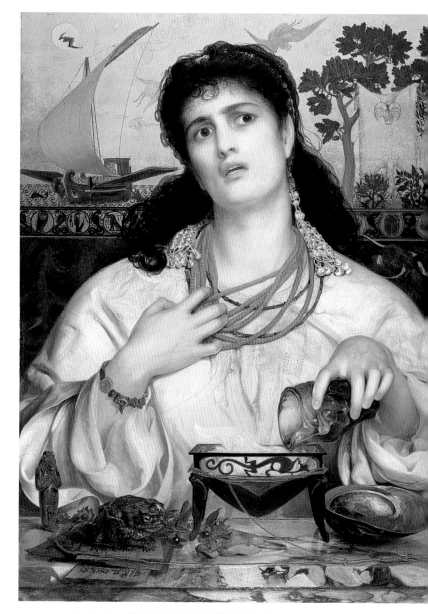

▲ Medea, FREDERICK SANDYS (1829–1904)
Medusa weaves a magical spell to restore youth to Jason's father Aeson, boiling him with virtuous herbs. Medea translates as "the cunning one." Sandys portrays her as dark and gypsylike.

thrown him into a deep sleep by a charm, had him laid on a bed of herbs, like one dead. Jason and all others were kept away from the place, that no profane eyes might look upon her mysteries. Then, with streaming hair, she thrice moved around the altars, dipped flaming twigs in the blood, and laid them thereon to burn. Meanwhile the caldron with its contents was got ready. In it she put magic herbs, with seeds and flowers of acrid juice, stones from the distant east, and sand from the shore of all-surrounding ocean; hoar frost, gathered by moonlight, a screech owl's head and wings, and the entrails of a wolf. She added fragments of the shells of tortoises, and the liver of stags—animals tenacious of life—and the head and beak of a crow, that outlives nine generations of men. These, with many other things "without a name," she boiled together for her purposed work, stirring them up with a dry olive branch; and behold! the branch when taken out instantly became green, and before long was covered with leaves and a plentiful growth of young olives; and as the liquor boiled and bubbled, and sometimes ran over, the grass wherever the sprinklings fell shot forth with a verdure like that of spring.

Seeing that all was ready, Medea cut the throat of the old man and let out all his blood, and poured into his mouth and into his wound the juices of her caldron. As soon as he had completely imbibed them, his hair and beard laid by their whiteness and assumed the blackness of youth; his paleness and emaciation were gone; his veins were full of blood, his limbs of vigor and robustness. Aeson is amazed at himself, and remembers that such as he now is, he was in his youthful days, forty years before.

Medea used her arts here for a good purpose, but not so in another instance where she made them the instruments of revenge. Pelias, our readers will recollect, was the usurping uncle of Jason, and had kept him out of his kingdom. Yet he must have had some good qualities, for his daughters loved him, and when they saw what Medea had done for Aeson, they wished her to do the same for their father. Medea pretended to consent and prepared her caldron as before. At her request an old sheep was brought and plunged into the caldron. Very soon a bleating was heard in the kettle, and when the cover was removed, a lamb jumped forth and ran frisking away into the meadow. The daughters of Pelias saw the experiment with delight, and appointed a time for their father to undergo the same operation. But Medea prepared her caldron for him in a very different way. She put in only water and a few simple herbs. In the night she with the sisters entered the bedchamber of the old king, while he and his guards slept soundly under the influence of a spell cast upon them by Medea. The daughters stood by the bedside with their weapons drawn, but hesitated to strike, till Medea chid their irresolution. Then, turning away their faces, and giving random blows, they smote him with their weapons. He, starting from his sleep, cried out, "My daughters, what are you doing? Will you kill your father?" Their hearts failed them, and the weapons fell from their hands, but Medea struck him a fatal blow and prevented his saying more.

Then they placed him in the caldron, and Medea hastened to depart in her serpent-drawn chariot before they discovered her treachery, or their vengeance would have been terrible. She escaped, however, but had little enjoyment of the fruits of her crime. Jason, for whom she had done so much, wishing to marry Creusa, Princess of Corinth, put away Medea. She, enraged at his ingratitude, called on the gods for vengeance, sent a poisoned robe as a gift to the bride, and then killing her own children and setting fire to the palace, mounted her serpent-drawn chariot and fled to Athens, where she married King Aegeus, the father of Theseus, and we shall meet her again when we come to the adventures of that hero.

There is another story of Medea almost too revolting for record even of a sorceress, a class of persons to whom both ancient and modern poets have been accustomed to attribute every degree of atrocity. In her flight from Colchis she had taken her young brother Absyrtus with her. Finding the pursuing vessels of Aetes gaining upon the Argonauts, she caused the lad to be killed and his limbs to be strewn over the sea. Aetes, on reaching the place found these sorrowful traces of his murdered son; but, while he tarried to collect the scattered fragments and bestow upon them an honorable interment, the Argonauts escaped.

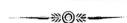

CHAPTER 18

MELEAGER · ATALANTA

ONE OF THE HEROES OF THE ARGONAUTIC expedition was Meleager, son of Oeneus and Althea, King and Queen of Calydon. Althea, when her son was born, beheld the three Destinies, who, as they spun their fatal thread, foretold that the life of the child should last no longer than a brand then burning upon the hearth. Althea seized and quenched the brand and carefully preserved it for years, while Meleager grew to boyhood, youth, and manhood. It chanced, then, that Oeneus, as he offered sacrifices to the gods, omitted to pay due honors to Diana; and she, indignant at the neglect, sent a wild boar of enormous size to lay waste the fields of Calydon. Its eyes shone with blood and fire, its bristles stood like threatening spears, its tusks were like those of Indian elephants. The growing corn was trampled, the vines and olive trees laid waste, the flocks and herds were driven in wild confusion by the slaughtering foe. All common aid seemed vain; but Meleager called on the heroes of Greece to join in a bold hunt for the ravenous monster. Theseus and his friend Pirithous, Jason, Peleus, afterward the father of Achilles, Telamon, the father of Ajax, Nestor, then a youth, but who in his age bore arms with Achilles and Ajax in the Trojan war—these and many more joined in the enterprise. With them came Atalanta, the daughter of Iasius, King of Arcadia. A buckle of polished gold confined her vest, an ivory quiver hung on her left shoulder, and her left hand bore the bow. Her face blent feminine beauty with the best graces of martial youth. Meleager saw and loved.

But now already they were near the monster's lair. They stretched strong nets from tree to tree; they uncoupled their dogs, they tried to find the footprints of their quarry in the grass. From the wood was a descent to marshy ground. Here the boar, as he lay among the reeds, heard the shouts of his pursuers and rushed forth against them. One and another is thrown down and slain. Jason throws his spear, with a prayer to Diana for success; and the favoring goddess allows the weapon to touch, but not to wound, removing the steel point of the spear even in its flight. Nestor, assailed, seeks and finds safety in the branches of a tree. Telamon rushes on, but stumbling at a projecting root, falls prone.

But an arrow from Atalanta at length for the first time tastes the monster's blood. It is a slight wound, but Meleager sees and joyfully proclaims it. Anceus, excited to envy by the praise given to a female, loudly proclaims his own valor and defies alike the boar and the goddess who had sent it; but as he rushes on, the infuriated beast lays him low with a mortal wound. Theseus throws his lance, but it is turned aside by a projecting bough. The dart of Jason misses its object and kills instead one of their own dogs. But Meleager, after one unsuccessful stroke, drives his spear into the monster's side, then rushes on and despatches him with repeated blows.

Then rose a shout from those around; they congratulated the conqueror, crowding to touch his hand. He, placing his foot upon the head of the slain boar, turned to Atalanta, and bestowed on her the head and the rough hide which were the trophies of his success. But at this, envy excited the rest to strife. Plexippus and Toxeus, the brothers of Meleager's mother, beyond the rest opposed the gift and snatched from the maiden the trophy she had received. Meleager, kindling with rage at the wrong done to himself, and still more at the insult offered to her whom he loved, forgot the claims of kindred and plunged his sword into the offenders' hearts.

As Althea bore gifts of thankfulness to the temples for the victory of her son, the bodies of her murdered brothers met her sight. She shrieks, and beats her breast, and hastens to change the garments of rejoicing for those of mourning. But when the author of the deed is known, grief gives way to the stern desire of vengeance on her son. The fatal brand, which once she rescued from the flames, the brand which the Destinies had linked with Meleager's life, she brings forth and commands a fire to be prepared. Then four times she essays to place the brand upon the pile; four times draws back, shuddering at the thought of bringing destruction on her son. The feelings of the mother and the sister contend within her. Now she is pale at the thought of the purposed deed, now flushed again with anger at the act of her son. As a vessel, driven in one direction by the wind and in the opposite by the tide, the mind of Althea hangs suspended in uncertainty.

But now the sister prevails above the mother, and she begins as she holds the fatal wood: "Turn, ye Furies, goddesses of punishment! Turn to behold the sacrifice I bring! Crime must atone for crime. Shall Oeneus rejoice in his victor son, while the house of Thestius is desolate? But, alas! to what deed am I borne along? Brothers, forgive a mother's weakness! My hand fails me. He deserves death, but not that I should destroy him. But shall he then live, and triumph, and reign over Calydon, while you, my brothers, wander unavenged among the shades? No! Thou hast lived by my gift; die, now, for thine own crime. Return the life which twice I gave thee, first at thy birth, again when I snatched this brand from the flames. Oh, that thou hadst then died! Alas! Evil is the conquest; but, brothers, ye have conquered." And, turning away her face, she threw the fatal wood upon the burning pile.

It gave, or seemed to give, a deadly groan. Meleager, absent and unknowing of the cause, felt a sudden pang. He burns, and only by courageous pride conquers the pain which destroys him. He mourns only that he perishes by a bloodless and unhonored death. With his last breath he calls upon his aged father, his brother, and his fond sisters, upon his beloved Atalanta, and upon his mother, the unknown cause of his fate. The flames increase, and with them the pain of the hero. Now both subside; now both are quenched. The brand is ashes, and the life of Meleager is breathed forth to the wandering winds.

Althea, when the deed was done, laid violent hands upon herself. The sisters of Meleager mourned their brother with uncontrollable grief; till Diana, pitying the sorrows of the house that once had aroused her anger, turned them into birds.

ATALANTA

The innocent cause of so much sorrow was a maiden whose face you might truly say was boyish for a girl, yet too girlish for a boy. Her fortune had been told, and it was to this effect: "Atalanta, do not marry; marriage will be your ruin." Terrified by this oracle, she fled the society of men and devoted herself to the sports of the chase. To all suitors (for she had many) she imposed a condition which was generally effectual in relieving her of their persecutions—"I will be the prize of him who shall conquer me in the race; but death must be the penalty of all who try and fail."

In spite of this hard condition some would try. Hippomenes was to be judge of the race. "Can it be possible that any will be so rash as to risk so much for a wife?" said he. But when he saw her lay aside her robe for the race, he changed his mind, and said, "Pardon me, youths, I knew not the prize you were competing for." As he surveyed them he wished them all to be beaten, and swelled with envy of anyone that seemed at all likely to win. While such were his thoughts, the virgin darted forward. As she ran she looked more beautiful than ever. The breezes seemed to give wings to her feet; her hair flew over her shoulders, and the gay fringe of her garment fluttered behind her. A ruddy hue tinged the whiteness of her skin, such as a crimson curtain casts on a marble wall. All her competitors were distanced, and were put to death without mercy. Hippomenes, not daunted by this result, fixing his eyes on the virgin, said, "Why boast of beating those laggards? I offer myself for the contest." Atalanta looked at him with a pitying countenance, and hardly knew whether she would rather conquer him or not. "What god can tempt one so young and handsome to throw himself away? I pity him, not for his beauty (yet he is beautiful), but for his youth. I wish he would give up the race, or if he will be so mad, I hope he may outrun me."

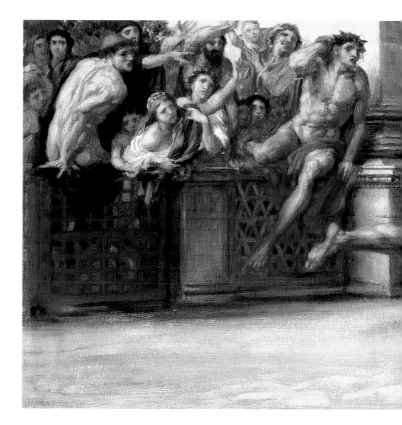

While she hesitates, revolving these thoughts, the spectators grow impatient for the race, and her father prompts her to prepare. Then Hippomenes addressed a prayer to Venus: "Help me, Venus, for you have led me on." Venus heard, and was propitious.

In the garden of her temple, in her own island of Cyprus, is a tree with yellow leaves and yellow branches, and golden fruit. Hence she gathered three golden apples, and, unseen by anyone else, gave them to Hippomenes and told him how to use them. The signal is given; each starts from the goal and skims over the sand. So light their tread, you would almost have thought they might run over the river surface or over the waving grain without sinking. The cries of the spectators cheered Hippomenes—"Now, now do your best! Haste, haste! You gain on her! Relax not! One more effort!" It was doubtful whether the youth or the maiden heard these cries with the greater pleasure. But his breath began to fail him, his throat was dry, the goal yet far off. At that moment he threw down one of the golden apples. The virgin was all amazement. She stopped to pick it up. Hippomenes shot ahead. Shouts burst forth from all sides. She redoubled her efforts and soon overtook him. Again he threw an apple. She stopped again, but again came up with him. The goal was near; one

chance only remained. "Now, goddess," said he, "prosper your gift!" and threw the last apple off at one side. She looked at it and hesitated; Venus impelled her to turn aside for it. She did so, and was vanquished. The youth carried off his prize.

But the lovers were so full of their own happiness that they forgot to pay due honor to Venus; and the goddess was provoked at their ingratitude. She caused them to give offence to Cybele. That powerful goddess was not to be insulted with impunity. She took from them their human form and turned them into animals of characters resembling their own: of the huntress-heroine, triumphing in the blood of her lovers, she made a lioness, and of her lord and master a lion, and yoked them to her ear, where they are still to be seen in all representations, in statuary or painting, of the goddess Cybele.

Cybele is the Latin name of the goddess called by the Greeks Rhea and Ops. She was the wife of Cronos and mother of Zeus. In works of art, she exhibits the matronly air which distinguishes Juno and Ceres. Sometimes she is veiled and seated on a throne with lions at her side, at other times riding in a chariot drawn by lions. She wears a mural crown, that is, a crown whose rim is carved in the form of towers and battlements. Her priests were called Corybantes.

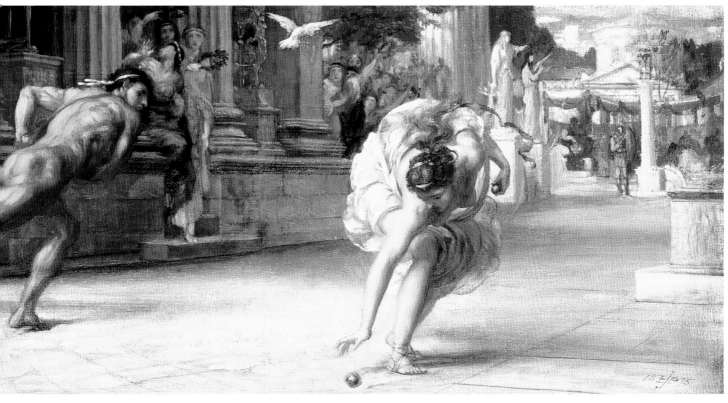

⋏ Atalanta's Race, SIR EDWARD JOHN POYNTER (1836–1919)
Atalanta was an Amazonian heroine who was raised by a she-bear—which accounted for her prowess at hunting and running.

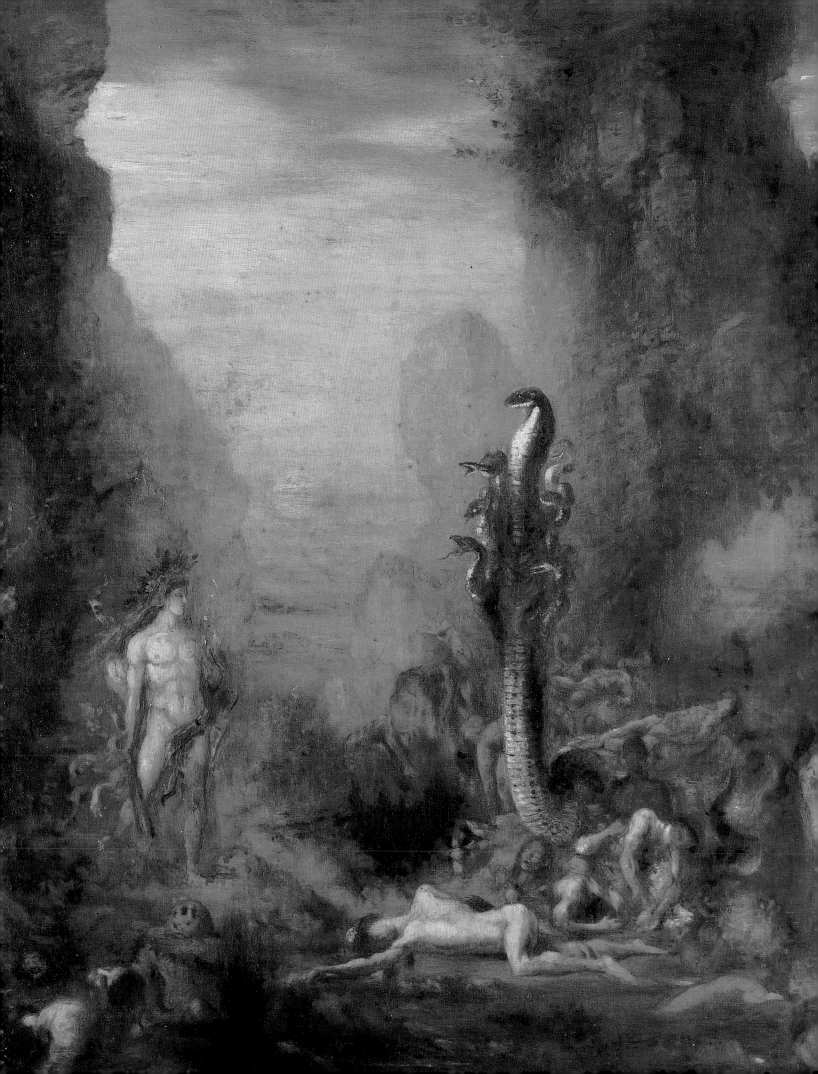

CHAPTER 19

HERCULES · HEBE AND GANYMEDE

HERCULES WAS THE SON OF JUPITER AND ALCMENA. As Juno was always hostile to the offspring of her husband by mortal mothers, she declared war against Hercules from his birth. She sent two serpents to destroy him as he lay in his cradle, but the precocious infant strangled them with his own hands. He was, however, by the arts of Juno rendered subject to Eurystheus and compelled to perform all his commands. Eurystheus enjoined upon him a succession of desperate adventures, which are called the twelve "Labors of Hercules." The first was the fight with the Nemean lion. The valley of Nemea was infested by a terrible lion. Eurystheus ordered Hercules to bring him the skin of this monster. After using in vain his club and arrows against the lion, Hercules strangled the animal with his hands. He returned carrying the dead lion on his shoulders; but Eurystheus was so frightened at the sight of it and at this proof of the prodigious strength of the hero, that he ordered him to deliver the account of his exploits in future outside the town.

His next labor was the slaughter of the Hydra. This monster ravaged the country of Argos, and dwelt in a swamp near the well of Amymone. This well had been discovered by Amymone when the country was suffering from drought, and the story was that Neptune, who loved her, had permitted her to touch the rock with his trident, and a spring of three outlets burst forth. Here the Hydra took up his position, and Hercules was sent to destroy him. The Hydra had nine heads, of which the middle one was immortal. Hercules struck off its heads with his club, but in the place of the head knocked off, two new ones grew forth each time. At length with the assistance of his faithful servant Iolaus, he burned away the heads of the Hydra and buried the ninth or immortal one under a huge rock.

Another labor was the cleaning of the Augean stables. Augeas, King of Elis, had a herd of three thousand oxen, whose stalls had not been cleansed

◄ *Hercules and the Hydra of Lerna,* GUSTAVE MOREAU (1826–1898): Hydra *means simply "water snake," but this creature could regenerate its numerous heads as soon as any were cut off. Hercules's strategy of cauterizing the wounded parts eventually destroyed the monster.*

for thirty years. Hercules brought the rivers Alpheus and Peneus through them and cleansed them thoroughly in one day.

His next labor was of a more delicate kind. Admeta, the daughter of Eurystheus, longed to obtain the girdle of the queen of the Amazons, and Eurystheus ordered Hercules to go and get it. The Amazons were a nation of women. They were very warlike and held several flourishing cities. It was their custom to bring up only the female children; the boys were either sent away to the neighboring nations or put to death. Hercules was accompanied by a number of volunteers, and after various adventures at last reached the country of the Amazons. Hippolyta, the queen, received him kindly, and consented to yield him her girdle, but Juno, taking the form of an Amazon, went and persuaded the rest that the strangers were carrying off their queen. They instantly armed and came in great numbers down to the ship. Hercules, thinking that Hippolyta had acted treacherously, slew her and, taking her girdle, made sail homeward.

Another task enjoined him was to bring to Eurystheus the oxen of Geryon, a monster with three bodies, who dwelt in the island Erytheia (the red), so called because it lay at the west, under the rays of the setting sun. This description is thought to apply to Spain, of which Geryon was king. After traversing various countries, Hercules reached at length the frontiers of Libya and Europe, where he raised the two mountains of Calpe and Abyla, as monuments of his progress, or according to another account rent one mountain into two and left half on each side, forming the Straits of Gibraltar, the two mountains being called the Pillars of Hercules. The oxen were guarded by the giant Eurytion and his two-headed dog, but Hercules killed the giant and his dog and brought away the oxen in safety to Eurystheus.

The most difficult labor of all was getting the golden apples of the Hesperides, for Hercules did not know where to find them. These were the apples which Juno had received at her wedding from the goddess of the earth, and which she had entrusted to the keeping of the daughters of Hesperus, assisted by a watchful dragon. After various adventures

Hercules arrived at Mount Atlas in Africa. Atlas was one of the Titans who had warred against the gods, and after they were subdued, Atlas was condemned to bear on his shoulders the weight of the heavens. He was the father of the Hesperides and, Hercules thought, might, if anyone could, find the apples and bring them to him. But how to send Atlas away from his post, or bear up the heavens while he was gone? Hercules took the burden on his own shoulders and sent Atlas to seek the apples. He returned with them and, though somewhat reluctantly, took his burden upon his shoulders again and let Hercules return with the apples to Eurystheus.

A celebrated exploit of Hercules was his victory over Antaeus. Antaeus, the son of Terra, the Earth, was a mighty giant and wrestler whose strength was invincible so long as he remained in contact with his mother Earth. He compelled all strangers who came to his country to wrestle with him, on condition that if conquered (as they all were) they should be put to death. Hercules encountered him, and finding that it was of no avail to throw him, for he always rose with renewed strength from every fall, he lifted him up from the earth and strangled him in the air.

Cacus was a huge giant who inhabited a cave on Mount Aventine and plundered the surrounding country. When Hercules was driving home the oxen of Geryon, Cacus stole part of the cattle while the hero slept. That their footprints might not serve to show where they had been driven, he dragged them backward by their tails to his cave, so their tracks all seemed to show that they had gone in the opposite direction. Hercules was deceived by this stratagem, and would have failed to find his oxen if it had not happened that in driving the remainder of the herd past the cave where the stolen ones were concealed, those within began to low, and were thus discovered. Cacus was slain by Hercules.

The last exploit we shall record was bringing Cerberus from the lower world. Hercules descended into Hades, accompanied by Mercury and Minerva. He obtained permission from Pluto to carry Cerberus to the upper air provided he could do it without the use of weapons; and in spite of the monster's struggling, he seized him, held him fast, and carried him to Eurystheus, and afterward brought him back again. When he was in Hades he obtained the liberty of Theseus, his admirer and imitator, who had been detained a prisoner there for an unsuccessful attempt to carry off Proserpine.

Hercules in a fit of madness killed his friend Iphitus, and was condemned for this offence to become the slave of Queen Omphale for three years. While in this service the hero's nature seemed changed. He lived effeminately, wearing at times the dress of a woman, and spinning wool with the handmaidens of Omphale, while the queen wore his lion's skin. When this service was ended he married Dejanira and lived in peace with her three years. On one occasion as he was traveling with his wife, they came to a river, across which the centaur Nessus carried travelers for a stated fee. Hercules himself forded the river, but gave Dejanira to Nessus to be carried across. Nessus attempted to run away with her, but Hercules heard her cries and shot an arrow into the heart of Nessus. The dying centaur told Dejanira to take a portion of his blood and keep it, as it might be used as a charm to preserve the love of her husband.

Dejanira did so and before long fancied she had occasion to use it. Hercules, in one of his conquests, had taken prisoner a fair maiden, named Iole, of whom he seemed more fond than Dejanira approved. When Hercules was about to offer sacrifices to the gods in honor of his victory, he sent to his wife for a white robe to use on the occasion. Dejanira, thinking it a good opportunity to try her love spell, steeped the garment in the blood of Nessus. We are to suppose she took care to wash out all traces of it, but the magic power remained, and as soon as the garment became warm on the body of Hercules, the poison penetrated into all his limbs and caused him the most intense agony. In his frenzy he seized Lichas, who had brought him the fatal robe, and hurled him into the sea. He wrenched off the garment, but it stuck to his flesh, and with it he tore away whole pieces of his body. In this state he embarked on board a ship and was conveyed home. Dejanira, on seeing what she had unwittingly done, hung herself. Hercules, prepared to die, ascended Mount Oeta, where he built a funeral pile of trees, gave his bow and arrows to Philoctetes, and laid himself down

The Abduction of Dejanira by the Centaur Nessus, ➤
GUIDO RENI (1575–1642): *In depicting the abduction of Dejanira, Reni makes the centaur's lustful desire central to his composition. Behind the struggling pair, Hercules prepares to shoot.*

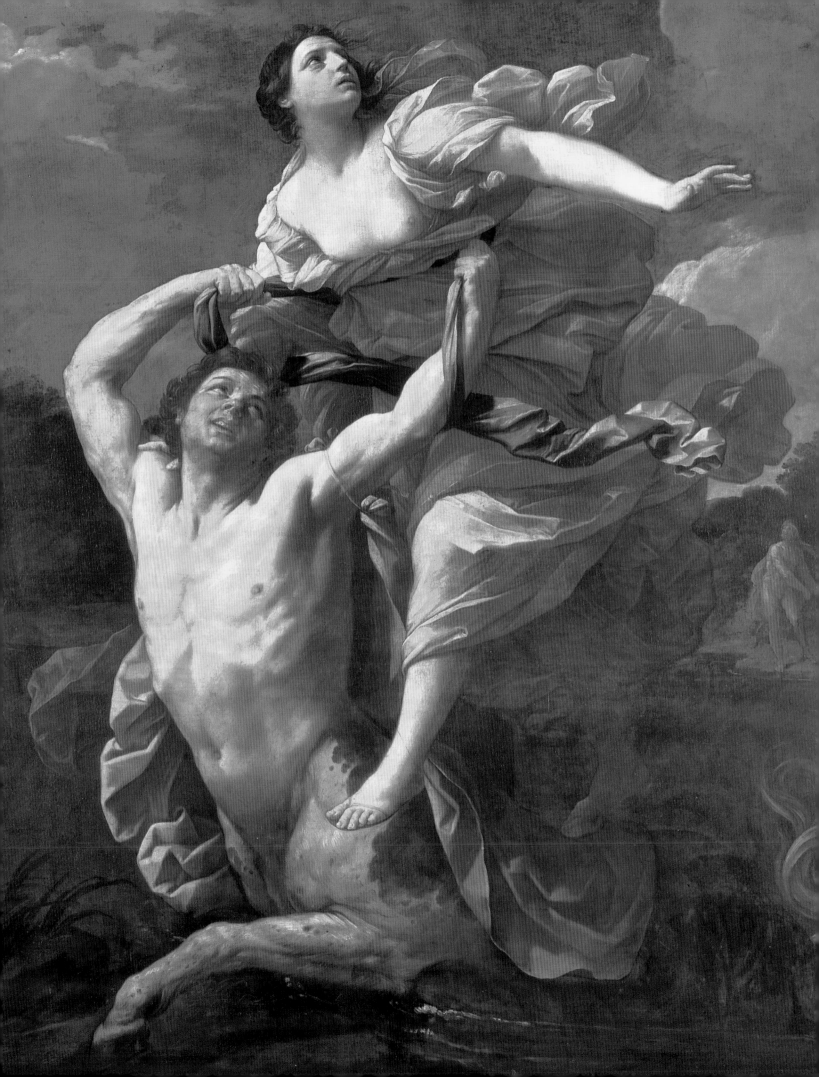

on the pile, his head resting on his club, and his lion's skin spread over him. With a countenance as serene as if he were taking his place at a festal board, he commanded Philoctetes to apply the torch. The flames spread apace and soon invested the whole mass.

The gods themselves felt troubled at seeing the champion of the earth so brought to his end. But Jupiter with cheerful countenance thus addressed them: "I am pleased to see your concern, my princes, and am gratified to perceive that I am the ruler of a loyal people and that my son enjoys your favor. For although your interest in him arises from his noble deeds, yet it is not the less gratifying to me. But now I say to you, Fear not. He who conquered all else is not to be conquered by those flames which you see blazing on Mount Oeta. Only his mother's share in him can perish; what he derived from me is immortal. I shall take him, dead to earth, to the heavenly shores, and I require of you all to receive him kindly. If any of you feel grieved at his attaining this honor, yet no one can deny that he has deserved it." The gods all gave their assent; Juno only heard the closing words with some displeasure that she should be so particularly pointed at, yet not enough to make her regret the determination of her husband. So when the flames had consumed the mother's share of Hercules, the diviner part, instead of being injured thereby, seemed to start forth with new vigor, to assume a more lofty port and a more awful dignity. Jupiter enveloped him in a cloud and took him up in a four-horse chariot to dwell among the stars. As he took his place in heaven, Atlas felt the added weight.

Juno, now reconciled to him, gave him her daughter Hebe in marriage.

HEBE AND GANYMEDE

Hebe, the daughter of Juno and goddess of youth, was cup bearer to the gods. The usual story is that she resigned her office on becoming the wife of Hercules. But there is another statement. According to this, Hebe was dismissed from her office in consequence of a fall which she met with one day when in attendance on the gods. Her successor was Ganymede, a Trojan boy whom Jupiter, in the disguise of an eagle, seized and carried off from the midst of his playfellows on Mount Ida, bore up to heaven, and installed in the vacant place.

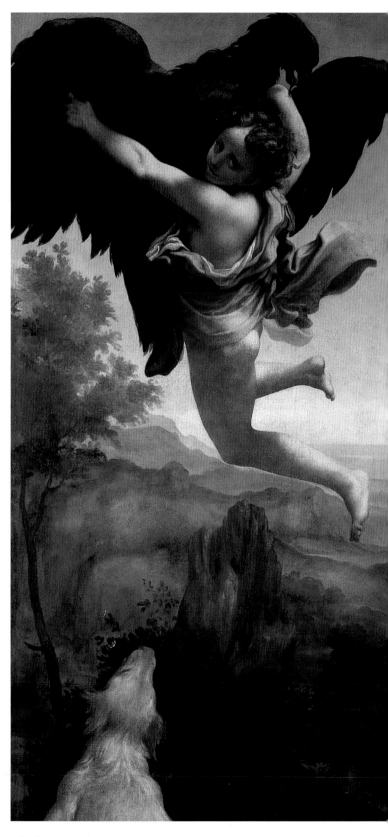

▲ The Rape of Ganymede, CORREGGIO (circa 1494; died 1534)
Jupiter, in the form of an eagle, selects his favorite boy for "cup-bearing duties." (Latinized, the name Ganymede gives us our term "catamite.")

THESEUS · DAEDALUS CASTOR AND POLLUX

THESEUS WAS THE SON OF AEGEUS, KING OF ATHENS, and of Aethra, daughter of the king of Troezen. He was brought up at Troezen, and when arrived at manhood, was to proceed to Athens and present himself to his father. Aegeus, on parting from Aethra, before the birth of his son, placed his sword and shoes under a large stone and directed her to send his son to him when he became strong enough to roll away the stone and take them from under it. When she thought the time had come, his mother led Theseus to the stone, and he removed it with ease and took the sword and shoes. As the roads were infested with robbers, his grandfather pressed him earnestly to take the shorter and safer way to his father's country, by sea; but the youth, feeling in himself the spirit and the soul of a hero, and eager to signalize himself like Hercules, with whose fame all Greece then rang, by destroying the evil doers and monsters that oppressed the country, determined on the more perilous and adventurous journey by land.

His first day's journey brought him to Epidaurus, where dwelt a man named Periphetes, a son of Vulcan. This ferocious savage always went armed with a club of iron, and all travelers stood in terror of his violence. When he saw Theseus approach, he assailed him, but speedily fell beneath the blows of the young hero, who took possession of his club and bore it ever afterward as a memorial of his first victory.

Several similar contests with the petty tyrants and marauders of the country followed, in all of which Theseus was victorious. One of these evildoers was called Procrustes, or the Stretcher. He had an iron bedstead on which he used to tie all travelers who fell into his hands. If they were shorter than the bed, he stretched their limbs to make them fit it; if they were longer than the bed, he lopped off a portion. Theseus served him as he had served others.

Having overcome all the perils of the road, Theseus at length reached Athens, where new dangers awaited him. Medea, the sorceress, who had fled from Corinth after her separation from Jason, had become the wife of Aegeus, the father of Theseus. Knowing by her arts who he was, and fearing the loss of her influence with her husband if Theseus should be acknowledged as his son, she filled the mind of Aegeus with suspicions of the young stranger and induced him to present him a cup of poison; but at the moment when Theseus stepped forward to take it, the sight of the sword which he wore discovered to his father who he was and prevented the fatal draught. Medea, detected in her arts, fled once more from deserved punishment and arrived in Asia, where the country afterward called Media received its name from her. Theseus was acknowledged by his father and declared his successor.

The Athenians were at that time in deep affliction, on account of the tribute which they were forced to pay to Minos, King of Crete. This tribute consisted of seven youths and seven maidens, who were sent every year to be devoured by the Minotaur, a monster with

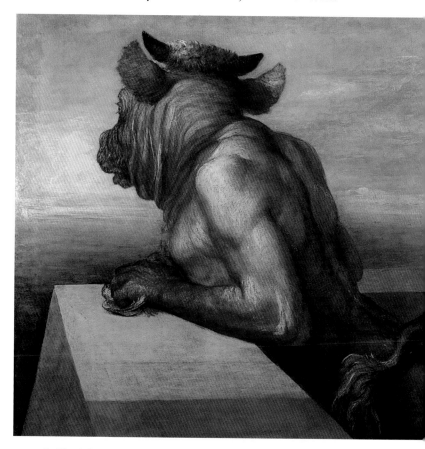

∧ The Minotaur, GEORGE FREDERICK WATTS (1817–1904)
Watts portrays the Minotaur with sympathy. Nevertheless, the beast is looking across the sea—anticipating the arrival of his human rations from Athens.

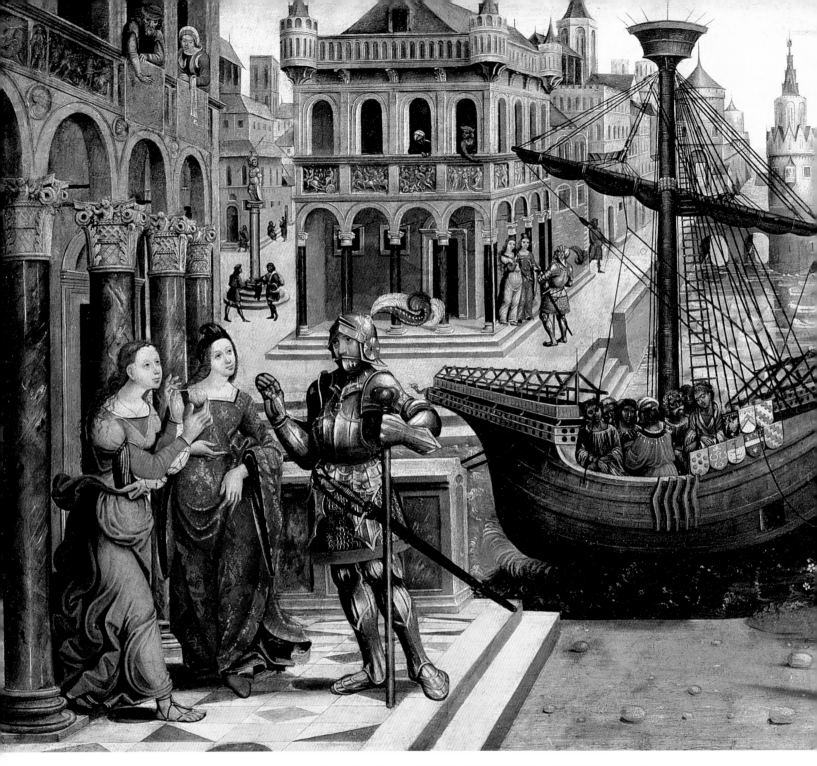

▲ History of Theseus: Ariadne Delivered by Theseus, MASTER OF THE CASSONI CAMPANA (early 16th century)
Theseus here becomes a chivalric knight, and the Cretan labyrinth a Renaissance garden maze.

a bull's body and a human head. It was exceedingly strong and fierce and was kept in a labyrinth constructed by Daedalus, so artfully contrived that whoever was enclosed in it could by no means find his way out unassisted. Here the Minotaur roamed, and was fed with human victims.

Theseus resolved to deliver his countrymen from this calamity, or to die in the attempt. Accordingly, when the time of sending off the tribute came, and

the youths and maidens were, according to custom, drawn by lot to be sent, he offered himself as one of the victims, in spite of the entreaties of his father. The ship departed under black sails, as usual, which Theseus promised his father to change for white, in case of his returning victorious. When they arrived in Crete, the youths and maidens were exhibited before Minos; and Ariadne, the daughter of the king, being present, became deeply enamored of Theseus, by

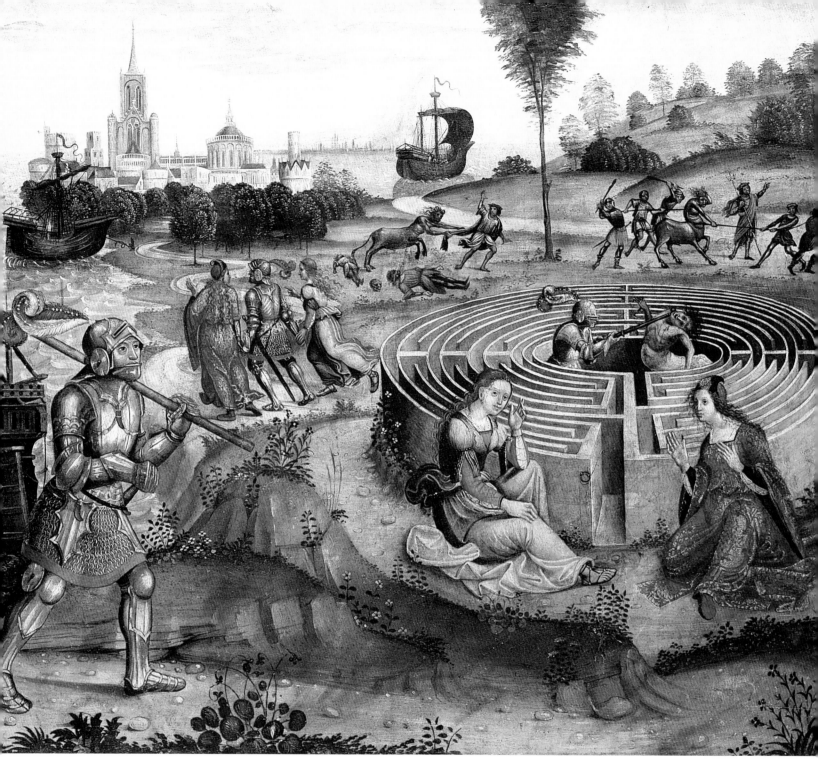

whom her love was readily returned. She furnished him with a sword, with which to encounter the Minotaur, and with a clew of thread by which he might find his way out of the labyrinth. He was successful, slew the Minotaur, escaped from the labyrinth, and taking Ariadne as the companion of his way, with his rescued companions sailed for Athens. On their way they stopped at the island of Naxos, where Theseus abandoned Ariadne, leaving her asleep. His excuse for this ungrateful treatment of his benefactress was that Minerva appeared to him in a dream and commanded him to do so.

On approaching the coast of Attica, Theseus forgot the signal appointed by his father and neglected to raise the white sails, and the old king, thinking his son had perished, put an end to his own life. Theseus thus became king of Athens.

One of the most celebrated of the adventures of Theseus is his expedition against the Amazons. He assailed them before they had recovered from the attack of Hercules, and carried off their queen Antiope. The Amazons in their turn invaded the country of Athens and penetrated into the city itself; and the final battle in which Theseus overcame them was fought in the very midst of the city. This battle was one of the favorite subjects of the ancient sculptors, and is commemorated in several works of art that are still extant.

The friendship between Theseus and Pirithous was of a most intimate nature, yet it originated in the midst of arms. Pirithous had made an irruption into the plain of Marathon and carried off the herds of the king of Athens. Theseus went to repel the plunderers. The moment Pirithous beheld him, he was seized with admiration; he stretched out his hand as a token of peace and cried, "Be judge thyself—what satisfaction dost thou require?" "Thy friendship," replied the Athenian, and they swore inviolable fidelity. Their deeds corresponded to their professions, and

they ever continued true brothers in arms. Each of them aspired to espouse a daughter of Jupiter. Theseus fixed his choice on Helen, then but a child, afterward so celebrated as the cause of the Trojan war, and with the aid of his friend he carried her off. Pirithous aspired to the wife of the monarch of Erebus; and Theseus, though aware of the danger, accompanied the ambitious lover in his descent to the underworld. But Pluto seized and set them on an enchanted rock at his palace gate, where they remained till Hercules arrived and liberated Theseus, leaving Pirithous to his fate.

After the death of Antiope, Theseus married Phaedra, daughter of Minos, King of Crete. Phaedra saw in Hippolytus, the son of Theseus, a youth endowed with all the graces and virtues of his father, and of an age corresponding to her own. She loved him,

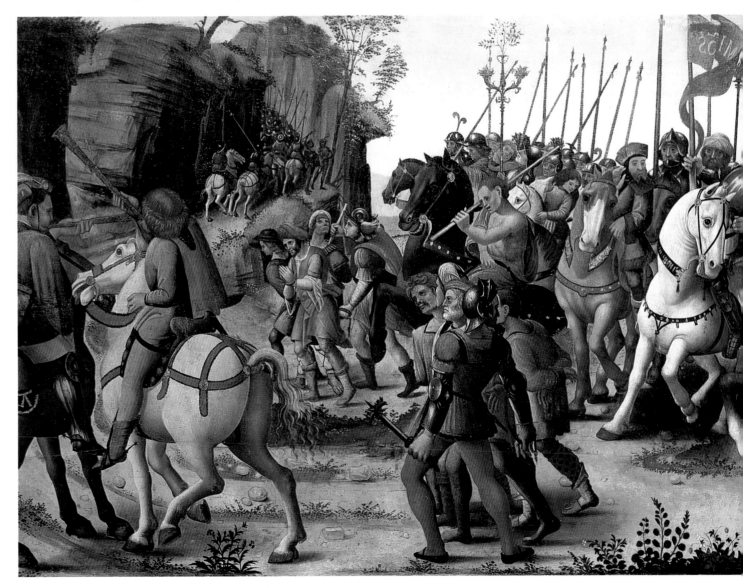

but he repulsed her advances, and her love was changed to hate. She used her influence over her infatuated husband to cause him to be jealous of his son, and he imprecated the vengeance of Neptune upon him. As Hippolytus was one day driving his chariot along the shore, a sea monster raised himself above the waters and frightened the horses so that they ran away and dashed the chariot to pieces. Hippolytus was killed, but by Diana's assistance Aesculapius restored him to life. Diana removed Hippolytus from the power of his deluded father and false stepmother, and placed him in Italy under the protection of the nymph Egeria.

Theseus at length lost the favor of his people and retired to the court of Lycomedes, King of Scyros, who at first received him kindly, but afterward treacherously slew him. In a later age the Athenian general Cimon discovered the place where his remains were laid, and caused them to be removed to Athens, where they were deposited in a temple called the Theseum, erected in honor of the hero.

DAEDALUS

The labyrinth from which Theseus escaped by means of the clew of Ariadne was built by Daedalus, a most skillful artificer. It was an edifice with numberless winding passages and turnings opening into one another, and seeming to have neither beginning nor end, like the river Maeander, which returns on itself, and flows now onward, now backward, in its course to the sea. Daedalus built the labyrinth for King Minos, but afterward lost the favor of the king, and was shut up in a tower. He contrived to make his escape from his prison, but could not leave the island by sea, as the king kept strict watch on all the vessels and permitted none to sail without being carefully searched. "Minos may control the land and sea," said Daedalus, "but not the regions of the air. I will try that way." So he set to work to fabricate wings for himself and his young son Icarus. He wrought feathers together, beginning with the smallest and adding larger, so as to form an increasing surface. The larger ones he secured with thread and the smaller with wax, and gave the whole a gentle curvature like the wings of a bird. Icarus, the boy, stood and looked on, sometimes running to gather up the feathers which the wind had blown away, and then handling the wax and working it over with his fingers, by his play impeding his father in his labors. When at last the work was done, the artist, waving his wings, found himself buoyed upward and hung suspended, poising himself on the beaten air. He next equipped his son in the same manner and taught him how to fly, as a bird tempts her young ones from the lofty nest into the air. When all was prepared for flight he said, "Icarus, my son, I charge you to keep at a moderate height, for if you fly too low the damp will clog your wings, and if too high the heat will melt them. Keep near me and you will be safe." While he gave him these instructions and fitted the wings to his shoulders, the face of the father was wet

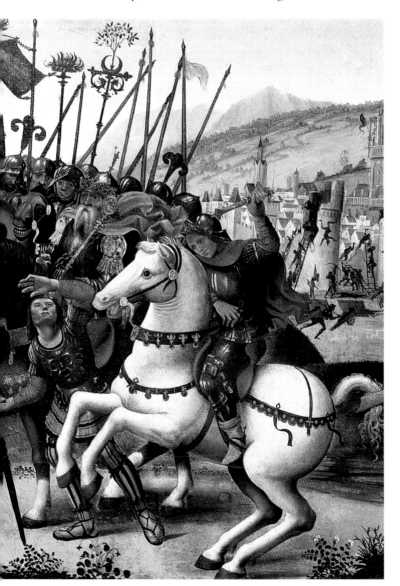

◄ History of Theseus: The Taking of Athens by Minos, MASTER OF THE CASSONI CAMPANA (early 16th century)
The stories of Theseus were probably composed in the sixth century BC, to provide Athenians with their own hero—a rival to Hercules.

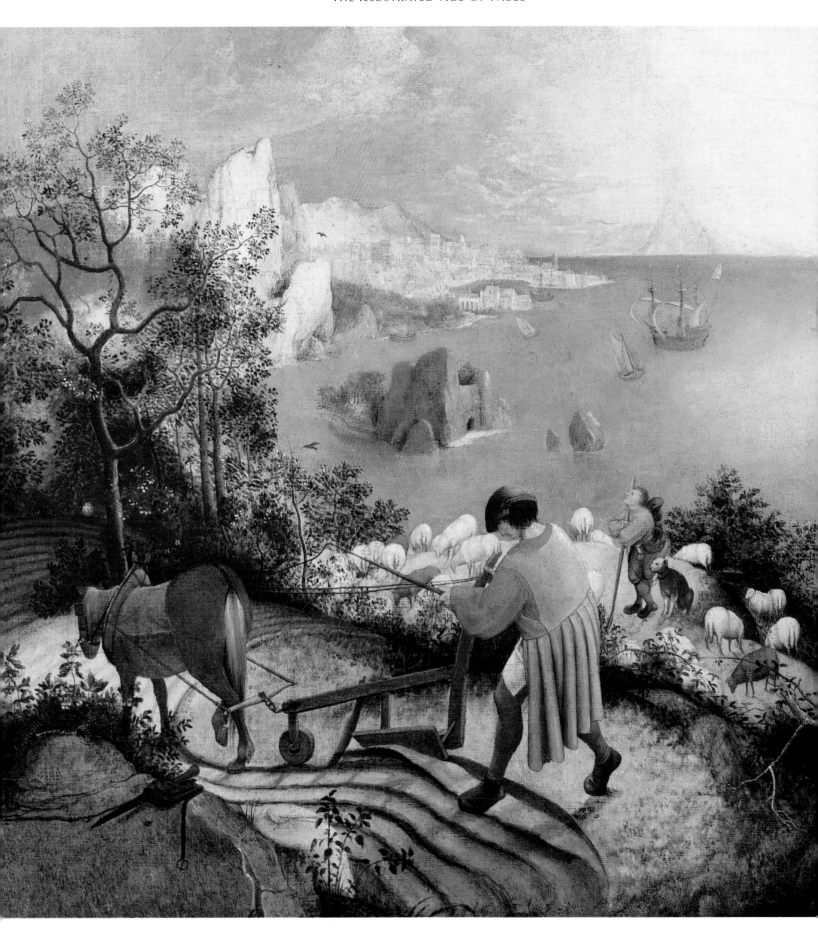

▲ Landscape with the Fall of Icarus, PIETER BRUEGEL THE ELDER (active 1550/1; died 1569)
*To the ancients, the fall of Icarus was a lesson in the perils of hubris or human vanity. Bruegel reduces it to
a pair of white legs disappearing into the sea—while the world goes on its way, regardless of the tragedy.*

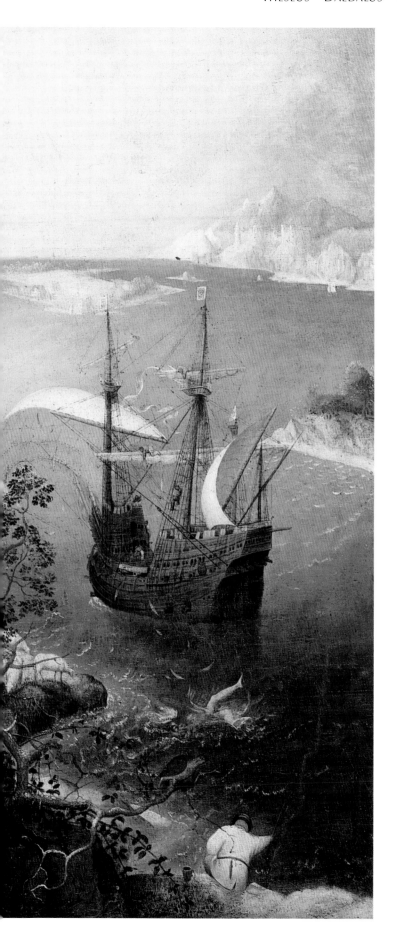

with tears, and his hands trembled. He kissed the boy, not knowing that it was for the last time. Then rising on his wings he flew off, encouraging him to follow, and looked back from his own flight to see how his son managed his wings. As they flew the plowman stopped his work to gaze, and the shepherd leaned on his staff and watched them, astonished at the sight, and thinking they were gods who could thus cleave the air.

They passed Samos and Delos on the left and Lebynthos on the right, when the boy, exulting in his career, began to leave the guidance of his companion and soar upward as if to reach heaven. The nearness of the blazing sun softened the wax which held the feathers together, and they came off. He fluttered with his arms, but no feathers remained to hold the air. While his mouth uttered cries to his father it was submerged in the blue waters of the sea, which thenceforth was called by his name. His father cried, "Icarus, Icarus, where are you?" At last he saw the feathers floating on the water, and bitterly lamenting his own arts, he buried the body and called the land Icaria in memory of his child. Daedalus arrived safe in Sicily, where he built a temple to Apollo and hung up his wings, an offering to the god.

Daedalus was so proud of his achievements that he could not bear the idea of a rival. His sister had placed her son Perdix under his charge to be taught the mechanical arts. He was an apt scholar and gave striking evidences of ingenuity. Walking on the seashore he picked up the spine of a fish. Imitating it, he took a piece of iron and notched it on the edge, and thus invented the saw. He put two pieces of iron together, connecting them at one end with a rivet and sharpening the other ends, and made a pair of compasses. Daedalus was so envious of his nephew's performances that he took an opportunity, when they were together one day on the top of a high tower, to push him off. But Minerva, who favors ingenuity, saw him falling, and arrested his fate by changing him into a bird called after his name, the Partridge. This bird does not build his nest in the trees, nor take lofty flights, but nestles in the hedges, and mindful of his fall, avoids high places.

CASTOR AND POLLUX

Castor and Pollux were the offspring of Leda and the swan, under which disguise Jupiter had concealed himself. Leda gave birth to an egg, from which sprang the twins. Helen, so famous afterward as the cause of the Trojan war, was their sister.

When Theseus and his friend Pirithous had carried off Helen from Sparta, the youthful heroes Castor and Pollux, with their followers, hastened to her rescue. Theseus was absent from Attica and the brothers were successful in recovering their sister.

Castor was famous for taming and managing horses, and Pollux for skill in boxing. They were united by the warmest affection and inseparable in all their enterprises. They accompanied the Argonautic expedition. During the voyage a storm arose, and Orpheus prayed to the Samothracian gods and played on his harp, whereupon the storm ceased and stars appeared on the heads of the brothers. From this incident, Castor and Pollux came afterward to be considered the patron deities of seamen and voyagers, and the lambent flames, which in certain states of the atmosphere play around the sails and masts of vessels, were called by their names.

After the Argonautic expedition, we find Castor and Pollux engaged in a war with Idas and Lynceus. Castor was slain, and Pollux, inconsolable for the loss of his brother, besought Jupiter to be permitted to give his own life as a ransom for him. Jupiter so far consented as to allow the two brothers to enjoy the boon of life alternately, passing one day under the earth and the next in the heavenly abodes. According to another form of the story Jupiter rewarded the attachment of the brothers by placing them among the stars as Gemini, the Twins.

They received divine honors under the name of Dioscuri (sons of Jove). They were believed to have appeared occasionally in later times, taking part with one side or the other, in hard-fought fields, and were said on such occasions to be mounted on magnificent white steeds. Thus in the early history of Rome they are said to have assisted the Romans at the battle of Lake Regillus, and after the victory a temple was erected in their honor on the spot where they appeared.

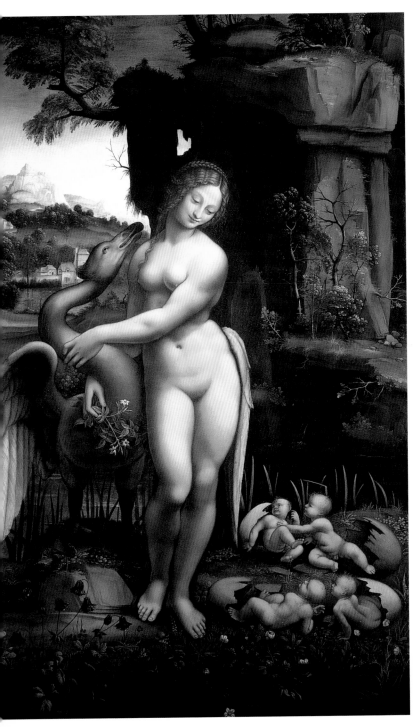

▲ Leda and the Swan, ARTIST UNKNOWN
(Italian, 15th century): *Leda was daughter of
a king of Aetolia; here her ravishment by Jupiter
in swan's guise has produced quadruple offspring:
Castor, Pollux, Helen, and Clytemnestra.*

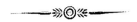

CHAPTER 21

BACCHUS · ARIADNE

Bacchus was the son of Jupiter and Semele. Juno, to gratify her resentment against Semele, contrived a plan for her destruction. Assuming the form of Beroë, her aged nurse, she insinuated doubts whether it was indeed Jove himself who came as a lover. Heaving a sigh, she said, "I hope it will turn out so, but I can't help being afraid. People are not always what they pretend to be. If he is indeed Jove, make him give some proof of it. Ask him to come arrayed in all his splendors, such as he wears in heaven. That will put the matter beyond a doubt." Semele was persuaded to try the experiment. She asks a favor, without naming what it is. Jove gives his promise, and confirms it with the irrevocable oath, attesting the River Styx, terrible to the gods themselves. Then she made known her request. The god

would have stopped her as she spake, but she was too quick for him. The words escaped, and he could neither unsay his promise nor her request. In deep distress he left her and returned to the upper regions. There he clothed himself in his splendors, not putting on all his terrors, as when he overthrew the giants, but what is known among the gods as his lesser panoply. Arrayed in this he entered the chamber of Semele. Her mortal frame could not endure the splendors of the immortal radiance. She was consumed to ashes.

Jove took the infant Bacchus and gave him in charge to the Nysaean nymphs, who nourished his infancy and childhood, and for their care were rewarded by Jupiter by being placed, as the Hyades, among the stars. When Bacchus grew up he discovered the culture of the vine and the mode of extracting

▼ The Infant Bacchus Entrusted to the Nymphs of Nysa: The Death of Echo and Narcis, NICOLAS POUSSIN (1594–1665)
The Greeks generally regarded Bacchus as a god from the East: Mount Nysa was variously located in Arabia, India, or Asia Minor.
The baby's careless father Jupiter is indicated aloft, sipping wine.

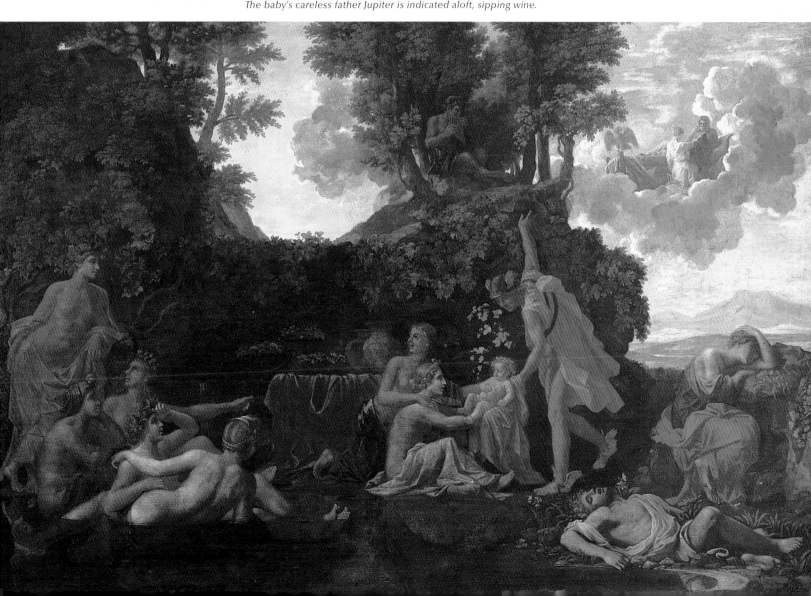

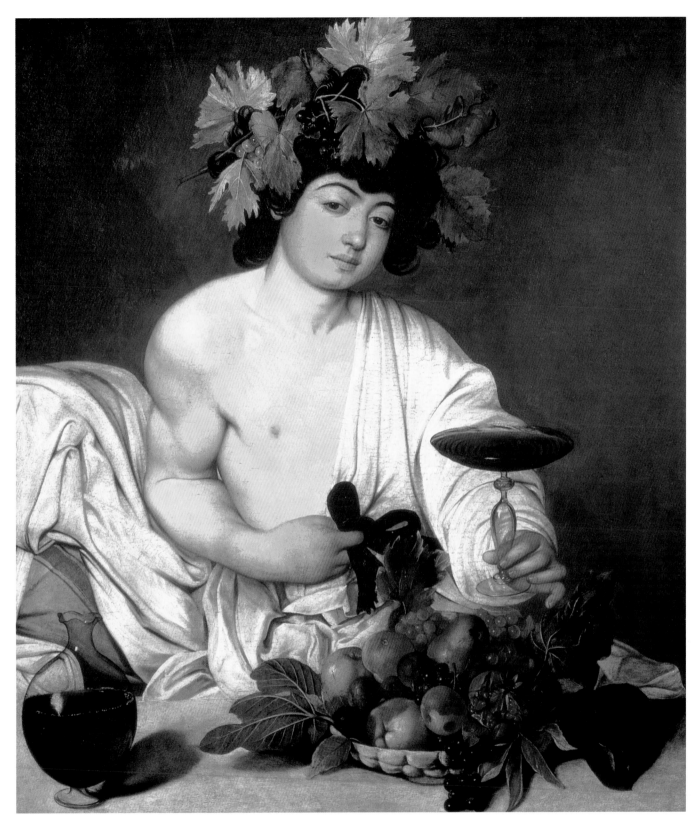

▲ The Young Bacchus, CARAVAGGIO (1571–1610)
As instigator of viticulture and presider over all formal drinking festivities in Greece, Bacchus was nicknamed
"the god who causes stumbling." Caravaggio's plump hedonist looks deceptively serene.

its precious juice; but Juno struck him with madness and drove him forth a wanderer through various parts of the earth. In Phrygia the goddess Rhea cured him and taught him her religious rites, and he set out on a progress through Asia teaching the people the cultivation of the vine. The most famous part of his wanderings is his expedition to India, which is said to have lasted several years. Returning in triumph, he undertook to introduce his worship into Greece, but was opposed by some princes who dreaded its introduction on account of the disorder and madness it brought with it.

As he approached his native city, Thebes, Pentheus the king, who had no respect for the new worship, forbade its rites to be performed. But when it was known that Bacchus was advancing, men and women, but chiefly the latter, young and old poured forth to meet him and to join his triumphal march.

It was in vain Pentheus remonstrated, commanded and threatened. "Go," said he to his attendants, "seize this vagabond leader of the rout and bring him to me. I will soon make him confess his false claim of heavenly parentage and renounce his counterfeit worship." It was in vain his nearest friends and wisest counselors remonstrated and begged him not to oppose the god. Their remonstrances only made him more violent.

But now the attendants returned whom he had despatched to seize Bacchus. They had been driven away by the Bacchanals, but had succeeded in taking one of them prisoner, whom, with his hands tied behind him, they brought before the king. Pentheus, beholding him with wrathful countenance, said, "Fellow! You shall speedily be put to death, that your fate may be a warning to others; but though I grudge the delay of your punishment, speak, tell us who you are, and what are these new rites you presume to celebrate."

The prisoner unterrified responded, "My name is Acetes; my country is Maeonia; my parents were poor people, who had no fields or flocks to leave me, but they left me their fishing rods and nets and their fisherman's trade. This I followed for some time, till growing weary of remaining in one place, I learned the pilot's art and how to guide my course by the stars. It happened, as I was sailing for Delos, we touched at the island of Dia and went ashore. Next morning I sent the men for fresh water and myself mounted the hill to observe the wind; when my men returned, bringing with them a prize, as they thought, a boy of delicate appearance, whom they had found asleep. They judged he was a noble youth, perhaps a king's son, and they might get a liberal ransom for him. I observed his dress, his walk, his face. There was something in them which I felt sure was more than mortal. I said to my men, 'What god there is concealed in that form I know not, but someone there certainly is. Pardon us, gentle deity, for the violence we have done you, and give success to our undertakings.' Dictys, one of my best hands for climbing the mast and coming down by the ropes, and Melanthus, my steersman, and Epopeus, the leader of the sailors' cry, one and all exclaimed, 'Spare your prayers for us.' So blind is the lust of gain! When they proceeded to put him on board I resisted them. 'This ship shall not be profaned by such impiety,' said I. 'I have a greater share in her than any of you.' But Lycabas, a turbulent fellow, seized me by the throat and attempted to throw me overboard, and I scarcely saved myself by clinging to the ropes. The rest approved the deed.

"Then Bacchus (for it was indeed he), as if shaking off his drowsiness, exclaimed, 'What are you doing with me? What is this fighting about? Who brought me here? Where are you going to carry me?' One of them replied, 'Fear nothing; tell us where you wish to go and we will take your there.' 'Naxos is my home,' said Bacchus; 'take me there and you shall be well rewarded.' They promised so to do and told me to pilot the ship to Naxos. Naxos lay to the right, and I was trimming the sails to carry us there, when some by signs and others by whispers signified to me their will that I should sail in the opposite direction, and take the boy to Egypt to sell him for a slave. I was confounded and said, 'Let someone else pilot the ship,' withdrawing myself from any further agency in their wickedness. They cursed me, and one of them, exclaiming, 'Don't flatter yourself that we depend on you for our safety,' took my place as pilot, and bore away from Naxos.

"Then the god, pretending that he had just become aware of their treachery, looked out over the sea and said in a voice of weeping, 'Sailors, these are not the shores you promised to take me to; yonder island is not my home. What have I done that you should treat me so? It is small glory you will gain by cheating a poor boy.' I wept to hear him, but the crew laughed at both of us and sped the vessel fast over the sea. All at once—strange as it may seem, it is true—the vessel stopped, in the mid sea, as fast as if it was fixed on the ground. The men, astonished, pulled at their oars, and spread more sail, trying to make progress by the aid of both, but all in vain. Ivy twined round the oars and hindered their motion, and clung to the sails, with heavy clusters of berries. A vine, laden with grapes, ran up the mast and along the sides of the vessel. The sound of flutes was heard, and the odor of fragrant wine spread all around. The god himself had a chaplet of vine leaves and bore in his hand a spear wreathed with ivy. Tigers crouched at his feet, and forms of lynxes and spotted panthers played around him. The men were seized with terror or madness; some leaped overboard; others preparing to do the same beheld their companions in the water undergoing a change, their bodies becoming flattened and ending in a crooked tail. One exclaimed, 'What miracle is this!' and as he spoke his mouth widened, his nostrils expanded, and scales covered all his body. Another, endeavoring to pull the oar, felt his hands shrink up and presently to be no longer hands but fins; another, trying to raise his arms to a rope, found he had no arms, and curving his mutilated body, jumped into the 'sea. What had been his legs became the two ends of a crescent-shaped tail. The whole crew became dolphins and swam about the ship, now upon the surface, now under it, scattering the spray and spouting the water from their broad nostrils. Of twenty men I alone was left. Trembling with fear, the god cheered me. 'Fear not,' said he; 'steer toward Naxos.' I obeyed, and when we arrived there, I kindled the altars and celebrated the sacred rites of Bacchus."

Pentheus here exclaimed, "We have wasted time enough on this silly story. Take him away and have him executed without delay." Acetes was led away by the attendants and shut up fast in prison; but while they were getting ready the instruments of execution, the prison doors came open of their own accord and the chains fell from his limbs, and when they looked for him he was nowhere to be found.

Pentheus would take no warning, but instead of sending others, determined to go himself to the scene of the solemnities. The mountain Cithaeron was all alive with worshippers, and the cries of the Bacchanals resounded on every side. The noise roused the anger of Pentheus as the sound of a trumpet does the fire of a war-horse. He penetrated through the wood and reached an open space where the chief scene of the orgies met his eyes. At the same moment the women saw him; and first among them his own mother, Agave, blinded by the god, cried out, "See there the wild boar, the hugest monster that prowls in these woods! Come on, sisters! I will be the first to strike the wild boar." The whole band rushed upon him, and while he now talks less arrogantly, now excuses himself, and now confesses his crime and implores pardon, they press upon and wound him. In vain he cries to his aunts to protect him from his mother. Autonoë seized one arm, Ino the other, and between them he was torn to pieces, while his mother shouted, "Victory! Victory! We have done it; the glory is ours!"

So the worship of Bacchus was established in Greece.

ARIADNE

We have seen in the story of Theseus how Ariadne, the daughter of King Minos, after helping Theseus to escape from the labyrinth, was carried by him to the island of Naxos and was left there asleep, while the ungrateful Theseus pursued his way home without her. Ariadne, on waking and finding herself deserted, abandoned herself to grief. But Venus took pity on her and consoled her with the promise that she should have an immortal lover, instead of the mortal one she had lost.

The island where Ariadne was left was the favorite island of Bacchus, the same that he wished the Tyrrhenian mariners to carry him to, when they so treacherously attempted to make prize of him. As Ariadne sat lamenting her fate, Bacchus found her, consoled her, and made her his wife. As a marriage present he gave her a golden crown, enriched with gems, and when she died, he took her crown and threw it up into the sky. As it mounted the gems grew brighter and were turned into stars, and preserving its form Ariadne's crown remains fixed in the heavens as a constellation, between the kneeling Hercules and the man who holds the serpent.

Bacchus and Ariadne, TITIAN (active circa 1506; died 1576) ➤
Titian's painting depicts the moment when Bacchus returns from taming tigers in India: among his drunken followers is the Satyr Silenus, lolling from a donkey. On the island of Naxos, Bacchus falls in love with Ariadne (deserted by Theseus) and transforms her crown into a constellation of stars above her head—signifying that he will love her eternally and make her immortal.

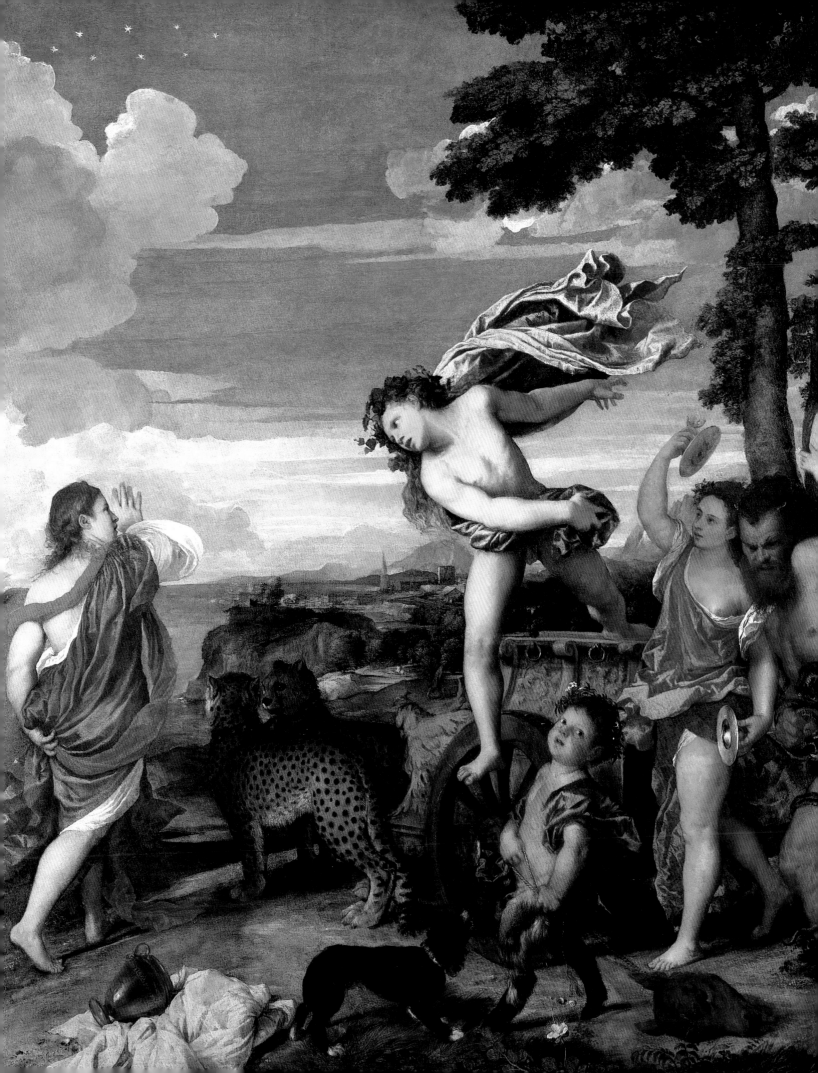

CHAPTER 22

THE RURAL DEITIES · ERISICHTHON RHOECUS · THE WATER DEITIES · THE WINDS

PAN, THE GOD OF WOODS AND FIELDS, OF FLOCKS and shepherds, dwelt in grottos, wandered on the mountains and in valleys, and amused himself with the chase or in leading the dances of the nymphs. He was fond of music, and was, as we have seen, the inventor of the syrinx, or shepherd's pipe, which he himself played in a masterly manner. Pan, like other gods who dwelt in forests, was dreaded by those whose occupations caused them to pass through the woods by night, for the gloom and loneliness of such scenes dispose the mind to superstitious fears. Hence sudden fright without any visible cause was ascribed to Pan and called a Panic terror.

As the name of the god signifies all, Pan came to be considered a symbol of the universe and personification of Nature; and later still to be

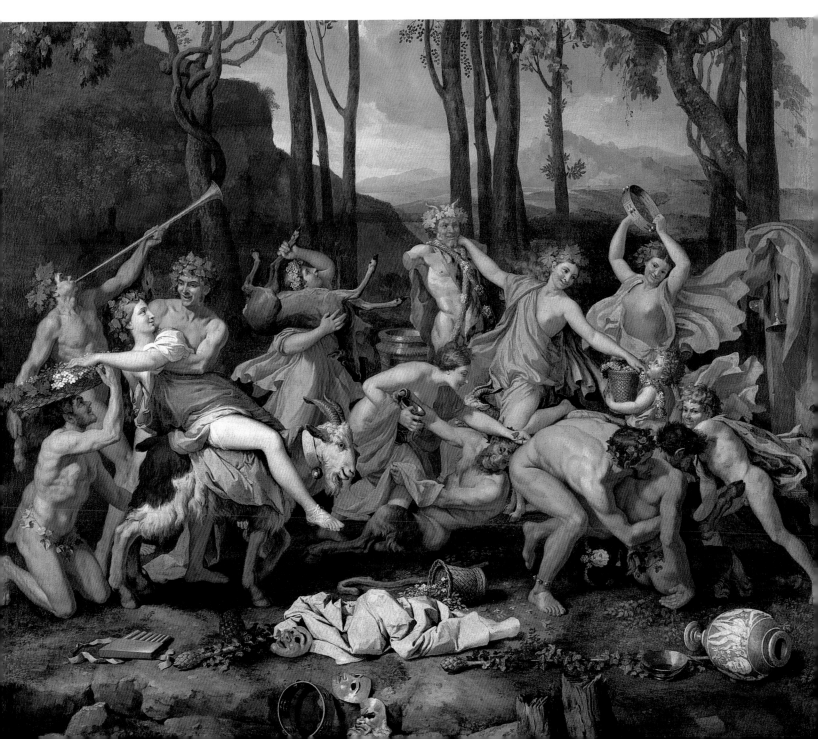

regarded as a representative of all the gods and of heathenism itself.

Sylvanus and Faunus were Latin divinities whose characteristics are so nearly the same as those of Pan that we may safely consider them as the same personage under different names.

The wood nymphs, Pan's partners in the dance, were but one class of nymphs. There were beside them the Naiads, who presided over brooks and fountains, the Oreads, nymphs of mountains and grottos, and the Nereids, sea nymphs. The three last named were immortal, but the wood nymphs, called Dryads or Hamadryads, were believed to perish with the trees which had been their abode, and with which they had come into existence. It was therefore an impious act to destroy a tree wantonly, and in some aggravated cases was severely punished, as in the instance of Erisichthon, which we are about to record.

ERISICHTHON

Erisichthon was a profane person and a despiser of the gods. On one occasion he presumed to violate with the axe a grove sacred to Ceres. There stood in this grove a venerable oak, so large that it seemed a wood in itself, its ancient trunk towering aloft, whereon votive garlands were often hung and inscriptions carved expressing the gratitude of suppliants to the nymph of the tree. Often had the Dryads danced around it hand in hand. Its trunk measured fifteen cubits round, and it overtopped the other trees as they overtopped the shrubbery. But for all that, Erisichthon saw no reason why he should spare it, and he ordered his servants to cut it down. When he saw them hesitate, he snatched an axe from one and thus impiously exclaimed: "I care not whether it be a tree beloved of the goddess or not; were it the goddess herself it should come down, if it stood in my way." So saying he lifted the axe, and the oak seemed to shudder and utter a groan. When the first blow fell upon the trunk, blood flowed from the wound. All the bystanders

◄ The Triumph of Pan, NICOLAS POUSSIN (1594–1665)
Pan, the god of nature, here takes part in an orgiastic, cloven-hoofed Bacchic ritual in the forest.
A set of discarded panpipes lies conspicuously in the foreground, along with masks of satyric drama.

were horror-struck, and one of them ventured to remonstrate and hold back the fatal axe. Erisichthon, with a scornful look, said to him, "Receive the reward of your piety;" and turned against him the weapon which he had held aside from the tree, gashed his body with many wounds, and cut off his head. Then from the midst of the oak came a voice, "I who dwell in this tree am a nymph beloved of Ceres, and dying by your hands, forewarn you that punishment awaits you." He desisted not from his crime, and at last the tree, sundered by repeated blows and drawn by ropes, fell with a crash and prostrated a great part of the grove in its fall.

The Dryads, in dismay at the loss of their companion and at seeing the pride of the forest laid low, went in a body to Ceres, all clad in garments of mourning, and invoked punishment upon Erisichthon. She nodded her assent, and as she bowed her head the grain ripe for harvest in the laden fields bowed also. She planned a punishment so dire that one would pity him, if such a culprit as he could be pitied—to deliver him over to Famine. As Ceres herself could not approach Famine, for the Fates have ordained that these two goddesses shall never come together, she called on Oread from her mountain and spoke to her in these words: "There is a place in the farthest part of ice-clad Scythia, a sad and sterile region without trees and without crops. Cold dwells there, and Fear, and Shuddering, and Famine. Go and tell the last to take possession of the bowels of Erisichthon. Let not abundance subdue her, nor the power of my gifts drive her away. Be not alarmed at the distance (for Famine dwells very far from Ceres) but take my chariot. The dragons are fleet and obey the rein, and will take you through the air in a short time." So she gave her the reins, and she drove away and soon reached Scythia. On arriving at Mount Caucasus she stopped the dragons and found Famine in a stony field, pulling up with teeth and claws the scanty herbage. Her hair was rough, her eyes sunk, her face pale, her lips blanched, her jaws covered with dust, and her skin drawn tight, so as to show all her bones. As the Oread saw her afar off (for she did not dare to come near), she delivered the commands of Ceres; and, though she stopped as short a time as possible, and kept her distance as well as she could, yet she began to feel hungry and turned the dragons' heads and drove back to Thessaly.

125

Famine obeyed the commands of Ceres and sped through the air to the dwelling of Erisichthon, entered the bedchamber of the guilty man, and found him asleep. She enfolded him with her wings and breathed herself into him, infusing her poison into his veins. Having discharged her task, she hastened to leave the land of plenty and returned to her accustomed haunts. Erisichthon still slept, and in his dreams craved food and moved his jaws as if eating. When he awoke his hunger was raging. Without a moment's delay he would have food set before him, of whatever kind earth, sea, or air produces; and complained of hunger even while he ate. What would have sufficed for a city or a nation was not enough for him. The more he ate the more he craved. His hunger was like the sea, which receives all the rivers, yet is never filled; or like fire that burns all the fuel that is heaped upon it, yet is still voracious for more.

His property rapidly diminished under the unceasing demands of his appetite, but his hunger continued unabated. At length he had spent all, and had only his daughter left, a daughter worthy of a better parent. Her too he sold. She scorned to be the slave of a purchaser, and as she stood by the seaside, raised her hands in prayer to Neptune. He heard her prayer, and, though her new master was not far off and had his eye upon her a moment before, Neptune changed her form and made her assume that of a fisherman busy at his occupation. Her master, looking for her and seeing her in her altered form, addressed her and said, "Good fisherman, whither went the maiden whom I saw just now, with hair dishevelled and in humble garb, standing about where you stand? Tell me truly; so may your luck be good, and not a fish nibble at your hook and get away." She perceived that her prayer was answered, and rejoiced inwardly at hearing herself enquired of about herself. She replied, "Pardon me, stranger, but I have been so intent upon my line that I have seen nothing else; but I wish I may never catch another fish if I believe any woman or other person except myself to have been hereabouts for some time." He was deceived and went his way, thinking his slave had escaped. Then she resumed her own form. Her father was well pleased to find her still with him, and the money too that he got by the sale of her; so he sold her again. But she was changed by the favor of Neptune as often as she was sold, now into a horse, now a bird,

now an ox, and now a stag—got away from her purchasers and came home. By this base method the starving father procured food; but not enough for his wants, and at last hunger compelled him to devour his limbs, and he strove to nourish his body by eating his body, till death relieved him from the vengeance of Ceres.

RHOECUS

The Hamadryads could appreciate services as well as punish injuries. The story of Rhoecus proves this. Rhoecus, happening to see an oak just ready to fall, ordered his servants to prop it up. The nymph, who had been on the point of perishing with the tree, came and expressed her gratitude to him for having saved her life and bade him ask what reward he would. Rhoecus boldly asked her love, and the nymph yielded to his desire. She at the same time charged him to be constant, and told him that a bee should be her messenger and let him know when she would admit his society. One time the bee came to Rhoecus when he was playing at draughts, and he carelessly brushed it away. This so incensed the nymph that she deprived him of sight.

THE WATER DEITIES

Oceanus and Tethys were the Titans who ruled over the watery element. When Jove and his brothers overthrew the Titans and assumed their power, Neptune and Amphitrite succeeded to the dominion of the waters in place of Oceanus and Tethys.

Neptune was the chief of the water deities. The symbol of his power was the trident, or spear with three points, with which he used to shatter rocks, to call forth or subdue storms, to shake the shores and the like. He created the horse and was the patron of horse races. His own horses had brazen hoofs and golden manes. They drew his chariot over the sea, which became smooth before him, while the monsters of the deep gambolled about his path.

Amphitrite was the wife of Neptune. She was the daughter of Nereus and Doris and the mother of Triton. Neptune, to pay his court to Amphitrite, came riding on a dolphin. Having won her, he rewarded the dolphin by placing him among the stars.

Nereus and Doris were the parents of the Nereids, the most celebrated of whom were Amphitrite, Thetis, the mother of Achilles, and Galatea, who

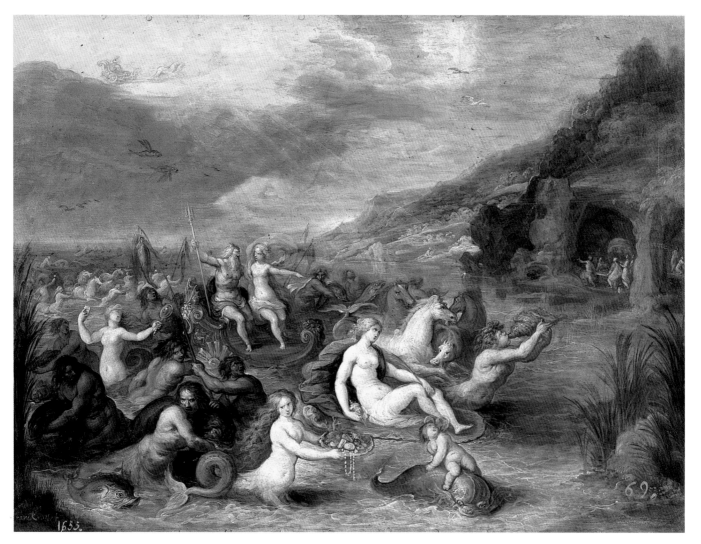

∧ The Triumph of Amphitrite, FRANS FRANCKEN THE YOUNGER (1581–1642)
*Neptune comes to pay court to his future wife with a serenade on conch shells. Neptune had other paramours too, notably the whirlpool Scylla
(traditionally located in the Straits of Messina, off Sicily). The baroque figures are executed in* contrapposto.

was loved by the Cyclops Polyphemus. Nereus was distinguished for his knowledge and his love of truth and justice, whence he was termed an elder; the gift of prophecy was also assigned to him.

Triton was the son of Neptune and Amphitrite, and the poets make him his father's trumpeter. Proteus was also a son of Neptune. He, like Nereus, is styled a sea-elder for his wisdom and knowledge of future events. His peculiar power was that of changing his shape at will.

Thetis, the daughter of Nereus and Doris, was so beautiful that Jupiter himself sought her in marriage; but having learned from Prometheus the Titan that Thetis should bear a son who would be greater than his father, Jupiter desisted from his suit and decreed that Thetis should be the wife of a mortal. By the aid of Chiron the centaur, Peleus succeeded in winning the goddess for his bride, and their son was the renowned Achilles. In our chapter on the Trojan war it will appear that Thetis was a faithful mother to him, aiding him in all difficulties and watching over his interests from the first to the last.

Ino, the daughter of Cadmus and wife of Athamas, flying from her frantic husband with her little son Melicertes in her arms, sprang from a cliff into the sea. The gods, out of compassion, made her a goddess of the sea, under the name of Leucothea, and him a god under that of Palaemon. Both were held powerful to save from shipwreck and were invoked by sailors. Palaemon was usually represented riding on a dolphin. The Isthmian games were celebrated in his honor. He was called Portunus by the Romans and believed to have jurisdiction over the ports and shores.

127

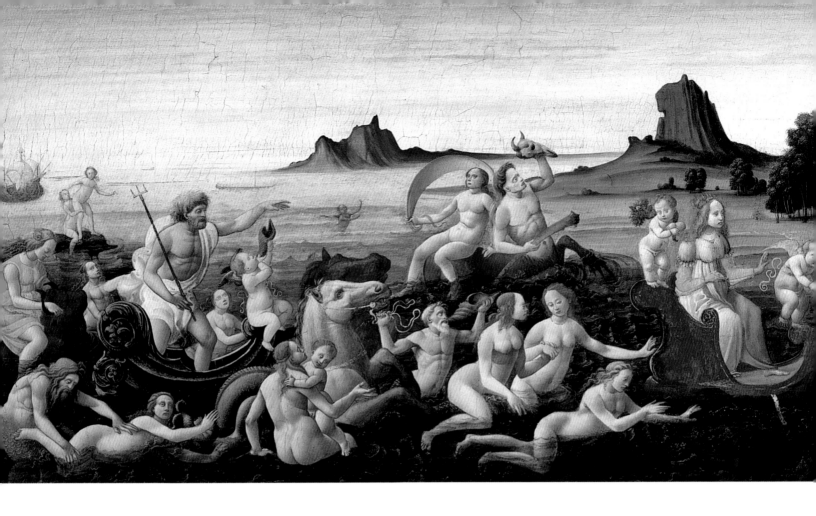

▲ The Cortège of Thetis, BARTOLOMEO DI GIOVANNI (late 15th to early 16th century)
*The wedding of Peleus and Thetis forms the central theme of one of the most ambitious
of all ancient Greek vases, the François Vase, now in Florence.*

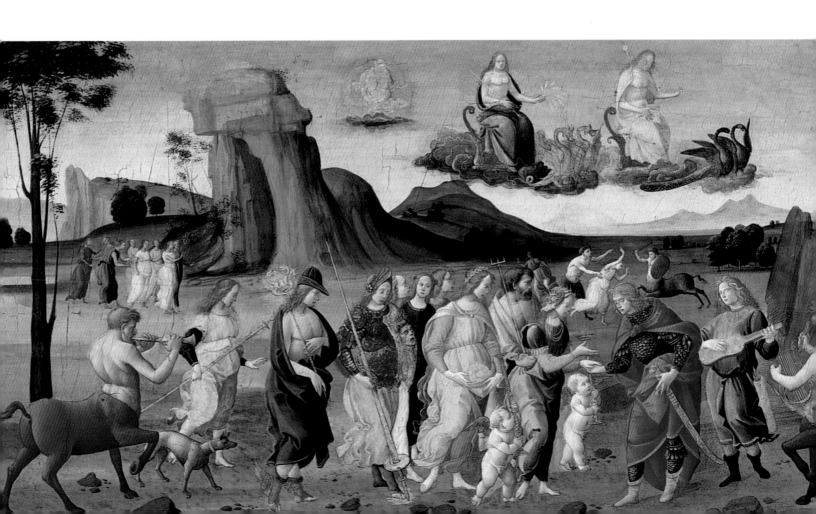

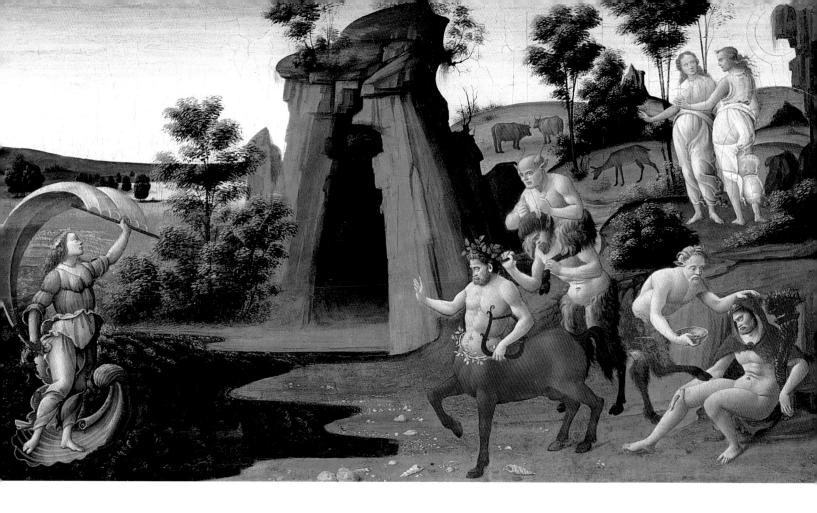

▼ The Marriage of Peleus and Thetis, BARTOLOMEO DI GIOVANNI
*Centaurs, musicians, and dogs alike join the nuptial procession in a frieze-like composition. Bartolomeo, a pupil
of Domenico Ghirlandaio, here shows more affiliation with medieval narratives than with the Florentine quattrocento.*

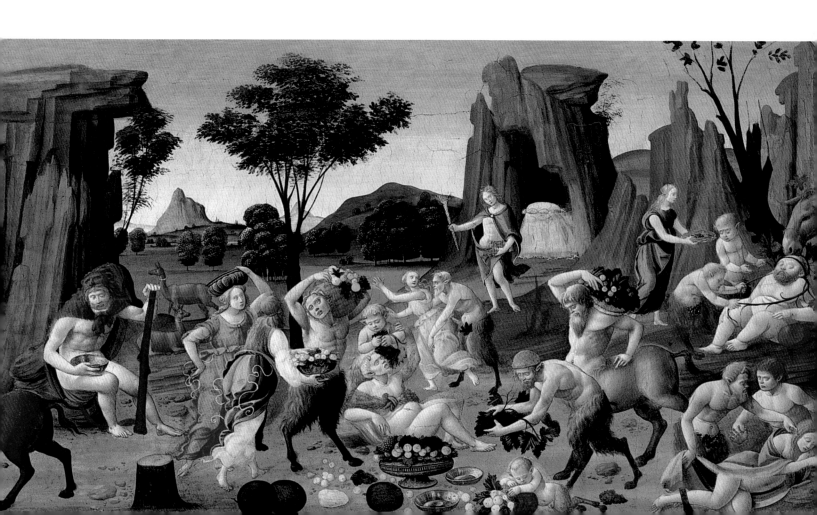

THE CAMENAE

By this name the Latins designated the Muses, but included under it also some other deities, principally nymphs of fountains. Egeria was one of them, whose fountain and grotto are still shown. It was said that Numa, the second king of Rome, was favored by this nymph with secret interviews, in which she taught him those lessons of wisdom and of law which he embodied in the institutions of his rising nation. After the death of Numa the nymph pined away and was changed into a fountain.

THE WINDS

When so many less active agencies were personified, it is not to be supposed that the winds failed to be so. They were Boreas or Aquilo, the north wind, Zephyrus or Favonius, the west, Notus or Auster, the south, and Eurus, the east. The first two have been chiefly celebrated by the poets, the former as the type of rudeness, the latter of gentleness. Boreas loved the nymph Orithyia and tried to play the lover's part, but met with poor success. It was hard for him to breathe gently, and sighing was out of the question. Weary at last of fruitless endeavors, he acted out his true character, seized the maiden, and carried her off. Their children were Zetes and Calais, winged warriors, who accompanied the Argonautic expedition and did good service in an encounter with those monstrous birds the Harpies.

Zephyrus was the lover of Flora.

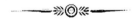

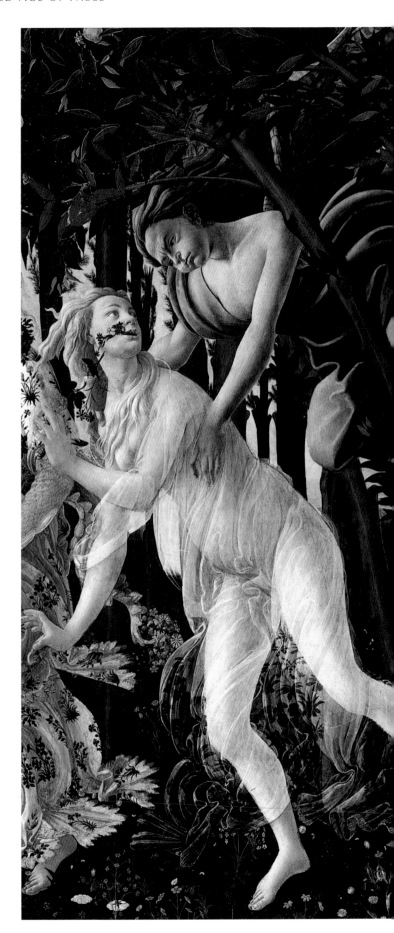

Primavera, SANDRO BOTTICELLI (circa 1445–1510) ➤
*The female members of Thetis's entourage were the Nereids—
celebrated in sculptural form by the wind-blown forms of the girls
on the Lycian Nereid monument (now in the British Museum).*

CHAPTER 23

ACHELOUS AND HERCULES
ADMETUS AND ALCESTIS
ANTIGONE · PENELOPE

THE RIVER GOD ACHELOUS TOLD THE STORY OF Erisichthon to Theseus and his companions, whom he was entertaining at his hospitable board, while they were delayed on their journey by the overflow of his waters. Having finished his story he added, "But why should I tell of other persons' transformations, when I myself am an instance of the possession of this power. Sometimes I become a serpent, and sometimes a bull, with horns on my head. Or I should say, I once could do so; but now I have but one horn, having lost one." And here he groaned and was silent.

Theseus asked him the cause of his grief and how he lost his horn. To which question the river god replied as follows: "Who likes to tell of his defeats? Yet I will not hesitate to relate mine, comforting myself with the thought of the greatness of my conqueror, for it was Hercules. Perhaps you have heard of the fame of Dejanira, the fairest of maidens, whom a host of suitors strove to win. Hercules and myself were of the number, and the rest yielded to us two. He urged in his behalf his descent from Jove and his labors, by which he had exceeded the exactions of Juno, his stepmother. I, on the other hand, said to the father of the maiden, 'Behold me, the king of the waters that flow through your land. I am no stranger from a foreign shore, but belong to the country, a part of your realm. Let it not stand in my way that royal Juno owes me no enmity, nor punishes me with heavy tasks. As for this man, who boasts himself the son of Jove, it is either a false pretence, or disgraceful to him if true, for it cannot be true except by his mother's shame.' As I said this, Hercules scowled upon me and, with difficulty, restrained his rage. 'My hand will answer better than my tongue,' said he. 'I yield you the victory in words, but trust my cause to the strife of deeds.' With that he advanced toward me, and I was ashamed, after what I had said, to yield. I threw off my green vesture and presented myself for the struggle. He tried to throw me, now attacking my head, now my body. My bulk was my protection,

and he assailed me in vain. For a time we stopped, then returned to the conflict. We each kept our position, determined not to yield, foot to foot, I bending over him, clinching his hands in mine, with my forehead almost touching his. Thrice Hercules tried to throw me off, and the fourth time he succeeded, brought me to the ground and himself upon my back. I tell you the truth, it was as if a mountain had fallen on me. I struggled to get my arms at liberty, panting and reeking with perspiration. He gave me no chance to recover, but seized my throat. My knees were on the earth and my mouth in the dust.

"Finding that I was no match for him in the warrior's art, I resorted to others, and glided away in the form of a serpent. I curled my body in a coil and hissed at him with my forked tongue. He smiled scornfully at this and said, 'It was the labor of my infancy to conquer snakes.' So saying he clasped my neck with his hands. I was almost choked, and struggled to get my neck out of his grasp. Vanquished in this form, I tried what alone remained to me, and assumed the form of a bull. He grasped my neck with his arm and, dragging my head down to the ground, overthrew me on the sand. Nor was this enough. His ruthless hand rent my horn from my head. The Naiads took it, consecrated it, and filled it with fragrant flowers. Plenty adopted my horn and made it her own, and called it cornucopia."

There is another account of the origin of the cornucopia. Jupiter at his birth was committed by his mother Rhea to the care of the daughters of Melisseus, a Cretan king. They fed the infant deity with the milk of the goat Amalthea. Jupiter broke off one of the horns of the goat and gave it to his nurses, and endowed it with the wonderful power of becoming filled with whatever the possessor might wish.

ADMETUS AND ALCESTIS

Aesculapius, the son of Apollo, was endowed by his father with such skill in the healing art that he even restored the dead to life. At this, Pluto took alarm and prevailed on Jupiter to launch a thunderbolt at Aesculapius. Apollo was indignant at the destruction of his son and wreaked his vengeance on the innocent workmen who had made the thunderbolt. These were the Cyclopes, who have their workshop under Mount Aetna, from which the smoke and flames of their furnaces are constantly issuing. Apollo shot his arrows at the Cyclopes, which so incensed Jupiter that he condemned him as a punishment to become the servant of a mortal for the space of one year. Accordingly Apollo went into the service of Admetus, King of Thessaly, and pastured his flocks for him on the verdant banks of the River Amphrysos.

Admetus was a suitor, with others, for the hand of Alcestis, the daughter of Pelias, who promised her to him who should come for her in a chariot drawn by lions and boars. This task Admetus performed by the assistance of his divine herdsman, and was made happy in the possession of Alcestis. But Admetus fell ill, and being near to death, Apollo prevailed on the Fates to spare him on condition that someone would consent to die in his stead. Admetus, in his joy at this reprieve, thought little of the ransom, and perhaps remembering the declarations of attachment which he had often heard from his courtiers and dependents, fancied that it would be easy to find a substitute. But it was not so. Brave warriors, who would willingly have periled their lives for their prince, shrunk from the thought of dying for him on the bed of sickness; and old servants who had experienced his bounty and that of his house from their childhood up were not willing to lay down the scanty remnant of their days to show their gratitude. Men asked, "Why does not one of his parents do it? They cannot in the course of nature live much longer, and who can feel like them the call to rescue the life they gave, from an untimely end?" But the parents, distressed though they were at the thought of losing him, shrunk from the call. Then Alcestis, with a generous self-devotion, proffered herself as the substitute. Admetus, fond as he was of life, would not have submitted to receive it at such a cost; but there was no remedy. The condition imposed by the Fates had been met, and the decree was irrevocable. Alcestis sickened as Admetus revived, and she was rapidly sinking to the grave.

Just at this time Hercules arrived at the palace of Admetus and found all the inmates in great distress for the impending loss of the devoted wife and beloved mistress. Hercules, to whom no labor was too arduous, resolved to attempt her rescue. He went and lay in wait at the door of the chamber of the dying queen, and when Death came for his prey, he seized him and forced him to resign his victim. Alcestis recovered, and was restored to her husband.

ANTIGONE

A large proportion, both of the interesting persons and of the exalted acts of legendary Greece, belongs to the female sex. Antigone was as bright an example of filial and sisterly fidelity as was Alcestis of connubial devotion. She was the daughter of Oedipus and Jocasta, who with all their descendants were the victims of an unrelenting fate, dooming them to destruction. Oedipus in his madness had torn out his eyes, and was driven forth from his kingdom Thebes, dreaded and abandoned by all men, as an object of divine vengeance. Antigone, his daughter, alone shared his wanderings and remained with him till he died, and then returned to Thebes.

Her brothers, Eteocles and Polynices, had agreed to share the kingdom between them and reign alternately year by year. The first year fell to the lot of Eteocles, who, when his time expired, refused to surrender the kingdom to his brother. Polynices fled to Adrastus, King of Argos, who gave him his daughter in marriage, and aided him with an army to enforce his claim to the kingdom. This led to the celebrated expedition of the "Seven against Thebes," which furnished ample materials for the epic and tragic poets of Greece.

Amphiaraus, the brother-in-law of Adrastus, opposed the enterprise, for he was a soothsayer and knew by his art that no one of the leaders except Adrastus would live to return. But Amphiaraus, on his marriage to Eriphyle, the king's sister, had agreed that whenever he and Adrastus should differ in opinion, the decision should be left to Eriphyle. Polynices, knowing this, gave Eriphyle the collar of Harmonia and thereby gained her to his interest. This collar or necklace was a present that Vulcan had given to Harmonia on her marriage with Cadmus, and Polynices had taken it with him on his flight from Thebes. Eriphyle could not resist so tempting a bribe, and by her decision the war was resolved on, and Amphiaraus went to his certain fate. He bore his part bravely in the contest, but could not avert his destiny. Pursued by the enemy, he fled along the river, when a thunderbolt launched by Jupiter opened the ground, and he, his chariot and his charioteer were swallowed up.

It would not be in place here to detail all the acts of heroism or atrocity that marked the contest; but we must not omit to record the fidelity of Evadne as an offset to the weakness of Eriphyle. Capaneus, the husband of Evadne, in the ardor of the fight, declared that he would force his way into the city in spite of Jove himself. Placing a ladder against the wall, he mounted, but Jupiter, offended at his impious language, struck him with a thunderbolt. When his obsequies were celebrated, Evadne cast herself on his funeral pile and perished.

Early in the contest Eteocles consulted the soothsayer Tiresias as to the issue. Tiresias in his youth had by chance seen Minerva bathing. The goddess in her wrath deprived him of his sight, but afterward relenting, gave him in compensation the knowledge of future events. When consulted by Eteocles, he declared that victory should fall to Thebes if Minoeceus, the son of Creon, gave himself as a voluntary victim. The heroic youth, learning the response, threw away his life in the first encounter.

The siege continued long, with various success. At length both hosts agreed that the brothers should decide their quarrel by single combat. They fought and fell by each other's hands. The armies then renewed the fight, and at last the invaders were forced to yield, and fled, leaving their dead unburied. Creon, the uncle of the fallen princes, now become king, caused Eteocles to be buried with distinguished honor, but suffered the body of Polynices to lie where it fell, forbidding everyone on pain of death to give it burial.

Antigone, the sister of Polynices, heard with indignation the revolting edict that consigned her brother's body to the dogs and vultures, depriving it of those rites that were considered essential to the repose of the dead. Unmoved by the dissuading counsel of an affectionate but timid sister, and unable to procure assistance, she determined to brave the hazard and to bury the body with her own hands. She was detected in the act, and Creon gave orders that she should be buried alive, as having deliberately set at nought the solemn edict of the city. Her lover, Haemon, the son of Creon,

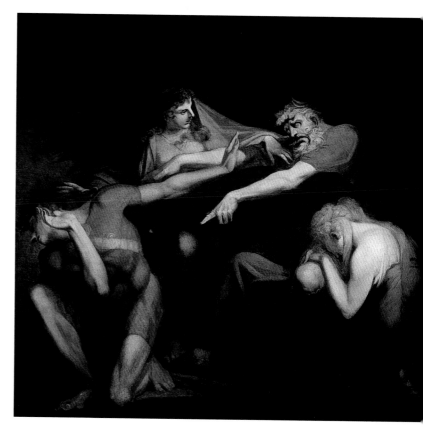

▲ Oedipus Cursing His Son, Polynices,
HENRY FUSELI (1741–1825)
Fuseli isolates the main characters of the Theban tragedy as if they were on stage. Polynices, who has expelled the blinded Oedipus from Thebes, leaving him a beggar, now comes to beg for his father's support in overthrowing his brother Eteocles.

unable to avert her fate, would not survive her, and fell by his own hand.

PENELOPE

Penelope is another of those mythic heroines whose beauties were rather those of character and conduct than of person. She was the daughter of Icarius, a Spartan prince. Ulysses, King of Ithaca, sought her in marriage, and won her over all competitors. When the moment came for the bride to leave her father's house, Icarius, unable to bear the thoughts of parting with his daughter, tried to persuade her to remain with him and not accompany her husband to Ithaca. Ulysses gave Penelope her choice, to stay or go with him. Penelope made no reply, but dropped her veil over her face. Icarius urged her no further, but when she was gone, erected a statue to Modesty on the spot where they parted.

Ulysses and Penelope had not enjoyed their union more than a year when it was interrupted by the events which called Ulysses to the Trojan war.

During his long absence, and when it was doubtful whether he still lived, and highly improbable that he would ever return, Penelope was importuned by numerous suitors, from whom there seemed no refuge but in choosing one of them for her husband. Penelope, however, employed every art to gain time, still hoping for Ulysses' return. One of her arts of delay was engaging in the preparation of a robe for the funeral canopy of Laertes, her husband's father.

She pledged herself to make her choice among the suitors when the robe was finished. During the day she worked at the robe, but in the night she undid the work of the day. This is the famous Penelope's web, which is used as a proverbial expression for anything which is perpetually doing but never done. The rest of Penelope's history will be told when we give an account of her husband's adventures.

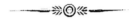

Y The Return of Ulysses, SIENESE SCHOOL (16th century)
*Penelope's faithfulness to her long-absent husband, and her devotion to the domestic duties of spinning and weaving,
have made her a paragon of bridal virtue, whether in classical Athens or courtly Siena;
so this is an appropriate subject for the decoration of a cassone or wedding chest.*

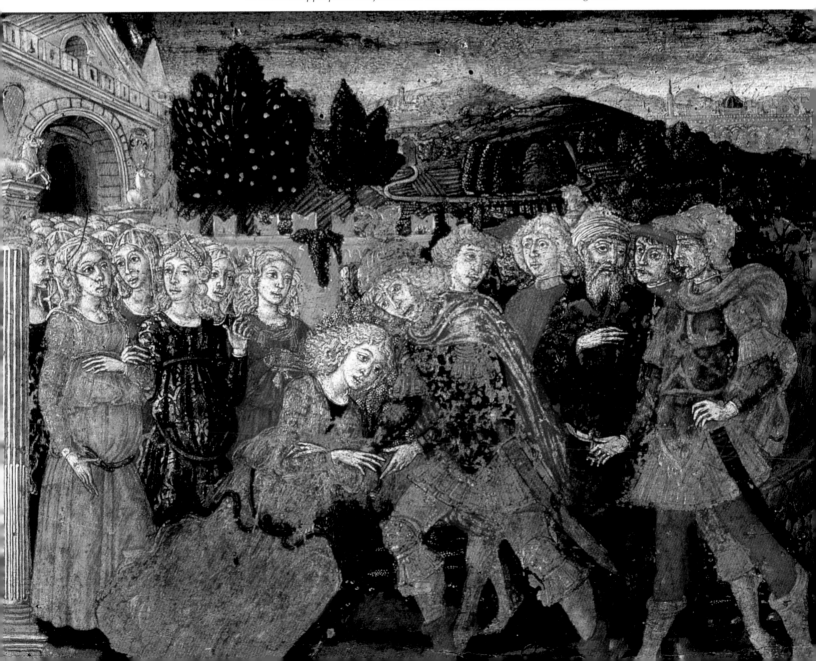

CHAPTER 24

ORPHEUS AND EURYDICE · ARISTAEUS AMPHION · LINUS · THAMYRIS MARSYAS · MELAMPUS · MUSAEUS

ORPHEUS WAS THE SON OF APOLLO AND THE MUSE Calliope. He was presented by his father with a lyre and taught to play upon it, which he did to such perfection that nothing could withstand the charm of his music. Not only his fellow mortals but wild beasts were softened by his strains, and gathering around him laid by their fierceness, and stood entranced with his lay. Nay, the very trees and rocks were sensible to the charm. The former crowded round him and the latter relaxed somewhat of their hardness, softened by his notes.

Hymen had been called to bless with his presence the nuptials of Orpheus with Eurydice; but though he attended, he brought no happy omens with him. His very torch smoked and brought tears into their eyes. In coincidence with such prognostics Eurydice, shortly after her marriage, while wandering with the nymphs, her companions, was seen by the shepherd Aristaeus, who was struck with her beauty, and made advances to her. She fled, and in flying trod upon a snake in the grass, was bitten in the foot, and died. Orpheus sang his grief to all who breathed the upper air, both gods and men, and finding it all unavailing, resolved to seek his wife in the regions of the dead. He descended by a cave situated on the side of the promontory of Taenarus and arrived at the Stygian realm. He passed through crowds of ghosts and presented himself before the throne of Pluto and Proserpine. Accompanying the words with the lyre, he sung, "O deities of the underworld, to whom all we who live must come, hear my words, for they are true. I come not to spy out the secrets of Tartarus, nor to try my strength against the three-headed dog with snaky hair who guards the entrance. I come to seek my wife, whose opening years the poisonous viper's fang has brought to an untimely end. Love has led me here, Love, a god all powerful with us who dwell on the earth, and, if old traditions say true, not less so here. I implore you by these abodes full of terror, these realms of silence and uncreated

things, unite again the thread of Eurydice's life. We all are destined to you, and sooner or later must pass to your domain. She, too, when she shall have filled her term of life, will rightly be yours. But till then grant her to me, I beseech you. If you deny me, I cannot return alone; you shall triumph in the death of us both."

As he sang these tender strains, the very ghosts shed tears. Tantalus, in spite of his thirst, stopped for a moment his efforts for water, Ixion's wheel stood still, the vulture ceased to tear the giant's liver, the daughters of Danaus rested from their task of drawing water in a sieve, and Sisyphus sat on his rock to listen. Then for the first time, it is said, the cheeks of the Furies were wet with tears. Proserpine could not resist, and Pluto himself gave way. Eurydice was called. She came from among the new arrived ghosts, limping with her wounded foot. Orpheus was permitted to take her away with him on one condition, that he should not turn around to look at her till they should have reached the upper air. Under this condition they proceeded on their way, he leading, she following, through passages dark and steep, in total silence, till they had nearly reached the outlet into the cheerful upper world, when Orpheus, in a moment of forgetfulness, to assure himself that she was still following, cast a glance behind him, when instantly she was borne away. Stretching out their arms to embrace one another, they grasped only the air! Dying now a second time she yet cannot reproach her husband, for how can she blame his impatience to behold her! "Farewell," she said, "a last farewell," and was hurried away so fast that the sound hardly reached his ears.

Orpheus endeavored to follow her and besought permission to return and try once more for her release;

Orpheus, ROELANDT SAVERY (1576–1639) ➤
Not only human beings, but wild animal and birds—even trees, plants and rocks—were mesmerized by the music of Orpheus, here set in a fantastical landscape, which was Savery's trademark.

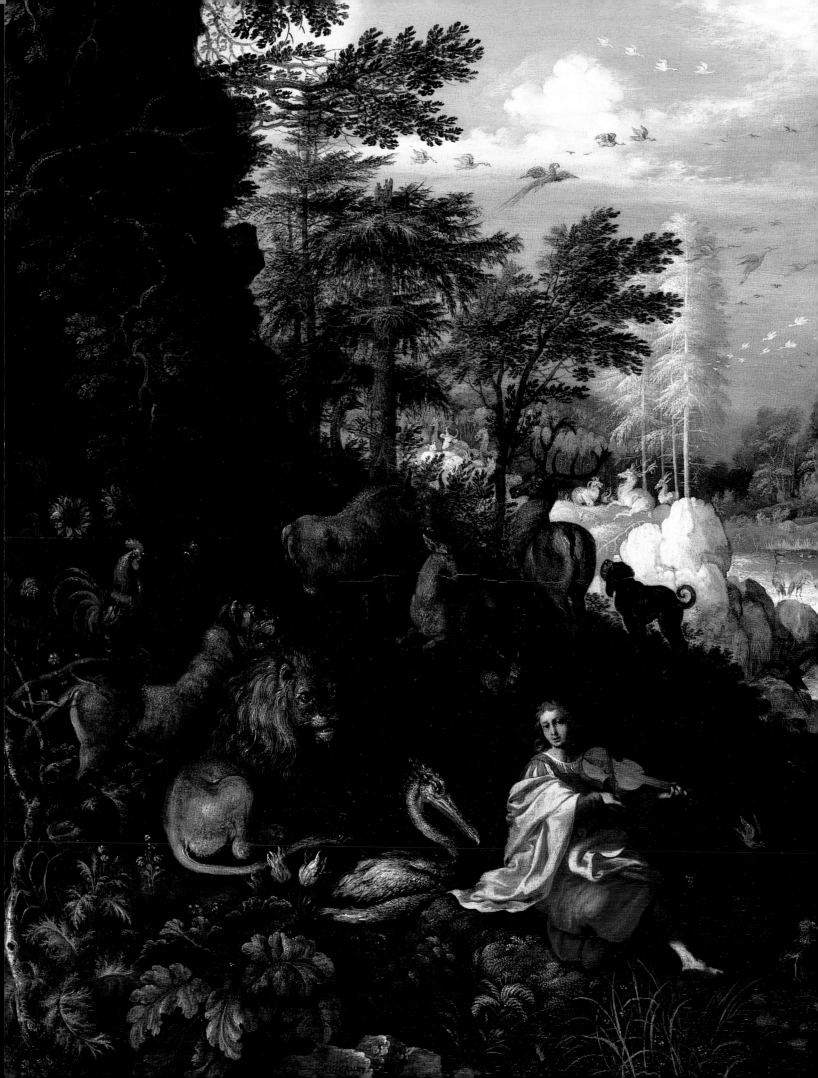

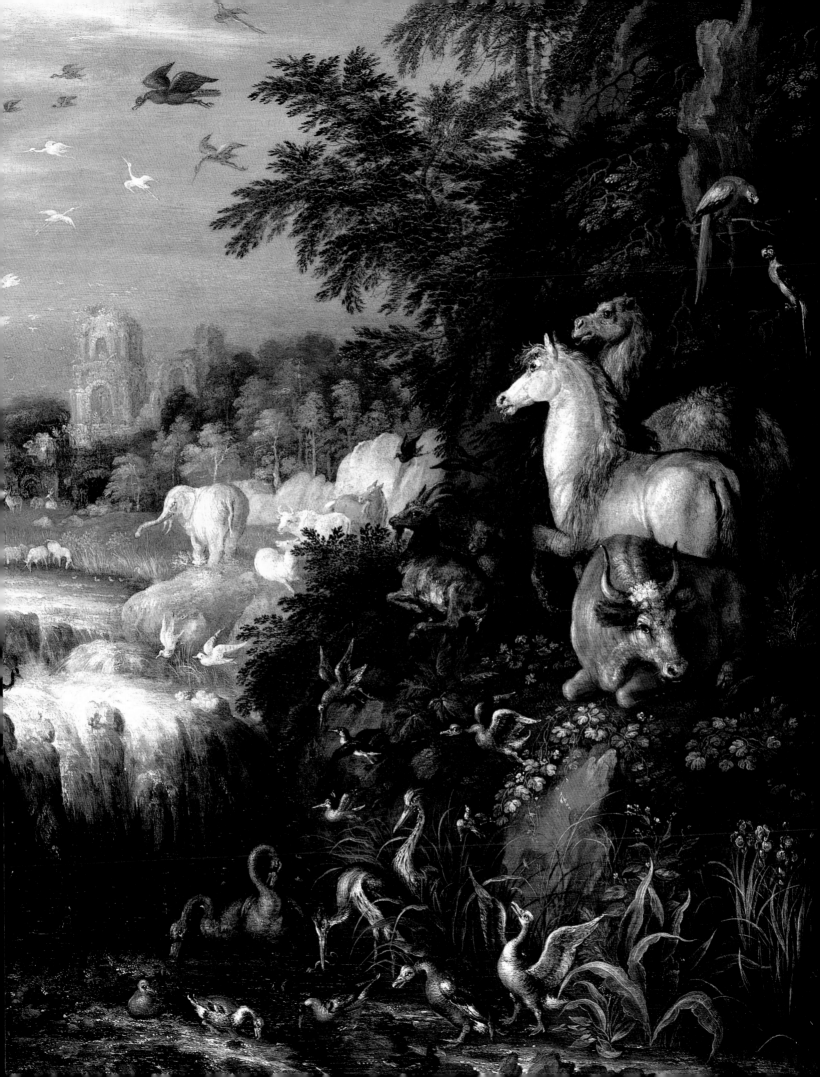

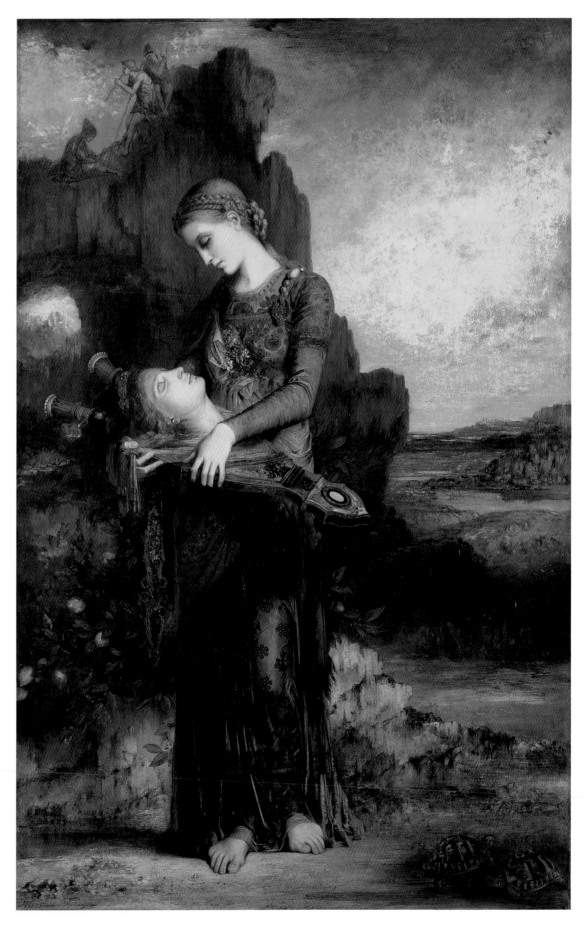

but the stern ferryman repulsed him and refused passage. Seven days he lingered about the brink, without food or sleep; then bitterly accusing of cruelty the powers of Erebus, he sang his complaints to the rocks and mountains, melting the hearts of tigers and moving the oaks from their stations. He held himself aloof from womankind, dwelling constantly on the recollection of his sad mischance. The Thracian maidens tried their best to captivate him, but he repulsed their advances. They bore with him as long as they could; but finding him insensible, one day, excited by the rites of Bacchus, one of them exclaimed, "See yonder our despiser!" and threw at him her javelin. The weapon, as soon as it came within the sound of his lyre, fell harmless at his feet. So did also the stones that they threw at him. But the women raised a scream and drowned the voice of the music, and then the missiles reached him and soon were stained with his blood. The maniacs tore him limb from limb, and threw his head and his lyre into the River Hebrus, down which they floated, murmuring sad music, to which the shores responded a plaintive symphony. The Muses gathered up the fragments of his body and buried them at Libethra, where the nightingale is said to sing over his grave more sweetly than in any other part of Greece. His lyre was placed by Jupiter among the stars. His shade passed a second time to Tartarus, where he sought out his Eurydice and embraced her, with eager arms. They roam the happy fields together now, sometimes he leading, sometimes she; and Orpheus gazes as much as he will upon her, no longer incurring a penalty for a thoughtless glance.

ARISTAEUS, OR THE BEE-KEEPER

Man avails himself of the instincts of the inferior animals for his own advantage. Hence sprang the art of keeping bees. Honey must first have been known as a wild product, the bees building their structures in hollow trees, or holes in the rocks, or any similar cavity that chance offered. Thus occasionally the carcass of a dead animal would be occupied by the bees for that purpose. It was no doubt from some

◄ The Prophetic Head and Lyre of Orpheus, GUSTAVE MOREAU (1826–1898): *When the Thracian Bacchantes tore lovesick Orpheus limb from limb, they tossed his head into a river, the banks of which echo his lament for Eurydice. The tortoises in the foreground of Moreau's picture symbolize the tortoise-shell lyre which was the favorite instrument of Orpheus.*

such incident that the superstition arose that the bees were engendered by the decaying flesh of the animal; and Virgil, in the following story, shows how this supposed fact may be turned to account for renewing the swarm when it has been lost by disease or accident.

Aristaeus, who first taught the management of bees, was the son of the water nymph Cyrene. His bees had perished, and he resorted for aid to his mother. He stood at the riverside and thus addressed her: "Oh, mother, the pride of my life is taken from me! I have lost my precious bees. My care and skill have availed me nothing, and you my mother have not warded off from me the blow of misfortune." His mother heard these complaints as she sat in her palace at the bottom of the river with her attendant nymphs around her. They were engaged in female occupations, spinning and weaving, while one told stories to amuse the rest. The sad voice of Aristaeus interrupting their occupation, one of them put her head above the water, and seeing him, returned and gave information to his mother, who ordered that he should be brought into her presence. The river at her command opened itself and let him pass in, while it stood curled like a mountain on either side. He descended to the region where the fountains of the great rivers lie; he saw the enormous receptacles of waters and was almost deafened with the roar, while he surveyed them hurrying off in various directions to water the face of the earth. Arriving at his mother's apartments he was hospitably received by Cyrene and her nymphs, who spread their table with the richest dainties. They first poured out libations to Neptune, then regaled themselves with the feast, and after that Cyrene thus addressed him: "There is an old prophet named Proteus, who dwells in the sea and is a favorite of Neptune whose herd of sea calves he pastures. We nymphs hold him in great respect, for he is a learned sage and knows all things, past, present and to come. He can tell you, my son, the cause of the mortality among your bees and how you may remedy it. But he will not do it voluntarily, however you may entreat him. You must compel him by force. If you seize him and chain him, he will answer your questions in order to get released, for he cannot by all his arts get away if you hold fast the chains. I will carry you to his cave, where he comes at noon to take his midday repose. Then you may easily secure him. But when he finds himself captured, his resort is to a power he possesses of changing himself into various forms. He will become a wild boar or a fierce tiger, a scaly dragon or lion with yellow mane. Or he will make a noise like the crackling of flames or the rush of water, so as to tempt you to let go the chain, when he will make his escape. But you have only to keep him fast bound, and at last when he finds all his arts unavailing, he will return to his own figure and obey your commands." So saying she sprinkled her son with fragrant nectar, the beverage of the gods, and immediately an unusual vigor filled his frame and courage his heart, while perfume breathed all around him.

The nymph led her son to the prophet's cave and concealed him among the recesses of the rocks, while she herself took her place behind the clouds. When noon came and the hour when men and herds retreat from the glaring sun to indulge in quiet slumber, Proteus issued from the water, followed by his herd of sea calves, which spread themselves along the shore. He sat on the rock and counted his herd; then stretched himself on the floor of the cave and went to sleep. Aristaeus hardly allowed him to get fairly asleep before he fixed the fetters on him and shouted aloud. Proteus, waking and finding himself captured, immediately resorted to his arts, becoming first a fire, then a flood, then a horrible wild beast, in rapid succession. But finding all would not do, he at last resumed his own form and addressed the youth in angry accents: "Who are you, bold youth, who thus invade my abode, and what do you want with me?" Aristaeus replied, "Proteus, you know already, for it is needless for any one to attempt to deceive you. And do you also cease your efforts to elude me. I am led hither by divine assistance, to know from you the cause of my misfortune and how to remedy it." At these words the prophet, fixing on him his gray eyes, with a piercing look, thus spoke: "You receive the merited reward of your deeds, by which Eurydice met her death, for in flying from you she trod upon a serpent, of whose bite she died. To avenge her death, the nymphs, her companions, have sent this destruction to your bees. You have to appease their anger, and thus it must be done: Select four bulls of perfect form and size, and four cows of equal beauty, build four altars to the nymphs, and sacrifice the animals, leaving their carcasses in the leafy grove. To Orpheus and Eurydice you shall pay such funeral honors as

may allay their resentment. Returning after nine days you will examine the bodies of the cattle slain and see what will befall." Aristaeus faithfully obeyed these directions. He sacrificed the cattle, he left their bodies in the grove, he offered funeral honors to the shades of Orpheus and Eurydice; then, returning on the ninth day, he examined the bodies of the animals, and, wonderful to relate! a swarm of bees had taken possession of one of the carcasses and were pursuing their labors there as in a hive.

The following are other celebrated mythical poets and musicians, some of whom were hardly inferior to Orpheus himself:

AMPHION

Amphion was the son of Jupiter and Antiope, Queen of Thebes. With his twin brother Zethus he was exposed at birth on Mount Cithaeron, where they grew up among the shepherds, not knowing their parentage. Mercury gave Amphion a lyre and taught him to play upon it, and his brother occupied himself in hunting and tending the flocks. Meanwhile Antiope, their mother, who had been treated with great cruelty by Lycus, the usurping king of Thebes, and by Dirce, his wife, found means to inform her children of their rights and to summon them to her assistance. With a band of their fellow herdsmen they attacked and slew Lycus, and tying Dirce by the hair of her head to a bull, let him drag her till she was dead. Amphion, having become king of Thebes, fortified the city with a wall. It is said that when he played on his lyre, the stones moved of their own accord and took their places in the wall.

LINUS

Linus was the instructor of Hercules in music, but having one day reproved his pupil rather harshly, he roused the anger of Hercules, who struck him with his lyre and killed him.

THAMYRIS

An ancient Thracian bard, who in his presumption challenged the Muses to a trial of skill, and being overcome in the contest, was deprived of his sight.

MARSYAS

Minerva invented the flute and played upon it to the delight of all the celestial auditors; but the mischievous urchin Cupid having dared to laugh at the queer face which the goddess made while playing, Minerva threw the instrument indignantly away, and it fell down to earth, and was found by Marsyas. He blew upon it and drew from it such ravishing sounds that he was tempted to challenge Apollo himself to a musical contest. The god, of course, triumphed and punished Marsyas by flaying him alive.

MELAMPUS

Melampus was the first mortal endowed with prophetic powers. Before his house there stood an oak tree containing a serpent's nest. The old serpents were killed by the servants, but Melampus took care of the young ones and fed them carefully. One day when he was asleep under the oak, the serpents licked his ears with their tongues. On awaking, he was astonished to find that he now understood the language of birds and creeping things. This knowledge enabled him to foretell future events, and he became a renowned soothsayer. At one time his enemies took him captive and kept him strictly imprisoned. Melampus, in the silence of the night, heard the wood worms in the timbers talking together and found out by what they said that the timbers were nearly eaten through and the roof would soon fall in. He told his captors and demanded to be let out, warning them also. They took his warning, and thus escaped destruction, and rewarded Melampus and held him in high honor.

MUSAEUS

A semi-mythological personage who was represented by one tradition to be the son of Orpheus. He is said to have written sacred poems and oracles.

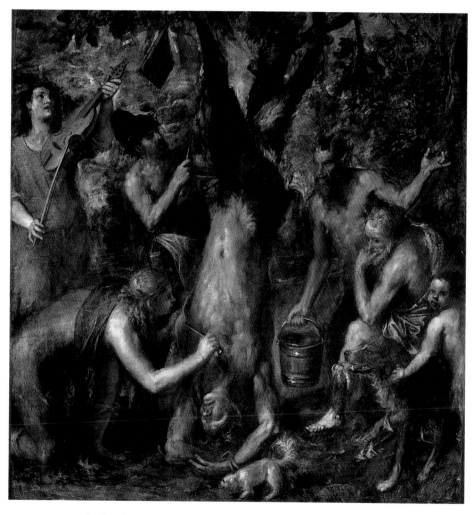

∧ The Flaying of Marysas, TITIAN (active circa 1506; died 1576)
To be flayed alive is to have bodily skin gradually sliced away from muscle and bones. The horror of the torture inflicted on Marsyas by Apollo is not spared by Titian; for the ancients, it would have been regarded as a very proper punishment for hubris.

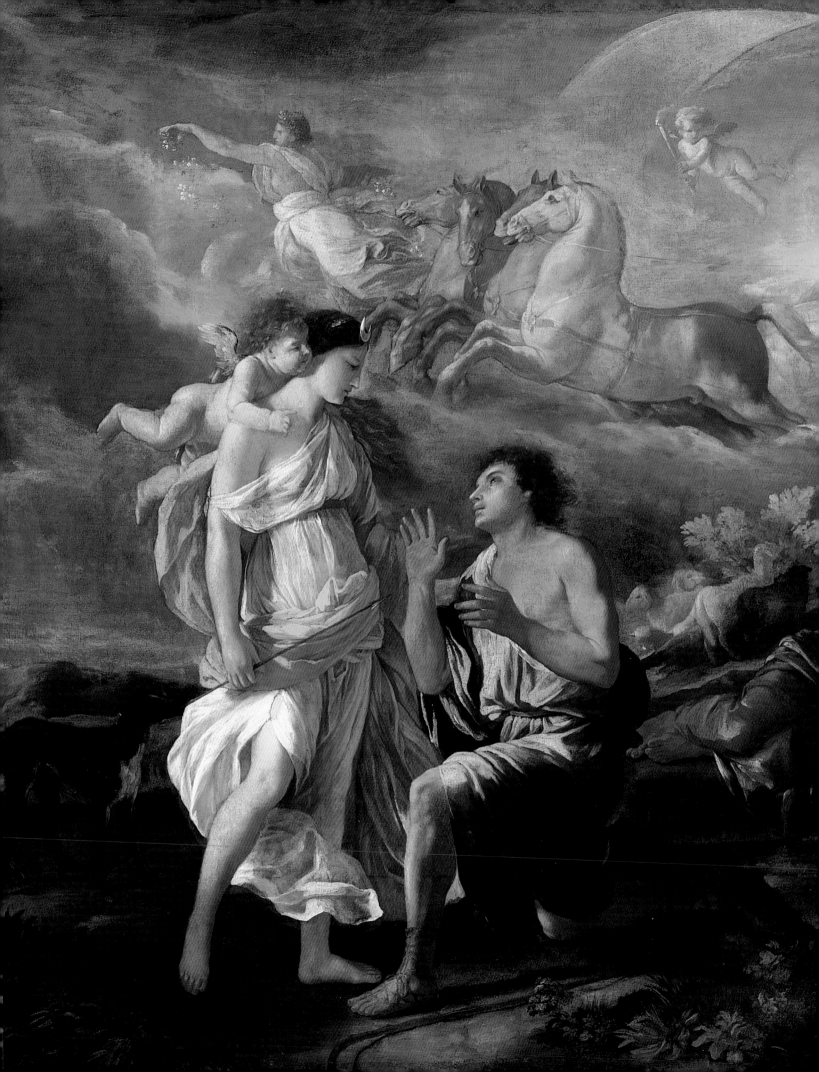

CHAPTER 25

ENDYMION · ORION
AURORA AND TITHONUS
ACIS AND GALATEA

ENDYMION WAS A BEAUTIFUL YOUTH WHO FED HIS flock on Mount Latmos. One calm, clear night, Diana, the Moon, looked down and saw him sleeping. The cold heart of the virgin goddess was warmed by his surpassing beauty, and she came down to him, kissed him, and watched over him while he slept.

Another story was that Jupiter bestowed on him the gift of perpetual youth united with perpetual sleep. Of one so gifted we can have but few adventures to record. Diana, it was said, took care that his fortunes should not suffer by his inactive life, for she made his flock increase and guarded his sheep and lambs from the wild beasts.

ORION

Orion was the son of Neptune. He was a handsome giant and a mighty hunter. His father gave him the power of wading through the depths of the sea, or as others say, of walking on its surface.

Orion loved Merope, the daughter of Oenopion, King of Chios, and sought her in marriage. He cleared the island of wild beasts and brought the spoils of the chase as presents to his beloved; but as Oenopion constantly deferred his consent, Orion attempted to gain possession of the maiden by violence. Her father, incensed at this conduct, having made Orion drunk, deprived him of his sight and cast him out on the seashore. The blinded hero followed the sound of a Cyclops's hammer till he reached Lemnos, and came to the forge of Vulcan, who, taking pity on him, gave him Kedalion, one of his men, to be his guide to the abode of the sun. Placing Kedalion on his shoulders, Orion proceeded to the east, and there, meeting the sun god, was restored to sight by his beam.

After this he dwelt as a hunter with Diana, with whom he was a favorite, and it is even said she was about to marry him. Her brother was highly displeased and often chid her, but to no purpose. One day, observing Orion wading through the sea with his head just above the water, Apollo pointed it out to his sister and maintained that she could not hit that black thing on the sea. The archer goddess discharged a shaft with fatal aim. The waves rolled the dead body of Orion to the land, and bewailing her fatal error with many tears, Diana placed him among the stars, where he appears as a giant, with a girdle, sword, lion's skin and club. Sirius, his dog, follows him, and the Pleiads fly before him.

The Pleiads were daughters of Atlas and nymphs of Diana's train. One day Orion saw them and became enamored and pursued them. In their distress they prayed to the gods to change their form, and Jupiter in pity turned them into pigeons and then made them a constellation in the sky. Though their number was seven, only six stars are visible, for Electra, one of them, it is said left her place that she might not behold the ruin of Troy, for that city was founded by her son Dardanus. The sight had such an effect on her sisters that they have looked pale ever since.

AURORA AND TITHONUS

The goddess of the dawn, like her sister the Moon, was at times inspired with the love of mortals. Her greatest favorite was Tithonus, son of Laomedon, King of Troy. She stole him away and prevailed on Jupiter to grant him immortality; but forgetting to have youth joined in the gift, after some time she began to discern, to her great mortification, that he was growing old. When his hair was quite white she left his society; but he still had the range of her palace, lived on ambrosial food, and was clad in celestial raiment.

◄ Diana and Endymion, NICOLAS POUSSIN (1594–1665)
As Dawn arrives, casting rose petals about her and closely followed by Apollo's sun chariot, so Diana takes leave of the transfigured Endymion. Her curious gift to him—perpetual sleep—is symbolized by the encroaching curtain of darkness.

Blind Orion Searching for the Rising Sun, NICOLAS POUSSIN ➤
Guided by the figure of Vulcan perched on his shoulder, the giant, blinded hunter Orion stumbles eastward to regain his sight from the rising sun, while the goddess Diana watches from the sky.

143

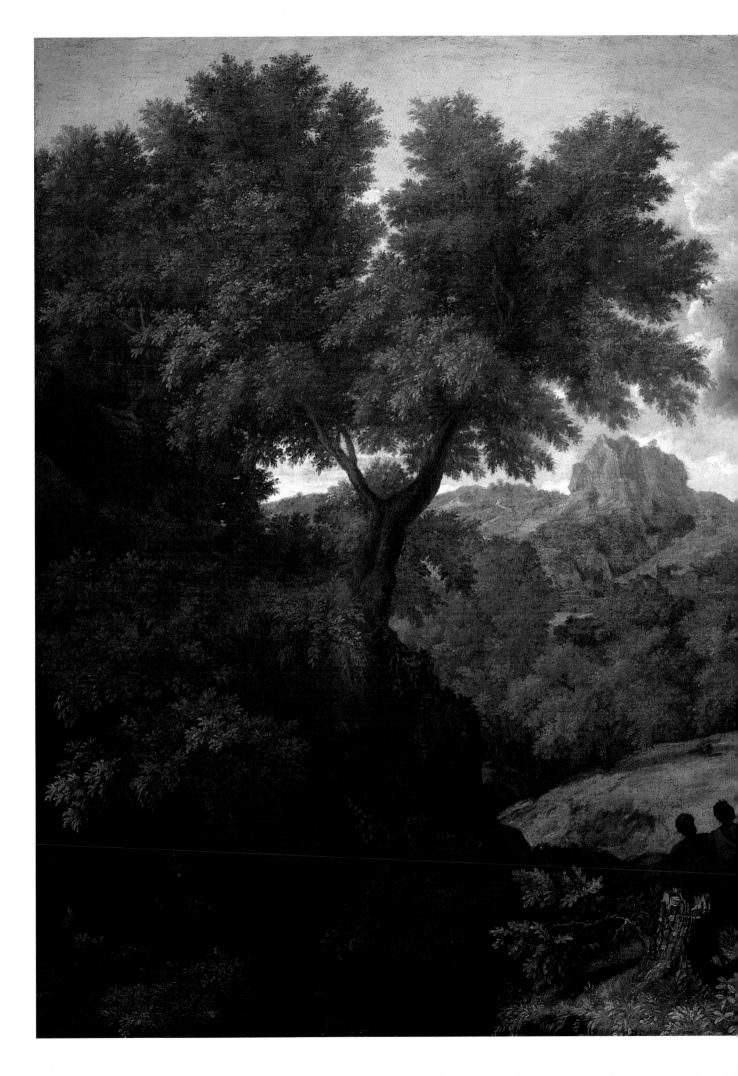

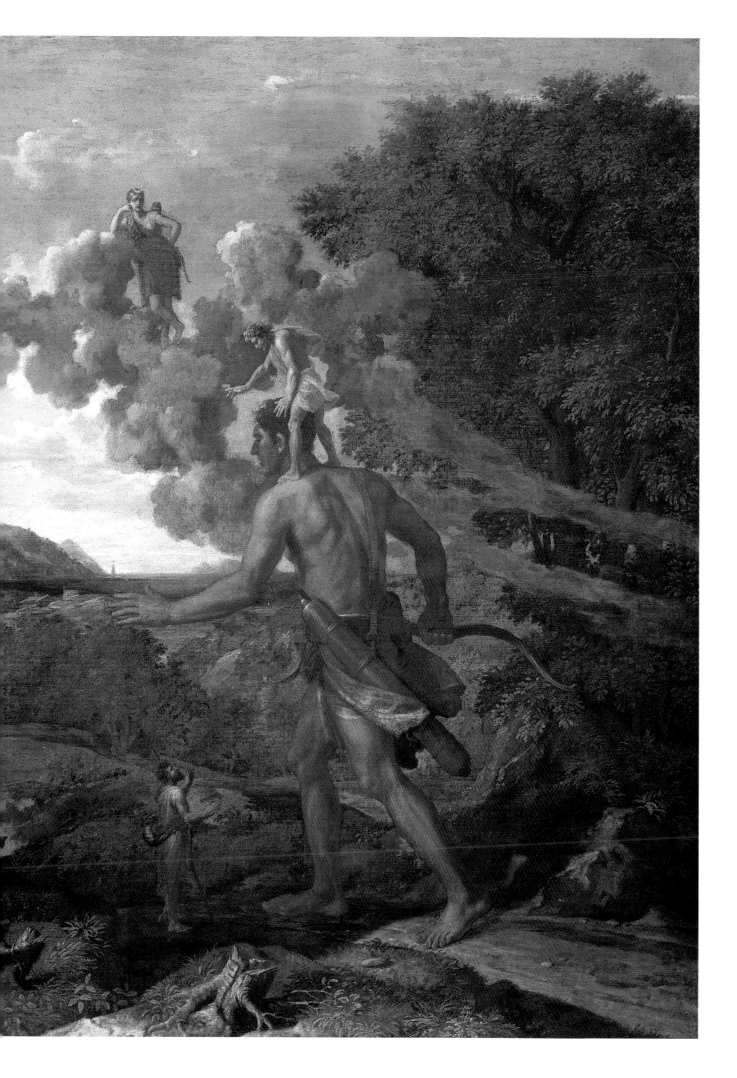

At length he lost the power of using his limbs, and then she shut him up in his chamber, whence his feeble voice might at times be heard. Finally she turned him into a grasshopper.

Memnon was the son of Aurora and Tithonus. He was king of the Aethiopians and dwelt in the extreme east, on the shore of Ocean. He came with his warriors to assist the kindred of his father in the war of Troy. King Priam received him with great honors and listened with admiration to his narrative of the wonders of the ocean shore.

The very day after his arrival, Memnon, impatient of repose, led his troops to the field. Antilochus, the brave son of Nestor, fell by his hand, and the Greeks were put to flight, when Achilles appeared and restored the battle. A long and doubtful contest ensued between him and the son of Aurora; at length, victory declared for Achilles, Memnon fell, and the Trojans fled in dismay.

Aurora, who from her station in the sky had viewed with apprehension the danger of her son, when she saw him fall directed his brothers the Winds to convey his body to the banks of the River Esepus in Paphlagonia. In the evening, Aurora came, accompanied by the Hours and the Pleiads, and wept and lamented over her son. Night, in sympathy with her grief, spread the heaven with clouds; all nature mourned for the offspring of the Dawn. The Aethiopians raised his tomb on the banks of the stream in the grove of the nymphs, and Jupiter caused the sparks and cinders of his funeral pile to be turned into birds, which, dividing into two flocks, fought over the pile till they fell into the flame. Every year at the anniversary of his death they return and celebrate his obsequies in like manner. Aurora remains inconsolable for the loss of her son. Her tears still flow and may be seen at early morning in the form of dewdrops on the grass.

ACIS AND GALATEA

Scylla was a fair virgin of Sicily, a favorite of the sea nymphs. She had many suitors, but repelled them all, and would go to the grotto of Galatea and tell her how she was persecuted. One day the goddess, while Scylla dressed her hair, listened to the story and then replied, "Yet, maiden, your persecutors are of the not ungentle race of men, whom if you will you can repel; but I, the daughter of Nereus, and protected by such a band of sisters, found no escape from the passion of the Cyclops but in the depths of the sea;" and tears stopped her utterance. When the pitying maiden had wiped them away with her delicate finger, and soothed the goddess, "Tell me, dearest," said she, "the cause of your grief." Galatea then said, "Acis was the son of Faunus and a Naiad. His father and mother loved him dearly, but their love was not equal to mine. For the beautiful youth attached himself to me alone, and he was just sixteen years old, the down just beginning to darken his cheeks. As much as I sought his society, so much did the Cyclops seek mine; and if you ask me whether my love for Acis or my hatred of Polyphemus was the stronger, I cannot tell you; they were in equal measure. O Venus, how great is thy power! This fierce giant, the terror of the woods, whom no hapless stranger escaped unharmed, who defied even Jove himself, learned to feel what love was and, touched with a passion for me, forgot his flocks and his well-stored caverns. Then for the first time he began to take some care of his appearance and to try to make himself agreeable; he harrowed those coarse locks of his with a comb, and mowed his beard with a sickle, looked at his harsh features in the water and composed his countenance. His love of slaughter, his fierceness and thirst of blood, prevailed no more, and ships that touched at his island went away in safety. He paced up and down the seashore, imprinting huge tracks with his heavy tread, and, when weary, lay tranquilly in his cave.

"There is a cliff that projects into the sea, which washes it on either side. Thither one day the huge Cyclops ascended and sat down while his flocks spread themselves around. Laying down his staff, which would have served for a mast to hold a vessel's sail, and taking his instrument compacted of numerous pipes, he made the hills and the waters echo the music of his song. I lay hid under a rock by the side of my beloved Acis and listened to the distant strain. It was full of extravagant praises of my beauty, mingled with passionate reproaches of my coldness and cruelty.

The Triumph of Galatea, RAPHAEL (1483–1520) ➤
The love song of Polyphemus for the sea nymph Galatea was a traditional theme of pastoral poets—for Polyphemus himself was a shepherd. Raphael shows Galatea escaping from the Cyclops's unwelcome courtship to the sea, where he cannot reach her.

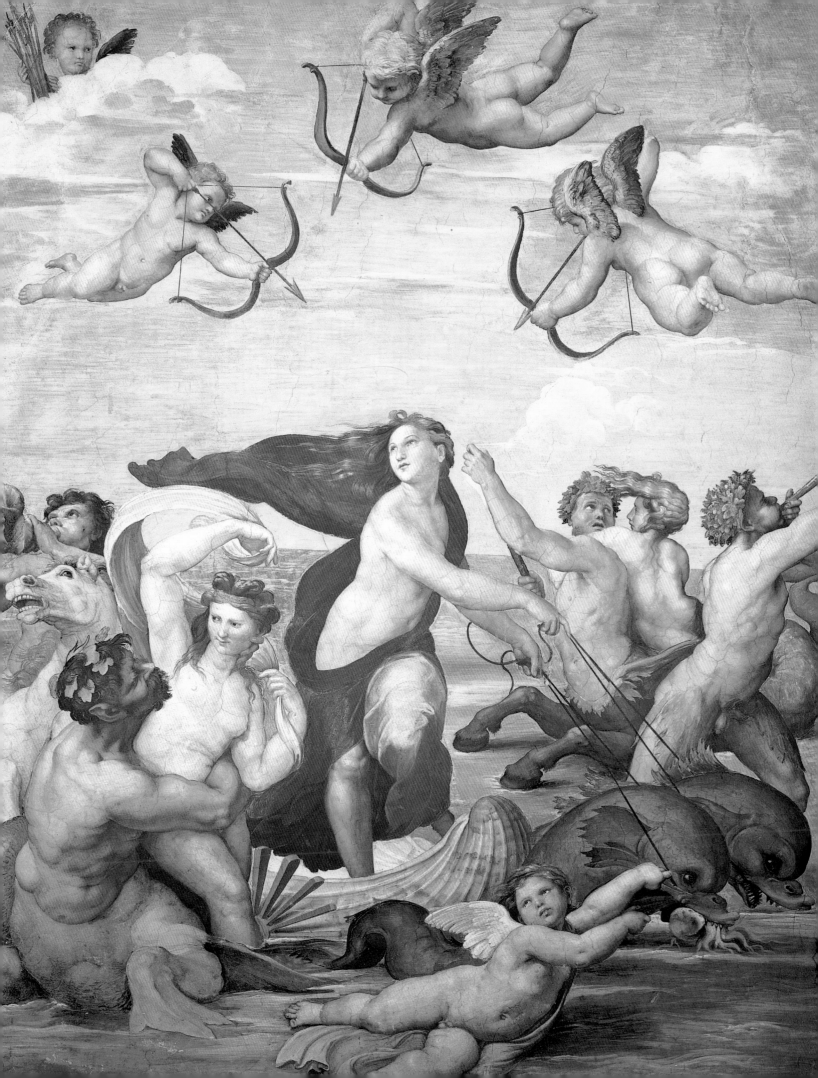

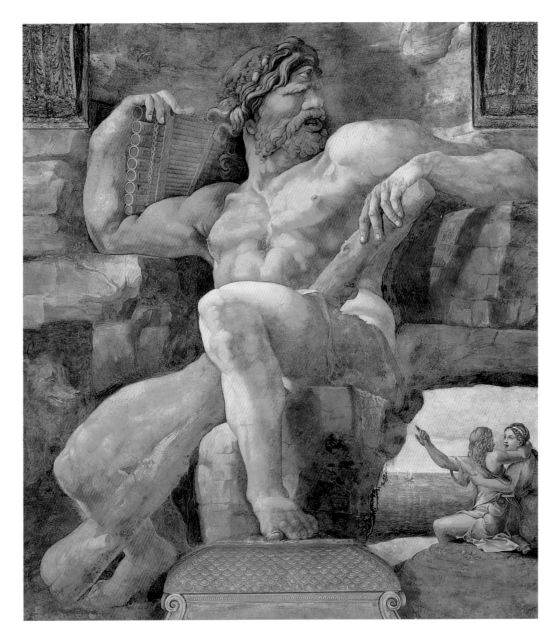

▲ Polyphemus, Acis and Galatea, GIULIO ROMANO (1492/9–1546)
Polyphemus brandishes his shepherd's pipes, but as his face and cudgel make clear,
he is an uncivilized monster who later will be tricked and blinded by Ulysses.

"When he had finished, he rose up and, like a raging bull that cannot stand still, wandered off into the woods. Acis and I thought no more of him, till on a sudden he came to a spot which gave him a view of us as we sat. 'I see you,' he exclaimed, 'and I will make this the last of your love meetings.' His voice was a roar such as an angry Cyclops alone could utter. Aetna trembled at the sound. I, overcome with terror, plunged into the water. Acis turned and fled, crying, 'Save me, Galatea, save me, my parents!' The Cyclops pursued him, and tearing a rock from the side of the mountain, hurled it at him.

Though only a corner of it touched him, it overwhelmed him.

"All that Fate left in my power I did for Acis. I endowed him with the honors of his grandfather the river god. The purple blood flowed out from under the rock, but by degrees grew paler and looked like the stream of a river rendered turbid by rains, and in time it became clear. The rock cleaved open, and the water, as it gushed from the chasm, uttered a pleasing murmur."

Thus Acis was changed into a river, and the river retains the name of Acis.

CHAPTER 26

THE TROJAN WAR · THE ILIAD

MINERVA WAS THE GODDESS OF WISDOM, BUT ON ONE occasion she did a very foolish thing: she entered into competition with Juno and Venus for the prize of beauty. It happened thus: At the nuptials of Peleus and Thetis all the gods were invited with the exception of Eris, or Discord. Enraged at her exclusion, the goddess threw a golden apple among the guests, with the inscription, "For the fairest." Thereupon Juno, Venus, and Minerva each claimed the apple. Jupiter, not willing to decide in so delicate a matter, sent the goddesses to Mount Ida, where the beautiful shepherd Paris was tending his flocks, and to him was committed the decision. The goddesses accordingly appeared before him. Juno promised him power and riches, Minerva glory and renown in war, and Venus the fairest of women for his wife, each attempting to bias his decision in her own favor. Paris decided in favor of Venus and gave her the golden apple, thus making the two other goddesses his enemies. Under the protection of Venus,

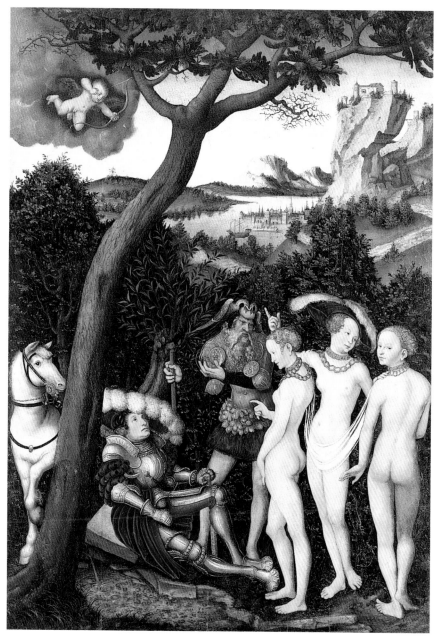

▲ The Judgment of Paris, LUCAS CRANACH THE ELDER (1472–1553)
Perceptions of female beauty vary from age to age, but the principle remains: The Judgment of Paris is a prime example of the "male gaze." The eventual prize was Helen—whose face was said to have launched a thousand ships.

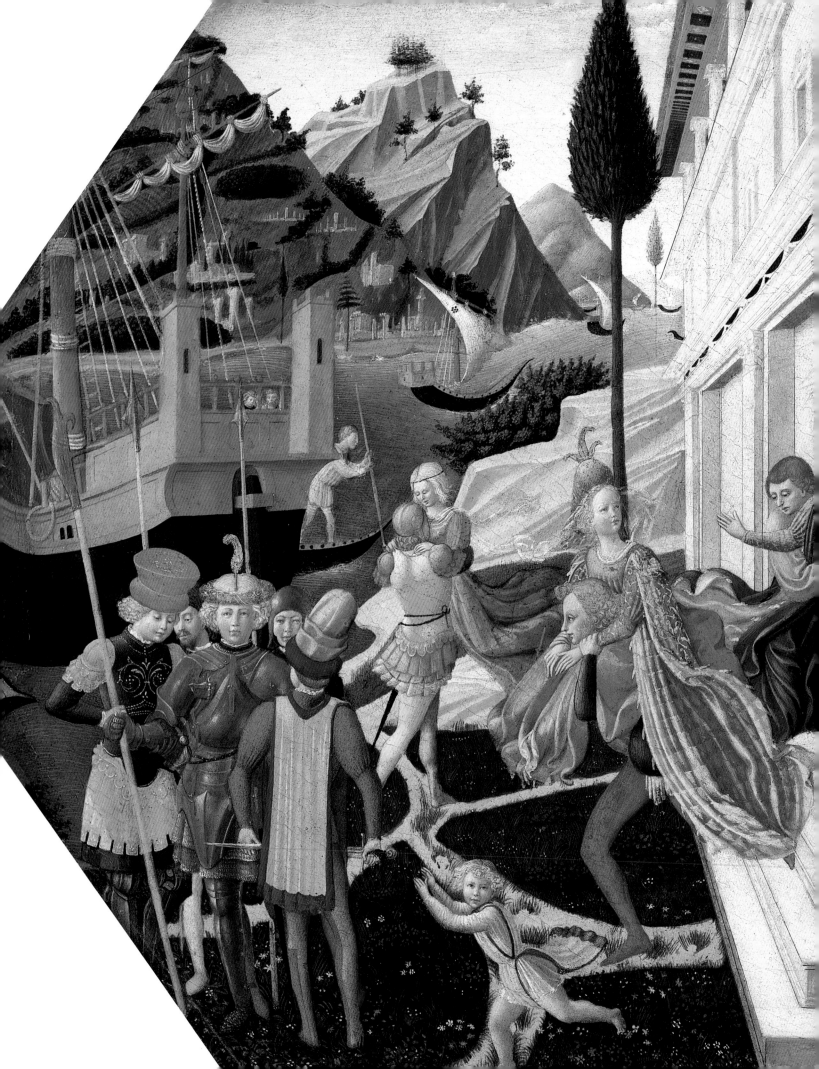

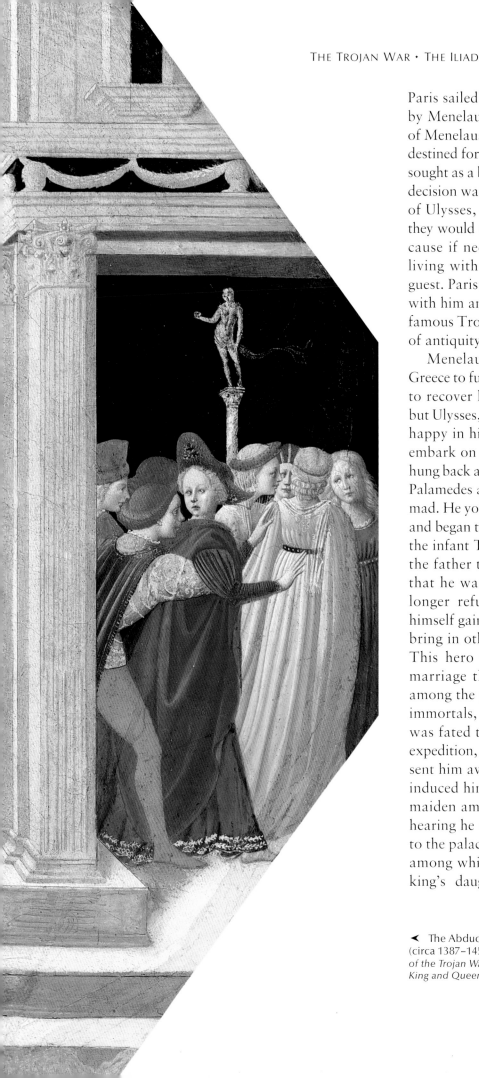

Paris sailed to Greece, and was hospitably received by Menelaus, King of Sparta. Now Helen, the wife of Menelaus, was the very woman whom Venus had destined for Paris, the fairest of her sex. She had been sought as a bride by numerous suitors, and before her decision was made known, they all, at the suggestion of Ulysses, one of their number, took an oath that they would defend her from all injury and avenge her cause if necessary. She chose Menelaus, and was living with him happily when Paris became their guest. Paris, aided by Venus, persuaded her to elope with him and carried her to Troy, whence arose the famous Trojan war, the theme of the greatest poems of antiquity, those of Homer and Virgil.

Menelaus called upon his brother chieftains of Greece to fulfil their pledge and join him in his efforts to recover his wife. They generally came forward, but Ulysses, who had married Penelope and was very happy in his wife and child, had no disposition to embark on such a troublesome affair. He therefore hung back and Palamedes was sent to urge him. When Palamedes arrived at Ithaca, Ulysses pretended to be mad. He yoked an ass and an ox together to the plow and began to sow salt. Palamedes, to try him, placed the infant Telemachus before the plow, whereupon the father turned the plow aside, showing plainly that he was no madman, and after that could no longer refuse to fulfill his promise. Being now himself gained for the undertaking he lent his aid to bring in other reluctant chiefs, especially Achilles. This hero was the son of that Thetis at whose marriage the apple of Discord had been thrown among the goddesses. Thetis was herself one of the immortals, a sea nymph, and knowing that her son was fated to perish before Troy if he went on the expedition, she endeavored to prevent his going. She sent him away to the court of King Lycomedes and induced him to conceal himself in the disguise of a maiden among the daughters of the king. Ulysses, hearing he was there, went disguised as a merchant to the palace and offered for sale female ornaments, among which he had placed some arms. While the king's daughters were engrossed with the other

◀ The Abduction of Helen by Paris, FOLLOWER OF FRA ANGELICO (circa 1387–1455): *The artist focuses on the direct cause of the Trojan War—the moment when Paris, son of Priam and Hecuba, King and Queen of Troy, carries off Helen of Sparta.*

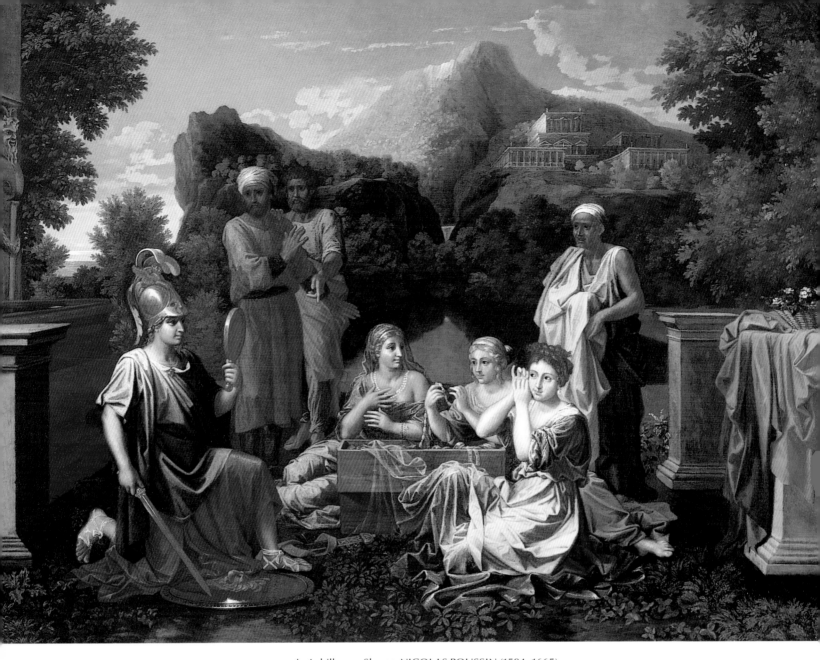

▲ Achilles on Skyros, NICOLAS POUSSIN (1594–1665)
Poussin portrays the daughers of Lycomedes as three Graces, festooning themselves with jewels from the casket. Achilles, dressed as a woman, chooses weapons instead, revealing his true identity. Ulysses watches from the background.

contents of the merchant's pack, Achilles handled the weapons and thereby betrayed himself to the keen eye of Ulysses, who found no great difficulty in persuading him to disregard his mother's prudent counsels and join his countrymen in the war.

Priam was king of Troy, and Paris, the shepherd and seducer of Helen, was his son. Paris had been brought up in obscurity, because there were certain ominous forebodings connected with him from his infancy that he would be the ruin of the state. These forebodings seemed at length likely to be realized, for the Grecian armament now in preparation was the greatest that had ever been fitted out. Agamemnon, King of Mycenae and brother of the injured Menelaus, was chosen commander-in-chief. Achilles

was their most illustrious warrior. After him ranked Ajax, gigantic in size and of great courage, but dull of intellect; Diomede, second only to Achilles in all the qualities of the hero; Ulysses, famous for his sagacity; and Nestor, the oldest of the Grecian chiefs and one to whom they all looked up for counsel. But Troy was no feeble enemy. Priam the king was now old, but he had been a wise prince and had strengthened his state by good government at home and numerous alliances with his neighbors. But the principal stay and support of his throne was his son Hector, one of the noblest characters painted by heathen antiquity. He felt, from the first, a presentiment of the fall of his country, but still persevered in his heroic resistance, yet by no means justified the wrong that brought this danger upon her. He was united in marriage with Andromache, and as a husband and father his character was not less admirable than as a warrior. The principal leaders on the side of the Trojans, besides Hector, were Aeneas and Deiphobus, Glaucus and Sarpedon.

After two years of preparation the Greek fleet and army assembled in the port of Aulis in Baeotia. Here Agamemnon in hunting killed a stag that was sacred to Diana, and the goddess in return visited the army with pestilence and produced a calm that prevented the ships from leaving the port. Calchas the soothsayer thereupon announced that the wrath of the virgin goddess could only be appeased by the sacrifice of a virgin on her altar, and that none other but the daughter of the offender would be acceptable. Agamemnon, however reluctant, yielded his consent, and the maiden Iphigenia was sent for under the pretence that she was to be married to Achilles. When she was about to be sacrificed the goddess relented and snatched her away, leaving a hind in her place, and Iphigenia, enveloped in a cloud, was carried to Tauris, where Diana made her priestess of her temple.

The wind now proving fair, the fleet made sail and brought the forces to the coast of Troy. The Trojans came to oppose their landing, and at the first onset Protesilaus fell by the hand of Hector. Protesilaus had left at home his wife Laodamia, who was most tenderly attached to him. When the news of his death reached her, she implored the gods to be allowed to converse with him only three hours. The request was granted. Mercury led Protesilaus back to the upper world, and when he died a second time, Laodamia died with him. There was a story that the nymphs planted elm trees round his grave which grew very well till they were high enough to command a view of Troy, and then withered away, while fresh branches sprang from the roots.

THE ILIAD

The war continued without decisive results for nine years. Then an event occurred which seemed likely to be fatal to the cause of the Greeks, and that was a quarrel between Achilles and Agamemnon. It is at this point that the great poem of Homer, the *Iliad*, begins. The Greeks, though unsuccessful against Troy, had taken the neighboring and allied cities, and in the division of the spoil a female captive, by name Chryseis, daughter of Chryses, priest of Apollo, had fallen to the share of Agamemnon. Chryses came bearing the sacred emblems of his office and begged the release of his daughter. Agamemnon refused. Thereupon Chryses implored Apollo to afflict the Greeks till they should be forced to yield their prey. Apollo granted the prayer of his priest and sent pestilence into the Grecian camp. Then a council was called to deliberate how to allay the wrath of the gods and avert the plague. Achilles boldly charged their misfortunes upon Agamemnon as caused by his withholding Chryseis. Agamemnon, enraged, consented to relinquish his captive, but demanded that Achilles should yield to him in her stead Briseis, a maiden who had fallen to Achilles' share in the division of the spoil. Achilles submitted but forthwith declared that he would take no further part in the war. He withdrew his forces from the general camp and openly avowed his intention of returning home to Greece.

The gods and goddesses interested themselves as much in this famous war as the parties themselves. It was well known to them that fate had decreed that Troy should fall, at last, if her enemies should persevere and not voluntarily abandon the enterprise. Yet there was room enough left for chance to excite by turns the hopes and fears of the powers above who took part with either side. Juno and Minerva, in consequence of the slight put upon their charms by Paris, were hostile to the Trojans; Venus for the opposite cause favored them. Venus enlisted her admirer Mars on the same side, but Neptune favored the Greeks. Apollo was neutral, sometimes taking one side, sometimes the other, and Jove himself, though he loved the good King Priam, yet exercised a degree of impartiality; not, however, without exceptions.

Thetis, the mother of Achilles, warmly resented the injury done to her son. She repaired immediately to Jove's palace and besought him to make the Greeks repent of their injustice to Achilles by granting success to the Trojan arms. Jupiter consented; and in the battle that ensued the Trojans were completely successful. The Greeks were driven from the field and took refuge in their ships.

Ulysses Returns Chryseis to Her Father, CLAUDE (1604/5–1682) ➤
The tale of Ulysses returning Chryseis to her father provided a perfect subject for Claude Lorrain, who delighted in painting ships at anchor in some stately port. Ulysses was known as "the cunning one" and his resourcefulness is well demonstrated in the story.

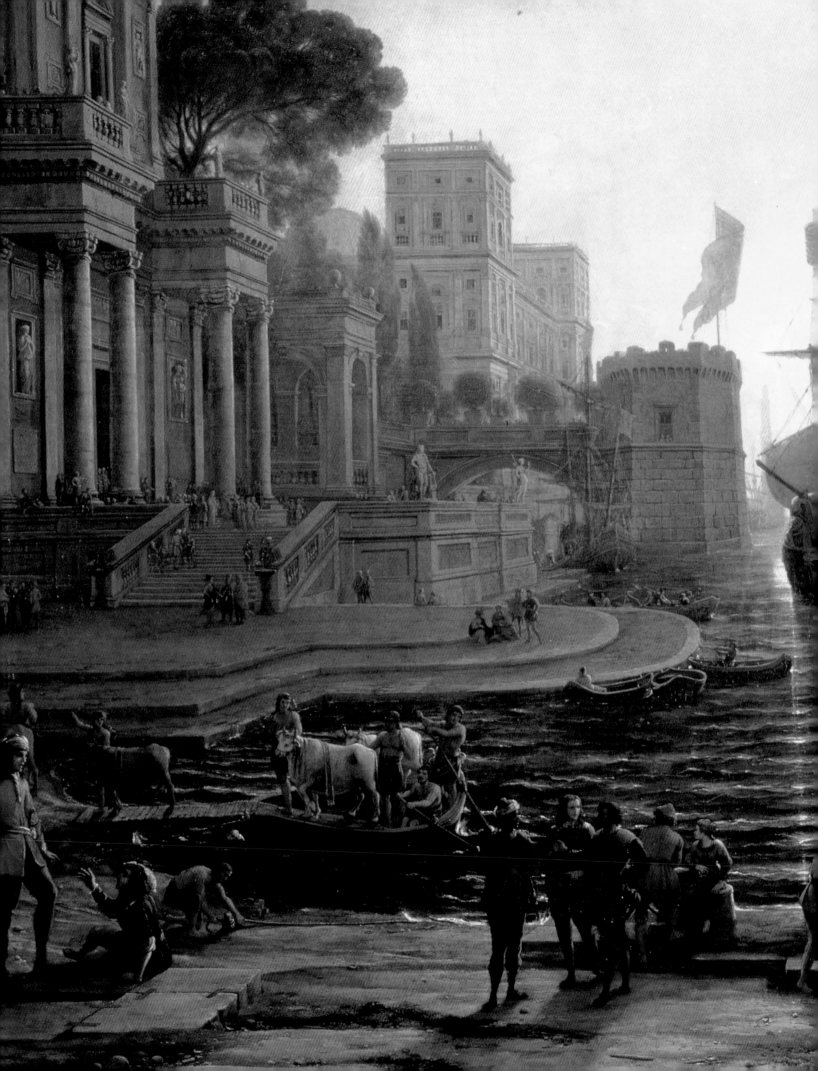

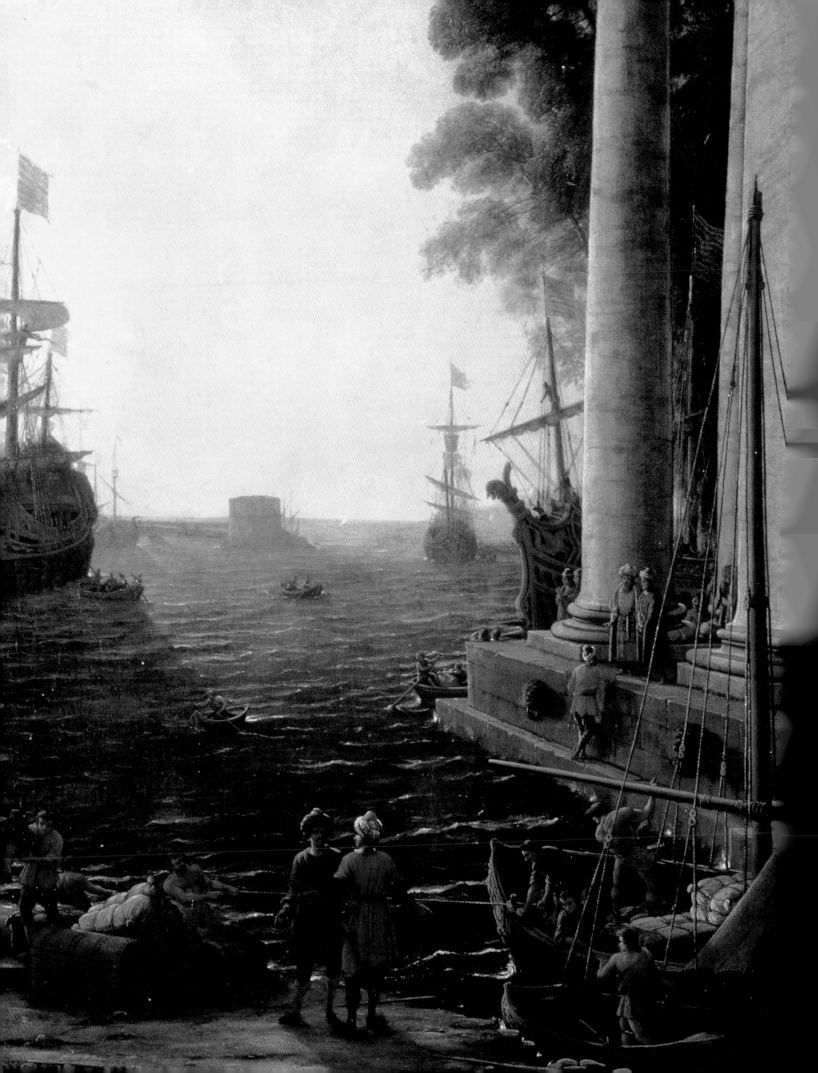

Then Agamemnon called a council of his wisest and bravest chiefs. Nestor advised that an embassy should be sent to Achilles to persuade him to return to the field; that Agamemnon should yield the maiden, the cause of the dispute, with ample gifts to atone for the wrong he had done. Agamemnon consented, and Ulysses, Ajax, and Phoenix were sent to carry to Achilles the penitent message. They performed that duty, but Achilles was deaf to their entreaties. He positively refused to return to the field and persisted in his resolution to embark for Greece without delay.

The Greeks had constructed a rampart around their ships, and now, instead of besieging Troy, they were in a manner besieged themselves, within their rampart. The next day after the unsuccessful embassy to Achilles, a battle was fought, and the Trojans, favored by Jove, were successful, and succeeded in forcing a passage through the Grecian rampart, and were about to set fire to the ships. Neptune, seeing the Greeks so pressed, came to their rescue. He appeared in the form of Calchas the prophet, encoraged the warriors with his shouts, and appealed to each individually till he raised their ardor to such a pitch that they forced the Trojans to give way. Ajax performed prodigies of valor and at length encountered Hector. Ajax shouted defiance, to which Hector replied, and hurled his lance at the huge warrior. It was well aimed, and struck Ajax where the belts that bore his sword and shield crossed each other on the breast. The double guard prevented its penetrating, and it fell harmless. Then Ajax, seizing a huge stone, one of those that served to prop the ships, hurled it at Hector. It struck him in the neck and stretched him on the plain. His followers instantly seized him and bore him off stunned and wounded.

While Neptune was thus aiding the Greeks and driving back the Trojans, Jupiter saw nothing of what was going on, for his attention had been drawn from the field by the wiles of Juno. That goddess had arrayed herself in all her charms, and to crown all had borrowed of Venus her girdle called Cestus, which had the effect to heighten the wearer's charms to such a degree that they were quite irresistible. So prepared, Juno went to join her husband, who sat on Olympus watching the battle. When he beheld her she looked so charming that the fondness of his early love

revived, and, forgetting the contending armies and all other affairs of state, he thought only of her and let the battle go as it would.

But this absorption did not continue long, and when, upon turning his eyes downward, he beheld Hector stretched on the plain almost lifeless from pain and bruises, he dismissed Juno in a rage, commanding her to send Iris and Apollo to him. When Iris came he sent her with a stern message to Neptune, ordering him instantly to quit the field. Apollo was despatched to heal Hector's bruises and to inspirit his heart. These orders were obeyed with such speed that while the battle still raged, Hector returned to the field and Neptune betook himself to his own dominions.

An arrow from Paris's bow wounded Machaon, son of Aesculapius, who inherited his father's art of healing, and was therefore of great value to the Greeks as their surgeon, besides being one of their bravest warriors. Nestor took Machaon in his chariot and conveyed him from the field. As they passed the ships of Achilles, that hero, looking out over the field, saw the chariot of Nestor and recognized the old chief, but could not discern who the wounded chief was. So calling Patroclus, his companion and dearest friend, he sent him to Nestor's tent to enquire.

Patroclus, arriving at Nestor's tent, saw Machaon wounded, and having told the cause of his coming, would have hastened away, but Nestor detained him, to tell him the extent of the Grecian calamities. He reminded him also how, at the time of departing for Troy, Achilles and himself had been charged by their respective fathers with different advice; Achilles to aspire to the highest pitch of glory, Patroclus, as the elder, to keep watch over his friend, and to guide his inexperience. "Now," said Nestor, "is the time for such influence. If the gods so please, thou mayest win him back to the common cause; but if not, let him at least send his soldiers to the field, and come thou Patroclus clad in his armor, and perhaps the very sight of it may drive back the Trojans."

Patroclus was strongly moved with this address, and hastened back to Achilles, revolving in his mind all he had seen and heard. He told the prince the sad condition of affairs at the camp of their late associates; Diomede, Ulysses, Agamemnon, Machaon, all wounded, the rampart broken down, the enemy among the ships preparing to burn them, and thus to cut off all means of return to Greece.

While they spoke, the flames burst forth from one of the ships. Achilles, at the sight, relented so far as to grant Patroclus his request to lead the Myrmidons (for so were Achilles' soldiers called) to the field, and to lend him his armor that he might thereby strike more terror into the minds of the Trojans. Without delay the soldiers were marshaled; Patroclus put on the radiant armor, and mounted the chariot of Achilles, and led forth the men ardent for battle. But before he went, Achilles strictly charged him that he should be content with repelling the foe. "Seek not," said he, "to press the Trojans without me, lest thou add still more to the disgrace already mine." Then, exhorting the troops to do their best, he dismissed them full of ardor to the fight.

Patroclus and his Myrmidons at once plunged into the contest where it raged hottest; at the sight of which the joyful Grecians shouted and the ships echoed the acclaim. The Trojans, at the sight of the well-known armor, struck with terror, looked everywhere for refuge. First, those who had got possession of the ship and set it on fire left and allowed the Grecians to retake it and extinguish the flames. Then the rest of the Trojans fled in dismay. Ajax, Menelaus, and the two sons of Nestor performed prodigies of valor. Hector was forced to turn his horses' heads and retire from the enclosure, leaving his men entangled in the fosse to escape as they could. Patroclus drove them before him, slaying many, none daring to make a stand against him.

At last Sarpedon, son of Jove, ventured to oppose himself in fight to Patroclus. Jupiter looked down upon him and would have snatched him from the fate that awaited him, but Juno hinted that if he did so it would induce all others of the inhabitants of heaven to interpose in like manner whenever any of their offspring were endangered; to which reason Jove yielded. Sarpedon threw his spear but missed Patroclus, but Patroclus threw his with better success. It pierced Sarpedon's breast, and he fell and, calling to his friends to save his body from the foe, expired. Then a furious contest arose for the possession of the corpse. The Greeks succeeded and stripped Sarpedon of his armor; but Jove would not allow the remains of his son to be dishonored, and by his command Apollo snatched from the midst of the combatants the body of Sarpedon and committed it to the care of the twin brothers Death

and Sleep, by whom it was transported to Lycia, the native land of Sarpedon, where it received due funeral rites.

Thus far Patroclus had succeeded to his utmost wish in repelling the Trojans and relieving his countrymen, but now came a change of fortune. Hector, borne in his chariot, confronted him. Patroclus threw a vast stone at Hector, which missed its aim, but smote Cebriones, the charioteer, and knocked him from the car. Hector leaped from the chariot to rescue his friend, and Patroclus also descended to complete his victory. Thus the two heroes met face to face. At this decisive moment the poet, as if reluctant to give Hector the glory, records that Phoebus took part against Patroclus. He struck the helmet from his head and the lance from his hand. At the same moment an obscure Trojan wounded him in the back, and Hector pressing forward pierced him with his spear. He fell mortally wounded.

Then arose a tremendous conflict for the body of Patroclus, but his armor was at once taken possession of by Hector, who, retiring a short distance, divested himself of his own armor and put on that of Achilles, then returned to the fight. Ajax and Menelaus defended the body, and Hector and his bravest warriors struggled to capture it. The battle raged with equal fortunes, when Jove enveloped the whole face of heaven with a dark cloud. The lightning flashed, the thunder roared, and Ajax, looking around for someone whom he might despatch to Achilles to tell him of the death of his friend and of the imminent danger that his remains would fall into the hands of the enemy, could see no suitable messenger. He prayed to Jupiter.

Jupiter heard the prayer and dispersed the clouds. Then Ajax sent Antilochus to Achilles with the intelligence of Patroclus's death and of the conflict raging for his remains. The Greeks at last succeeded in bearing off the body to the ships, closely pursued by Hector and Aeneas and the rest of the Trojans.

Achilles heard the fate of his friend with such distress that Antilochus feared for a while that he would destroy himself. His groans reached the ears of his mother Thetis, far down in the deeps of ocean where she abode, and she hastened to him to enquire the cause. She found him overwhelmed with self-reproach that he had indulged his resentment so far and suffered his friend to fall a victim to it.

But his only consolation was the hope of revenge. He would fly instantly in search of Hector. But his mother reminded him that he was now without armor and promised him, if he would but wait till the morrow, she would procure for him a suit of armor from Vulcan more than equal to that he had lost. He consented, and Thetis immediately repaired to Vulcan's palace. She found him busy at his forge making tripods for his own use, so artfully constructed that they moved forward of their own accord when wanted, and retired again when dismissed. On hearing the request of Thetis, Vulcan immediately laid aside his work and hastened to comply with her wishes. He fabricated a splendid suit of armor for Achilles, first a shield adorned with elaborate devices, then a helmet crested with gold, then a corselet and greaves of impenetrable temper, all perfectly adapted to his form and of consummate workmanship. It was all done in one night, and Thetis, receiving it, descended with it to earth and laid it down at Achilles' feet at the dawn of day.

The first glow of pleasure that Achilles had felt since the death of Patroclus was at the sight of this splendid armor. And now arrayed in it, he went forth into the camp calling all the chiefs to council. When they were all assembled he addressed them. Renouncing his displeasure against Agamemnon and bitterly lamenting the miseries that had resulted from it, he called on them to proceed at once to the field. Agamemnon made a suitable reply, laying all the blame on Ate, the goddess of discord, and thereupon complete reconcilement took place between the heroes.

Then Achilles went forth to battle inspired with a rage and thirst for vengeance that made him irresistible. The bravest warriors fled before him or fell by his lance. Hector, cautioned by Apollo, kept aloof; but the god, assuming the form of one of Priam's sons, Lycaon, urged Aeneas to encounter the terrible warrior. Aeneas, though he felt himself unequal, did not decline the combat. He hurled his spear with all his force against the shield, the work of Vulcan. It was formed of five metal plates; two were of brass, two of tin, and one of gold. The spear pierced two thicknesses, but was stopped in the third. Achilles threw his with better success. It pierced through the shield of Aeneas, but glanced near his shoulder and made no wound. Then Aeneas

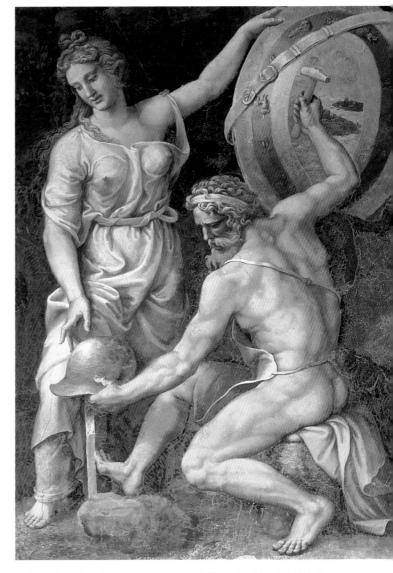

▲ Vulcan Forging the Armor of Achilles, GIULIO ROMANO AND WORKSHOP (1492/9–1546): *Vulcan's power as master of metals is heightened here by Romano's sculptural sense of form. Later, after Achilles had been slain, possession of the armor was hotly disputed by Ajax and Ulysses.*

seized a stone, such as two men of modern times could hardly lift, and was about to throw it, and Achilles, with sword drawn, was about to rush upon him, when Neptune, who looked out upon the contest, moved with pity for Aeneas, who he saw would surely fall a victim if not speedily rescued, spread a cloud between the combatants, and lifting Aeneas from the ground, bore him over the heads of warriors and steeds to the rear of the battle. Achilles, when the mist cleared away, looked round in vain for his adversary, and acknowledging the prodigy, turned his arms against other champions. But none dared stand before him, and Priam, looking down from his city walls, beheld his whole army in full flight toward the city. He gave command to open wide the gates to receive the fugitives and to shut them as soon as the Trojans should have passed, lest the enemy should enter likewise. But Achilles was so close in pursuit that that would have been impossible if Apollo had not, in the form of Agenor, Priam's son, encountered Achilles for a while, then turned to fly, and taken the way apart from the city. Achilles pursued and had chased his supposed victim far from the walls, when Apollo disclosed himself, and Achilles, perceiving how he had been deluded, gave up the chase.

But when the rest had escaped into the town, Hector stood without, determined to await the combat. His old father called to him from the walls and begged him to retire nor tempt the encounter. His mother, Hecuba, also besought him to the same effect, but all in vain. "How can I," said he to himself, "by whose command the people went to this day's contest, where so many have fallen, seek safety for myself against a single foe? But what if I offer him to yield up Helen and all her treasures and ample of our own beside? Ah no! it is too late. He would not even hear me through, but slay me while I spoke." While he thus ruminated, Achilles approached, terrible as Mars, his armor flashing lightning as he moved. At that sight Hector's heart failed him and he fled. Achilles swiftly pursued. They ran, still keeping near the walls, till they had thrice encircled the city. As often as Hector approached the walls Achilles intercepted him and forced him to keep out in a wider circle. But Apollo sustained Hector's strength and would not let him sink in weariness. Then Pallas, assuming the form of Deiphobus, Hector's bravest brother, appeared suddenly at his side. Hector saw him with delight and, thus strengthened, stopped his flight and turned to meet Achilles. Hector threw his spear, which struck the shield of Achilles and bounded back. He turned to receive another from the hand of Deiphobus, but Deiphobus was gone. Then Hector understood his doom and said, "Alas! It is plain this is my hour to die! I thought Deiphobus at hand, but Pallas deceived me, and he is still in Troy. But I will not fall inglorious." So saying he drew his falchion from his side and rushed at once to combat. Achilles, secured behind his shield, waited the approach of Hector. When he came within reach of his spear, Achilles, choosing with his eye a vulnerable part where the armor leaves the neck uncovered, aimed his spear at that part, and Hector fell, death-wounded, and feebly said, "Spare my body! Let my parents ransom it, and let me receive funeral rites from the sons and daughters of Troy." To which Achilles replied, "Dog, name not ransom nor pity to me, on whom you have brought such dire distress. No! Trust me, nought shall save thy carcass from the dogs. Though twenty ransoms and thy weight in gold were offered, I would refuse it all."

So saying he stripped the body of its armor and, fastening cords to the feet, tied them behind his chariot, leaving the body to trail along the ground. Then, mounting the chariot, he lashed the steeds and so dragged the body to and fro before the city. What words can tell the grief of King Priam and Queen Hecuba at this sight! His people could scarce restrain the old king from rushing forth. He threw himself in the dust and besought them each by name to give him way. Hecuba's distress was not less violent. The citizens stood round them weeping. The sound of the mourning reached the ears of Andromache, the wife of Hector, as she sat among her maidens at work, and anticipating evil she went forth to the wall. When she saw the sight there presented, she would have thrown herself headlong from the wall, but fainted and fell into the arms of her maidens. Recovering, she bewailed her fate, picturing to herself her country ruined, herself a captive, and her son dependent for his bread on the charity of strangers.

When Achilles and the Greeks had taken their revenge on the killer of Patroclus, they busied themselves in paying due funeral rites to their friend. A pile was erected, and the body burned with due solemnity; and then ensued games of strength and skill, chariot races, wrestling, boxing, and archery. Then the chiefs sat down to the funeral banquet and after that retired to rest. But Achilles neither partook of the feast nor of sleep. The recollection of his lost friend kept him awake, remembering their companionship in toil and dangers, in battle or on the perilous deep. Before the earliest dawn he left his tent, and joining to his chariot his swift steeds, he fastened Hector's body to be dragged behind. Twice he dragged him round the tomb of Patroclus, leaving him at length stretched in the dust. But Apollo would not permit the body to be torn or disfigured with all this abuse, but preserved it free from all taint or defilement.

While Achilles indulged his wrath in thus disgracing brave Hector, Jupiter in pity summoned Thetis to his presence. He told her to go to her son and prevail on him to restore the body of Hector to his friends. Then Jupiter sent Iris to King Priam to encourage him to go to Achilles and beg the body of his son. Iris delivered her message, and Priam immediately prepared to obey. He opened his treasuries and took out rich garments and cloths, with ten talents in gold and two splendid tripods and a golden cup of matchless workmanship. Then he called to his sons and bade them draw forth his litter and place in it the various articles designed for a ransom to Achilles. When all was ready, the old king, with a single companion as aged as himself, the herald Idaeus, drove forth from the gates, parting there with Hecuba his queen and all his friends, who lamented him as going to certain death.

But Jupiter, beholding with compassion the venerable king, sent Mercury to be his guide and protector. Mercury, assuming the form of a young warrior, presented himself to the aged couple, and while at the sight of him they hesitated whether to fly or yield, the god approached and, grasping Priam's hand, offered to be their guide to Achilles' tent. Priam gladly accepted his offered service, and he, mounting the carriage, assumed the reins and soon conveyed them to the tent of Achilles. Mercury's wand put to sleep all the guards, and without hindrance he introduced Priam into the tent where Achilles sat, attended by two of his warriors. The old king threw himself at the feet of Achilles and kissed those terrible hands which had destroyed so many of his sons. "Think, oh, Achilles," he said, "of thy own father, full of days like me, and trembling on the gloomy verge of life. Perhaps even now some neighbor chief oppresses him and there is none at hand to succor him in his distress. Yet, doubtless knowing that Achilles lives, he still rejoices, hoping that one day he shall see thy face again. But no comfort cheers me,

▼ The Siege of Troy 1: The Death of Hector, BIAGIO DI ANTONIO (about 1445–1510)
Although for many centuries Homer's Iliad was regarded as a work of imagination, excavations at Troy (located by Heinrich Schliemann in the 19th century) indicate that the city was indeed sacked and set on fire around 1250 BC.

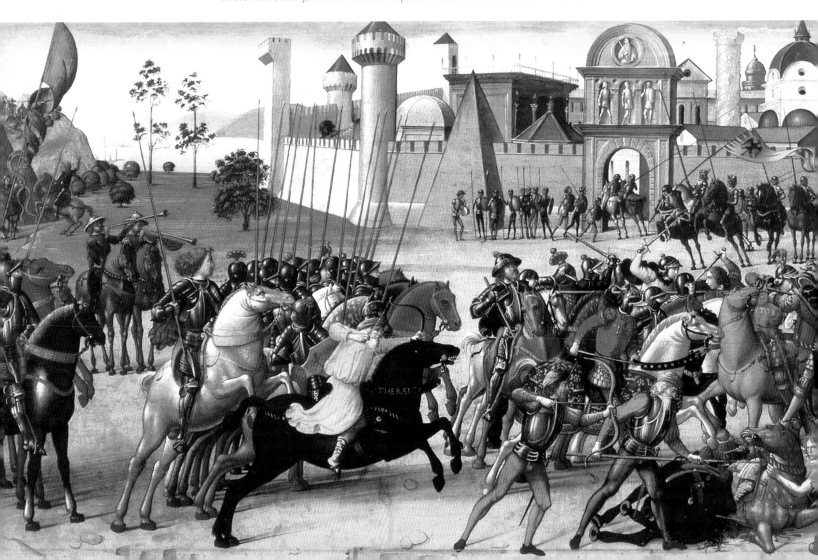

whose bravest sons, so late the flower of Ilium, all have fallen. Yet one I had, one more than all the rest the strength of my age whom, fighting for his country, thou hast slain. I come to redeem his body, bringing inestimable ransom with me. Achilles! Reverence the gods! Recollect thy father! For his sake show compassion to me!" These words moved Achilles and he wept; remembering by turns his absent father and his lost friend. Moved with pity of Priam's silver locks and beard, he raised him from the earth and thus spake: "Priam, I know that thou hast reached this place conducted by some god, for without aid divine no mortal even in his prime of youth had dared the attempt. I grant thy request; moved thereto by the evident will of Jove." So saying he arose, and went forth with his two friends, and unloaded of its charge the litter, leaving two mantles and a robe for the covering of the body, which they placed on the litter, and spread the garments over it, that not unveiled it should be

borne back to Troy. Then Achilles dismissed the old king with his attendants, having first pledged himself to allow a truce of twelve days for the funeral solemnities.

As the litter approached the city and was descried from the walls, the people poured forth to gaze once more on the face of their hero. Foremost of all, the mother and the wife of Hector came and, at the sight of the lifeless body, renewed their lamentations. The people all wept with them, and to the going down of the sun there was no pause or abatement of their grief.

The next day, preparations were made for the funeral solemnities. For nine days the people brought wood and built the pile, and on the tenth they placed the body on the summit and applied the torch; while all Troy thronging forth encompassed the pile. When it had completely burned, they quenched the cinders with wine, collected the bones, and placed them in a golden urn, which they buried in the earth, and reared a pile of stones over the spot.

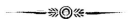

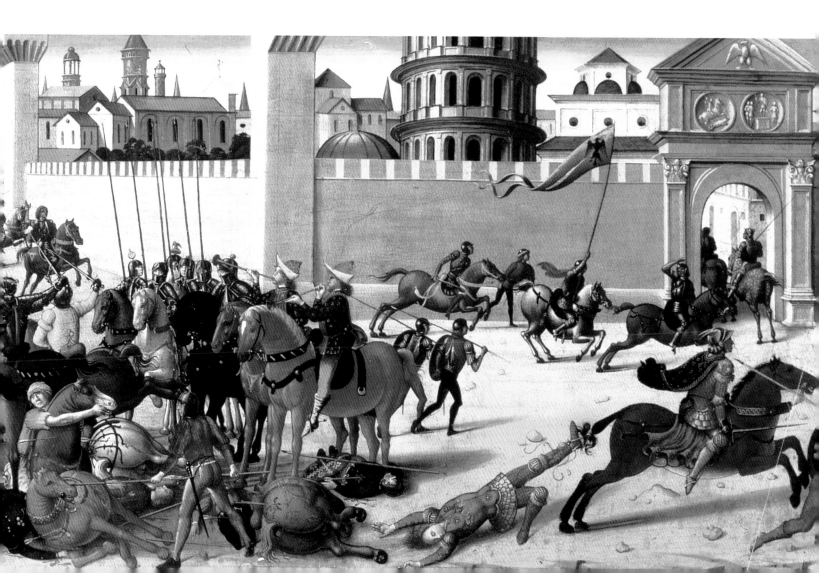

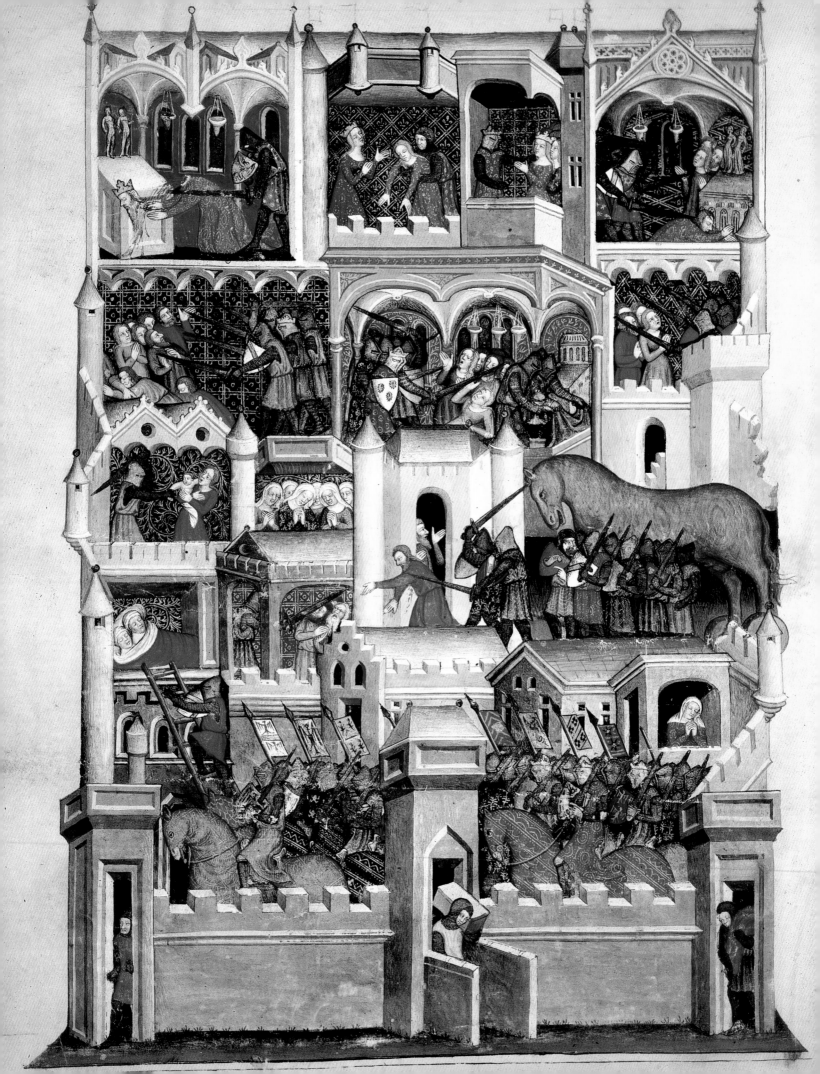

THE FALL OF TROY · MENELAUS AND HELEN · AGAMEMNON, ORESTES, AND ELECTRA

THE STORY OF THE *ILIAD* ENDS WITH THE DEATH of Hector, and it is from the *Odyssey* and later poems that we learn the fate of the other heroes. After the death of Hector, Troy did not immediately fall, but receiving aid from new allies still continued its resistance. One of these allies was Memnon, the Aethiopian prince, whose story we have already told. Another was Penthesilea, Queen of the Amazons, who came with a band of female warriors. All the authorities attest their valor and the fearful effect of their war cry. Penthesilea slew many of the bravest warriors, but was at last slain by Achilles. But when the hero bent over his fallen foe and contemplated her beauty, youth, and valor, he bitterly regretted his victory. Thersites, an insolent brawler and demagogue, ridiculed his grief, and was in consequence slain by the hero.

Achilles by chance had seen Polyxena, daughter of King Priam, perhaps on occasion of the truce that was allowed the Trojans for the burial of Hector. He was captivated with her charms, and to win her in marriage agreed to use his influence with the Greeks to grant peace to Troy. While in the temple of Apollo, negotiating the marriage, Paris discharged at him a poisoned arrow, which, guided by Apollo, wounded Achilles in the heel, the only vulnerable part about him. For Thetis, his mother, had dipped him when an infant in the River Styx, which made every part of him invulnerable except the heel by which she held him.

The body of Achilles so treacherously slain was rescued by Ajax and Ulysses. Thetis directed the Greeks to bestow her son's armor on the hero who of all the survivors should be judged most deserving of it. Ajax and Ulysses were the only claimants; a select number of the other chiefs were appointed to award the prize. It was awarded to Ulysses, thus placing wisdom before valor; whereupon Ajax slew himself. On the spot where his blood sank into the earth a flower sprang up, called the hyacinth, bearing on its leaves the first two letters of the name of Ajax, *Ai*, the Greek for "woe." Thus Ajax is a claimant with the boy Hyacinthus for the honor of giving birth to this flower. There is a species of larkspur that represents the hyacinth of the poets in preserving the memory of this event, the *Delphinium Ajacis*—Ajax's Larkspur.

It was now discovered that Troy could not be taken but by the aid of the arrows of Hercules. They were in possession of Philoctetes, the friend who had been with Hercules at the last and lighted his funeral pyre. Philoctetes had joined the Grecian expedition against Troy, but had accidentally wounded his foot with one of the poisoned arrows, and the smell from his wound proved so offensive that his companions carried him to the isle of Lemnos and left him there. Diomed was now sent to induce him to rejoin the army. He succeeded. Philoctetes was cured of his wound by Machaon, and Paris was the first victim of the fatal arrows. In his distress Paris bethought him of one whom in his prosperity he had forgotten. This was the nymph Oenone, whom he had married when a youth and had abandoned for the fatal beauty Helen. Oenone, remembering the wrongs she had suffered, refused to heal the wound, and Paris went back to Troy and died. Oenone quickly repented and hastened after him with remedies, but came too late, and in her grief hung herself.

There was in Troy a celebrated statue of Minerva called the Palladium. It was said to have fallen from heaven, and the belief was that the city could not be taken so long as this statue remained within it. Ulysses and Diomed entered the city in disguise and succeeded in obtaining the Palladium, which they carried off to the Grecian camp.

But Troy still held out, and the Greeks began to despair of ever subduing it by force, and on advice

◄ Scene from the Trojan War, HISTOIRE ANCIENNE JUSQU'A CESAR (late 14th century): *Following a pattern set by Roman artists (in the so-called* Tabula Iliaca*), medieval artists showed the Trojan epic as a series of friezes, mixing horizontal and bird's-eye perspectives.*

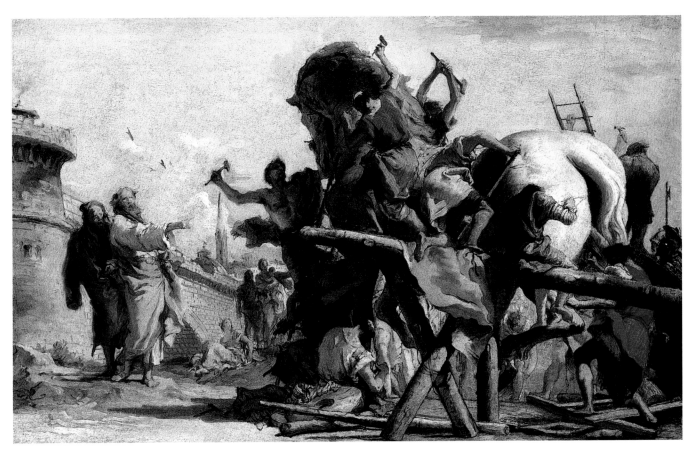

▲ The Building of the Trojan Horse, GIOVANNI DOMENICO TIEPOLO (1727–1804)
For decades the Greeks battled and lay siege outside the walls of Troy, but without success.
In the end, they built the famed wooden horse, and gained entry to the city by this deception.

of Ulysses resolved to resort to stratagem. They pretended to be making preparations to abandon the siege, and a portion of the ships were withdrawn and lay hid behind a neighboring island. The Greeks then constructed an immense wooden horse, which they gave out was intended as a propitiatory offering to Minerva, but in fact was filled with armed men. The remaining Greeks then betook themselves to their ships and sailed away, as if for a final departure. The Trojans, seeing the encampment broken up and the fleet gone, concluded the enemy to have abandoned the siege. The gates were thrown open, and the whole population issued forth, rejoicing at the long-prohibited liberty of passing freely over the scene of the late encampment. The great horse was the chief object of curiosity. All wondered what it could be for. Some recommended to take it into the city as a trophy; others felt afraid of it.

While they hesitate, Laocoön, the priest of Neptune, exclaims, "What madness, citizens, is this! Have you not learned enough of Grecian fraud to be on your guard against it? For my part I fear the Greeks even when they offer gifts." So saying, he threw his lance at the horse's side. It struck, and a hollow sound reverberated like a groan. Then perhaps the people might have taken his advice and destroyed the fatal horse and all its contents; but just at that moment a group of people appeared, dragging forward one who seemed a prisoner and a Greek. Stupefied with terror, he was brought before the chiefs, who reassured him, promising that his life should be spared on condition of his returning true answers to the questions asked him. He informed them that he was a Greek, Sinon by name, and that in consequence of the malice of Ulysses he had been left behind by his countrymen at their departure. With regard to the wooden horse, he told them that it was a propitiatory offering to Minerva, and made so huge for the express purpose of preventing its being carried within the city; for Calchas the prophet had told them that if the Trojans took possession of it, they would assuredly triumph over the Greeks. This language turned the tide of the people's feelings, and they began to think how they might best secure the monstrous horse and the

164

favorable auguries connected with it, when suddenly a prodigy occurred that left no room to doubt. There appeared advancing over the sea two immense serpents. They came upon the land, and the crowd fled in all directions. The serpents advanced directly to the spot where Laocoön stood with his two sons. They first attacked the children, winding round their bodies and breathing their pestilential breath in their faces. The father attempting to rescue them is next seized and involved in the serpents' coils. He struggles to tear them away, but they overpower all his efforts and strangle him and the children in their poisonous folds. This event was regarded as a clear indication of the displeasure of the gods at Laocoön's irreverent treatment of the wooden horse, which they no longer hesitated to regard as a sacred object and prepared to introduce with due solemnity into the city. This was done with songs and triumphal acclamations and the day closed with festivity. In the night the armed men who were enclosed in the body of the horse, being let out by the traitor Sinon, opened the gates of the city to their friends who had returned under cover of the night. The city was set on fire, the people, overcome with feasting and sleep, put to the sword, and Troy completely subdued.

King Priam lived to see the downfall of his kingdom, and was slain at last on the fatal night when the Greeks took the city. He had armed himself and was about to mingle with the combatants, but was prevailed on by Hecuba, his aged queen, to take refuge with herself and his daughters as a suppliant at the altar of Jupiter. While there, his youngest son, Polites, pursued by Pyrrhus, the son of Achilles, rushed in, wounded, and expired at the feet of his father; whereupon Priam, overcome with indignation, hurled his spear with feeble hand against Pyrrhus, and was forthwith slain by him.

Queen Hecuba and her daughter Cassandra were carried captives to Greece. Cassandra had been loved by Apollo, and he gave her the gift of prophecy; but afterward, offended with her, he rendered the gift unavailing by ordaining that her predictions should never be believed. Polyxena, another daughter who had been loved by Achilles, was demanded by the ghost of that warrior, and was sacrificed by the Greeks upon his tomb.

▼ The Procession of the Trojan Horse into Troy, GIOVANNI DOMENICO TIEPOLO
The priest Laocoön's fear was justified: once the treacherous wooden horse was dragged inside Troy, the city was doomed.

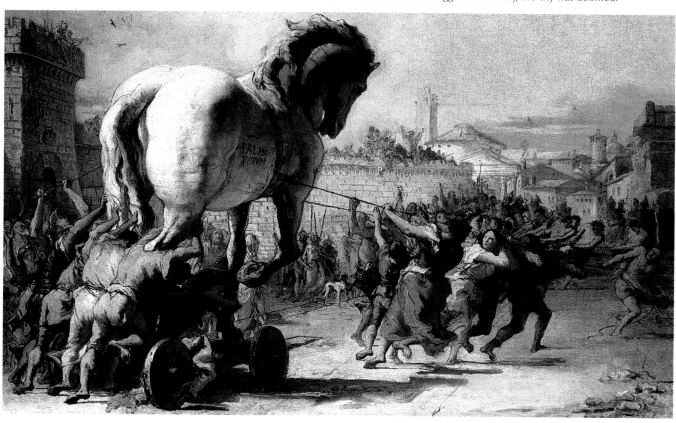

165

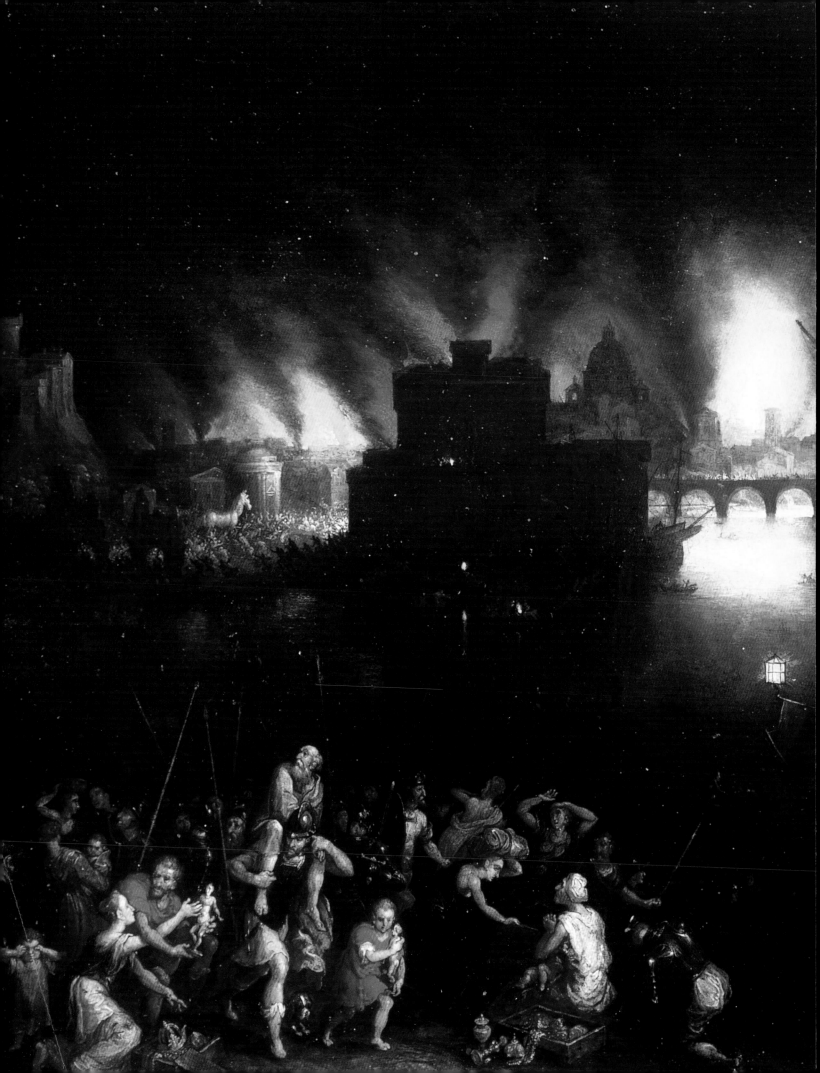

MENELAUS AND HELEN

Our readers will be anxious to know the fate of Helen, the fair but guilty occasion of so much slaughter. On the fall of Troy, Menelaus recovered possession of his wife, who had not ceased to love him, though she had yielded to the might of Venus and deserted him for another. After the death of Paris she aided the Greeks secretly on several occasions, and in particular when Ulysses and Diomed entered the city in disguise to carry off the Palladium. She saw and recognized Ulysses, but kept the secret and even assisted them in obtaining the image. Thus she became reconciled to her husband, and they were among the first to leave the shores of Troy for their native land. But having incurred the displeasure of the gods they were driven by storms from shore to shore of the Mediterranean, visiting Cyprus, Phoenicia, and Egypt. In Egypt they were kindly treated and presented with rich gifts, of which Helen's share was a golden spindle and a basket on wheels. The basket was to hold the wool and spools for the queen's work.

Menelaus and Helen at length arrived in safety at Sparta, resumed their royal dignity, and lived and reigned in splendor; and when Telemachus, the son of Ulysses, in search of his father, arrived at Sparta, he found Menelaus and Helen celebrating the marriage of their daughter Hermione to Neoptolemus, son of Achilles.

AGAMEMNON, ORESTES, AND ELECTRA

Agamemnon, the general-in-chief of the Greeks, the brother of Menelaus, and who had been drawn into the quarrel to avenge his brother's wrongs, not his own, was not so fortunate in the issue. During his absence his wife Clytemnestra had been false to him, and when his return was expected, she, with her paramour, Aegisthus, laid a plan for his destruction and, at the banquet given to celebrate his return, murdered him. It was intended by the conspirators to slay his son Orestes also, a lad not yet old enough to be an object of apprehension, but from whom, if he should be suffered to grow up, there might be danger. Electra, the sister of Orestes, saved her brother's

◄ The Burning Troy, JAN BRUEGHEL THE ELDER (1568–1625)
The fall of Troy provided a favorite theme for tragic poets;
the emperor Nero recited such an epic as he watched Rome burn.

life by sending him secretly away to his Uncle Strophius, King of Phocis. In the palace of Strophius Orestes grew up with the king's son, Pylades, and formed with him that ardent friendship which has become proverbial. Electra frequently reminded her brother by messengers of the duty of avenging his father's death, and when grown up he consulted the oracle of Delphi, which confirmed him in his design. He therefore repaired in disguise to Argos, pretending to be a messenger from Strophius, who had come to announce the death of Orestes and brought the ashes of the deceased in a funeral urn. After visiting his father's tomb and sacrificing upon it, according to the rites of the ancients, he made himself known to his sister Electra, and soon after slew both Aegisthus and Clytemnestra.

This revolting act, the slaughter of a mother by her son, though alleviated by the guilt of the victim and the express command of the gods, did not fail to awaken in the breasts of the ancients the same abhorrence that it does in ours. The Eumenides, avenging deities, seized upon Orestes and drove him frantic from land to land. Pylades accompanied him in his wanderings and watched over him. At length, in answer to a second appeal to the oracle, he was directed to go to Tauris in Scythia, and to bring thence a statue of Diana that was believed to have fallen from heaven. Accordingly Orestes and Pylades went to Tauris, where the barbarous people were accustomed to sacrifice to the goddess all strangers who fell into their hands. The two friends were seized and carried bound to the temple to be made victims. But the priestess of Diana was no other than Iphigenia, the sister of Orestes, who, our readers will remember, was snatched away by Diana, at the moment when she was about to be sacrificed. Ascertaining from the prisoners who they were, Iphigenia disclosed herself to them, and the three made their escape with the statue of the goddess, and returned to Mycenae.

But Orestes was not yet relieved from the vengeance of the Erinnyes. At length he took refuge with Minerva at Athens. The goddess afforded him protection, and appointed the court of Areopagus to decide his fate. The Erinnyes brought forward their accusation, and Orestes made the command of the Delphic oracle his excuse. When the court voted and the voices were equally divided, Orestes was acquitted by the command of Minerva.

CHAPTER 28

ADVENTURES OF ULYSSES · THE CYCLOPES THE LAESTRYGONIANS · CIRCE · THE SIRENS SCYLLA AND CHARYBDIS · CALYPSO

THE ROMANTIC POEM OF THE *ODYSSEY* IS NOW TO engage our attention. It narrates the wanderings of Ulysses (Odysseus in the Greek language) in his return from Troy to his own kingdom, Ithaca.

From Troy the vessels first made land at Ismarus, city of the Ciconians, where, in a skirmish with the inhabitants, Ulysses lost six men from each ship. Sailing thence they were overtaken by a storm which drove them for nine days along the sea till they reached the country of the Lotus-eaters. Here, after watering, Ulysses sent three of his men to discover who the inhabitants were. These men, on coming among the Lotus-eaters, were kindly entertained by them and were given some of their own food, the lotus plant, to eat. The effect of this food was such that those who partook of it lost all thoughts of home and wished to remain in that country. It was by main force that Ulysses dragged these men away, and he was even obliged to tie them under the benches of his ship.

THE CYCLOPES

They next arrived at the country of the Cyclopes. The Cyclopes were giants, who inhabited an island of which they were the only possessors. The name means "round eye," and these giants were so called because they had but one eye, and that placed in the middle of the forehead. They dwelt in caves and fed on the wild products of the island and on what their flocks yielded, for they were shepherds. Ulysses left the main body of his ships at anchor and, with one vessel, went to the Cyclopes' island to explore for supplies. He landed with his companions, carrying with them a jar of wine for a present; and coming to a large cave, they entered it; and finding no one within, examined its contents. They found it stored with the riches of the flock, quantities of cheese, pails and bowls of milk, lambs and kids in their pens, all in nice order. Presently arrived the master of the cave, Polyphemus, bearing an immense bundle of firewood, which he threw down before the cavern's mouth. He then drove into the cave the sheep and goats to be milked, and, entering, rolled to the cave's mouth an enormous rock, that twenty oxen could not draw. Next he sat down and milked his ewes, preparing a part for cheese and setting the rest aside for his customary drink. Then turning around his great eye, he discerned the strangers and growled out to them, demanding who they were and where from. Ulysses replied most humbly, stating that they were Greeks, from the great expedition that had lately won so much glory in the conquest of Troy; that they were now on their way home, and finished by imploring his hospitality in the name of the gods. Polyphemus deigned no answer, but reaching out his hand seized two of the Greeks, whom he hurled against the side of the cave, and dashed out their brains. He proceeded to devour them with great relish and, having made a hearty meal, stretched himself out on the floor to sleep. Ulysses was tempted to seize the opportunity and plunge his sword into him as he slept, but recollected that it would only expose them all to certain destruction, as the rock with which the giant had closed up the door was far beyond their power to remove, and they would therefore be in hopeless imprisonment.

Next morning the giant seized two more of the Greeks and despatched them in the same manner as their companions, feasting on their flesh till no fragment was left. He then moved away the rock from the door, drove out his flocks, and went out, carefully replacing the barrier after him. When he was gone, Ulysses planned how he might take vengeance for his murdered friends and effect his escape with his surviving companions. He made his men prepare a massive bar of wood cut by the Cyclops for a staff, which they found in the cave. They sharpened the end of it, and seasoned it in the fire, and hid it under the straw on the cavern floor. Then four of the boldest were selected, with whom Ulysses joined himself as a fifth. The Cyclops came home at evening, rolled away the stone, and drove in his flocks as usual. After milking them and making his arrangements as before, he seized two more of Ulysses' companions, and dashed their brains out, and made his evening meal upon them as he had on the others. After he had supped, Ulysses, approaching him, handed him a bowl of wine, saying, "Cyclops, this is wine; taste and drink after thy meal of man's flesh." He took and drank it, and was hugely delighted with it, and called for more. Ulysses supplied him once and again, which pleased the giant so much that he promised him as a favor that he should be the last of the party devoured. He asked his name, to which Ulysses replied, "My name is Noman."

After his supper the giant lay down to repose, and was soon sound asleep. Then Ulysses with his four select friends thrust the end of the stake into the fire till it was all one burning coal, then poising it exactly above the giant's only eye, they buried it deeply into the socket, twirling it around as a carpenter does his auger. The howling monster with his outcry filled the cavern, and Ulysses with his aids nimbly got out of his way and concealed themselves in the cave. He, bellowing, called aloud on all the Cyclopes dwelling in the caves around him, far and near. They, on his cry, flocked round the den and enquired what grievous hurt had caused him to sound such an alarm and break their slumbers. He replied, "Oh, friends, I die, and Noman gives the blow." They answered, "If no man hurts thee, it is the stroke of Jove, and thou must bear it." So saying, they left him groaning.

Next morning the Cyclops rolled away the stone to let his flock out to pasture, but planted himself in the door of the cave to feel of all as they went out, that Ulysses and his men should not escape with them. But Ulysses had made his men harness the rams of the flock three abreast, with osiers which they found on the floor of the cave. To the middle ram of the three one of the Greeks suspended himself, so protected by the exterior rams on either side. As they passed, the giant felt of the animals' backs and sides, but never thought of their bellies; so the men all passed safe, Ulysses himself being on the last one that passed. When they had got a few paces from the cavern, Ulysses and his friends released themselves from their rams, and drove a good part of the flock down to the shore to their boat. They put them aboard with all haste, then pushed off from the shore, and when at a safe distance Ulysses shouted out, "Cyclops, the gods have well requited thee for thy

atrocious deeds. Know it is Ulysses to whom thou owest thy shameful loss of sight." The Cyclops, hearing this, seized a rock that projected from the side of the mountain, and rending it from its bed, he lifted it high in the air, then exerting all his force, hurled it in the direction of the voice. Down came the mass, just clearing the vessel's stern. The ocean, at the plunge of the huge rock, heaved the ship toward the land, so that it barely escaped being swamped by the waves. When they had with the utmost difficulty pulled off shore, Ulysses was about to hail the giant again, but his friends besought him not to do so. He could not forbear, however, letting the giant know that they had escaped his missile, but waited till they had reached a safer distance than before. The giant answered them with curses, but Ulysses and his friends plied their oars vigorously and soon regained their companions.

Ulysses next arrived at the island of Aeolus. To this monarch Jupiter had entrusted the government of the winds, to send them forth or retain them at his will. He treated Ulysses hospitably, and at his departure gave him, tied up in a leathern bag with a silver string, such winds as might be hurtful and dangerous, commanding fair winds to blow the barks toward their country. Nine days they sped before the wind, and all that time Ulysses had stood at the helm, without sleep. At last, quite exhausted, he lay down to sleep. While he slept, the crew conferred together about the mysterious bag and concluded it must contain treasures given by the hospitable King Aeolus to their commander. Tempted to secure some portion for themselves, they loosed the string, when immediately the winds rushed forth. The ships were driven far from their course and back again to the island they had just left. Aeolus was so indignant at their folly that he refused to assist them further, and they were obliged to labor over their course once more by means of their oars.

THE LAESTRYGONIANS

Their next adventure was with the barbarous tribe of Laestrygonians. The vessels all pushed into the harbor, tempted by the secure appearance of the cove, completely landlocked; only Ulysses moored his vessel without. As soon as the Laestrygonians found the ships completely in their power, they attacked them, heaving huge stones, which broke and overturned them, and with their spears despatched the seamen as they struggled in the water. All the vessels with their crews were destroyed, except Ulysses' own ship, which had remained outside, and finding no safety but in flight, he exhorted his men to ply their oars vigorously, and they escaped.

CIRCE

With grief for their slain companions mixed with joy at their own escape, they pursued their way till they arrived at the Aeaean isle, where Circe dwelt, the daughter of the sun. Landing here, Ulysses climbed a hill and, gazing round, saw no signs of habitation except in one spot at the center of the island, where he perceived a palace embowered with trees. He sent forward one half of his crew, under the command of Eurylochus, to see what prospect of hospitality they might find. As they approached the palace, they found themselves surrounded by lions, tigers, and wolves, not fierce, but tamed by Circe's art, for she was a powerful magician. All these animals had once been men, but had been changed by Circe's enchantments into the forms of beasts. The sounds of soft music were heard from within, and a sweet female voice singing. Eurylochus called aloud, and the goddess came forth and invited them in; they all gladly entered, except Eurylochus, who suspected danger. The goddess conducted her guests to a seat and had them served with wine and other delicacies. When they had feasted heartily, she touched them one by one with her wand, and they became immediately changed into swine, in "head, body, voice, and bristles," yet with their intellects as before. She shut them in her sties and supplied them with acorns and such other things as swine love.

Eurylochus hurried back to the ship and told the tale. Ulysses thereupon determined to go himself and try if by any means he might deliver his companions. As he strode onward alone, he met a youth who addressed him familiarly, appearing to be acquainted with his adventures. He announced himself as Mercury, and informed Ulysses of the arts of Circe and of the danger of approaching her. As Ulysses was not to be dissuaded from his attempt, Mercury provided him with a sprig of the plant moly, of wonderful power to resist sorceries, and instructed him how to act. Ulysses proceeded, and reaching the palace was courteously received by Circe, who entertained him as she had done his companions, and after he had eaten and drunk, touched him with her wand,

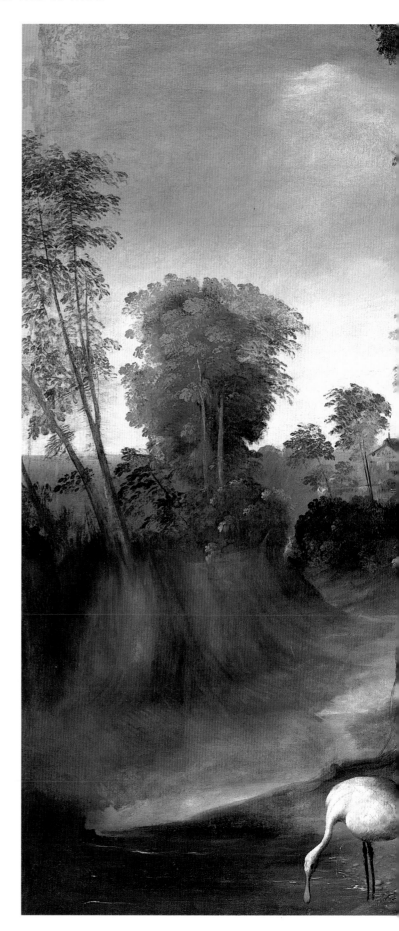

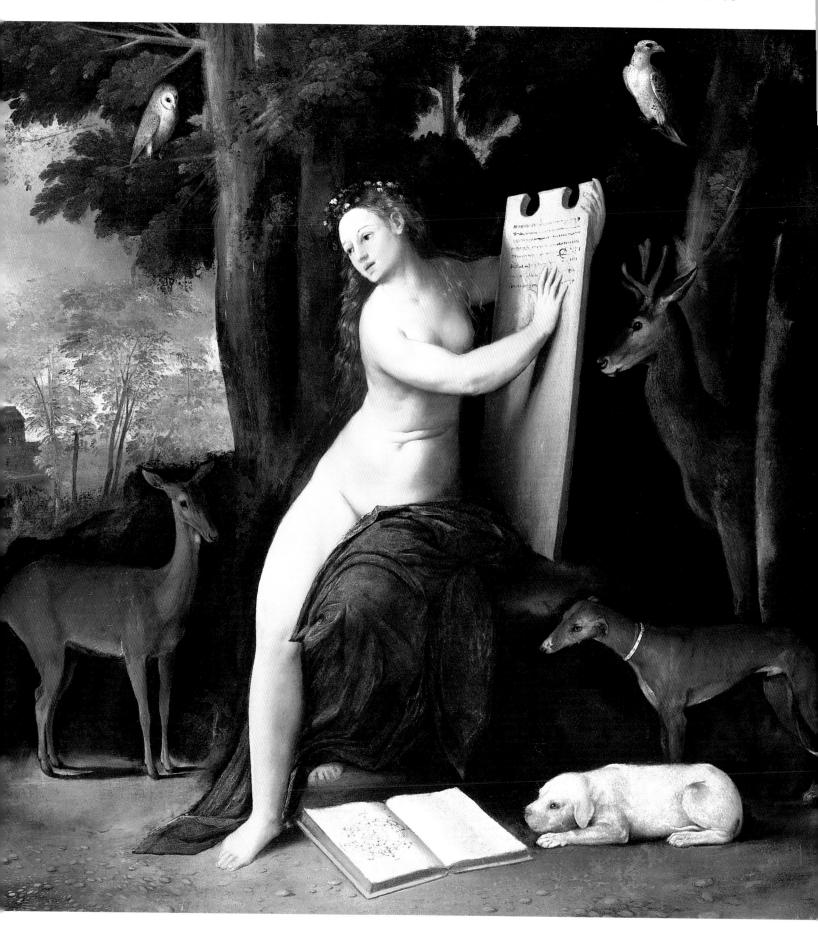

▲ Circe and Her Lovers in a Landscape, DOSSI DOSSO (active 1512; died 1542)
The sorceress Circe is shown taming the deer, dogs, and birds she has magically transformed from human form. Dosso makes clear that her intellectual powers were compounded by sexual allure.

saying, "Hence, seek the sty and wallow with thy friends." But he, instead of obeying, drew his sword and rushed upon her with fury in his countenance. She fell on her knees and begged for mercy. He dictated a solemn oath that she would release his companions and practice no further harm against him or them; and she repeated it, at the same time promising to dismiss them all in safety after hospitably entertaining them. She was as good as her word. The men were restored to their shapes, the rest of the crew summoned from the shore, and the whole magnificently entertained day after day, till Ulysses seemed to have forgotten his native land and to have reconciled himself to an inglorious life of ease and pleasure.

THE SIRENS

At length, his companions recalled him to nobler sentiments, and he received their admonition gratefully. Circe aided their departure and instructed them how to pass safely by the coast of the Sirens. The Sirens were sea nymphs who had the power of charming by their song all who heard them, so that the unhappy mariners were irresistibly impelled to cast themselves into the sea to their destruction. Circe directed Ulysses to fill the ears of his seamen with wax, so that they should not hear the strain; and to cause himself to be bound to the mast, and his people to be strictly enjoined, whatever he might say or do, by no means to release him till they should have passed the Sirens' island. Ulysses obeyed these directions. He filled the ears of his people with wax and suffered them to bind him with cords firmly to the mast. As they approached the Siren's island, the sea was calm, and over the waters came the notes of music so ravishing and attractive that Ulysses struggled to get loose and, by cries and signs to his people, begged to be released; but they, obedient to his previous orders, sprang forward and bound him still faster. They held on their course, and the music grew fainter till it ceased to be heard, when with joy Ulysses gave his companions the signal to unseal their ears, and they relieved him from his bonds.

SCYLLA AND CHARYBDIS

Ulysses had been warned by Circe of the two monsters Scylla and Charybdis. We have already met with Scylla, in the story of Glaucus, and remember that she was once a beautiful maiden and was changed into a snaky monster by Circe. She dwelt in a cave high up on the cliff, from whence she was accustomed to thrust forth her long necks (for she had six heads), and in each of her mouths to seize one of the crew of every vessel passing within reach. The other terror, Charybdis, was a gulf, nearly on a level with the water. Thrice each day the water rushed into a frightful chasm, and thrice was disgorged. Any vessel coming near the whirlpool when the tide was rushing in must inevitably be engulfed; not Neptune himself could save it.

On approaching the haunt of the dread monsters, Ulysses kept strict watch to discover them. The roar of the waters as Charybdis engulfed them gave warning at a distance, but Scylla could nowhere be discerned. While Ulysses and his men watched with anxious eyes the dreadful whirlpool, they were not equally on their guard from the attack of Scylla, and the monster, darting forth her snaky heads, caught six of his men and bore them away shrieking to her den. It was the saddest sight Ulysses had yet seen: to behold his friends thus sacrificed and hear their cries, unable to afford them any assistance.

Circe had warned him of another danger. After passing Scylla and Charybdis the next land he would make was Thrinakia, an island whereon were pastured the cattle of Hyperion, the sun, tended by his daughters Lampetia and Phaëthusa. These flocks must not be violated, whatever the wants of the voyagers might be. If this injunction were transgressed, destruction was sure to fall on the offenders.

Ulysses would willingly have passed the island of the sun without stopping, but his companions so urgently pleaded for the rest and refreshment that would be derived from anchoring and passing the night on shore that Ulysses yielded. He bound them, however, with an oath that they would not touch one of the animals of the sacred flocks and herds, but content themselves with what provision they yet had left of the supply which Circe had put on board. So long as this supply lasted the people kept their oath, but contrary winds detained them at the island for a month, and after consuming all their stock of provisions, they were forced to rely upon the birds and fishes they could catch. Famine pressed them, and at length one day, in the absence of Ulysses, they slew some of the cattle, vainly attempting to make amends for the deed by offering from them a portion to the offended powers. Ulysses, on his return, was horror-struck at perceiving what they had done, and the more so on account of the portentous signs that followed. The skins crept on the ground, and the joints of meat lowed on the spits while roasting.

The wind becoming fair, they sailed from the island. They had not gone far when the weather changed, and a storm of thunder and lightning ensued. A stroke of lightning shattered their mast, which in its fall killed the pilot. At last the vessel itself came to pieces. The keel and mast floating side by side, Ulysses formed of them a raft, to which he clung, and, the wind changing, the waves bore him to Calypso's island. All the rest of the crew perished.

CALYPSO

Calypso was a sea nymph, which name denotes a numerous class of female divinities of lower rank, yet sharing many of the attributes of the gods. Calypso received Ulysses hospitably, entertained him magnificently, became enamored of him, and wished to retain him forever, conferring on him immortality. But he persisted in his resolution to return to his country and his wife and son. Calypso at last received the command of Jove to dismiss him. Mercury brought the message to her and found her in her grotto.

Calypso, with much reluctance, proceeded to obey the commands of Jupiter. She supplied Ulysses with the means of constructing a raft, provisioned it well for him, and gave him a favoring gale. He sped on his course prosperously for many days, till at length, when in sight of land, a storm arose that broke his mast and threatened to rend the raft asunder. In this crisis he was seen by a compassionate sea nymph, who in the form of a cormorant alighted on the raft and presented him a girdle, directing him to bind it beneath his breast, and if he should be compelled to trust himself to the waves, it would buoy him up and enable him by swimming to reach the land.

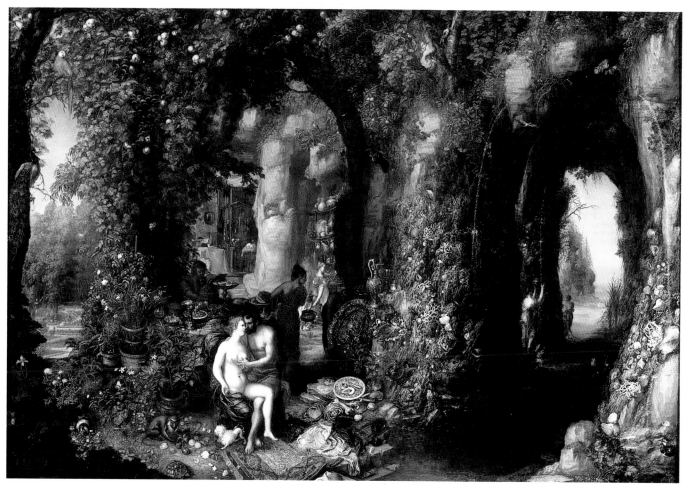

⋏ A Fantastic Cave with Odysseus and Calypso, JAN BRUEGHEL THE ELDER (1568–1625)
The name Calypso translates as "she who conceals." Her cave is a trap for the shipwrecked Ulysses, but it is not without its delights—as suggested by this luxuriant grotto. Burgeoning flowers and fruit reinforce the theme of ripening love.

CHAPTER 29

THE PHAEACIANS
THE FATE OF THE SUITORS

ULYSSES CLUNG TO THE RAFT WHILE ANY OF ITS timbers kept together, and when it no longer yielded him support, binding the girdle around him, he swam. Minerva smoothed the billows before him and sent him a wind that rolled the waves toward the shore. The surf beat high on the rocks and seemed to forbid approach; but at length finding calm water at the mouth of a gentle stream, he landed, spent with toil, breathless and speechless and almost dead. After some time reviving he kissed the soil rejoicing, yet at a loss what course to take. At a short distance he perceived a wood, to which he turned his steps. There, finding a covert sheltered by intermingling branches alike from the sun and the rain, he collected a pile of leaves and formed a bed on which he stretched himself and, heaping the leaves over him, fell asleep.

The land where he was thrown was Scheria, the country of the Phaeacians. These people dwelt originally near the Cyclopes; but being oppressed by that savage race, they migrated to the isle of Scheria, under the conduct of Nausithous their king. They were, the poet tells us, a people akin to the gods, who appeared manifestly and feasted among them when they offered sacrifices and did not conceal themselves from solitary wayfarers when they met them. They had abundance of wealth and lived in the enjoyment of it undisturbed by the alarms of war, for as they dwelt remote from gain-seeking man, no enemy ever approached their shores, and they did not even require to make use of bows and quivers. Their chief employment was navigation. Their ships, which went with the velocity of birds, were endued with intelligence; they knew every port and needed no pilot. Alcinous, the son of Nausithous, was now their king, a wise and just sovereign, beloved by his people.

Now it happened that the very night on which Ulysses was cast ashore on the Phaeacian island, and while he lay sleeping on his bed of leaves, Nausicaa, the daughter of the king, had a dream sent by Minerva, reminding her that her wedding day was not far distant and that it would be but a prudent preparation for that event to have a general washing of the clothes of the family. This was no slight affair, for the fountains were at some distance and the garments must be carried thither. On awaking, the princess hastened to her parents to tell them what was on her mind; not alluding to her wedding day, but finding other reasons equally good. Her father readily assented and ordered the grooms to furnish forth a wagon for the purpose. The clothes were put therein, and the queen mother placed in the wagon likewise an abundant supply of food and wine. The princess took her seat and plied the lash, her attendant virgins following her on foot. Arrived at the riverside, they turned out the mules to graze, and unlading the carriage, bore the garments down to the water, and working with cheerfulness and alacrity, soon despatched their labor. Then, having spread the garments on the shore to dry, and having themselves bathed, they sat down to enjoy their meal; after which they rose and amused themselves with a game of ball, the princess singing to them while they played. But when they had refolded the apparel and were about to resume their way to the town, Minerva caused the ball thrown by the princess to fall into the water, whereat they all screamed and Ulysses awaked at the sound.

Now we must picture to ourselves Ulysses, a shipwrecked mariner, but a few hours escaped from the waves and utterly destitute of clothing, awaking and discovering that only a few bushes were interposed between him and a group of young maidens whom by their deportment and attire he discovered to be not mere peasant girls, but of a higher class. Sadly needing help, how could he yet venture naked as he was to discover himself and make his wants known? It certainly was a case worthy of the interposition of his patron goddess Minerva, who never failed him at a crisis. Breaking off a leafy branch from a tree he held it before him and stepped out from the thicket. The virgins at sight of him fled in all directions, Nausicaa alone excepted, for her Minerva aided and endowed with courage and discernment. Ulysses, standing respectfully aloof, told his sad case and besought the fair object (whether queen or goddess he professed he knew not) for food and clothing. The princess replied courteously, promising present relief and her father's hospitality when he should become acquainted with the facts. She called back her scattered maidens, chiding their alarm and reminding them that the Phaeacians had no enemies to fear. This man, she told them, was an unhappy wanderer, whom it was a duty to cherish, for the poor and stranger are from Jove. She bade them bring food and clothing, for some of her brothers' garments were among the contents of the wagon. When this was done, and Ulysses, retiring to a sheltered place, had washed his body free from the sea foam, clothed and refreshed himself with food, Pallas dilated his form and diffused grace over his ample chest and manly brows.

The princess, seeing him, was filled with admiration, and scrupled not to say to her damsels that she wished the gods would send her such a husband. To Ulysses she recommended that he should repair to the city, following herself and train so far as the way lay through the fields; but when they should approach the city she desired that he would no longer be seen in her company, for she feared the remarks that rude and vulgar people might make on seeing her return accompanied by such a gallant stranger. To avoid that she directed him to stop at a grove adjoining the city, in which were a farm and garden belonging to the king. After allowing time for the princess and her companions to reach the city, he was then to pursue his way thither, and would be easily guided by any he might meet to the royal abode.

Ulysses obeyed the directions and in due time proceeded to the city, on approaching which he met a young woman bearing a pitcher forth for water. It was Minerva, who had assumed that form. Ulysses accosted her and desired to be directed to the palace of Alcinous the king. The maiden replied respectfully, offering to be his guide; for the palace she informed him stood near her father's dwelling. Under the guidance of the goddess and by her power enveloped in a cloud which shielded him from observation, Ulysses passed among the busy crowd, and with wonder observed their harbor, their ships, their forum (the resort of heroes), and their battlements, till they came to the palace, where the goddess, having first given him some information of the country, king, and people he was about to meet, left him. Ulysses, before entering the courtyard of the palace, stood and surveyed the scene. Its splendor astonished him. Brazen walls stretched from the entrance to the interior house, of which the doors were gold, the door posts silver, the lintels silver ornamented with gold. On either side were figures of mastiffs wrought in gold and silver, standing in rows as if to guard the approach. Along the walls were seats spread through all their length with mantles of finest texture, the work of Phaeacian maidens. On these seats the princes sat and feasted, while golden statues of graceful youths held in their hands lighted torches, which shed radiance over the scene. Full fifty female menials served in household offices, some employed to grind the corn, others to wind off the purple wool or ply the loom; for the Phaeacian women as far exceeded all other women in household arts as the mariners of that country did the rest of mankind in the management of ships. Without the court a spacious garden lay, four acres in extent. In it grew many a lofty tree, pomegranate, pear, apple, fig and olive. Neither winter's cold nor summer's drought arrested their growth, but they flourished in constant succession, some budding while others were maturing. The vineyard was equally prolific. In one quarter, you might see the vines, some in blossom, some loaded with ripe grapes, and in another observe the vintagers treading the wine press. On the garden's borders, flowers of all hues bloomed all the year round, arranged with neatest art. In the midst, two fountains poured forth their waters, one flowing by artificial channels over all the garden, the other conducted through the courtyard of the palace, whence every citizen might draw his supplies.

Ulysses stood gazing in admiration, unobserved himself, for the cloud which Minerva spread around him still shielded him. At length, having sufficiently observed the scene, he advanced with rapid step into the hall where the chiefs and senators were assembled, pouring libation to Mercury, whose worship followed the evening meal. Just then Minerva dissolved the cloud and disclosed him to the assembled chiefs. Advancing to the place where the queen sat, he knelt at her feet and implored her favor and assistance to enable him to return to his native country. Then withdrawing, he seated himself in the manner of suppliants, at the hearthside.

For a time none spoke. At last an aged statesman, addressing the king, said, "It is not fit that a stranger who asks our hospitality should be kept waiting in suppliant guise, none welcoming him. Let him therefore be led to a seat among us and supplied with food and wine." At these words the king, rising, gave his hand to Ulysses and led him to a seat, displacing thence his own son to make room for the stranger. Food and wine were set before him and he ate and refreshed himself.

The king then dismissed his guests, notifying them that the next day he would call them to council to consider what had best be done for the stranger.

When the guests had departed and Ulysses was left alone with the king and queen, the queen asked him who he was and whence he came, and (recognizing the clothes which he wore as those which her maidens and herself had made) from whom he received those garments. He told them of his residence in Calypso's isle and his departure thence; of the wreck of his raft, his escape by swimming, and of the relief afforded by the princess. The parents heard approvingly, and the king promised to furnish a ship in which his guest might return to his own land.

The next day the assembled chiefs confirmed the promise of the king. A bark was prepared and a crew of stout rowers selected, and all betook themselves to the palace, where a bounteous repast was provided. After the feast the king proposed that the young men should show their guest their proficiency in manly sports, and all went forth to the arena for games of running, wrestling and other exercises. After all had done their best, Ulysses, being challenged to show what he could do, at first declined, but being taunted by one of the youths, seized a quoit of weight far heavier than any the Phaeacians had thrown and sent it farther than the utmost throw of theirs. All were astonished, and viewed their guest with greatly increased respect.

After the games they returned to the hall, and the herald led in Demodocus, the blind bard. He took for his theme the wooden horse, by means of which the Greeks found entrance into Troy. Apollo inspired him, and he sang so feelingly the terrors and the exploits of that eventful time that all were delighted, but Ulysses was moved to tears. Observing which, Alcinous, when the song was done, demanded of him why at the mention of Troy his sorrows awaked. Had he lost there a father, or brother, or any dear friend? Ulysses replied by announcing himself by his true name, and at their request, recounted the adventures that had befallen him since his departure from Troy. This narrative raised the sympathy and admiration of the Phaeacians for their guest to the highest pitch. The king proposed that all the chiefs should present him with a gift, himself setting the example. They obeyed and vied with one another in loading the illustrious stranger with costly gifts.

The next day Ulysses set sail in the Phaeacian vessel and in a short time arrived safe at Ithaca, his own island. When the vessel touched the strand, he was asleep. The mariners, without waking him, carried him on shore and landed with him the chest containing his presents, and then sailed away.

Neptune was so displeased at the conduct of the Phaeacians in thus rescuing Ulysses from his hands that on the return of the vessel to port he transformed it into a rock, right opposite the mouth of the harbor.

THE FATE OF THE SUITORS

Ulysses had now been away from Ithaca for twenty years, and when he awoke, he did not recognize his native land. Minerva appeared to him in the form of a young shepherd, informed him where he was, and told him the state of things at his palace. More than a hundred nobles of Ithaca and of the neighboring islands had been for years suing for the hand of Penelope, his wife, imagining him dead, and lording it over his palace and people, as if they were owners of both. That he might be able to take vengeance upon them, it was important that he should not be recognized. Minerva accordingly metamorphosed him into an unsightly beggar, and as such he was kindly received by Eumaeus, the swineherd, a faithful servant of his house.

Telemachus, his son, was absent in quest of his father. He had gone to the courts of the other kings, who had returned from the Trojan expedition. While on the search, he received counsel from Minerva to return home. He arrived and sought Eumaeus to learn something of the state of affairs at the palace before presenting himself among the suitors. Finding a stranger with Eumaeus, he treated him courteously, though in the garb of a beggar, and promised him assistance. Eumaeus was sent to the palace to inform Penelope privately of her son's arrival, for caution was necessary with regard to

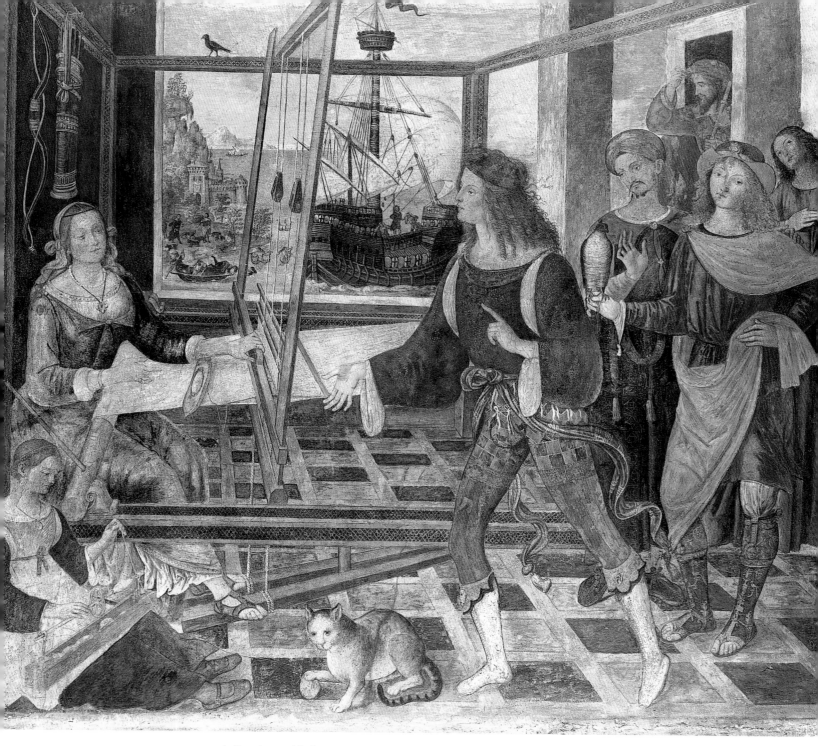

▲ Penelope with the Suitors, PINTORICCHIO (active 1481; died 1513)
Penelope's persistent suitors press toward her. Ulysses enters at the back of the room, disguised as a beggar, his bow at his shoulder.
Past episodes from the Odyssey are featured in the background.

the suitors, who, as Telemachus had learned, were plotting to intercept and kill him. When Eumaeus was gone, Minerva presented herself to Ulysses and directed him to make himself known to his son. At the same time she touched him, removed at once from him the appearance of age and penury, and gave him the aspect of vigorous manhood that belonged to him. Telemachus viewed him with astonishment and at first thought he must be more than mortal. But Ulysses announced himself as his father and

accounted for the change of appearance by explaining that it was Minerva's doing.

The father and son took counsel together how they should get the better of the suitors and punish them for their outrages. It was arranged that Telemachus should proceed to the palace and mingle with the suitors as formerly; that Ulysses should also go as a beggar, a character which in the rude old times had different privileges from what we concede to it now. As traveler and storyteller, the beggar was admitted in the halls of chieftains and often treated like a guest; though sometimes also, no doubt, with contumely. Ulysses charged his son not to betray, by any display of unusual interest in him, that he knew him to be other than he seemed, and even if he saw him insulted, or beaten, not to interpose otherwise than he might do for any stranger. At the palace they found the usual scene of feasting and riot going on. The suitors pretended to receive Telemachus with joy at his return, though secretly mortified at the failure of their plots to take his life. The old beggar was permitted to enter and provided with a portion from the table. A touching incident occurred as Ulysses entered the courtyard of the palace. An old dog lay in the yard almost dead with age and, seeing a stranger enter, raised his head, with ears erect. It was Argus, Ulysses' own dog, that he had in other days often led to the chase.

As Ulysses sat eating his portion in the hall, the suitors began to exhibit their insolence to him. When he mildly remonstrated, one of them raised a stool and with it gave him a blow. Telemachus had hard work to restrain his indignation at seeing his father so treated in his own hall, but remembering his father's injunctions, said no more than what became him as master of the house, though young, and protector of his guests.

Penelope had protracted her decision in favor of either of her suitors so long that there seemed to be no further pretence for delay. The continued absence of her husband seemed to prove that his return was no longer to be expected. Meanwhile her son had grown up, and was able to manage his own affairs. She therefore consented to submit the question of her choice to a trial of skill among the suitors. The test selected was shooting with the bow. Twelve rings were arranged in a line, and he whose arrow was sent through the whole twelve was to have the queen for his prize. A bow that one of his brother heroes had given to Ulysses in former times was brought from the armory and, with its quiver full of arrows, was laid in the hall. Telemachus had taken care

that all other weapons should be removed, under pretence that in the heat of competition, there was danger, in some rash moment, of putting them to an improper use.

All things being prepared for the trial, the first thing to be done was to bend the bow in order to attach the string. Telemachus endeavored to do it, but found all his efforts fruitless; and modestly confessing that he had attempted a task beyond his strength, he yielded the bow to another. He tried it with no better success, and, amidst the laughter and jeers of his companions, gave it up. Another tried it and another; they rubbed the bow with tallow, but all to no purpose; it would not bend. Then spoke Ulysses, humbly suggesting that he should be permitted to try; for, said he, "beggar as I am, I was once a soldier, and there is still some strength in these old limbs of mine." The suitors hooted with derision and commanded to turn him out of the hall for his insolence. But Telemachus spoke up for him and, merely to gratify the old man, bade him try. Ulysses took the bow and handled it with the hand of a master. With ease he adjusted the cord to its notch, then fitting an arrow to the bow, he drew the string and sped the arrow unerring through the rings.

Without allowing them time to express their astonishment, he said, "Now for another mark!" and aimed direct at the most insolent one of the suitors. The arrow pierced through his throat and he fell dead. Telemachus, Eumaeus, and another faithful follower, well-armed, now sprang to the side of Ulysses. The suitors, in amazement, looked round for arms, but found none, neither was there any way of escape, for Eumaeus had secured the door. Ulysses left them not long in uncertainty; he announced himself as the long-lost chief, whose house they had invaded, whose substance they had squandered, whose wife and son they had persecuted for ten long years; and told them he meant to have ample vengeance. All were slain, and Ulysses was left master of his palace and possessor of his kingdom and his wife.

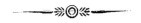

CHAPTER 30

ADVENTURES OF AENEAS
THE HARPIES · DIDO · PALINURUS

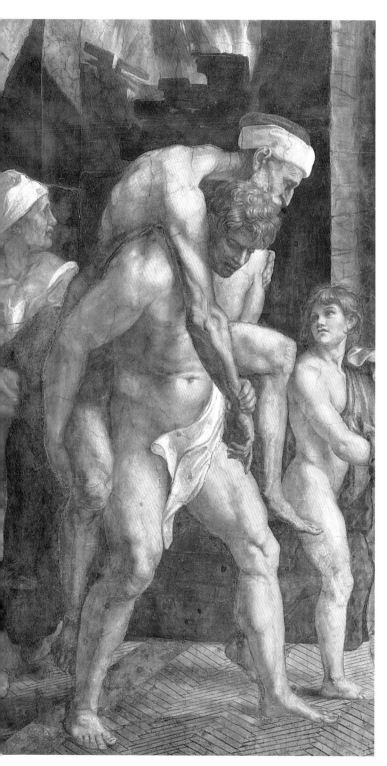

▲ The Fire in the Borgo, SCHOOL OF RAPHAEL (1483–1520)
*As Troy blazes, Aeneas hoists his father Anchises onto
his shoulders to begin the long journey westward.
Aeneas's son Ascanius accompanies them.*

WE HAVE FOLLOWED ONE OF THE GRECIAN HEROES, Ulysses, in his wanderings on his return home from Troy, and now we propose to share the fortunes of the remnant of the conquered people, under their chief Aeneas, in their search for a new home, after the ruin of their native city. On that fatal night when the wooden horse disgorged its contents of armed men, and the capture and conflagration of the city were the result, Aeneas made his escape from the scene of destruction with his father and his wife and young son. The father, Anchises, was too old to walk with the speed required, and Aeneas took him upon his shoulders. Thus burdened, leading his son and followed by his wife, he made the best of his way out of the burning city; but, in the confusion, his wife was swept away and lost.

On arriving at the place of rendezvous, numerous fugitives of both sexes were found, who put themselves under the guidance of Aeneas. Some months were spent in preparation, and at length they embarked. They first landed on the neighboring shores of Thrace, and were preparing to build a city, but Aeneas was deterred by a prodigy. Preparing to offer sacrifice, he tore some twigs from one of the bushes. To his dismay the wounded part dropped blood. When he repeated the act, a voice from the ground cried out to him, "Spare me, Aeneas; I am your kinsman, Polydore, here murdered with many arrows, from which a bush has grown, nourished with my blood." These words recalled to the recollection of Aeneas that Polydore was a young prince of Troy, whom his father had sent with ample treasures to the neighboring land of Thrace, there to be brought up, at a distance from the horrors of war. The king to whom he was sent had murdered him and seized his treasures. Aeneas and his companions, considering the land accursed by the stain of such a crime, hastened away.

They next landed on the island of Delos, which was once a floating island, till Jupiter fastened it by adamantine chains to the bottom of the sea. Apollo and Diana were born there, and the island was sacred to Apollo. Here Aeneas consulted the oracle of Apollo

179

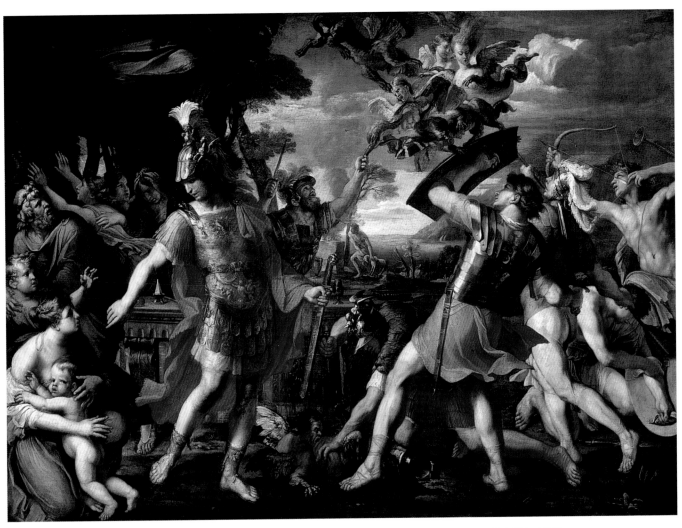

▲ Aeneas and His Companions Fight against the Harpies, FRANÇOIS PERRIER (1590–1650)
Virgil's Aeneid *furnished the Romans with their own equivalent of Homer's Greek epics. Aeneas and his men therefore face similar perils
to those of Ulysses and his crew—including the predatory half-bird, half-human Harpies.*

and received an answer, ambiguous as usual—"Seek your ancient mother; there the race of Aeneas shall dwell and reduce all other nations to their sway." The Trojans heard with joy and immediately began to ask one another, "Where is the spot intended by the oracle?" Anchises remembered that there was a tradition that their forefathers came from Crete, and thither they resolved to steer. They arrived at Crete and began to build their city, but sickness broke out among them, and the fields that they had planted failed to yield a crop. In this gloomy aspect of affairs, Aeneas was warned in a dream to leave the country and seek a western land, called Hesperia, whence Dardanus, the true founder of the Trojan race, had originally migrated. To Hesperia, now called Italy, therefore, they directed their future course, and not

till after many adventures, and the lapse of time sufficient to carry a modern navigator several times round the world, did they arrive there.

THE HARPIES

Their first landing was at the island of the Harpies. These were disgusting birds, with the heads of maidens, with long claws and faces pale with hunger. They were sent by the gods to torment a certain Phineus, whom Jupiter had deprived of his sight in punishment of his cruelty; and whenever a meal was placed before him, the Harpies darted down from the air and carried it off. They were driven away from Phineus by the heroes of the Argonautic expedition and took refuge in the island where Aeneas now found them.

When they entered the port, the Trojans saw herds of cattle roaming over the plain. They slew as many as they wished and prepared for a feast. But no sooner had they seated themselves at the table than a horrible clamor was heard in the air, and a flock of these odious Harpies came rushing down upon them, seizing in their talons the meat from the dishes and flying away with it. Aeneas and his companions drew their swords and dealt vigorous blows among the monsters, but to no purpose, for they were so nimble it was almost impossible to hit them, and their feathers were like armor impenetrable to steel. One of them, perched on a neighboring cliff, screamed out, "Is it thus, Trojans, you treat us innocent birds, first slaughter our cattle and then make war on ourselves?" She then predicted dire sufferings to them in their future course, and having vented her wrath flew away. The Trojans made haste to leave the country and next found themselves coasting along the shore of Epirus. Here they landed and, to their astonishment, learned that certain Trojan exiles, who had been carried there as prisoners, had become rulers of the country. Andromache, the widow of Hector, became the wife of one of the victorious Grecian chiefs, to whom she bore a son. Her husband dying, she was left regent of the country, as guardian of her son, and had married a fellow captive, Helenus, of the royal race of Troy. Helenus and Andromache treated the exiles with the utmost hospitality and dismissed them loaded with gifts.

From hence Aeneas coasted along the shore of Sicily and passed the country of the Cyclopes. Here they were hailed from the shore by a miserable object, whom by his garments, tattered as they were, they perceived to be a Greek. He told them he was one of Ulysses' companions, left behind by that chief in his hurried departure. He related the story of Ulysses' adventure with Polyphemus and besought them to take him off with them, as he had no means of sustaining his existence where he was but wild berries and roots, and lived in constant fear of the Cyclopes. While he spoke, Polyphemus made his appearance; a terrible monster, shapeless, vast, whose only eye had been put out. He walked with cautious steps, feeling his way with a staff, down to the seaside, to wash his eye socket in the waves. When he reached the water, he waded out toward them, and his immense height enabled him to advance far into the sea, so that the Trojans, in terror, took to their oars to get out of his way. Hearing the oars, Polyphemus shouted after them, so that the shores resounded, and at the noise the other Cyclopes came forth from their caves and woods and lined the shore, like a row of lofty pine trees. The Trojans plied their oars and soon left them out of sight.

Aeneas had been cautioned by Helenus to avoid the strait guarded by the monsters Scylla and Charybdis. There Ulysses, the reader will remember, had lost six of his men, seized by Scylla, while the navigators were wholly intent upon avoiding Charybdis. Aeneas, following the advice of Helenus, shunned the dangerous pass and coasted along the island of Sicily.

Juno, seeing the Trojans speeding their way prosperously toward their destined shore, felt her old grudge against them revive, for she could not forget the slight that Paris had put upon her, in awarding the prize of beauty to another. In heavenly minds can such resentments dwell! Accordingly she hastened to Aeolus, the ruler of the winds—the same who supplied Ulysses with favoring gales, giving him the contrary ones tied up in a bag. Aeolus obeyed the goddess and sent forth his sons, Boreas, Typhon, and the other winds, to toss the ocean. A terrible storm ensued, and the Trojan ships were driven out of their course toward the coast of Africa. They were in imminent danger of being wrecked and were separated, so that Aeneas thought that all were lost except his own.

At this crisis, Neptune, hearing the storm raging and knowing that he had given no orders for one, raised his head above the waves and saw the fleet of Aeneas driving before the gale. Knowing the hostility of Juno, he was at no loss to account for it, but his anger was not the less at this interference in his province. He called the winds and dismissed them with a severe reprimand. He then soothed the waves and brushed away the clouds from before the face of the sun. Some of the ships that had got on the rocks he pried off with his own trident, while Triton and a sea nymph, putting their shoulders under others, set them afloat again. The Trojans, when the sea became calm, sought the nearest shore, which was the coast of Carthage, where Aeneas was so happy as to find that one by one the ships all arrived safe, though badly shaken.

DIDO

Carthage, where the exiles had now arrived, was a spot on the coast of Africa opposite Sicily, where at that time a Tyrian colony under Dido, their queen, was laying the foundations of a state destined in later ages to be the rival of Rome itself. Dido was the daughter of Belus, King of Tyre, and sister of Pygmalion, who succeeded his father on the throne. Her husband was Sichaeus, a man of immense wealth, but Pygmalion, who coveted his treasures, caused him to be put to death. Dido, with a numerous body of friends and followers, both men and women, succeeded in effecting their escape from Tyre in several vessels, carrying with them the treasures of Sichaeus. On arriving at the spot which they selected as the seat of their future home, they asked of the natives only so much land as they could enclose with a bull's hide. When this was readily granted, she caused the hide to be cut into strips, and with them enclosed a spot on which she built a citadel, and called it Byrsa (a hide). Around this fort, the city of Carthage rose and soon became a powerful and flourishing place.

Such was the state of affairs when Aeneas with his Trojans arrived there. Dido received the illustrious exiles with friendliness and hospitality. "Not unacquainted with distress," she said, "I have learned to succor the unfortunate." The queen's hospitality displayed itself in festivities at which games of strength and skill were exhibited. The strangers contended for the palm with her own subjects, on equal terms, the queen declaring that whether the victor were "Trojan or Tyrian should make no difference to her." At the feast that followed the games, Aeneas gave at her request a recital of the closing events of the Trojan history and his own adventures after the fall of the city. Dido was charmed with his discourse and filled with admiration of his exploits. She conceived an ardent passion for him, and he for his part seemed well content to accept the fortunate chance that appeared to offer him at once a happy termination of his wanderings, a home, a kingdom, and a bride.

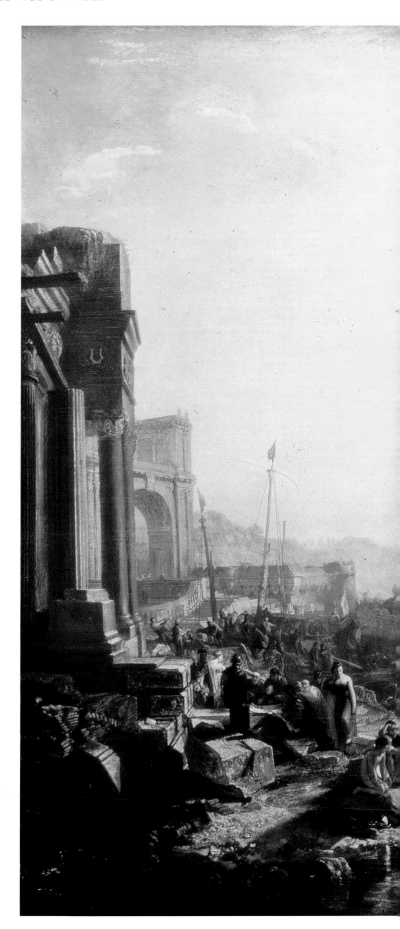

Dido Building Carthage ➤
JOSEPH MALLORD WILLIAM TURNER (1775–1851)
On the left bank of the bay, Dido supervises architects and masons.
The rising sun and children playing symbolize the rising power
and future generations of the fabulous city.

182

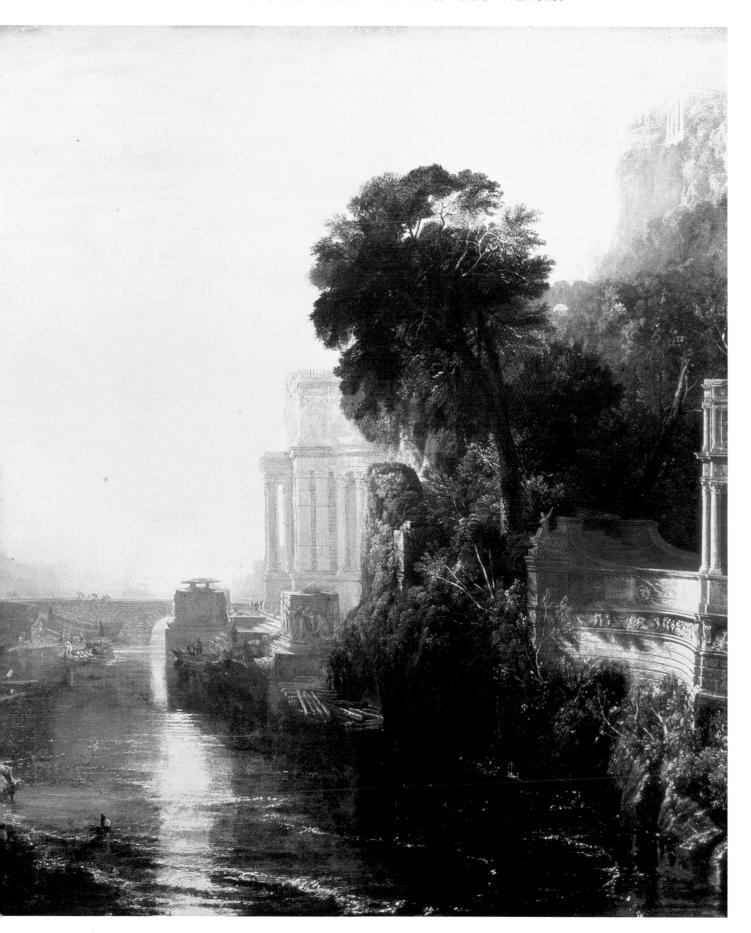

Months rolled away in the enjoyment of pleasant intercourse, and it seemed as if Italy and the empire destined to be founded on its shores were alike forgotten. Seeing which, Jupiter despatched Mercury with a message to Aeneas, recalling him to a sense of his high destiny and commanding him to resume his voyage.

Aeneas parted from Dido, though she tried every allurement and persuasion to detain him. The blow to her affection and her pride was too much for her to endure, and when she found that he was gone, she mounted a funeral pile which she had caused to be prepared, and, having stabbed herself, was consumed with the pile. The flames rising over the city were seen by the departing Trojans, and though the cause was unknown, gave to Aeneas some intimation of the fatal event.

PALINURUS

After touching at the island of Sicily, where Acestes, a prince of Trojan lineage, bore sway, who gave them a hospitable reception, the Trojans reembarked and held on their course for Italy. Venus now interceded with Neptune to allow her son at last to attain the wished-for goal and find an end of his perils on the deep. Neptune consented, stipulating only for one life as a ransom for the rest. The victim was Palinurus, the pilot. As he sat watching the stars, with his hand on the helm, Somnus, sent by Neptune, approached in the guise of Phorbas and said, "Palinurus, the breeze is fair, the water smooth, and the ship sails steadily on her course. Lie down a while and take needful rest. I will stand at the helm in your place." Palinurus replied, "Tell me not of smooth seas or favoring winds—me who have seen so much of their treachery. Shall I trust Aeneas to the chances of the weather and the winds?" And he continued to grasp the helm and to keep his eyes fixed on the stars. But Somnus waved over him a branch moistened with Lethaean dew, and his eyes closed in spite of all his efforts. Then Somnus pushed him overboard and he fell; but

keeping his hold upon the helm, it came away with him. Neptune was mindful of his promise and kept the ship on her track without helm or pilot, till Aeneas discovered his loss, and sorrowing deeply for his faithful steersman took charge of the ship himself.

The ships at last reached the shores of Italy, and joyfully did the adventurers leap to land. While his people were employed in making their encampment Aeneas sought the abode of the Sibyl. It was a cave connected with a temple and grove, sacred to Apollo and Diana. While Aeneas contemplated the scene, the Sibyl accosted him. She seemed to know his errand, and under the influence of the deity of the place, burst forth in a prophetic strain, giving dark intimations of labors and perils through which he was destined to make his way to final success. She closed with the encouraging words that have become proverbial: "Yield not to disasters, but press onward the more bravely." Aeneas replied that he had prepared himself for whatever might await him. He had but one request to make. Having been directed in a dream to seek the abode of the dead in order to confer with his father, Anchises, to receive from him a revelation of his future fortunes and those of his race, he asked her assistance to enable him to accomplish the task. The Sibyl replied, "The descent to Avernus is easy; the gate of Pluto stands open night and day; but to retrace one's steps and return to the upper air, that is the toil, that the difficulty." She instructed him to seek in the forest a tree on which grew a golden branch. This branch was to be plucked off and borne as a gift to Proserpine, and if fate was propitious it would yield to the hand and quit its parent trunk, but otherwise no force could rend it away. If torn away, another would succeed.

Aeneas followed the directions of the Sibyl. His mother, Venus, sent two of her doves to fly before him and show him the way, and by their assistance he found the tree, plucked the branch, and hastened back with it to the Sibyl.

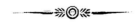

CHAPTER 31

THE INFERNAL REGIONS
ELYSIUM · THE SIBYL

As at the commencement of our series we have given the pagan account of the creation of the world, so as we approach its conclusion we present a view of the regions of the dead, depicted by one of their most enlightened poets, who drew his doctrines from their most esteemed philosophers.

The region where Virgil locates the entrance into this abode is perhaps the most strikingly adapted to excite ideas of the terrific and preternatural of any on the face of the earth. It is the volcanic region near Vesuvius, where the whole country is cleft with chasms from which sulphurous flames arise, while the ground is shaken with pent-up vapors, and mysterious sounds issue from the bowels of the earth. The lake Avernus is supposed to fill the crater of an extinct volcano. It is circular, half a mile wide, and very deep, surrounded by high banks which, in Virgil's time, were covered with a gloomy forest. Mephitic vapors rise from its waters, so that no life is found on its banks and no birds fly over it. Here, according to the poet, was the cave that afforded access to the infernal regions, and here Aeneas offered sacrifices to the infernal deities, Proserpine, Hecate, and the Furies.

Then a roaring was heard in the earth, the woods on the hilltops were shaken, and the howling of dogs announced the approach of the deities. "Now," said the Sibyl, "summon up your courage, for you will need it." She descended into the cave, and Aeneas followed. Before the threshold of hell they passed through a group of beings who are enumerated as Griefs and avenging Cares, pale Diseases and melancholy Age, Fear and Hunger that tempt to crime, Toil, Poverty, and Death, forms horrible to view. The Furies spread their couches there, and Discord, whose hair was of vipers tied up with a bloody fillet. Here also were the monsters, Briareus with his hundred arms, Hydras hissing, and Chimaeras breathing fire. Aeneas shuddered at the sight, drew his sword and would have struck, but the Sibyl restrained him.

They then came to the black river Cocytus, where they found the ferryman, Charon, old and squalid, but strong and vigorous, who was receiving passengers of all kinds into his boat, magnanimous heroes, boys and unmarried girls, as numerous as the leaves that fall at autumn or the flocks that fly southward at the approach of winter. They stood pressing for a passage and longing to touch the opposite shore. But the stern ferryman took in only such as he chose, driving the rest back. Aeneas, wondering at the sight, asked the Sibyl, "Why this discrimination?" She answered, "Those who are taken on board the bark are the souls of those who have received due burial rites; the host of others who have remained unburied are not permitted to pass the flood, but wander a hundred years and flit to and fro about the shore, till at last they are taken over." Aeneas grieved at recollecting some of his own companions who had perished in the storm. At that moment he beheld Palinurus, his pilot, who fell overboard and was drowned. He addressed him and asked him the cause of his misfortune. Palinurus replied that the rudder was carried away and he, clinging to it, was swept away with it. He besought Aeneas most urgently to extend to him his hand and take him in company to the opposite shore. But the Sibyl rebuked him for the wish thus to transgress the laws of Pluto; but consoled him by informing him that the people of the shore where his body had been wafted by the waves should be stirred up by prodigies to give it due burial, and that the promontory should bear the name of Cape Palinurus, which it does to this day.

Leaving Palinurus consoled by these words, they approached the boat. Charon, fixing his eyes sternly upon the advancing warrior, demanded by what right he, living and armed, approached that shore. To which the Sibyl replied that they would commit no violence, that Aeneas's only object was to see his father, and finally exhibited the golden branch, at sight of which Charon's wrath relaxed, and he made haste to turn his bark to the shore and receive them on board. The boat, adapted only to the light freight of bodiless spirits, groaned under the weight of the hero. They were soon conveyed to the opposite shore.

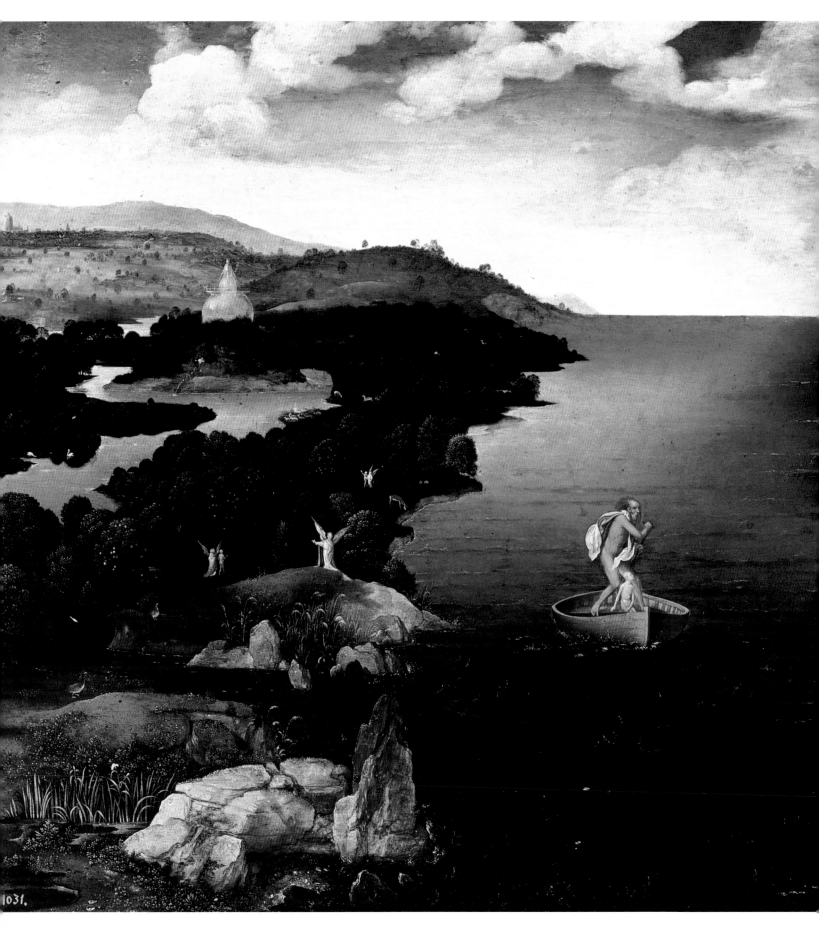

▲ The Crossing of the Styx, JOACHIM PATENIER (active 1515; died not later than 1524)
Charon the ferryman, Etruscan in origin, is shown here as a malignant and isolated figure on the black waters of Hades,
ferrying his passengers through limbo.

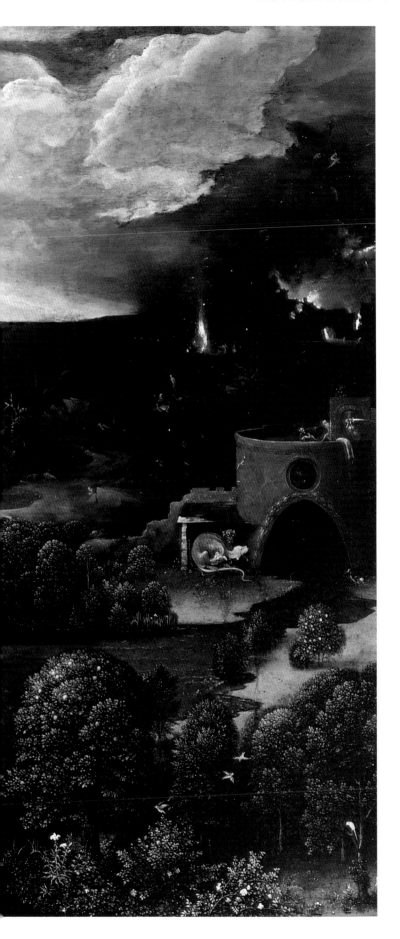

There they were encountered by the three-headed dog Cerberus, with his necks bristling with snakes. He barked with all his three throats till the Sibyl threw him a medicated cake, which he eagerly devoured and then stretched himself out in his den and fell asleep. Aeneas and the Sibyl sprang to land. The first sound that struck their ears was the wailing of young children, who had died on the threshold of life, and near to these were they who had perished under false charges. Minos presides over them as judge and examines the deeds of each. The next class was of those who had died by their own hand, hating life and seeking refuge in death. Oh, how willingly would they now endure poverty, labor and any other infliction, if they might but return to life! Next were situated the regions of sadness, divided off into retired paths, leading through groves of myrtle. Here roamed those who had fallen victims to unrequited love, not freed from pain even by death itself. Among those, Aeneas thought he descried the form of Dido, with a wound still recent. In the dim light he was for a moment uncertain, but approaching, perceived it was indeed herself. Tears fell from his eyes, and he addressed her in the accents of love. "Unhappy Dido! was then the rumor true that you had perished? And was I, alas! the cause? I call the gods to witness that my departure from you was reluctant and in obedience to the commands of Jove; nor could I believe that my absence would have cost you so dear. Stop, I beseech you, and refuse me not a last farewell." She stood for a moment, with averted countenance and eyes fixed on the ground, and then silently passed on, as insensible to his pleadings as a rock. Aeneas followed for some distance; then, with a heavy heart, rejoined his companion and resumed his route.

They next entered the fields where roam the heroes who have fallen in battle. Here they saw many shades of Grecian and Trojan warriors. The Trojans thronged around him and could not be satisfied with the sight. They asked the cause of his coming and plied him with innumerable questions. But the Greeks, at the sight of his armor glittering through the murky atmosphere, recognised the hero and, filled with terror, turned their backs and fled, as they used to do on the plains of Troy.

Aeneas would have lingered long with his Trojan friends, but the Sibyl hurried him away. They next came to a place where the road divided, the one

187

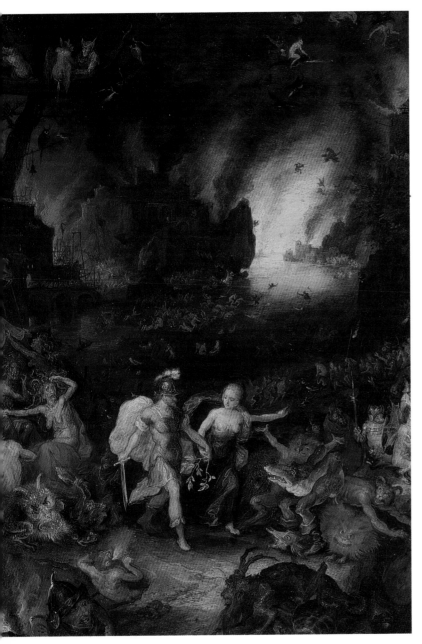

▲ Aeneas in Hades, JAN BRUEGHEL THE ELDER (1568–1625)
Book VI of Virgil's Aeneid *describes the descent of Aeneas into Hades.*
Monsters and specters are not all that Aeneas will encounter:
in this underworld he will also see a procession
of future builders of the Roman empire.

whose punishments produced the sounds he heard?

The Sibyl answered, "Here is the judgment hall of Rhadamanthus, who brings to light crimes done in life, which the perpetrator vainly thought impenetrably hid. Tisiphone applies her whip of scorpions and delivers the offender over to her sister Furies. At this moment with horrid clang the brazen gates unfolded, and Aeneas saw within a Hydra with fifty heads, guarding the entrance. The Sibyl told him that the gulf of Tartarus descended deep, so that its recesses were as far beneath their feet as heaven was high above their heads. In the bottom of this pit, the Titan race, who warred against the gods, lie prostrate; Salmoneus, also, who presumed to vie with Jupiter and built a bridge of brass over which he drove his chariot that the sound might resemble thunder, launching flaming brands at his people in imitation of lightning, till Jupiter struck him with a real thunderbolt and taught him the difference between mortal weapons and divine. Here, also, is Tityus, the giant, whose form is so immense that as he lies, he stretches over nine acres, while a vulture preys upon his liver, which as fast as it is devoured grows again, so that his punishment will have no end.

Aeneas saw groups seated at tables loaded with dainties, while nearby stood a Fury who snatched away the viands from their lips as fast as they prepared to taste them. Others beheld suspended over their heads huge rocks, threatening to fall, keeping them in a state of constant alarm. These were they who had hated their brothers, or struck their parents, or defrauded the friends who trusted them, or who, having grown rich, kept their money to themselves and gave no share to others; the last being the most numerous class. Here also were those who had violated the marriage vow, or fought in a bad cause, or failed in fidelity to their employers. Here was one who had sold his country for gold, another who perverted the laws, making them say one thing today and another tomorrow.

Ixion was there, fastened to the circumference of a wheel ceaselessly revolving; and Sisyphus, whose task was to roll a huge stone up to a hilltop, but when the steep was well-nigh gained, the rock, repulsed by some sudden force, rushed again headlong down to the plain. Again he toiled at it, while the sweat bathed all his weary limbs, but all to no effect. There was Tantalus, who stood in a pool, his chin level with

leading to Elysium, the other to the regions of the condemned. Aeneas beheld on one side the walls of a mighty city, around which Phlegethon rolled its fiery waters. Before him was the gate of adamant that neither gods nor men can break through. An iron tower stood by the gate, on which Tisiphone, the avenging Fury, kept guard. From the city were heard groans, and the sound of the scourge, the creaking of iron, and the clanking of chains. Aeneas, horror-struck, enquired of his guide what crimes were those the water, yet he was parched with thirst and found nothing to assuage it; for when he bowed his hoary head, eager to quaff, the water fled away, leaving the ground at his feet all dry. Tall trees laden with fruit stooped their heads to him, pears, pomegranates, apples and luscious figs; but when with a sudden grasp he tried to seize them, winds whirled them high above his reach.

The Sibyl now warned Aeneas that it was time to turn from these melancholy regions and seek the city of the blessed. They passed through a middle tract of darkness and came upon the Elysian fields, the groves where the happy reside. They breathed a freer air and saw all objects clothed in a purple light. The region has a sun and stars of its own. The inhabitants were enjoying themselves in various ways, some in sports on the grassy turf, in games of strength or skill, others dancing or singing. Orpheus struck the chords of his lyre and called forth ravishing sounds. Here Aeneas saw the founders of the Trojan state, magnanimous heroes who lived in happier times. He gazed with admiration on the war chariots and glittering arms now reposing in disuse. Spears stood fixed in the ground, and the horses, unharnessed, roamed over the plain. The same pride in splendid armor and generous steeds which the old heroes felt in life accompanied them here. He saw another group feasting and listening to the strains of music. They were in a laurel grove, whence the great river Po has its origin and flows out among men. Here dwelt those who fell by wounds received in their country's cause, holy priests also, and poets who have uttered thoughts worthy of Apollo, and others who have contributed to cheer and adorn life by their discoveries in the useful arts and have made their memory blessed by rendering service to mankind. They wore snow-white fillets about their brows. The Sibyl addressed a group of these and enquired where Anchises was to be found. They were directed where to seek him and soon found him in a verdant valley, where he was contemplating the ranks of his posterity, their destinies and worthy deeds to be achieved in coming times. When he recognized Aeneas approaching, he stretched out both hands to him, while tears flowed freely. "Have you come at last," said he, "long expected, and do I behold you after such perils past? Oh, my son, how have I trembled for you as I have watched your career!" To which

Aeneas replied, "Oh, father! Your image was always before me to guide and guard me." Then he endeavored to enfold his father in his embrace, but his arms enclosed only an unsubstantial image.

Aeneas perceived before him a spacious valley, with trees gently waving to the wind, a tranquil landscape, through which the river Lethe flowed. Along the banks of the stream wandered a countless multitude, numerous as insects in the summer air. Aeneas, with surprise, enquired who were these. Anchises answered, "They are souls to which bodies are to be given in due time. Meanwhile, they dwell on Lethe's bank and drink oblivion of their former lives." "Oh, father!" said Aeneas, "is it possible that any can be so in love with life as to wish to leave these tranquil seats for the upper world?" Anchises replied by explaining the plan of creation. The Creator, he told him, originally made the material of which souls are composed, of the four elements, fire, air, earth and water, all which when united took the form of the most excellent part, fire, and became flame. This material was scattered like seed among the heavenly bodies, the sun, moon, and stars. Of this seed the inferior gods created man and all other animals, mingling it with various proportions of earth, by which its purity was alloyed and reduced. Thus the more earth predominates in the composition, the less pure is the individual; and we see men and women with their full-grown bodies have not the purity of childhood. So in proportion to the time which the union of body and soul has lasted is the impurity contracted by the spiritual part. This impurity must be purged away after death, which is done by ventilating the souls in the current of winds, or merging them in water, or burning out their impurities by fire. Some few, of whom Anchises intimates that he is one, are admitted at once to Elysium, there to remain. But the rest, after the impurities of earth are purged away, are sent back to life endowed with new bodies, having had the remembrance of their former lives effectually washed away by the waters of Lethe. Some, however, there still are, so thoroughly corrupted that they are not fit to be entrusted with human bodies, and these are made into brute animals, lions, tigers, cats, dogs, monkeys, etc. This is what the ancients called metempsychosis, or the transmigration of souls; a doctrine that is still held by the natives of India, who scruple to destroy the life, even of the most

189

insignificant animal, not knowing but it may be one of their relations in an altered form.

Anchises, having explained so much, proceeded to point out to Aeneas individuals of his race who were hereafter to be born, and to relate to him the exploits they should perform in the world. After this he reverted to the present and told his son of the events that remained to him to be accomplished before the complete establishment of himself and his followers in Italy. Wars were to be waged, battles fought, a bride to be won, and in the result a Trojan state founded, from which should rise the Roman power, to be in time the sovereign of the world.

Aeneas and the Sibyl then took leave of Anchises and returned by some short cut, which the poet does not explain, to the upper world.

ELYSIUM

Virgil, we have seen, places his Elysium under the earth and assigns it for a residence to the spirits of the blessed. But in Homer Elysium forms no part of the realms of the dead. He places it on the west of the earth, near Ocean, and describes it as a happy land, where there is neither snow, nor cold, nor rain, and always fanned by the delightful breezes of Zephyrus. Hither favored heroes pass without dying and live happy under the rule of Rhadamanthus. The Elysium of Hesiod and Pindar is in the Isles of the Blessed, or Fortunate Islands, in the Western Ocean. From these sprang the legend of the happy island Atlantis.

THE SIBYL

As Aeneas and the Sibyl pursued their way back to earth, he said to her, "Whether thou be a goddess or a mortal beloved of the gods, by me thou shalt always be held in reverence. When I reach the upper air, I will cause a temple to be built to thy honor, and will myself bring offerings." "I am no goddess," said the Sibyl; "I have no claim to sacrifice or offering. I am mortal; yet if I could have accepted the love of Apollo, I might have been immortal. He promised me the fulfillment of my wish, if I would consent to be his. I took a handful of sand and, holding it forth, said, 'Grant me to see as many birthdays as there are

sand grains in my hand.' Unluckily I forgot to ask for enduring youth. This also he would have granted, could I have accepted his love, but offended at my refusal, he allowed me to grow old. My youth and youthful strength fled long ago. I have lived seven hundred years, and to equal the number of the sand grains, I have still to see three hundred springs and three hundred harvests. My body shrinks up as years increase, and in time I shall be lost to sight, but my voice will remain, and future ages will respect my sayings."

These concluding words of the Sibyl alluded to her prophetic power. In her cave she was accustomed to inscribe on leaves gathered from the trees the names and fates of individuals. The leaves thus inscribed were arranged in order within the cave, and might be consulted by her votaries. But if perchance at the opening of the door the wind rushed in and dispersed the leaves, the Sibyl gave no aid to restoring them again, and the oracle was irreparably lost.

The following legend of the Sibyl is fixed at a later date. In the reign of one of the Tarquins there appeared before the king a woman who offered him nine books for sale. The king refused to purchase them, whereupon the woman went away and burned three of the books, and returning, offered the remaining books for the same price she had asked for the nine. The king again rejected them; but when the woman, after burning three books more, returned and asked for the three remaining the same price which she had before asked for the nine, his curiosity was excited, and he purchased the books. They were found to contain the destinies of the Roman state. They were kept in the temple of Jupiter Capitolinus, presented in a stone chest, and allowed to be inspected only by especial officers appointed for that duty, who on great occasions consulted them and interpreted their oracles to the people.

There were various Sibyls; but the Cumaean Sibyl, of whom Ovid and Virgil write, is the most celebrated of them. Ovid's story of her life protracted to one thousand years may be intended to represent the various Sibyls as being only reappearances of one and the same individual.

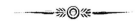

CHAPTER 32

AENEAS IN ITALY · THE GATES OF JANUS
CAMILLA · EVANDER · INFANT ROME
NISUS AND EURYALUS
MEZENTIUS · TURNUS

ENEAS, HAVING PARTED FROM THE SIBYL AND rejoined his fleet, coasted along the shores of Italy and cast anchor in the mouth of the Tiber. The poet, having brought his hero to this spot, the destined termination of his wanderings, invokes his Muse to tell him the situation of things at that eventful moment. Latinus, third in descent from Saturn, ruled the country. He was now old and had no male descendant, but had one charming daughter, Lavinia, who was sought in marriage by many neighboring chiefs, one of whom, Turnus, King of the Rutulians, was favored by the wishes of her parents. But Latinus had been warned in a dream by his father, Faunus, that the destined husband of Lavinia should come from a foreign land. From that union should spring a race destined to subdue the world.

Our readers will remember that in the conflict with the Harpies, one of those half-human birds had threatened the Trojans with dire sufferings. In particular she predicted that before their wanderings ceased they should be pressed by hunger to devour their tables. This portent now came true; for as they took their scanty meal, seated on the grass, the men placed their hard biscuit on their laps and put thereon whatever their gleanings in the woods supplied. Having despatched the latter, they finished by eating the crusts. Seeing which, the boy Iulus said playfully, "See, we are eating our tables." Aeneas caught the words and accepted the omen. "All hail, promised land!" he exclaimed. "This is our home, this our country!" He then took measures to find out who were the present inhabitants of the land, and who their rulers. A hundred chosen men were sent to the village of Latinus, bearing presents and a request for friendship and alliance. They went and were favorably received. Latinus immediately concluded that the Trojan hero was no other than the promised son-in-law announced by the oracle. He cheerfully granted his alliance and sent back the messengers mounted on steeds from his stables and loaded with gifts and friendly messages.

Juno, seeing things go thus prosperously for the Trojans, felt her old animosity revive, summoned Alecto from Erebus, and sent her to stir up discord. The Fury first took possession of the queen, Amata, and roused her to oppose in every way the new alliance. Alecto then speeded to the city of Turnus and, assuming the form of an old priestess, informed him of the arrival of the foreigners and of the attempts of their prince to rob him of his bride. Next she turned her attention to the camp of the Trojans. There she saw the boy Iulus and his companions amusing themselves with hunting. She sharpened the scent of the dogs and led them to rouse up from the thicket a tame stag, the favorite of Silvia, the daughter of Tyrrheus, the king's herdsman. A javelin from the hand of Iulus wounded the animal, and he had only strength left to run homeward, and die at his mistress's feet. Her cries and tears roused her brothers and the herdsmen, and they, seizing whatever weapons came to hand, furiously assaulted the hunting party. These were protected by their friends, and the herdsmen were finally driven back with the loss of two of their number.

These things were enough to rouse the storm of war, and the queen, Turnus, and the peasants all urged the old king to drive the strangers from the country. He resisted as long as he could, but finding his opposition unavailing, finally gave way and retreated to his retirement.

THE GATES OF JANUS

It was the custom of the country, when war was to be undertaken, for the chief magistrate, clad in his robes of office, with solemn pomp to open the gates of the temple of Janus, which were kept shut as long as peace endured. His people now urged the old king to perform that solemn office, but he refused to do so. While they contested, Juno herself, descending from the skies, smote the doors with irresistible force and burst them open. Immediately the whole country was in a flame. The people rushed from every side breathing nothing but war.

Turnus was recognized by all as leader; others joined as allies, chief of whom was Mezentius, a brave and able soldier, but of detestable cruelty. He had been the chief of one of the neighboring cities, but his people drove him out. With him was joined his son Lausus, a generous youth worthy of a better sire.

CAMILLA

Camilla, the favorite of Diana, a huntress and warrior, after the fashion of the Amazons, came with her band of mounted followers, including a select number of her own sex, and ranged herself on the side of Turnus. This maiden had never accustomed her fingers to the distaff or the loom, but had learned to endure the toils of war and in speed to outstrip the wind. It seemed as if she might run over the standing corn without crushing it, or over the surface of the water without dipping her feet. Camilla's history had been singular from the beginning. Her father, Metabus, driven from his city by civil discord, carried with him in his flight his infant daughter. As he fled through the woods, his enemies in hot pursuit, he reached the bank of the River Amazenus, which, swelled by rains, seemed to debar a passage. He paused for a moment, then decided what to do. He tied the infant to his lance with wrappers of bark and, poising the weapon in his upraised hand, thus addressed Diana: "Goddess of the woods! I consecrate this maid to you;" then hurled the weapon with its burden to the opposite bank. The spear flew across the roaring water. His pursuers were already upon him, but he plunged into the river and swam across, and found the spear, with the infant safe on the other side. Thenceforth he lived among the shepherds and brought up his daughter in woodland arts. While a child she was taught to use the bow and throw the javelin. With her sling she could bring down the crane or the wild swan. Her dress was a tiger's skin. Many mothers sought her for a daughter-in-law, but she continued faithful to Diana and repelled the thought of marriage.

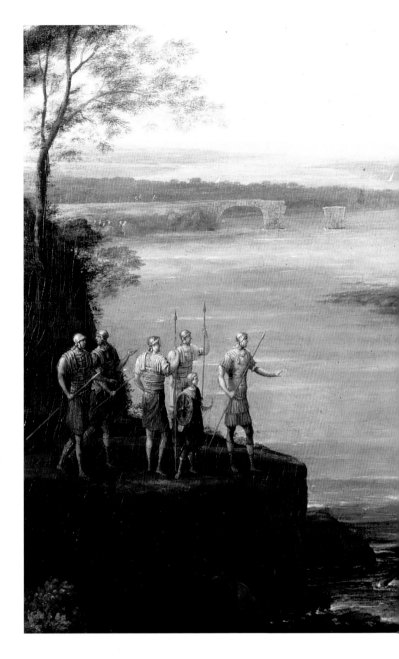

EVANDER

Such were the formidable allies that ranged themselves against Aeneas. It was night, and he lay stretched in sleep on the bank of the river, under the open heavens. The god of the stream, Father Tiber, seemed to raise his head above the willows and to say, "O goddess-born, destined possessor of the Latin realms, this is the promised land, here is to be your home, here shall terminate the hostility of the heavenly powers, if only you faithfully persevere. There are friends not far distant. Prepare your boats and row up my stream; I will lead you to Evander the Arcadian chief. He had long been at strife with Turnus

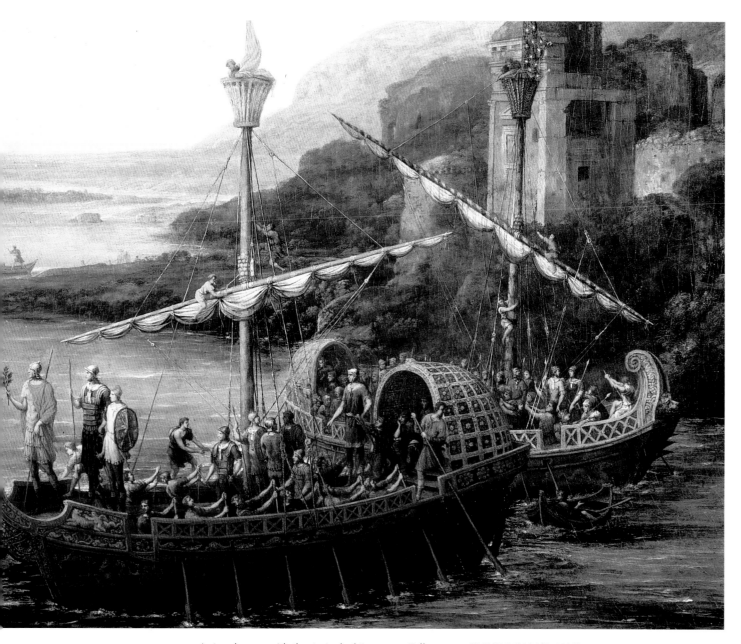

▲ Landscape with the Arrival of Aeneas at Pallanteum, CLAUDE (1604/5–1682)
The settlement of Aeneas in the territory of the Latin peoples rooted Rome, mythically speaking, in the golden age of classical legend.
Romulus and Remus are still to come; here Aeneas signals his peaceful intentions, holding an olive branch before him.

and the Rutulians, and is prepared to become an ally of yours. Rise! Offer your vows to Juno, and deprecate her anger. When you have achieved your victory then think of me." Aeneas woke and paid immediate obedience to the friendly vision. He sacrificed to Juno and invoked the god of the river and all his tributary fountains to lend their aid. Then for the first time a vessel filled with armed warriors floated on the stream of the Tiber. The river smoothed its waves, and bade its current flow gently, while, impelled by the vigorous strokes of the rowers, the vessel shot rapidly up the stream.

About the middle of the day they came in sight of the scattered buildings of the infant town where in aftertimes the proud city of Rome grew, whose glory reached the skies. By chance the old king, Evander, was that day celebrating annual solemnities in honor of Hercules and all the gods. Pallas, his son, and all the chiefs of the little commonwealth stood by. When they saw the tall ship gliding onward through the wood, they were alarmed at the sight, and rose from the tables. But Pallas forbade the solemnities to be interrupted and, seizing a weapon, stepped forward to the river's bank. He called aloud, demanding who they were and what their object. Aeneas, holding forth an olive branch, replied, "We are Trojans, friends to you and enemies to the Rutulians. We seek Evander and offer to join our arms with yours." Pallas, in amaze at the sound of so great a name, invited them to land, and when Aeneas touched the shore, he seized his hand and held it long in friendly grasp. Proceeding through the wood, they joined the king and his party, and were most favorably received. Seats were provided for them at the tables, and the repast proceeded.

INFANT ROME

When the solemnities were ended, all moved toward the city. The king, bending with age, walked between his son and Aeneas, taking the arm of one or the other of them and, with much variety of pleasing talk, shortening the way. Aeneas with delight looked and listened, observing all the beauties of the scene and learning much of heroes renowned in ancient times. Evander said, "These extensive groves were once inhabited by fauns and nymphs and a rude race of men who sprang from the trees themselves, and had neither laws nor social culture. They knew not how to yoke the cattle nor raise a harvest, nor provide from present abundance for future want; but browsed like beasts upon the leafy boughs, or fed voraciously on their hunted prey. Such were they when Saturn, expelled from Olympus by his sons, came among them and drew together the fierce savages, formed them into society, and gave them laws. Such peace and plenty ensued that men ever since have called his reign the golden age; but, by degrees, four other times succeeded, and the thirst of gold and the thirst of blood prevailed. The land was a prey to successive tyrants, till fortune and resistless destiny brought me hither, an exile from my native land, Arcadia."

Having thus said, he showed him the Tarpeian rock, and the rude spot then overgrown with bushes where in aftertimes the Capitol rose in all its magnificence. He next pointed to some dismantled walls and said, "Here stood Janiculum, built by Janus, and there Saturnia, the town of Saturn." Such discourse brought them to the cottage of poor Evander, whence they saw the lowing herds roaming over the plain where now the proud and stately Forum stands. They entered, and a couch was spread for Aeneas, well stuffed with leaves and covered with the skin of a Libyan bear.

Next morning, awakened by the dawn and the shrill song of birds beneath the eaves of his low mansion, old Evander rose. Clad in a tunic, and a panther's skin thrown over his shoulders, with sandals on his feet and his good sword girded to his side, he went forth to seek his guest. Two mastiffs followed him, his whole retinue and bodyguard. He found the hero attended by his faithful Achates, and, Pallas soon joining them, the old king spoke thus:

"Illustrious Trojan, it is but little we can do in so great a cause. Our state is feeble, hemmed in on one side by the river, on the other by the Rutulians. But I propose to ally you with a people numerous and rich, to whom fate has brought you at the propitious moment. The Etruscans hold the country beyond the river. Mezentius was their king, a monster of cruelty, who invented unheard-of torments to gratify his vengeance. He would fasten the dead to the living, hand to hand and face to face, and leave the wretched victims to die in that dreadful embrace. At length the people cast him out, him and his house. They burned his palace and slew his friends. He escaped and took refuge with Turnus, who protects him with arms. The Etruscans demand that he shall be given up to deserved punishment, and would ere now have attempted to enforce their demand; but their priests restrain them, telling them that it is the will of heaven that no native of the land shall guide them to victory and that their destined leader must come from across the sea. They have offered the crown to me, but I am too old to undertake such great affairs, and my son is native-born, which precludes him from the choice. You, equally by birth and time of life, and fame in arms, pointed out by the gods, have but to appear to be hailed at once as their leader. With you I will join Pallas, my son, my only hope and comfort. Under you he shall learn the art of war and strive to emulate your great exploits."

Then the king ordered horses to be furnished for the Trojan chiefs, and Aeneas, with a chosen band of followers and Pallas accompanying, mounted and took the way to the Etruscan city, having sent back the rest of his party in the ships. Aeneas and his band safely arrived at the Etruscan camp, and were received with open arms by Tarchon and his countrymen.

NISUS AND EURYALUS

In the meanwhile Turnus had collected his bands and made all necessary preparations for the war. Juno sent Iris to him with a message inciting him to take advantage of the absence of Aeneas and surprise the Trojan camp. Accordingly the attempt was made, but the Trojans were found on their guard, and having received strict orders from Aeneas not to fight in his absence, they lay still in their entrenchments and resisted all the effort of the Rutulians to draw them into the field. Night coming on, the army of Turnus, in high spirits at their fancied superiority, feasted and enjoyed themselves and finally stretched themselves on the field and slept secure.

In the camp of the Trojans things were far otherwise. There all was watchfulness and anxiety and impatience for Aeneas's return. Nisus stood guard at the entrance of the camp, and Euryalus, a youth distinguished above all in the army for graces of person and fine qualities, was with him. These two were friends and brothers in arms. Nisus said to his friend, "Do you perceive what confidence and carelessness the enemy display? Their lights are few and dim, and the men seem all oppressed with wine or sleep. You know how anxiously our chiefs wish to send to Aeneas and to get intelligence from him. Now I am strongly moved to make my way through the enemy's camp and to go in search of our chief. If I succeed, the glory of the deed will be reward enough for me, and if they judge the service deserves anything more, let them pay it to you."

Euryalus, all on fire with the love of adventure, replied, "Would you then, Nisus, refuse to share your enterprise with me? And shall I let you go into such danger alone? Not so my brave father brought me up, nor so have I planned for myself when I joined the standard of Aeneas and resolved to hold my life cheap in comparison with honor." Nisus replied, "I doubt it not, my friend; but you know the uncertain event of such an undertaking, and whatever may happen to me, I wish you to be safe. You are younger than I and have more of life in prospect. Nor can I be the cause of such grief to your mother, who has chosen to be here in the camp with you rather than stay and live in peace with the other matrons in Acestes' city." Euryalus replied, "Say no more. In vain you seek arguments to dissuade me. I am fixed in the resolution to go with you. Let us lose no time." They called the guard and, committing the watch to them, sought the general's tent. They found the chief officers in consultation, deliberating how they should send notice to Aeneas of their situation. The offer of the two friends was gladly accepted, themselves loaded with praises and promised the most liberal rewards in case of success. Iulus especially addressed Euryalus, assuring him of his lasting friendship. Euryalus replied, "I have but one boon to ask. My aged mother is with me in the camp. For me she left the Trojan soil, and would not stay behind with the other matrons at the city of Acestes. I go now without taking leave of her. I could not bear her tears nor set at nought her entreaties. But do thou, I beseech you, comfort her in her distress. Promise me that, and I shall go more boldly into whatever dangers may present themselves." Iulus and the other chiefs were moved to tears, and promised to do all his request. "Your mother shall be mine," said Iulus, "and all that I have promised to you shall be made good to her, if you do not return to receive it."

The two friends left the camp and plunged at once into the midst of the enemy. They found no watch, no sentinels posted, but all about the sleeping soldiers strewn on the grass and among the wagons. The laws of war at that early day did not forbid a brave man to slay a sleeping foe, and the two Trojans slew, as they passed, such of the enemy as they could without exciting alarm. In one tent Euryalus made prize of a helmet brilliant with gold and plumes. They had passed through the enemy's ranks without being discovered, but now suddenly appeared a troop directly in front of them, which, under Volscens, their leader, were approaching the camp. The glittering helmet of Euryalus caught their attention, and Volscens hailed the two and demanded who and whence they were. They made no answer, but plunged into the wood. The horsemen scattered in all directions to intercept their flight. Nisus had eluded pursuit and was out of danger, but Euryalus being missing, he turned back to seek him. He again entered the wood and soon came within sound of voices. Looking through the thicket he saw the whole band surrounding Euryalus with noisy questions. What should he do! How extricate the youth! Or would it be better to die with him?

Raising his eyes to the moon, which now shone clear, he said, "Goddess! Favor my effort!" and aiming his javelin at one of the leaders of the troop, struck him in the back and stretched him on the plain with a death blow. In the midst of their amazement another weapon flew and another of the party fell dead. Volscens, the leader, ignorant whence the darts came, rushed sword in hand upon Euryalus. "You shall pay the penalty of both," he said, and would have plunged the sword into his bosom, when Nisus, who from his concealment saw the peril of his friend, rushed forward exclaiming, "'Twas I, 'twas I; turn your swords against me, Rutulians; I did it; he only followed me as a friend." While he spoke the sword fell and pierced the comely bosom of Euryalus. His head fell over on his shoulder, like a flower cut down by the plow. Nisus rushed upon Volscens and plunged his sword into his body, and was himself slain on the instant by numberless blows.

MEZENTIUS

Aeneas, with his Etrurian allies, arrived on the scene of action in time to rescue his beleaguered camp; and now the two armies being nearly equal in strength, the war began in good earnest. We cannot find space for all the details, but must simply record the fate of the principal characters whom we have introduced to our readers. The tyrant Mezentius, finding himself engaged against his revolted subjects, raged like a wild beast. He slew all who dared to withstand him and put the multitude to flight wherever he appeared. At last he encountered Aeneas, and the armies stood still to see the issue. Mezentius threw his spear, which, striking Aeneas's shield, glanced off and hit Anthor. He was a Grecian by birth, who had left Argos, his native city, and followed Evander into Italy. The poet says of him with simple pathos that has made the words proverbial, "He fell, unhappy, by a wound intended for another, looked up to the skies, and dying remembered sweet Argos." Aeneas now in turn hurled his lance. It pierced the shield of Mezentius and wounded him in the thigh. Lausus, his son, could not bear the sight, but rushed forward and interposed himself, while the followers pressed around Mezentius and bore him away. Aeneas held his sword suspended over Lausus and delayed to strike, but the furious youth pressed on, and he was compelled to deal the fatal blow. Lausus fell, and Aeneas bent over him in pity. "Hapless youth," he said, "what can I do for you worthy of your praise?

Keep those arms in which you glory, and fear not but that your body shall be restored to your friends and have due funeral honors." So saying, he called the timid followers and delivered the body into their hands.

Mezentius, meanwhile, had been borne to the riverside, and washed his wound. Soon the news reached him of Lausus's death, and rage and despair supplied the place of strength. He mounted his horse and dashed into the thickest of the fight, seeking Aeneas. Having found him, he rode him in a circle, throwing one javelin after another, while Aeneas stood fenced with his shield, turning every way to meet them. At last, after Mezentius had three times made the circuit, Aeneas threw his lance directly at the horse's head. It pierced his temples and he fell, while a shout from both armies rent the skies. Mezentius asked no mercy, but only that his body might be spared the insults of his revolted subjects and be buried in the same grave with his son. He received the fatal stroke not unprepared, and poured out his life and his blood together.

TURNUS

While these things were doing in one part of the field, in another Turnus encountered the youthful Pallas. The contest between champions so unequally matched could not be doubtful. Pallas bore himself bravely, but fell by the lance of Turnus. The victor almost relented when he saw the brave youth lying dead at his feet, and spared to use the privilege of a conqueror in despoiling him of his arms. The belt only, adorned with studs and carvings of gold, he took and clasped round his own body. The rest he remitted to the friends of the slain.

After the battle there was a cessation of arms for some days to allow both armies to bury their dead. In this interval Aeneas challenged Turnus to decide the contest by single combat, but Turnus evaded the challenge. Another battle ensued, in which Camilla, the virgin warrior, was chiefly conspicuous. Her deeds of valor surpassed those of the bravest warriors, and many Trojans and Etruscans fell pierced with her darts or struck down by her battle-ax. At last an Etruscan named Aruns, who had watched her long, seeking for some advantage, observed her pursuing a flying enemy whose splendid armor offered a tempting prize. Intent on the chase, she observed not her danger, and the javelin of Aruns struck her and inflicted a fatal wound. She fell and breathed her last in the arms of her attendant maidens. But Diana, who beheld her fate, suffered not her slaughter to be unavenged. Aruns, as he stole away, glad but frightened, was struck by a secret arrow, launched by one of the nymphs of Diana's train, and died ignobly and unknown.

At length the final conflict took place between Aeneas and Turnus. Turnus had avoided the contest as long as he could, but at last impelled by the ill success of his arms, and by the murmurs of his followers, he braced himself to the conflict. It could not be doubtful. On the side of Aeneas were the expressed decree of destiny, the aid of his goddess-mother at every emergency, and impenetrable armor fabricated by Vulcan, at her request, for her son. Turnus, on the other hand, was deserted by his celestial allies, Juno having been expressly forbidden by Jupiter to assist him any longer. Turnus threw his lance, but it recoiled harmless from the shield of Aeneas. The Trojan hero then threw his, which penetrated the shield of Turnus and pierced his thigh. Then Turnus's fortitude forsook him and he begged for mercy; and Aeneas would have given him his life, but at the instant his eye fell on the belt of Pallas, which Turnus had taken from the slaughtered youth. Instantly his rage revived, and exclaiming, "Pallas immolates thee with this blow," he thrust him through with his sword.

Here the poem of the *Aeneid* closes, and we are left to infer that Aeneas, having triumphed over his foes, obtained Lavinia for his bride. Tradition adds that he founded his city and called it after her name, Lavinium. His son Iulus founded Alba Longa, which was the birthplace of Romulus and Remus and the cradle of Rome itself.

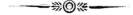

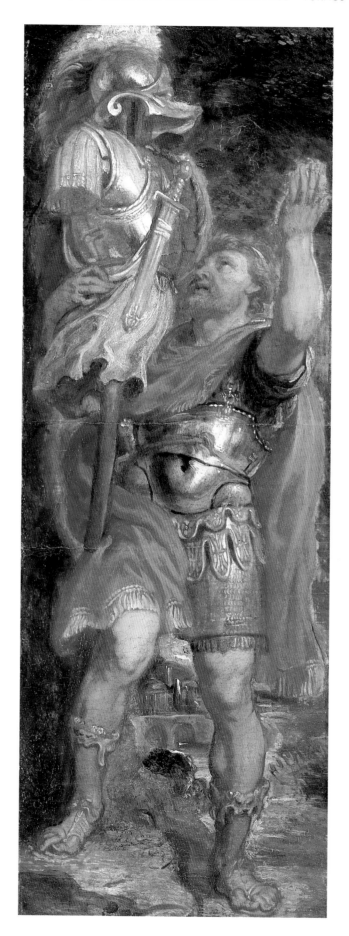

Aeneas with the Arms of Mezentius, ➤
PETER PAUL RUBENS (1577–1640)
Aeneas flourishes the arms of Mezentius as if they were the spolia optima, *or ultimate trophy, coveted in battle by every Roman general.*

197

FAMILY TREE OF THE GREEK GODS

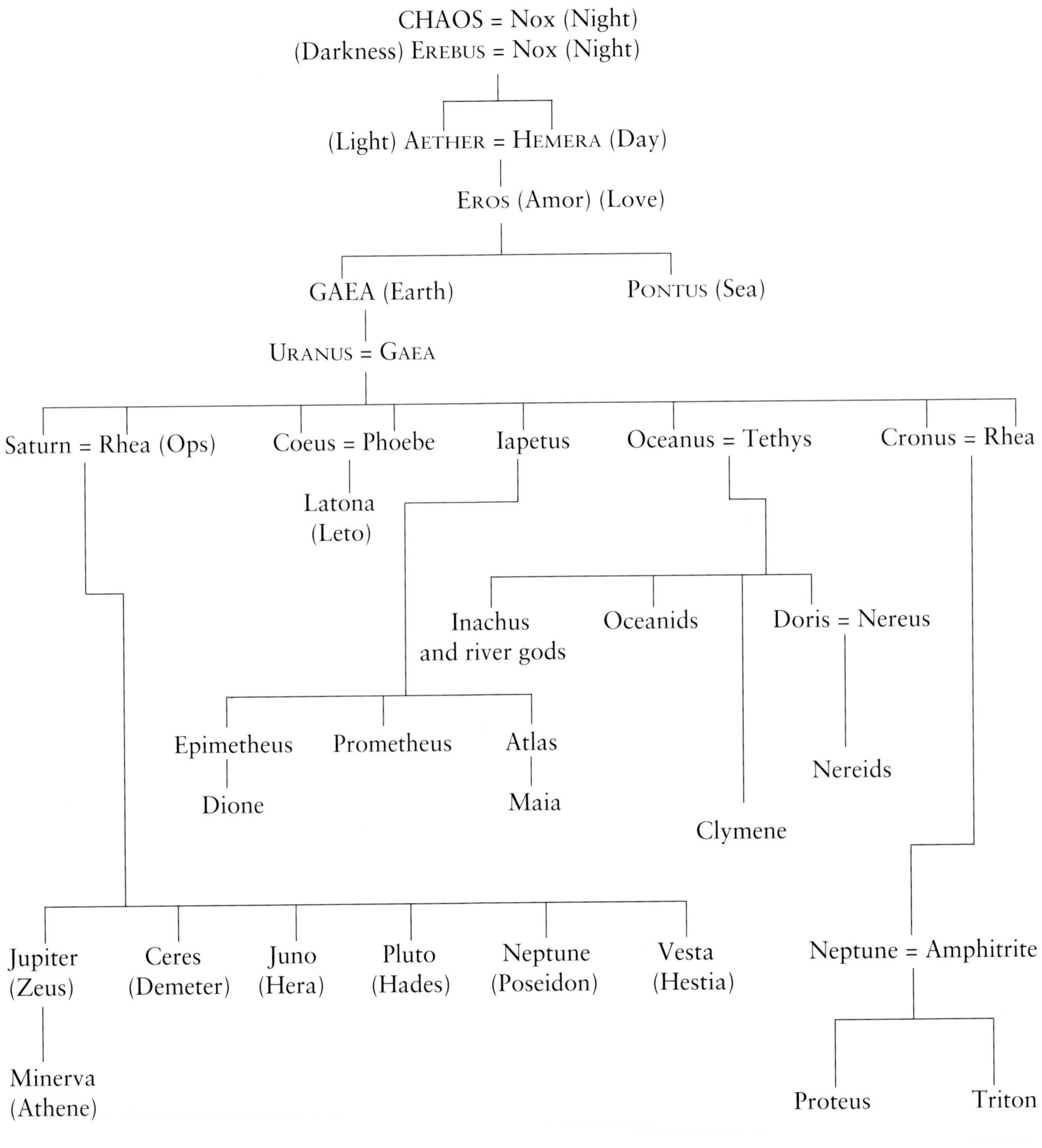

CHAOS = Nox (Night)

(Darkness) EREBUS = Nox (Night)

(Light) AETHER = HEMERA (Day)

EROS (Amor) (Love)

GAEA (Earth)   PONTUS (Sea)

URANUS = GAEA

Saturn = Rhea (Ops)   Coeus = Phoebe   Iapetus   Oceanus = Tethys   Cronus = Rhea

Latona
(Leto)

Inachus   Oceanids   Doris = Nereus
and river gods

Epimetheus   Prometheus   Atlas

Dione   Maia

Nereids

Clymene

Jupiter   Ceres   Juno   Pluto   Neptune   Vesta   Neptune = Amphitrite
(Zeus)   (Demeter)   (Hera)   (Hades)   (Poseidon)   (Hestia)

Minerva
(Athene)

Proteus   Triton

198

THE CHILDREN OF EARTH & SEA

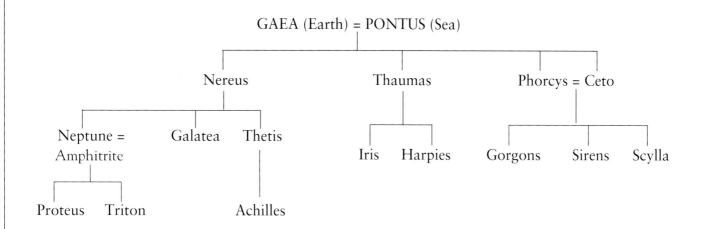

GAEA (Earth) = PONTUS (Sea)

Nereus Thaumas Phorcys = Ceto

Neptune = Amphitrite Galatea Thetis

Iris Harpies

Gorgons Sirens Scylla

Proteus Triton

Achilles

THE CHILDREN OF JUPITER

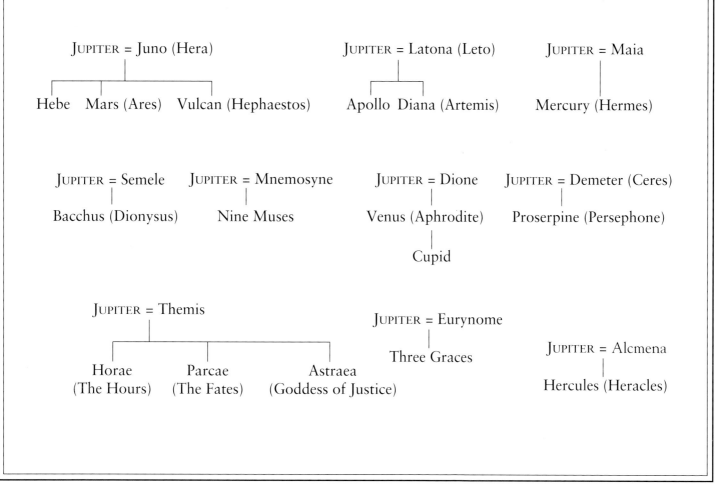

JUPITER = Juno (Hera)

Hebe Mars (Ares) Vulcan (Hephaestos)

JUPITER = Latona (Leto)

Apollo Diana (Artemis)

JUPITER = Maia

Mercury (Hermes)

JUPITER = Semele

Bacchus (Dionysus)

JUPITER = Mnemosyne

Nine Muses

JUPITER = Dione

Venus (Aphrodite)

Cupid

JUPITER = Demeter (Ceres)

Proserpine (Persephone)

JUPITER = Themis

Horae
(The Hours) Parcae
(The Fates) Astraea
(Goddess of Justice)

JUPITER = Eurynome

Three Graces

JUPITER = Alcmena

Hercules (Heracles)

INDEX OF ARTISTS AND PAINTINGS

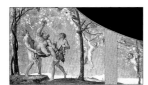

p. 1 **Silenus Gathering Grapes**
(*detail*)
ANNIBALE CARRACCI
1560-1609
The National Gallery, London

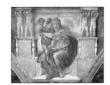

p. 8 **Delphic Sibyl** (*detail*)
MICHELANGELO
1475-1564
Sistine Chapel, The Vatican, Rome

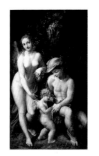

p. 14 **Venus with Mercury and
Cupid ("The School of Love")**
CORREGGIO
circa 1494; died 1534
The National Gallery, London

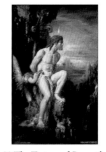

p. 20 **The Torture of Prometheus**
GUSTAVE MOREAU
1826-1898
Musée Gustave Moreau, Paris

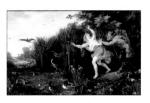

pp. 30-31 **Landscape
with Pan and Syrinx**
PETER PAUL RUBENS
AND JAN BRUEGHEL
THE ELDER
1577-1640 and 1568-1625
Private Collection

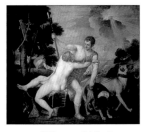

p. 3 **Venus and Adonis**
TITIAN
active circa 1506; died 1576
Prado, Madrid

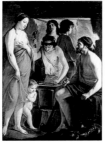

p. 10 **Venus at Vulcan's Forge**
MATHIEU LE NAIN
circa 1607-1677
Musée des Beaux-Arts, Reims

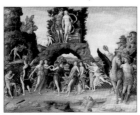

p. 15 **Mars and Venus,
Known as Parnassus**
ANDREA MANTEGNA
circa 1430/1-1506
Louvre, Paris

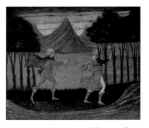

p. 23 **Daphne Pursued by Apollo**
MASTER OF THE JUDGMENT
OF PARIS
Italian, active mid-15th century
*The Barber Institute of Fine Arts,
University of Birmingham*

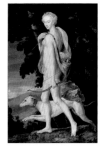

p. 33 **Diana the Huntress**
SCHOOL OF FONTAINEBLEAU
circa 1530-1560
Louvre, Paris

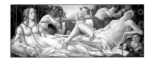

pp. 4-5 **Venus and Mars**
SANDRO BOTTICELLI
circa 1445-1510
The National Gallery, London

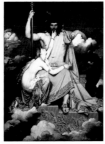

p. 11 **Jupiter and Thetis**
JEAN-AUGUSTE-DOMINIQUE
INGRES
1780-1867
Musée Granet, Aix-en-Provence

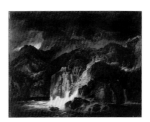

p. 17 **Prometheus**
ARNOLD BÖCKLIN
1827-1901
Private Collection

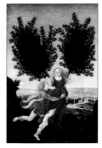

p. 24 **Apollo and Daphne**
ANTONIO DEL POLLAIUOLO
circa 1432-1498
The National Gallery, London

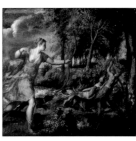

p. 34 **The Death of Actaeon**
TITIAN
active circa 1506; died 1576
The National Gallery, London

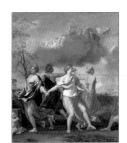

p. 6 **A Dance to the Music of Time**
NICOLAS POUSSIN
1594-1665
Wallace Collection, London

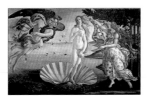

pp. 12-13 **The Birth of Venus**
SANDRO BOTTICELLI
circa 1445-1510
Uffizi, Florence

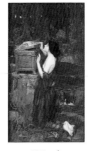

p. 18 **Pandora**
JOHN WILLIAM WATERHOUSE
1849-1917
Private Collection

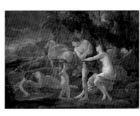

pp. 26-27 **Cephalus and Aurora**
NICOLAS POUSSIN
1594-1665
The National Gallery, London

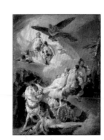

p. 37 **Phaëton and Apollo**
GIAMBATTISTA TIEPOLO
1696-1770
*Gemäldegalerie Akademie der
Bildenden Kunste, Vienna*

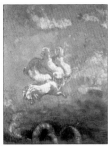

p. 39 **Phaëton and Apollo**
ODILON REDON
1840-1916
Louvre, Paris

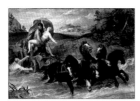

p. 47 **The Rape of Proserpine**
CHRISTOPH SCHWARTZ
1545-1592
*Fitzwilliam Museum,
University of Cambridge*

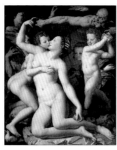

p. 53 **An Allegory
with Venus and Cupid**
BRONZINO
1503-1572
The National Gallery, London

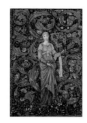

p. 62 **Pomona Tapestry Design**
SIR EDWARD BURNE-JONES
1833-1898
*The National Trust,
Wightwick Manor*

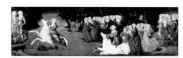

pp. 72-73 **Europa and the Bull**
LIBERALE DA VERONA
circa 1445-1527/9
Louvre, Paris

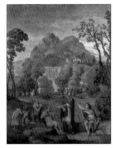

p. 41 **Midas at the Source
of the Pactolus**
NICOLAS POUSSIN
1594-1665
Museé Fesch, Ajaccio, Corsica

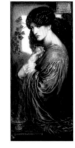

p. 48 **Proserpine** (*detail*)
DANTE GABRIEL ROSSETTI
1828-1882
Private Collection

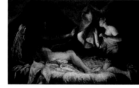

pp. 54-55 **Venus Weeping
over Adonis**
NICOLAS POUSSIN
1594-1665
Musée des Beaux Arts, Caen

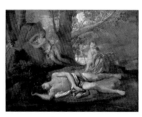

pp. 66-67 **Landscape with Psyche
outside the Palace of Cupid
("The Enchanted Castle")**
CLAUDE
1604/5-1682
The National Gallery, London

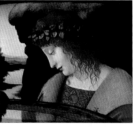

p. 77 **Narcissus**
FOLLOWER OF LEONARDO
1452-1519
The National Gallery, London

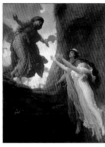

p. 43 **The Judgment of Midas**
DOMENICHINO
AND ASSISTANTS
1581-1641
The National Gallery, London

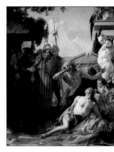

p. 49 **The Return of Persephone**
LORD FREDERIC LEIGHTON
1830-1896
Leeds City Art Gallery

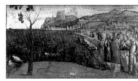

p. 56 **The Death of Hyacinth**
GIAMBATTISTA TIEPOLO
1696-1770
*Museo Thyssen-Bornemisza,
Madrid*

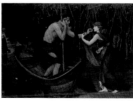

p. 69 **Cupid and Psyche**
GIUSEPPE MARIA CRESPI
1665-1747
Uffizi, Florence

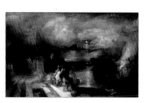

pp. 78-79 **Echo and Narcissus**
NICOLAS POUSSIN
1594-1665
Louvre, Paris

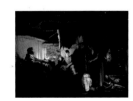

p. 44 **Jupiter and Mercury beside
Philemon and Baucis**
ADAM ELSHEIMER
1578-1610
Gemäldegalerie, Dresden

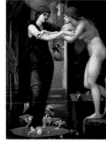

p. 51 **The Godhead Fires**
SIR EDWARD BURNE-JONES
1833-1898
Private Collection

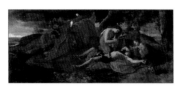

pp. 60-61 **The Metamorphosis
of Alcyone**
VITTORE CARPACCIO
active 1490; died 1523/6
*Philadelphia Museum of Art
(The John G. Johnson Collection)*

p. 71 **Charon and Psyche** (*detail*)
JOHN SPENCER STANHOPE
1829-1908
Private Collection

p. 80 **The Parting
of Hero and Leander**
JOSEPH MALLORD WILLIAM
TURNER
1775-1851
The National Gallery, London

201

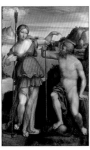

p. 81 **Neptune and Minerva**
GAROFALO
circa 1481-1559
Gemäldegalerie, Dresden

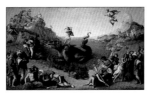

pp. 88-89 **Andromeda Saved
by Perseus**
PIERO DI COSIMO
circa 1462-1521
Uffizi, Florence

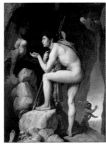

p. 94 **Oedipus Explains the Riddle
of the Sphinx**
JEAN-AUGUSTE-DOMINIQUE
INGRES
1780-1867
Louvre, Paris

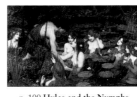

p. 100 **Hylas and the Nymphs**
JOHN WILLIAM WATERHOUSE
1849-1917
Manchester City Art Galleries

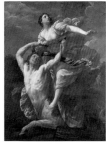

p. 109 **The Abduction of Dejanira
by the Centaur Nessus**
GUIDO RENI
1575-1642
Louvre, Paris

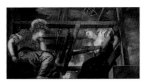

pp. 82-83 **Minerva and Arachne**
JACOPO TINTORETTO
1518-1594
*Collection Contini Bonacossi,
Florence*

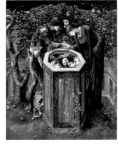

p. 91 **The Baleful Head**
SIR EDWARD BURNE-JONES
1833-1898
Southampton City Art Gallery

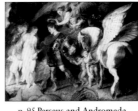

p. 95 **Perseus and Andromeda**
(detail)
PETER PAUL RUBENS
1577-1640
The Hermitage, St Petersburg

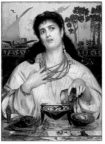

p. 101 **Medea**
FREDERICK SANDYS
1829-1904
*Birmingham Museum
and Art Gallery*

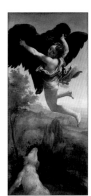

p. 110 **The Rape
of Ganymede**
CORREGGIO
circa 1494; died 1534
*Kunsthistorisches Museum,
Vienna*

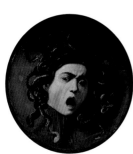

p. 86 **Medusa**
CARAVAGGIO
1571-1610
Uffizi, Florence

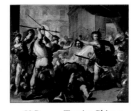

p. 92 **Perseus Turning Phineas
and His Followers to Stone**
LUCA GIORDANO
1634-1705
The National Gallery, London

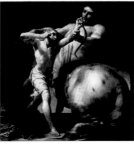

p. 96 **The Centaur Chiron Teaches
the Young Achilles Archery**
GIUSEPPE MARIA CRESPI
1665-1747
Kunsthistorisches Museum, Vienna

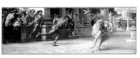

pp. 104-105 **Atalanta's Race**
SIR EDWARD JOHN POYNTER
1836-1919
Private Collection

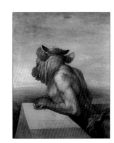

p. 111 **The Minotaur**
GEORGE FREDERICK WATTS
1817-1904
Tate Gallery, London

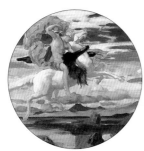

p. 87 *Study for* **Perseus on Pegasus
Hastening to the Rescue of
Andromeda**
LORD FREDERIC LEIGHTON
1830-1896
Private Collection

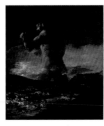

p. 93 **The Colossus**
FRANCISCO DE GOYA
1746-1828
Prado, Madrid

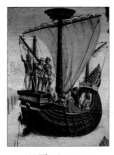

p. 98 **The Argonauts
Leaving Colchis**
ERCOLE de'ROBERTI
active 1479; died 1496
*Museo Thyssen-Bornemisza,
Madrid*

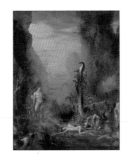

p. 106 **Hercules and the Hydra
of Lerna**
GUSTAVE MOREAU
1826-1898
*Musée Nationale Gustave Moreau,
Paris*

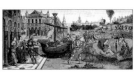

pp. 112-113 **History of Theseus:
Ariadne Delivered by Theseus**
MASTER OF THE CASSONI
CAMPANA
early 16th century
Musée du Petit-Palais, Avignon

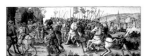

pp. 114-115 **History of Theseus:**
The Taking of Athens by Minos
MASTER OF THE CASSONI
CAMPANA
early 16th century
Musée du Petit-Palais, Avignon

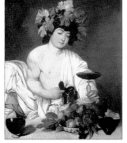

p. 120 **The Young Bacchus**
CARAVAGGIO
1571-1610
Uffizi, Florence

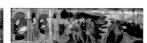

pp. 128-129 *(above)*
The Cortège of Thetis
BARTOLOMEO DI GIOVANNI
late 15th to early 16th century
Louvre, Paris

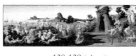

p. 134 **The Return of Ulysses** *(detail)*
SIENESE SCHOOL
16th century
Chateau Ecouen, Paris

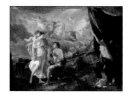

p. 142 **Diana and Endymion** *(detail)*
NICOLAS POUSSIN
1594-1665
The Detroit Institute of Arts
(Founders Society Purchase,
General Membership Fund)

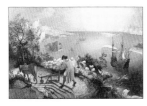

pp. 116-117 **Landscape with**
the Fall of Icarus
PIETER BRUEGEL THE ELDER
active 1550/1; died 1569
Royal Museums of Fine Arts,
Brussels

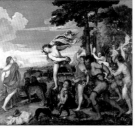

p. 123 **Bacchus and Ariadne** *(detail)*
TITIAN
active circa 1506; died 1576
The National Gallery, London

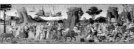

pp. 128-129 *(below)* **The Marriage of**
Peleus and Thetis
BARTOLOMEO DI GIOVANNI
late 15th to early 16th century
Louvre, Paris

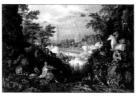

pp. 136-137 **Orpheus**
ROELANDT SAVERY
1576-1639
The National Gallery, London

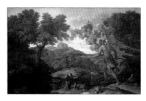

pp. 144-145 **Blind Orion**
Searching for the Rising Sun
NICOLAS POUSSIN
1594-1665
The Metropolitan Museum of Art

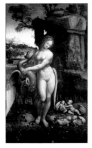

p. 118 **Leda and the Swan**
ARTIST UNKNOWN
Italian, 15th century
Uffizi, Florence

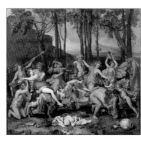

p. 124 **The Triumph of Pan**
NICOLAS POUSSIN
1594-1665
The National Gallery, London

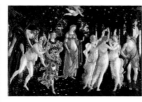

p. 130 **Primavera** *(detail)*
SANDRO BOTTICELLI
circa 1445-1510
Uffizi, Florence

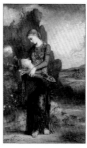

p. 138 **The Prophetic Head**
and Lyre of Orpheus
GUSTAVE MOREAU
1826-1898
Louvre, Paris

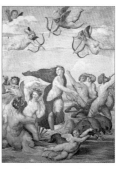

p. 147 **The Triumph of Galatea**
RAPHAEL
1483-1520
Villa Farnesina, Rome

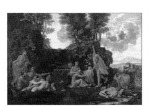

p. 119 **The Infant Bacchus**
Entrusted to the Nymphs of Nysa:
The Death of Echo and Narcis
NICOLAS POUSSIN
1594-1665
Fogg Art Museum, Cambridge,
Massachusetts
(Mrs Samuel Sachs in memory of
Mr Samuel Sachs)

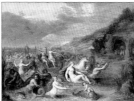

p. 127 **The Triumph of Amphitrite**
FRANS FRANCKEN
THE YOUNGER
1581-1642
Prado, Madrid

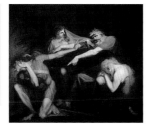

p. 133 **Oedipus Cursing**
His Son, Polynices
HENRY FUSELI
1741-1825
The National Gallery of Art,
Washington
(Paul Mellon Collection)

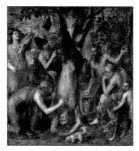

p. 141 **The Flaying of Marsyas**
TITIAN
active circa 1506; died 1576
The Archbishop's Palace, Kromeriz

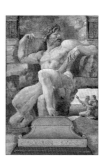

p. 148 **Polyphemus,**
Acis and Galatea *(detail)*
GIULIO ROMANO
1492/9-1546
Palazzo del Tei, Mantua
The Metropolitan Museum of Art
(Rogers Fund, 1928. 28.221)

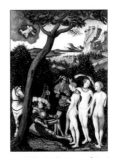

p. 149 **The Judgment of Paris**
LUCAS CRANACH THE ELDER
1472-1553
The Metropolitan Museum of Art
(Rogers Fund, 1928. 28.221)

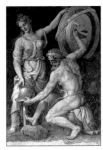

p. 158 **Vulcan Forging
the Armour of Achilles**
GIULIO ROMANO
AND WORKSHOP
1492/9-1546
Palazzo Ducale, Mantua

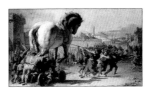

p. 165 **The Procession of
the Trojan Horse into Troy**
GIOVANNI DOMENICO
TIEPOLO
1727-1804
The National Gallery, London

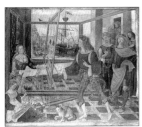

p. 177 **Penelope with the Suitors**
PINTORICCHIO
active 1481; died 1513
The National Gallery, London

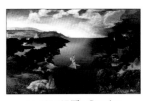

pp. 186-187 **The Crossing
of the Styx**
JOACHIM PATENIER
active 1515; died not later than 1524
Prado, Madrid

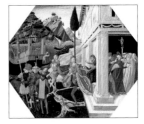

pp. 150-151 **The Abduction
of Helen by Paris**
FOLLOWER OF FRA ANGELICO
circa 1387-1455
The National Gallery, London

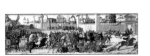

pp. 160-161 **The Siege of Troy 1:
The Death of Hector**
BIAGIO DI ANTONIO
circa 1445-1510
*Fitzwilliam Museum,
University of Cambridge*

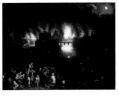

p. 166 **The Burning Troy**
JAN BRUEGHEL THE ELDER
1568-1625
Alte Pinakothek, Munich

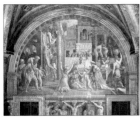

p. 179 **The Fire in the Borgo** (*detail*)
SCHOOL OF RAPHAEL
1483-1520
Vatican, Rome

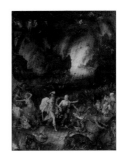

p. 188 **Aeneas in Hades**
JAN BRUEGHEL THE ELDER
1568-1625
Museum of Fine Arts, Budapest

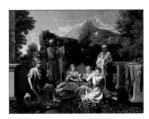

p. 152 **Achilles on Skyros**
NICOLAS POUSSIN
1594-1665
*Virginia Museum of Fine Arts,
Richmond
(The Arthur and Margaret Glasgow
Fund, #57.2)*

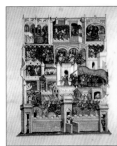

p. 162 **Scene from
the Trojan War**
HISTOIRE ANCIENNE
JUSQU'A CESAR
late 14th century
Bibliothèque Nationale, Paris

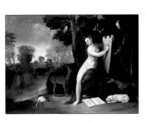

pp. 170-171 **Circe and Her Lovers
in a Landscape**
DOSSO DOSSI
active 1512; died 1542
*The National Gallery of Art,
Washington
(Samuel H. Kress Collection)*

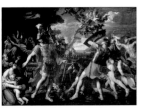

p. 180 **Aeneas and His Companions
Fight against the Harpies**
FRANÇOIS PERRIER
1590-1650
Louvre, Paris

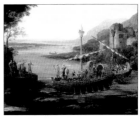

pp. 192-193 **Landscape with
the Arrival of Aeneas at Pallanteum**
CLAUDE
1604/5-1682
*The National Trust,
Anglesey Abbey*

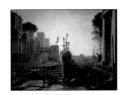

pp. 154-155 **Ulysses Returns
Chryseis to Her Father**
CLAUDE
1604/5-1682
Louvre, Paris

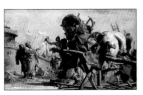

p. 164 **The Building
of the Trojan Horse**
GIOVANNI DOMENICO
TIEPOLO
1727-1804
The National Gallery, London

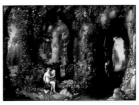

p. 173 **A Fantastic Cave
with Odysseus and Calypso**
JAN BRUEGHEL THE ELDER
1568-1625
*Johnny van Haeften Gallery,
London*

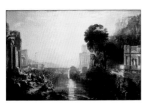

pp. 182-183 **Dido Building Carthage**
JOSEPH MALLORD WILLIAM
TURNER
1775-1851
The National Gallery, London

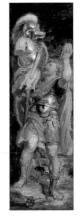

p. 197 **Aeneas with the Arms
of Mezentius**
PETER PAUL RUBENS
1577-1640
Dulwich Picture Gallery, London

INDEX

Absyrtus, 102
Abyla, 107
Acestes, 184, 195
Acetes, 121-2
Achates, 194
Achelous, 131
Achilles, 74, 103, 127, 146, 151-2, 153, 156-61, 163
Acis, 146-8
Aconteus, 92
Acrisius, 86
Actaeon, 32-5, 74
Admeta, 107
Admetus, King of Thessaly, 131-2
Adonis, 52-7
Adrastus, King of Argos, 132
Aeacus, King of Aegina, 74-5
Aeaean isle, 170
Aegean Sea, 60
Aegeus, King of Athens, 102, 111, 113
Aegina, 74
Aegis, 12
Aegisthus, 167
Aeneas, 50, 153, 157, 158, 179-84, 185-90, 191, 192-7
Aeneid, 197
Aeolus, 58, 61, 169, 181
Aesculapius (Asclepius), 97, 115, 131, 156
Aeson, King, 99, 101-2
Aetes, 99, 100, 102
Aethiopians, 9, 39, 87, 146
Aethra, 111
Aetna, Mount, 39, 46, 93, 132, 148
Africa, 108, 181, 182
Agamemnon, King of Mycenae, 152, 153, 156, 158, 167
Agave, 122
Agenor, King of Phoenicia, 72
Agenor (son of Priam), 159
Aglaia, 14
Ajax, 103, 152, 156, 157, 163
Alba Longa, 197
Alcestis, 131-2
Alcinous, 174, 175-6
Alcmena, 107
Alecto, 15, 191
Aleian field, 95
Alexander the Great, 42
Alphenor, 85
Alpheus, 48
Alpheus, River, 107
Alps, 39
Althea, 103-4
Amalthea, 131
Amathos, 52
Amazenus, River, 192
Amazons, 107, 113-14, 163, 192

Ammon, 93
Amphiaraus, 132-3
Amphion, 85, 140
Amphitrite, 126, 127
Amphrysos, River, 132
Ampyx, 92
Amymone, 107
Anaxarete, 63-4
Anchises, 179, 180, 184, 189-90
Andraemon, 52
Andromache, 153, 159, 181
Andromeda, 87-90
Anemone, 57
Antaeus, 93, 108
Antea, 95
Anteros, 14
Anthor, 196
Antigone, 132-3
Antilochus, 146, 157
Antiope, Queen of the Amazons, 113
Antiope, Queen of Thebes, 140
Apennines, 39
Aphrodite *see* Venus
Apollo, 10, 14, 18, 76, 184, 190; and Aesculapius, 132; and Cassandra, 165; and Chiron, 97; and Clytie, 80; contest with Pan, 42; and Daphne, 22-5; and Delos, 179-80; hides from giants, 93; and Hyacinthus, 57; and Marsyas, 141; and Niobe, 84-5; oracle of, 58, 65, 72, 179-80; and Orion, 143; and Orpheus, 135; and Phaëton, 36-9; and the Trojan War, 153, 156, 159, 163
Aquilo, 130
Arachne, 81-4
Arcadia, 15, 103, 194
Areopagus, 167
Ares *see* Mars
Arethusa, 48
Argo, 99, 101
Argonauts, 99, 102, 118, 130, 180
Argos, 107, 167, 196
Argus, 29-30, 99
Argus (dog), 178
Ariadne, 112-13, 115, 122
Arimaspians, 97
Aristaeus, 135, 139-40
Artemis *see* Diana
Aruns, 196-7
Asia, 99, 111, 121
Astraea, 19
Astyages, 92
Atalanta, 54, 103, 104-5
Ate, 158
Athamas, 99, 127
Athene *see* Minerva

Athens, 81, 102, 111, 113-14, 115, 167
Athos, 39
Atlantis, 190
Atlas, 10, 40, 86-7, 108, 110, 143
Atropos, 14
Attica, 113, 118
Augean stables, 107
Augeas, King of Elis, 107
Augustus, Emperor, 16
Aulis, 153
Aurora, 25, 26, 46, 59, 143-6
Auster, 130
Autonoë, 122
Autumn, 36
Aventine, Mount, 108
Avernus, 184, 185

Babylonia, 25, 39
Bacchanals, 121, 122
Bacchus (Dionysus, Liber), 14, 16, 41-2, 93, 119-22, 139
Baeotia, 153
Baucis, 42-5
Bellerophon, 95
Bellona, 16
Belus, King of Tyre, 182
Beroë, 119
Black Sea, 99
Boötes, 38
Boreas, 130, 181
Bosphorus, 30
Brazen Age, 19
Briareus, 46, 93, 185
Briseis, 153
Byrsa, 182

Cacus, 108
Cadmus, 32, 72-4, 99, 127
Caicus, 39
Calais, 130
Calchas, 153, 156, 164
Calliope, 14, 135
Callisto, 30-2
Calpe, 107
Calydon, 103-4
Calydonian boar, 103
Calypso, 173, 176
Camenae, 130
Camilla, 192, 196-7
Capaneus, 133
Carthage, 181, 182-4
Cassandra, 165
Cassiopeia, 87
Castor, 117-18
Caucasus, Mount, 21, 39, 125
Caÿster, River, 39
Cebriones, 157
Cecrops, King of Athens, 81
Celeus, 46-7, 49

centaurs, 95-7
Cephalus, 26-8
Cephalus, King of Athens, 74-5
Cepheus, 87, 90
Cephisus, 72
Cerberus, 71, 108, 187
Ceres, 14, 46-9, 70, 105, 125-6
Cestus, 12, 156
Ceyx, 58-61
Chaos, 10, 17, 40
Charon, 71, 185
Charybdis, 172, 181
Chimaera, 93, 94-5, 185
Chios, 143
Chiron, 97, 127
Chryseis, 153
Chryses, 153
Ciconians, 168
Cimmerians, 30
Cimon, 115
Circe, 50, 170-2
Cithaeron, Mount, 122, 140
Claros, 58
Clio, 14
Clotho, 14
Clymene, 36
Clytemnestra, 167
Clytie, 80
Cnidos, 52
Cocytus, River, 185
Colchis, 99, 102
Corinth, 111
Corybantes, 105
Creon, 133
Crete, 74, 76, 84, 111-13, 114, 180
Creusa, 102
Crocale, 32
Cronos *see* Saturn
Cumaean Sibyl, 190
Cupid (Eros, Love), 10, 12-14, 46, 141; Apollo and Daphne, 22; and Psyche, 65-71; Venus and Adonis, 52
Cyane, River, 46, 47
Cybele, 105
Cyclopes, 93, 132, 143, 146-8, 168-9, 174, 181
Cyprus, 12, 51, 55, 63, 105, 167
Cyrene, 139-40

Daedalus, 112, 115-17
Danaë, 83, 86
Danaus, 107
Daphne, 22-5
Dardanelles, 99
Dardanus, 143, 180
Dawn, 9, 10, 38, 146
Daystar *see* Hesperus
Deiphobus, 153, 159
Dejanira, 108, 131

Delos, 117, 121, 179
Delphi, 9, 167
Demeter *see* Ceres
Demodocus, 176
Destinies, 103
Deucalion, 21
Dia, 121
Diana (Artemis), 12, 46, 184; and Actaeon, 32-5; birth, 179; and Camilla, 192, 197; and Chiron, 97; and Echo, 77; and Endymion, 143; hides from giants, 93; and Hippolytus, 115; and Iphigenia, 153, 167; and Meleager, 103, 104; and Niobe, 84; and Orion, 143; and Pan, 29-30; and Procris, 26; rescues Arethusa, 48
Dictys, 121
Dido, 182-4, 187
Diomed, 163, 167
Diomede, 152, 156
Dione, 12
Dionysus *see* Bacchus
Dioscori, 118
Dirce, 140
Dis *see* Pluto
Dorceus, 34
Doris, 40, 126, 127
Dryads, 125, 126
Dryope, 52

Echo, 77-9
Egeria, 115, 130
Egypt, 93, 121, 167
Electra, 143, 167
Eleusinian mysteries, 49
Eleusis, 46, 49
Elis, 48, 107
Elysian fields, 9, 189
Elysium, 188, 189, 190
Enceladus, 46, 93
Enchelians, 74
Endymion, 143
Enna, 46
Epidaurus, 111
Epimetheus, 18
Epirus, 181
Epopeus, 121
Erato, 14
Erebus, 10, 48, 71, 114, 139, 191
Eridanus, 40
Erinnyes *see* Furies
Eriphyle, 132-3
Eris, 149
Erisichthon, 125-6, 131
Eros *see* Cupid
Erytheia, 107
Eryx, Mount, 46

Esepus, River, 146
Eteocles, 132, 133
Etruscans, 194, 196
Eumacus, 176-7, 178
Eumenides, 15, 167
Euphrates, River, 39
Euphrosyne, 14
Europa, 72, 83-4
Europe, 99, 107
Eurus, 130
Euryalus, 195-6
Eurydice, 135-9, 140
Eurylochus, 170
Eurynome, 10
Eurystheus, 97, 107, 108
Eurytion, 95, 107
Euterpe, 14
Euxine Sea, 9, 99
Evadne, 133
Evander, 192-4, 196

Famine, 125-6
Fates, 14, 48, 55, 125, 132
Fauns, 16, 63
Faunus, 16, 35, 125, 146, 191
Favonius, 130
Flora, 16, 130
Fortunate Isles, 9, 190
Furies (Erinnyes), 15, 135, 167, 185, 188, 191

Galatea, 127, 146-8
Ganges, River, 39
Ganymede, 110
Gemini, 118
Genius, 16
Geryon, 107, 108
giants, 93
Gibraltar, Straits of, 107
Glaucus, 49-50, 153
Golden Age, 15, 19
golden fleece, 99-101
Gordian knot, 42
Gordius, 42
Gorgon, 86, 87, 90-2
Graces, 10, 14
Graeae , 86
Great Bear, 32, 38
Greece, 9-15
griffin (gryphon), 97

Hades, 108
Haemon, 133
Haemus, Mount, 30, 39
Halcyone, 58-61
Hamadryads, 63, 125, 126
Harmonia, 74, 132
Harpies, 130, 180-1,191
Hebe, 9, 101, 110
Hebrus, River, 139
Hecate, 99, 101, 185
Hector, 152-3, 156, 157-8, 159-61, 163
Hecuba, 159, 160, 165

Helen, 63, 114, 118, 151-2, 159, 163, 167
Helenus, 181
Heliades, 40
Helicon, 39, 94
Hellas, 9
Helle, 99
Hellespont, 99
Hephaestos see Vulcan
Hera see Juno
Hercules (Heracles), 97, 99, 101, 107-10, 111, 122, 131, 132, 140, 163, 193
Hermes see Mercury
Hermione, 167
Hero, 80
Hesiod, 190
Hesperia, 180
Hesperides, 41, 107-8
Hesperus (Daystar), 38, 46, 58, 59, 107
Hestia see Vesta
Hippocrene, 94
Hippodamia, 95
Hippolyta, 107
Hippolytus, 114-15
Hippomenes, 54, 104-5
Homer, 97, 151, 153, 190
Hours, 38, 146
Hyacinthus, 57, 163
Hyades, 119
Hyale, 32
Hydra, 107, 185, 188
Hylas, 101
Hymen, 22, 135
Hymettus, 51
Hyperboreans, 9
Hyperion, 10, 172

Iapetus, 10
Icarius, 133
Icarus, 115-17
Icelos, 59
Ida, Mount, 39, 110, 149
Idaeus, 160
Idas, 118
Iliad, 153-61, 163
Ilioneus, 85
Illyria, 30
Inachus, 29
India, 36, 97, 121, 189-90
Infernal Regions, 185-90
Ino, 74, 127
Io, 29, 30
Iobates, 95
Iolaus, 107
Iole, 52, 108
Ionia, 58
Ionian Sea, 30
Iphigenia, 153, 167
Iphis, 63-4
Iphitus, 108
Iris, 12, 59, 156, 160, 195
Iron Age, 19
Isaius, King of Arcadia, 103
Isles of the Blessed, 9, 190

Ismarus, 168
Ismenos, 84
Isthmian games, 127
Italy, 115, 180, 184, 190, 191
Ithaca, 133, 151, 168, 176
Iulus, 191, 195, 197
Ixion, 135, 188

Janus, 16, 191-2
Jason, 99-102, 103, 111
Jocasta, 94, 132
Jove see Jupiter
Juno (Hera), 12, 16, 65, 105, 131, 191-2; and Aeneas, 181, 193, 195, 197; and Bacchus, 121; Ceyx and Halcyone, 59; and Echo, 77; and Hercules, 107, 110; hides from giants, 93; jealousy, 29-32, 35; the judgment of Paris, 149; and Semele, 119; and the Trojan War, 153, 156, 157
Jupiter (Zeus, Jove), 9, 10-12, 14, 15, 86; and Aeneas, 184; and Aesculapius, 97; anger with mankind, 19-21; and Apollo, 132; Baucis and Philemon, 42-5; and Calypso, 173; Castor and Pollux, 118; cornucopia, 131; Cupid and Psyche, 71; and Delos, 179; and Endymion, 143; and Europa, 72, 83-4; and Ganymede, 110; and Hercules, 110; hides from giants, 93; Juno and her rivals, 29-32; and Leda, 83, 118; and Minerva, 81, 83; and the Myrmidons, 75; and Pandora, 18, 19; and the Pleiads, 143; and Proserpine, 48; and Semele, 119; and Thetis, 127; and the Trojan War, 153, 156, 157, 160; war in Thebes, 133

Kedalion, 143

Lachesis, 14
Laertes, 134
Laestrygonians, 169-70
Laius, King of Thebes, 94
Lake Regillus, battle of, 118
Lampetia, 172
Laocoön, 164, 165
Laodamia, 153
Laomedon, King of Troy, 143
Lapithae, 97
Lares (Lars), 16
Larva, 16
Latinus, 191
Latmos, Mount, 143
Latona, 12, 35, 84, 85
Lausus, 192, 196

Lavinia, 191, 197
Lavinium, 197
Law see Themis
Leander, 80
Lebynthos, 117
Leda, 83, 117-18
Lelaps, 26-8, 34
Lemnos, 12, 99, 143, 163
Lemur, 16
Lethe, River, 59, 189
Leucothea, 127
Liber see Bacchus
Libethra, 139
Libya, 39, 107
Lichas, 108
Linus, 140
Little Bear, 32, 38
Lotis, 52
Lotus-eaters, 168
Love see Cupid
Lucina, 16
Lycabas, 121
Lycaon, 158
Lycia, 35, 94-5, 157
Lycomedes, King of Scyros, 115, 151
Lycus, King of Thebes, 140
Lynceus, 118

Machaon, 156, 163
Maeander, River, 39, 115
Maeonia, 121
Maia, 14
Marathon, 114
Mars (Ares), 12, 74, 81, 100, 153, 159
Marsyas, 140-1
Medea, 99-100, 101-2, 111
Media, 111
Mediterranean Sea, 9, 167
Medusa, 86, 94
Megaera, 15
Megara, 76
Melampus (dog), 34
Melampus (prophet), 141
Melanthus, 121
Meleager, 103-4
Melicertes, 127
Melisseus, 131
Melpomene, 14
Memnon, 146, 163
Memory see Mnemosyne
Menelaus, King of Sparta, 151, 152, 157, 167
Mercury (Hermes) 14, 18, 86, 153, 175; and Aeneas, 184; and Amphion, 140; Baucis and Philemon, 42-5; Cupid and Psyche, 71; and the golden fleece, 99; hides from giants, 93; and the labors of Hercules, 108; plays Syrinx, 29-30; and Proserpine, 48; and the Trojan War, 160; and Ulysses, 170
Merope, 143

Metabus, 192
Metanira, 46-7
Metis (Prudence), 10
Mezentius, 192, 196
Midas, 41-2
Milky Way, 19
Minerva (Pallas Athene), 10, 14, 18, 44, 46, 108; blinds Tiresius, 133; invents thunderbolts, 93; the judgment of Paris, 149; and Marsyas, 140-1; and Medusa, 86; and Orestes, 167; and Pegasus, 94, 95; and Perdix, 117; spinning competition with Arachne, 81-4; and Theseus, 113; and the Trojan War, 153, 164; and Ulysses, 174, 175, 176, 177
Minoeceus, 133
Minos, 187
Minos, King of Crete, 74, 76-7, 111-12, 114, 115, 122
Minotaur, 111-13
Mnemosyne (Memory), 10, 14
Momus, 15
monsters, 93-7
Moon, 9, 10, 38, 143
Morpheus, 59-60
Mulciber see Vulcan
Musaeus, 141
Muses, 10, 14, 39, 94, 130, 139, 140
Mycenae, 152
Myrmidons, 74-5, 157
Mysia, 99, 101

Naiads, 35, 40, 125, 131, 146
Nape, 34
Narcissus, 77-9
Nausicaa, 174-5
Nausithous, 174
Naxos, 113, 121, 122
Nemean lion, 107
Nemesis, 15
Neoptolemus, 167
Nephele, 32, 99
Neptune (Poseidon), 10, 12, 40, 101, 139; and Aeneas, 181, 184; and Amphitrite, 126; and Amymone, 107; floods Earth, 19, 21; and Hippolytus, 115; and Minerva, 81, 82-3; and Orion, 143; sons, 127; and the Trojan War, 153, 156, 158; and Ulysses, 176
Nereids, 40, 125, 126
Nereus, 40, 126-7, 146
Nessus, 108
Nestor, 99, 103, 146, 152, 156
Night, 146
Nile, River, 30, 39, 97
Niobe, 84-5
Nisus, King of Megara, 76-7
Nisus (Trojan), 195-6

Notus, 130
Numa, King of Rome, 16, 130
Nymphs, 101, 125
Nysaean nymphs, 119

Ocean, 9, 40, 146, 190
Oceanus, 10, 32, 49, 126
Ocyroe, 97
Odysseus see Ulysses
Odyssey, 163, 168-73, 174-8
Oedipus, 94, 132
Oeneus, 103, 104
Oenone, 163
Oenopion, King of Chios, 143
Oeta, Mount, 39, 108-10
Olympus, Mount, 9-10, 12, 39, 74, 156
Omphale, Queen, 108
Ophion, 10
Ops see Rhea
Oreads, 125
Orestes, 167
Orion, 93, 143
Orithyia, 130
Orpheus, 99, 118, 135-9, 140, 141, 189
Ossa, 39, 93
Ovid, 190

Pactolus, River, 41-2
Palaemon, 127
Palamedes, 151
Pales, 16
Palinurus, 184, 185
Palladium, 163, 167
Pallas, 65, 159, 175, 193-4, 196, 197
Pallas Athene see Minerva
Pamphagus, 34
Pan, 15, 29-30, 42, 63, 124-5
Pandean pipes, 29
Pandora, 18-19
Panope, 72
Paphlagonia, 146
Paphos, 52
Paris, 149-51, 152, 156, 163, 167, 181
Parnassus, Mount, 21, 22, 39
Partridge, 117
Patroclus, 156-8, 159
Pegasus, 94, 95
Peleus, 103, 127, 149
Pelias, 99, 101, 102, 132
Pelion, 93
Penates, 16
Penelope, 63, 133-4, 151, 176-8
Peneus, 22, 23
Peneus, River, 107
Penthesilea, Queen of the Amazons, 163
Pentheus, King of Thebes, 74, 121, 122
Penus, 16
Perdix, 117

Periphetes, 111
Persephone see Proserpine
Perseus, 86-92, 94
Phaeacians, 174-6
Phaedra, 114-15
Phaëthusa, 172
Phaëton, 36-40
Phantasos, 59
Philemon, 42-5
Philoctetes, 108-10, 163
Phineus, 90, 92, 99, 180
Phlegethon, 188
Phocis, 167
Phoebus, 12, 36, 57, 59, 72, 157
Phoenicians, 74, 167
Phoenix, 156
Phorbus, 184
Phrygia, 42, 84, 121
Phryxus, 99
Pillars of Hercules, 107
Pindar, 190
Pindus, 39
Pirene, 95
Pirithous, 95, 103, 114, 118
Pleasure, 71
Pleiads, 143, 146
Plexippus, 103
Pluto (Dis), 12, 14, 101, 108, 114; and Aesculapius, 97, 131-2; Cupid and Psyche, 71; Orpheus and Eurydice, 135; and Proserpine, 46, 47, 48-9
Plutus, 15
Po, River, 189
Polites, 165
Pollux, 117-18
Polydectes, 86
Polydore, 179
Polyhymnia, 14
Polyidus, 95
Polynices, 132, 133
Polyphemus, 127, 146-8, 168-9, 181
Polyxena, 163, 165
Pomona, 16, 63-4
Panope, 72
Portunus, 127
Poseidon see Neptune
Priam, King of Troy, 146, 152, 153, 158-9, 160-1, 163, 165
Procris, 26-8
Procrustes, 111
Proetus, 95
Prometheus, 17-21, 127
Proserpine (Persephone), 14, 46-9, 70-1, 108, 135, 184, 185
Protesilaus, 153
Proteus, 127, 139-40
Prudence see Metis
Psyche, 65-71
Pygmalion, 51-2, 182
Pygmies, 97
Pylades, 167
Pyramus, 25-6
Pyrrha, 21
Pyrrhus, 165
Pythian games, 22

Python, 22

Quirinus, 16

Remus, 197
Rhadamanthus, 188, 190
Rhea (Ops), 10, 14, 105, 121, 131
Rhodope, 39
Rhoecus, 126
Roman Empire, 9, 15-16
Rome, 19-34, 197
Romulus, 16, 197
Rutulians, 191, 193, 194, 195-6

Sagittarius, 97
Salamis, 64
Salmoneus, 188
Samos, 117
Samothrace, 118
Sarpedon, 153, 157
Saturn (Cronos), 101-2, 14, 15-16, 105, 194
Saturnalia, 15-16
Satyrs, 15, 16, 63
Scheria, 174
Scorpion, 39
Scylla, 49-50, 76-7, 146, 172, 181
Scyros, 115
Scythia, 30, 39, 97, 125, 167
sea monster, 87-90
Seasons, 9, 12
Semele, 14, 74, 119
Semiramis, 25
Seriphus, 86
Serpent, 38
Sibyl, 184, 185, 187-8, 189, 190
Sichaeus, 182
Sicily, 47-8, 50, 117, 146, 181, 182, 184
Silenus, 41
Silver Age, 19
Silvia, 191
Sinon, 164, 165
Sirens, 172
Sirius, 143
Sisyphus, 135, 188
Somnus, 59, 184
Spain, 107
Sparta, 118, 151, 167
Sphinx, 93, 94
Spring, 36
Strophius, King of Phocis, 167
Stygian realm, 135
Styx, River, 79, 119, 163
Summer, 36
Sun, 9, 10, 36
Sylvanus, 63, 125
Symplegades, 99
Syrinx, 29-30, 124

Taenarus, 135
Tagus, River, 39
Tanais, 39
Tantalus, 84, 135, 188-9
Tarchon, 194
Tarquin, 190
Tartarus, 10, 39, 46, 135, 139, 188
Tauris, 153, 167
Taurus, 39
Telamon, 75, 103
Telemachus, 151, 167, 176-8
Tellus (Gaea), 101
Terminus, 16
Terpsichore, 14
Terra, 108
Tethys, 32, 36, 49, 126
Thalia, 14
Thamyris, 140
Thebes, 72, 74, 84, 94, 121, 132-3
Themis (Law), 10, 14
Theron, 34
Thersites, 163
Thescelus, 92
Theseus, 99, 102, 103, 108, 111-15, 118, 122, 131
Thessaly, 9, 58, 99, 101, 126
Thetis, 127, 149, 151, 153, 157-8, 160, 163
Thisbe, 25-6
Thrace, 99, 179
Thracian strait, 30
Thrinakia, 172
Tiber, Father, 192-3
Tiber, River, 191, 193
Tigris, 34
Tiresias, 133
Tisiphone, 15, 188
Titans, 10, 18, 46, 108, 126, 188
Tithonius, 143-6
Tityus, 93, 188
Tmolus, 39, 42
Toxeus, 103
Trachine, 59
Triptolemus, 49
Triton, 21, 126, 127, 181
Troezen, 111
Trojan Horse, 164-5, 176, 179
Trojan War, 74, 103, 114, 118, 133, 146, 151-61, 163-7,
Troy, 143, 151-61, 163-7, 168, 176, 179, 180, 182, 187, 189
Turnus, King of the Rutulians, 191-3, 194, 195, 196, 197
Typhon, 46, 93, 181
Tyre, 182
Tyrrheus, 191

Ulysses (Odysseus), 50, 63, 133-4, 151-2, 156, 163, 164, 167, 168-73, 174-8, 179, 181
Urania, 14

Venus (Aphrodite), 12-14, 18; and Adonis, 52-7; and Aeneas, 184; and Ariadne, 122; and Atalanta, 105; Cupid and Psyche, 65, 70-1; fall of the Titans, 46; girdle, 156; hides from giants, 93; jealousy, 65; the judgment of Paris, 149-51; and Pygmalion, 51-2; and the Trojan War, 153
Vertumnus, 63-4
Vesta (Hestia), 16
Vestals, 16
Vesuvius, 185
Virgil, 139, 151, 185, 190
Volscens, 195, 196
Vulcan (Hephaestos, Mulciber), 10, 12, 16, 111; Aeneas's armour, 197; Harmonia's necklace, 74, 132; and Orion, 143; palace of the Sun, 36; thunderbolts, 93; and the Trojan War, 158

Winds, 130, 146, 169, 181
Winter, 36

Xanthus, 39

Zephyrus (zephyr), 65, 68, 69, 57, 130, 190
Zetes, 130
Zethus, 140
Zeus see Jupiter

Photographic Acknowledgments

For permission to reproduce the paintings on the following pages and for supplying photographs, the Publishers would like to thank:

AKG London: 11, 17, 44, 81, 93, 95, 166, 180; Erich Lessing: 10, 78-79, 96, 110, 138, 141, 154-155

Birmingham Museums & Art Gallery: 101

Bridgeman Art Library: 3, 6, 23, 37, 47, 49, 51 (Julian Hartnoll), 86, 91, 100, 109 (photo Peter Willi), 120, 127, 158, 160-161, 162, 173, 182-183, 188, 192-193

Christie's Images: 48, 104-105

Photograph 1997 The Detroit Institute of Arts: 142

Dulwich Picture Gallery (by permission of the Trustees): 197

Musée Fesch: 41 (photo Jean Harixcalde)

Fine Art Photographs: 18, 71, 87

Giraudon: 106, 112-113, 114-115

Giraudon/Bridgeman Art Library: 39, 54-55, 94, 134

Harvard University Art Museums: 119

The Metropolitan Museum of Art: 144-145, 149 (photo Schecter Lee)

The National Gallery, London: 1, 4-5, 14, 24, 26-27, 34, 43, 53, 66-67, 77, 80, 92, 123, 124, 136-137, 150-151, 164, 165, 177

National Gallery of Art, Washington (© 1998 Board of Trustees): 133, 170-171

National Trust Photographic Library/Derrick E. Witty: 62

Philadelphia Museum of Art: 60-61

© Photo RMN: 33, 72-73 (photo Arnaudet), 128-129 (photos J.G. Berizzi)

Roger-Viollet, Paris/Bridgeman Art Library: 20

Scala, Florence: 8, 12-13, 15, 69, 82-83, 88-89, 116-117, 118, 130, 147, 148, 179, 186-187

Sotheby's Picture Library: 30-31

© Tate Gallery, London: 111

© Museo Thyssen-Bornemisza, Madrid: 56, 98

© 1999 Virginia Museum of Fine Arts: 152 (photo Katherine Wetzel)